Contents

Handbook of Tests and Measurement in Education and the Social Sciences

2nd edition

This book is due for return on or before the last date shown below.

SCARECROW PRESS, INC.
Technomic Books

Published in the United States of America
by Scarecrow Press, Inc.
A wholly owned subsidary of The Rowman & Littlefield Publishing Group, Inc.
4501 Forbes Boulevard, Suite 200, Lanham, Maryland 20706
www.scarecrowpress.com

PO Box 317
Oxford
OX2 9RU, UK

British Library Cataloguing in Publication Information Available

Library of Congress Cataloging-in-Publication Data

Lester, Paula E.
  Handbook of tests and measurement in education and the social sciences / Paula E. Lester, Lloyd K. Bishop — 2nd ed.
    p.   cm.
  Includes bibliographical references and indexes.
  ISBN 0-8108-3863-X (paper : alk. paper)
  1. Educational tests and measurement—Handbooks, manuals, etc. 2. Social sciences—Methodology—Handbooks, manuals, etc. I. Bishop, Lloyd K. II. Title.
  LB3051 .L4543 2000
  371.26—dc21

00-041964

Introduction

In 1993, Bishop and Lester compiled an anthology of instruments in education and the social sciences for Garland Publishing, Inc. Bibliographic references were provided for over 700 instruments developed over the last 40 years in over 30 related areas. This anthology was based on more than a dozen major reference books that were written in the 1960s and 1970s. Many of these books are presently not in print and no longer available. These reference books varied in the amount of information provided. Some sources included the actual instruments, while others provided only a summary of the psychometric characteristics. Still other sources presented critiques of instruments and general bibliographic information. Consequently, there was a need to include in one book not only the specific psychometric information about the instruments and bibliographic references related to the instrument, but the actual instrument (published and/or unpublished). The original handbook was published in 1997 for that purpose. In several cases, only sample items were provided with the approval of the publisher of the instrument. This revised handbook expands upon and updates the original handbook.

Structure of the Handbook

Instruments Included

The original handbook contained over 70 instruments arranged under 30 topics. The revised handbook contains over 120 instruments arranged under the following 36 topics. Eight topics were added or modified for the revised handbook.

Alienation	Morale
Anxiety/frustration	Motivation/money
Change/innovation	Needs/need deficiency
Climate	Organizational assessment/effectiveness
Communication	Organizational structure
Conflict/conflict management	Politics
Culture	Power/authority/control
Decision-making/problem solving	Professional performance/autonomy
Dogmatism	Role/role conflict/ambiguity
Ethics	Self-actualization
Honesty/trust	Self concept
Interpersonal relations	Self efficacy
Job commitment	Self esteem
Job involvement	Sex roles/gender identification
Job satisfaction	Supervisory/managerial behavior
Leadership/leader style/behavior	Stress/burnout
Locus of control	Teacher attitudes/beliefs
Mentoring	Total quality management

Two types of indices are included: author and title. Consequently, if the researcher knows the name of the author, he/she can use the author index. Similarly, if the researcher knows the name of the instrument, he/she can use the title index. Also, the revised handbook contains a section that identifies instruments available through commercial organizations.

In addition, there is a section on **measurement and measurement theory** that includes information on measurement problems and scaling; instrumentation construction and evaluation; basic measurement procedures; validity; reliability; relation of validity to reliability; reliability of difference, change, or growth scores; and selected references.

Also, a section in this revised handbook provides an introduction with examples of three important psychometric procedures that are frequently used in the development of "good" measurement. These include the **Reliability** procedure with an explanation and interpretation of the Cronbach Alpha coefficient as an estimate of reliability. The **Item Analysis** techniques included in the reliability procedure are also discussed and interpreted in terms of analyzing the effectiveness of individual items in a scale. Finally, a discussion of **Factor Analysis** with examples and explanations is included. The SPSS statistical program was used for all examples and data analysis. These three techniques are discussed because they form the minimum tests expected in the development of "good" measurement. At least one measure of reliability should be used. Techniques for evaluating the effectiveness of individual items in a scale are necessary. And most importantly, at least one method of obtaining construct validity should be documented. Factor Analysis is a procedure frequently used in evaluating instruments that measure complex, multidimensional concepts that have some type of subscale structure.

Instruments Not Included

This handbook still does not include instruments that focus exclusively on personality or psychology.

Reference Sources

Three major databases were searched to locate instruments and/or references to existing instruments. The first was ERIC (Educational Resources Information Center), which contains published and unpublished documents. In addition, it also contains papers from national and local conferences that were written by researchers from numerous institutions. Another was Dissertation Abstracts International, which provides references to dissertations that focus on developing instruments and also provide references to existing instruments. Finally, Psychological Abstracts was used to discover information about new or existing instruments.

In addition, a concise annotated bibliography for each of the reference sources follows:

Bishop, L., and P.E. Lester. 1993. *Instrumentation in Education: An Anthology*. New York: Garland Publishing, Inc.
Identifies approximately 700 instruments in the areas of organizational administration and school effectiveness. From one to three instruments are described in detail and include sample items in each of the 31 main categories.

Bonjean, C., et al. 1968. *Sociological Measurement*. San Francisco: Chandler Publishing Company.
Refers to over 2,000 questionnaires, although only 50 questionnaires are described in detail.

Conoley, J.C., and J.C. Impara, eds. 1995. *The Twelfth Mental Measurements Yearbook*. Lincoln, Nebraska: Buros Institute of Mental Measurements, University of Nebraska, Lincoln.
Provides a complete bibliography and review of tests. Entries include a test title, purpose, description of the groups for which the test is intended, date of publication, special comments, part scores, forms, cost, author, publisher, and cross-references.

ETS Test Collection. 1990. *Annotated Bibliography of Tests*. Princeton, NJ: Educational Testing Service.

Provides annotated bibliographies for many areas related to education. Each reference contains some of the following information: name of the instrument, personal or institutional author, year test was published or copyrighted, test publisher or distributor, components within the overall test that assess particular skills or factors, target audience, and a description of the test and its purposes.

Keyser, D.J., and R.C. Sweetland, eds. 1993. *Test Critiques*. Austin, TX: Pro-Ed.

Reports psychometric information in three sections: introduction (development of the test and its historical significance), practical applications and uses (information about the sample, administration, scoring, and interpretation), and technical aspects (information about reliability and validity studies). An overall critique is provided at the end of each review.

Lake, D.G., et al. eds. 1973. *Measuring Human Behavior*. New York: Teachers College Press, Teachers College, Columbia University.

Reviews 84 instruments related to personal variables (cognitive-perceptual, affective-motivational, and overt behavior), interpersonal variables, group variables, and organizational variables.

Miller, D.C. 1970. *Handbook of Research Design and Social Measurement*. New York: David McKay Company, Inc.

Provides scales and indexes that focus on: social status, group structure and dynamics, morale and job satisfaction, community, social participation, leadership in the work organization, scales of attitudes, values, and norms, family and marriage, and personality measures.

————1991. *Handbook of Research Design and Social Measurement*. Newbury Park: Sage Publications.

Includes scales and indexes that focus on social indicators and measures of organizational structure.

Price, J.L. 1972. *Handbook of Organizational Measurement*. Massachusetts: D.C. Heath and Company.

Identifies measures of absenteeism, administrative staff, alienation, autonomy, centralization, communication, complexity, consensus, coordination, dispersion, distributive justice, effectiveness, formalization, innovation, mechanization, motivation, bases of power, routinization, satisfaction, size, span of control, and succession.

Robinson, J.P., et al. 1969. *Measures of Occupational Attitudes and Occupational Characteristics*. Ann Arbor, MI: Institute for Social Research, University of Michigan.

Includes instruments assessing general job satisfaction, job satisfaction with specific job features, concepts related to job satisfaction, occupational values, leadership styles, other work-relevant attitudes, vocational interest measures, and occupational status measures.

Robinson, J.P., and P.R. Shaver. 1978. *Measures of Social Psychological Attitudes*. Ann Arbor, MI: Institute for Social Research, University of Michigan.

Provides instruments assessing self esteem and related constructs, internal-external locus of control, alienation and anomia, authoritarianism, dogmatism, and related measures, other sociopolitical attitudes, values, general attitudes toward people, religious attitudes, and methodological scales.

3

————1972. *Measures of Political Attitudes.* Ann Arbor, MI: Institute for Social Research, University of Michigan.

Includes instruments assessing liberalism-conservatism, democratic principles, domestic government policies, racial and ethnic attitudes, international affairs, hostility-related national attitudes, community-based political attitudes, political information, political participation, and attitudes toward the political process.

Shaw, M.E., and J.M. Wright. 1967. *Scales for the Measurement of Attitudes.* New York: McGraw-Hill Book Company.

Discusses methods of scale construction as well as scales that focus on social practices, social issues and problems, international issues, abstract concepts, political and religious attitudes, ethnic and national groups, significant others, and social institutions.

Sweetland, R.C., and D.J. Keyser, eds. 1986. *Tests.* Kansas City: Test Corporation of America.

Provides concise descriptions of thousands of instruments. Entries contain the following information: test title and author, purpose, major features, scoring method, cost, availability, and primary publisher.

Criteria for Inclusion

This handbook includes instruments for each of the major constructs identified by the authors. In general, an instrument is included because it provides adequate support for its reliability and validity. In other words, the instrument is psychometrically sound. In some cases, an instrument is included because it is most representative of the construct under study. In addition, some instruments are included because they are the most frequently cited. Occasionally, an instrument is included because it was recently developed and the potential exists for additional research. Some instruments were not included because the authors were either unable to receive permission from the test publisher or because the organization or journal that holds the copyright wanted substantial fees in order to grant permission. Researchers and school administrators should obtain permission from the author(s) of the instrument(s) and/or original publisher(s) prior to their research.

Format of Entries

The authors sought to provide each entry with the following information. Where the information was not readily available or was inapplicable, the category was omitted.

Title: Identifies instrument in bold print.

Source: Provides a primary reference. Tells where the instrument is available.

Comments: Describes what the instrument measures as well as the number of items in the instrument. Includes comments and/or suggestions by the original author(s). Points out strengths and/or weaknesses. Provides general information.

Scale Construction: Describes how the instrument was developed including the theoretical basis for the instrument.

Sample: Describes the original sample who participated in developing the instrument as well as additional normative data.

Reliability: Discusses internal consistency coefficients, equivalent forms, and other data analysis techniques.

Validity: Describes the types of validity addressed: concurrent, construct, content, discriminant, and predictive.

Factor Analysis: Reports the results of factor analytic procedures. Contains information about the subscales and the number of items for each scale (item numbers are included in parentheses).

References: Provides references to articles, books, dissertations, and ERIC documents that describe the development of the instrument or its use. Provides no more than five representative references.

Scoring: Describes how to score the instrument.

Measurement in Education and the Social Sciences

This section emphasizes the importance of measurement in educational research. A basic understanding of measurement concepts, of measurement theory, and of correct psychometric procedures provides the foundation for educational research. It is axiomatic that if one's research variables cannot be appropriately measured, then one cannot conduct empirical research. The development of new, and the refinement of existing instruments, are basic research activities. **A researcher should not assume that an existing measure, or a measure published or reported in the literature, is a psychometrically sound tool.** Basic procedures of acceptable test construction are frequently violated in the reported research literature in the social sciences. For this reason, competent researchers must understand and develop the skills required for correct test construction in order to either develop their own tools, or critically evaluate those which are available. The purpose of this section is to provide a review of the basic information concerning the development of tests and measures in education and the social sciences. This information can be used also to evaluate the efficacy of many of the instruments found in this book.

Measurement and Measurement Theory

Measurement is the assigning of numbers (quantification) to individuals in a systematic way as a means of representing properties of the individuals. These numbers must be assigned according to a carefully prescribed, repeatable procedure. The particular test generates scores by using the same instructions, questions, and scoring procedure for each subject. Numbers can be assigned based on the properties to be measured utilizing various forms depending upon the type of scale to be generated. That is, numbers can be assigned to subjects in categories forming nominal scales, in ranks forming ordinal scales, or as continuous scores forming either interval or ratio scales.

Measurement theory is a branch of applied statistics that attempts to describe, categorize, and evaluate the quality of measurements (tests, instruments, scales, etc.). It attempts to improve the usefulness, accuracy, and meaningfulness of instruments. It proposes methods for developing new and better measurement tools. Several disciplines in the social and behavioral sciences have adopted, or created, their own unique measurement approaches with an accompanying label. For example, in psychology and education, these measurement approaches are referred to as **psychometrics**, in economics as **econometrics**, and in sociology as **sociometrics**. Although most of the foundation for present-day measurement theory was completed by the 1950s, research and development into newer approaches to psychological measurement (or psychometrics) continues. As stated, psychometrics tends to dominate measurement approaches in the behavioral sciences and education, as opposed to econometrics, which are used in business and economics.

Overview to Measurement Problems and Scaling

Measurement in the social sciences is by no means an exact science. A number of techniques are used to obtain measures (observations) from human subjects. Such techniques are **paper and pencil tests** (questionnaires, instruments, inventories, scales), **interviews, observations, ratings, and tests.** Because paper and pencil tests (questionnaires or instruments) are so frequently used in education to obtain information from respondents, these tests will be emphasized primarily in this section.

In order to obtain an objective quantitative indication from each respondent to the items, or statements, in a questionnaire or instrument, some method of scoring these statements is required. This is referred to as **scaling**. That is, scales, or **anchors,** are devices employed by test developers to quantify the responses of a subject on a particular item, or statement, of a test. Several of the more commonly used scales are:

Forced Choice	(True-False)
Likert	(Summated-rating)
Thurstone	(Equal-appearing interval)
Guttman	(Cumulative scale)
Semantic Differential	(Bipolar adjectives)

Forced-Choice Scale

The forced-choice scale accomplishes what the name implies. It forces the respondent generally to one of two (or three) possible choices. The **true-false** response is typical of this type scale. Numerical values of either one (true response) or zero (false response) are assigned. This type scale, or some slight modification, is often used with personality tests. Responses such as like—dislike, agree—disagree might be used. A third neutral response may be used also: like—undecided—dislike. The scale could be numerically coded either $1 =$ dislike, $2 =$ undecided, $3 =$ like; or $-1 =$ dislike, $0 =$ undecided, $+1 =$ like.

Likert Scale

The Likert scale, or **summated-rating scale,** is perhaps the most frequently used in the social sciences. Any measure obtained by adding together the response scores of a number of items is referred to as a Likert or summated scale. Alternately, the terms **linear composite, homogeneous scale, composite scale,** or **additive scale** may be used to characterize the Likert scale. Typically, this scale contains a set of items, or statements, that are considered approximately equal in attitude or value. The number of items may be as few as five or six, or as many as 30 to 40. The subject responds with varying degrees of intensity on a five-point scale ranging between extremes. For example, statements such as Strongly Agree—Agree—Undecided—Disagree—Strongly Disagree may be used. The scale can be expanded to seven or more positions, or used as a modified forced-choice scale, by eliminating the middle (undecided) position.

Briefly, a Likert scale can be described as follows. A set of items composed of approximately an equal number of favorable and unfavorable responses concerning the attitude, event, phenomenon, or object to be measured is given to a group of subjects. They respond to each statement in terms of their degree of agreement or disagreement by generally selecting one of five responses (anchors) from Strongly Agree to Strongly Disagree. Each subject's responses to the set of items are combined (summated, yielding a composite score) so that the most favorable attitude will have the highest score while the least favorable will have the lowest score. A major assumption of this scale is the ability to **linearly combine** the items in the scale producing a **homogeneous** measure. All items to be linearly combined must be related to a single common factor. The sum of these items is expected to contain all the important information contained in the individual items. This suggests three important and interrelated tasks necessary for constructing Likert measures: 1) item construction, 2) item selection, and 3) item scoring. Likert suggested two methods of **item analysis** in order to evaluate the ability of the individual items to measure the attitude, or object, measured by the total scale: correlation analysis, and analysis based on the criterion of internal consistency. Each of these procedures will be discussed later in this section.

Thurstone Scale

The Thurstone scale is referred to as an **equal-appearing interval** scale. In the case of the Likert scale, each item within a set of items is considered to be approximately equal in attitude or value to be assessed. With the Thurstone Scale, items are scaled along the attitude to be measured. Each item is assigned a scale value indicating the strength of attitude for an agreement response to the item. The items in the scale are assumed to be **differentially ordered, rather than equal**. It is more difficult to construct a Thurstone Scale than the Likert, summated scale, and both scales yield similar results. Table 1 below illustrates a Thurstone Scale.

Table 1
ATTITUDE TOWARD DIVORCE
(Thurstone Scale)

The following statements express opinions about divorce. Please indicate your agreement, or disagreement, with each of the statements by marking them as follows:

(✓) Mark with a check if you agree with the statement.
(X) Mark with an X if you disagree with the statement.

Scale
Value

0.5	1. Divorce is disgraceful.
0.8	2. Divorce is legalized adultery.
1.2	3. Lenient divorce is equivalent to polygamy.
1.6	4. Divorce lowers the standard of morality.
3.3	5. Divorce should be discouraged in order to stabilize society.
3.7	6. Divorce is justifiable only after all efforts to mend the union have failed.
4.2	7. Divorce should be discouraged but not forbidden.
5.8	8. The evils of divorce should not prevent us from seeing its benefits.
6.2	9. A divorce is justifiable or not, depending on the desires of the persons involved.
7.1	10. Divorce should be permitted so long as the rights of all parties are insured.
8.1	11. Permanence in marriage is unnecessary for social stability.
8.4	12. Divorce is desirable for adjusting errors in marriage.
8.8	13. Easy divorce leads to a more intelligent understanding of marriage.
9.4	14. The marriage contract should be as easily broken as made.
9.8	15. Divorce should be granted for the asking.
10.1	16. A person should have the right to marry and divorce as often as he or she chooses.

The scale was taken from Shaw and Wright (1967). The original scale contained 22 statements. For the sake of brevity some items were omitted.

The respondent checks the items with which he agrees. The points (scale value) corresponding to each item are totaled and then divided by the number of answered items to yield an average score for each respondent. A high score indicates a favorable attitude toward divorce.

The construction of a Thurstone Scale and the assignment of scale values is accomplished through the use of **judges**. After the collection of a series of short, concise statements reflecting various degrees of the attitude to be measured, these are subjected to a group of judges working independently. They sort the statements into eleven piles according to their relative degree of favorableness to unfavorableness. The scale above was created using 26 judges. Shaw and Wright (1967) indicate that it has been shown that as few as 20 judges can be used to compute reliable scale values.

Guttman Scale

The Guttman Scale is referred to as a **cumulative scale**. This scale consists of a relatively small set of homogeneous items that are considered to be **unidimensional**, measuring one, and only one, attitude, event, or phenomenon. Items are ordered in difficulty or complexity, so that to answer correctly or approve the last implies success, or approval, on all the preceding items. Table 2 below is an example of a Guttman-type scale.

Table 2
HOMOSEXUALITY ATTITUDE SCALE
(Guttman Scale)

Homosexual relations between two consenting adult males should be dealt with in which of the following ways? Respond to each statement using the following key:

1: Strongly Disagree	4: Agree
2: Disagree	5: Strongly Agree
3: Not Sure	

_____ 1. They should be punished by execution.
_____ 2. They should serve at least five years in prison.
_____ 3. They should be given a short prison sentence.
_____ 4. They should be required to accept treatment or go to jail.
_____ 5. They should be offered treatment if they want it but not punished in any way, but warned not to recruit others.
_____ 6. They should not be made to feel deviant or warned about recruiting others.
_____ 7. They should be praised for choosing their own form of sexual satisfaction as long as it does not interfere with others.
_____ 8. They should be praised and encouraged to recruit others into homosexuality.

The scale was taken from Gorden (1977).

Semantic Differential Scale

The Semantic Differential is an attitude-type scale developed by Osgood, Suci, and Tannenbaum in 1957. It is a method for measuring the meanings of concepts, and it has two applications: 1) to measure the semantic properties of words and concepts, and 2) as an attitude scale restricting its focus to the affective domain and the evaluative dimension. In applying the method, the respondent is asked to rate an object, for example, school, teacher, supervisor, etc., on a series of bipolar adjectives anchored by a seven-point scale. The respondent is instructed to put a check in the position indicating both the direction and intensity of his feelings toward the object.

Osgood and Suci, using factor analysis, established three general factors of meaning measured by the semantic differential: an **evaluative factor** (bipolar adjectives such as good-bad, wise-foolish, kind-cruel), a **potency factor** (hard-soft, strong-weak), and an **activity factor** (hot-cold, fast-slow). Pairs of these bipolar adjectives are selected according to the purpose of the research, and the emphasis upon either evaluative, potency, or activity dimensions. Approximately fifteen to twenty adjective pairs should be selected with the concept to be rated placed at the top of the combined scale (see Table 3).

The semantic differential yields a large amount of data with a relatively short questionnaire, and with minimum effort. In variance terms, it produces three main sources of variance: **concepts, scales,** and **subjects.** Thus, scores can be produced and analyzed for differences between **concepts** (school, teacher, and supervisor); **scales** (evaluative, potency, and activity dimensions); and among **subjects,** or analyses may be conducted in any combination of the three.

Table 3
SUPERVISOR
(Semantic Differential Scale)

Good	:	:	:	:	:	:	Bad
Slow	:	:	:	:	:	:	Fast
Large	:	:	:	:	:	:	Small
Ugly	:	:	:	:	:	:	Beautiful
Clean	:	:	:	:	:	:	Dirty
Weak	:	:	:	:	:	:	Strong
Dark	:	:	:	:	:	:	Bright

In this example, the respondent is instructed to rate the concept supervisor according to how he or she perceives, or feels, toward the supervisor at the moment by placing an X someplace along the seven-point scale.

Instrumentation Construction and Evaluation

As suggested earlier, the measurement of research variables is perhaps one of the greatest weaknesses in conducting meaningful and useful research in the social and behavioral sciences. Much research in education, when evaluated against appropriate psychometric and measurement procedures, must be discounted, if not totally rejected. Thus, the development of new measures, and the refinement of existing instruments are fundamental research activities. Again, one should not assume that a measure that is published, or reported, in the research literature is necessarily a psychometrically sound tool, including many of the instruments included here. Basic procedures of acceptable test construction are frequently violated or totally ignored. This was aptly reported by Mitchell (April, 1985) in a recent survey of the research literature. Some 21% of studies did not report reliability, and only 26% provided information on construct validity. Both measures of reliability, and procedures for obtaining validity are essential, and required, types of information that should be reported in all quantitative research studies.

The purpose of this section is to provide information on several specific procedures that are useful in instrumentation development. It should be noted that these techniques can be used whether one is interested in developing their own instrument, or in the process of critiquing and evaluating an existing tool. First, an outline will be provided listing in order the major steps one should following in instrumentation construction. Second, several of these procedures will be discussed in greater detail providing, where appropriate, specific statistical procedures that can be employed. Six steps are listed below that should be considered in good scale construction.

Steps in Instrumentation Construction and Evaluation

1. **A theory and accompanying concepts** (or a taxonomy) should be selected first. Many instruments developed in the social sciences and education have no conceptual or theoretical basis to serve as a guide in the selection of items, and the construction of scales. The concepts to be measured should be defined as carefully and precisely as possible, and considered in relation to the specific population (selection of subjects) to be studied. An example of an instrument developed without a conceptual foundation is the *Organizational Climate Description Index* (Halpin, 1963). On the other hand, examples of instruments employing a theoretical base are the Stern climate indices, which used the Murray Need-Press Model.

2. Next, an **item pool** should be written. This will be accomplished based on the theoretical and conceptual framework provided in step one. Statements, or items, will be created to which subjects may respond, and will serve as **stimuli** to the content or subject matter to be measured. One may obtain items from a variety of sources: review of the theoretical and research literature, other instruments, documents, through observation of the phenomena, behavior, trait, or attitude to be studied. In writing items, one should be sensitive to the following: 1) frame of reference and item formats; 2) content and population specificity; 3) descriptive vs. evaluative items; 4) items that are clear, concise, and as unambiguous as possible; and 5) simple, as opposed to compound statements.

Frame of Reference—Smith, et al. (1969) provided the research evidence that indicates that **perceptual selectivity** in human judgments is dramatic. When two individuals with different frames of reference are exposed to the same object or stimulus, they will select different aspects and provide different summary evaluations of the situation. Van de Ven and Ferry (1980) have suggested that frames of reference are the cognitive filters (perceptual screens) a person uses in describing or evaluating a situation. They indicate that for the purpose of instrumentation construction and evaluation that there are three issues to be examined relative to a respondent's frame of reference: 1) the characteristics of the stimulus a person is exposed to; 2) the systematic; and 3) the unsystematic individual differences and biases that respondents bring to a stimulus as a result of their prior experiences, predilections, expectations, and personalities.

The first issue deals with the interaction between a respondent's frame of reference and the **composition of the instrument** (item format). Specifically, such features as test length, complexity of items, time perspective, and anchor points on an answer scale have been found to significantly influence a respondent's frame of reference at the point of measurement (Smith, et al., 1969).

There are also effects due to composition and item selection of an instrument on the frame of reference of respondents due to position, past experiences, and predilections of the individual. For example in studies of job satisfaction, climate or morale perceptions have been found to differ

11

systematically among respondents of different age, sex, education, social background, and job tenure (Smith, et al., 1969). Unsystematic biases of respondents on frame of references are expected to be randomly and normally distributed among a sample, and therefore, they will cancel out statistically when judgments are averaged together (Van de Ven and Ferry, 1980). This suggests that more accurate responses may be made by respondents if one is careful in constructing unambiguous statements that are sensitive to the following:

Content and population specificity suggests that the item wording should be specific to a particular population, or selection of subjects. Measurement created in one test situation may not be appropriate for another. Items should be rewritten to be **situationally specific**.

Descriptive and evaluative items should be distinguished during test construction. Van de Ven (1980) suggested that descriptive items are positive and value-free focusing on the factual characteristics and behaviors that actually exist. Evaluative items are normative and value-laden and ask a respondent to provide an opinion about the strengths or weaknesses, likes or dislikes of events or behaviors. They indicate that evaluative statements are more susceptible to variation in frames of reference and perceptions of respondents than descriptive items.

Number of scale points (anchors) on the answer sheet may also influence response bias. If too few scale points are used, the answer scale is a coarse one and much information may be lost because the scale does not discriminate sufficiently among respondents. However, if too many scale points are used, the scale points may be graded so finely that it is beyond the ability of respondents to discriminate among response cues. The effect of the number of scale points on the reliability of measures has received much attention and considerable empirical investigation. To summarize these findings, Van de Ven (1980) indicates for homogeneous, Likert-type measures, there is very little increase in scale reliability beyond five scale points for a single (unipolar) scale, and nine points for a bipolar scale.

Simple vs. compound statements should be analyzed. Compound items are generally more ambiguous statements, and lead to greater response bias. A compound item is one in which two or more, somewhat mutually exclusive, pieces of information are addressed in one statement. The following is an example of a compound item with inherent ambiguity due to its complexity: "The goals of education should be dictated by children's interests and needs, as well as by the larger demands of society." A respondent could have varying attitudes on three different aspects of the item: 1) goals of education dictated by children's *interests*, 2) goals dictated by children's *needs*, and 3) goals dictated by the *larger demands of society*. Such compound statements appear frequently in many attitude questionnaires. These statements should be rewritten into simple statements with only one idea (stimulus or cue) for each item.

It has been recommended that one should create approximately twice as many statements in the initial item pool, as the number to be retained in the final test (Thorndike, 1982). However, twice as many items is probably a low estimate. To ensure high quality selection in the refinement of items and scales, it would be better if the initial item pool contained three or four times the number required in the final instrument.

3. **Content validation** should be used with the item pool. (Even though this procedure is only mentioned once, it is not uncommon for one to repeat this step several times in the process of refining the item pool.) Determining content validity, sometimes referred to as **subject matter** validity, is primarily a judgmental process. Generally, a panel of five to seven experts (judges) will be selected who are experts in the area of study and with the concepts to be measured. At this stage the researcher is attempting to accomplish at least two objectives: 1) to determine which items from the

item pool are most representative of the total universe of items that could be selected dealing with the subject matter to be measured—to determine if voids in statements exist (new items should be included), and if items should be discarded or rewritten; 2) if the theory to be measured is multiconceptual (most social science theories are), then to determine which items logically cluster or deal with which subconcepts. To accomplish this, each judge should work independently, rating each statement in the item pool and categorizing it under the appropriate concept or subconcept. Usually, a criterion of at least 80% agreement among judges is established for the inclusion of an item in the final or revised pool.

4. **A pilot study** should be conducted with the statements retained from step three for the purpose of performing some initial item analyses. The items can be appropriately "packaged" and administered to a small sample of subjects similar to those to be used in the final study (subjects for whom the instrument was designed). Generally, 25-40 subjects should be sufficient for a pilot study. Reliability estimates can be obtained, and several item analyses can be performed with the data (to be discussed in a following section in more detail).

Note: The steps listed above may be repeated several times in the process of developing and refining a reasonably sound tool. It may be necessary to use a new panel of judges, or to administer the test to additional subjects for further pilot study.

5. The **final study** will be conducted. In the case of most dissertation research, the instrument developed from steps one through four will be administered to the final study sample. Depending on the concepts to be measured, 40 to 50 items may survive the initial screening. One need not be too critical in rejecting statements during steps three and four because much of this work will be repeated with the final study sample. This provides for a refinement of the instrument repeating statistical procedures with a much larger selection of subjects. Also, some statistical procedures, such as factor analysis, can be used with a larger study sample which is not possible with the smaller pilot group. It is important to recognize that no instrument should be considered the "final" or "completed" version; additional and continued refinement to any instrument is generally always useful and necessary.

6. With the larger study sample, a number of additional statistical techniques can be used for further instrument refinement. These are only listed briefly inasmuch as each procedure is discussed at length in the following sections. These techniques include: 1) establishing **criterion-related validity** both in terms of concurrent and predictive validity; 2) establishing **construct validity** both convergent and discriminant validity; 3) obtaining final **reliability estimates** for total scale and all subscales, and the reliability of raters if appropriate; and 4) conducting additional item analysis procedures in particular tests of item-to-scale homogeneity.

Basic Measurement Procedures

Item Analysis

Each item analysis procedure discussed provides a way of using item data from a number of respondents to evaluate the quality and usefulness of test items. These techniques provide a means of choosing the "best" items for inclusion in the refined version of the measure. Sometimes, item analysis can offer information also about ways that poor items may be made better. Because of the overwhelming occurrence of Likert-type scales in education measurement, techniques useful in creating Likert scales will be emphasized. Texts are listed at the end of this section that deal with procedures for developing other scale types, i.e., Guttman, Thurstone, or Semantic Differential scales.

The **Item-Difficulty Index** (P) is used to determine the proportion of respondents (examinees) who get the item correct compared to those who missed the item. This technique is most useful in developing classroom tests and has little utility in creating other types of instrumentation. The best range is a ratio of 0.3 to 0.7.

Several **Item Discrimination Indices** are available, and are useful, in evaluating items individually or collectively. Generally, these procedures are used to assess the difference between the proportion of **high-scoring** respondents, those who score high on the attitude, to **low-scoring** respondents. Several techniques are discussed below.

Critical Ratio (t-test) compares the upper 25% of respondents with the lower 25% of the respondents on the means of the two groups on each item. If the low scoring group has a low mean on an item, when compared to a high mean of the high scoring group, which is statistically significant, one then concludes that the individual item is discriminating properly between high and low scoring subjects. With this procedure, each item can be analyzed in three ways: 1) low scoring 25% with a low mean—high scoring 25% with a high mean, the difference between the two means is statistically significant at the .05 level; 2) the difference between means in the low 25% and high 25% is not statistically significant; and 3) there is statistical significance between the means, but the low scoring group has the high mean and the high scoring group has the low mean, indicating a reverse in the intended response pattern.

The first example above indicates that the item is discriminating correctly between low and high scoring respondents. The second case indicates that the item does not discriminate between low and high respondents. The little difference in means between the two groups could have occurred by chance. The third example suggests that the item is stimulating a reversed response pattern from each subject. Both examples two and three indicate that either the item should be discarded from the test, or rewritten in an attempt to correct the problem of proper discrimination among subjects.

Corrected Item-Total Correlations compare each individual item in the scale with the total composite score for the scale. This technique correlates each individual item in the test with the composite score of all of the remaining items. A low item-to-total score correlation indicates that the individual item fails to measure that which the other items measure. Again, the item should be either discarded or rewritten. This procedure is regarded also as a test of item-to-scale **homogeneity**. Likert regarded this procedure as being essential in developing Likert-type scales. The method evaluates the ability of the individual items to measure the attribute measured by the total scale. It should be noted that this test is found in many statistical programs.

Item Means and Variances (standard deviations) may be used also to obtain an initial indication of the item's ability to discriminate along the Likert scale (anchor). For example, if a five-point (1-5) scale is used, one would like an item mean of about 3.0, and a standard deviation of at least 1.0, in order to ensure a reasonable degree of dispersion of responses along the scale. In contrast, a high mean of 4.5 and standard deviation of less than 1.0 (i.e., .5), or a low mean of 1.5, would suggest a skewed response pattern (either high or low) to the item.

Item Frequency Distributions may be computed for each item in the scale. One hopes to obtain a fairly normal distribution of responses across the five-point Likert scale. Responses to scale anchors two, three, and four would be greater than to anchors one and five.

Reliability Estimates are extremely useful for evaluating the internal consistency of items within a scale. Likert stressed the importance of using the criterion of internal consistency in developing homogeneous scales. Two statistical procedures are available to satisfy this test—the **Alpha Coefficient**, and either the **KR-20** or **KR-21** formulas. The **split-halves** method, also known as the **Spearman-Brown Prophecy Formula**, is also available as a test of internal consistency. However, Alpha is preferred as an estimate of scale reliability. Alpha is the generalized form of the estimate based on the **interitem correlation matrix**, and it is used with Likert-type scales. The KR-20 and KR-21 formulas are special cases of reliability estimates used with forced-choice scales.

For example, the SPSS RELIABILITY procedure provides an individual item analysis technique referred to as "**If Item Deleted**." This evaluates the reliability contribution of the individual item against the total overall reliability estimate of the scale. If the item (if item deleted) reliability estimate is several points greater than the total scale reliability, this suggests that the item **is not** contributing to the internal consistency of the other scale items as a whole. Potentially, the item should be discarded or rewritten based on this test.

Finally, **Factor Analysis** can also be a useful procedure for conducting item analysis in determining the individual contribution of items to total scale consistency and homogeneity. Items with large factor loadings would contribute more to the measurement of the particular scale than items with small factor loadings (less than .30). Also, items that load somewhat equally on two or more factors show tendencies toward ambiguity, and might be discarded. Again, factor analysis is useful for developing homogeneous scales where measures have inherent **multidimensionality**.

Validity

The general definition of validity refers to whether an instrument accurately measures what it is intended to measure. Three types of validity are discussed in the literature and will be reviewed briefly. These are **content validity, construct validity**, and **criterion-related validity**. Criterion-related validity includes two types: **concurrent validity and predictive validity**. Of the three general types of validity, construct validity is by far the most important to establish for most instruments in the social sciences and education. This is sometimes the most difficult to accomplish while content validity, which provides the least information concerning the validity of the scale, is generally the easiest to operationalize.

Nunnally (1978) indicates that scientific generalization is at the heart of understanding and applying validity to measurement methods. Each type of validity constitutes different issues concerning scientific generalization. That is, each type addresses a different aspect of validating a scale, and each should not be used interchangeably. Nunnally continues that of the three types, the logical issues of relating construct validity to scientific generalization are considerably more complex than those in criterion or content validity.

Content Validity

Content validity is concerned with the extent to which an instrument reflects a specific domain of content. That is, the extent to which items appear to be logical and understandable indicators of the constructs or concepts under consideration. Test items should be a *sample of all possible items taken from a universe of content* dealing with the concepts to be measured. It is sometimes referred to as **subject matter** validity. The operationalization of content validity of any instrument ultimately rests with the degree of **consensus** that can be obtained from a heterogeneous group of judges, who are experts in the field. Thus, content validity is established by individual, subjective judgments of expert reviewers. A minimum of five to seven individuals should be used; each working independently with an 80% criterion level of agreement being reached on the appropriateness of each item in the measure.

Criterion-Related Validity

This deals with the degree of correspondence, or correlation, between the instrument and some other measure of the same concepts or attributes. This may be obtained by correlating the instrument with other measures of similar characteristics or attributes, or in some cases using what is referred to as a **known-group** procedure. Individuals are used who are known to possess varying degrees of the attribute or behavior to be measured by the test. Thorndike (1982) suggested that if we are dealing with two extreme groups, then the ability of the measure to discriminate between the two groups can be expressed as a point-biserial correlation. Nevertheless, this type of criterion-related validity is referred to as **concurrent validity**. **Predictive validity** is obtained in those instances when the test must be used to predict to some future behavior, or the future acquisition of some skill. An example would be the predictive validity of the SAT test battery to predict successful completion of the freshman year of college.

Construct Validity

Construct validity focuses on the extent that a measure (scale or subscales within a larger instrument) perform in accordance with **theoretical expectations**. Construct validity has limited application unless the instrument has been developed from some theoretical base—a theoretical system (conceptual or taxonomic system) underlies the scales development. **Factor analysis** is an often used statistical procedure for establishing construct validity (sometimes called factorial validity). When using factor analysis, the questions addressed are: How well do items designed to measure a construct (concept) **converge** by loading together as a single factor? This may also be referred to as **convergent validity**. Next, How well do items designed to measure other constructs **discriminate** by breaking out as different factors? This is sometimes referred to as **discriminate validity** (Carmines and Zeller, 1979, 54).

Thorndike (1982) indicated that there are at least four methods of obtaining evidence for the construct validity of a measure. One is judgmental—using judgmental comparisons of behavior or attributes to be measured and the test items. Next is correlational—obtaining correlations between the test and other measures. One's test should show substantially higher correlations with other measures designed to assess the same attribute than with measures designed to assess other attributes. This can be accomplished through factor analysis. The third is group difference data—comparing subgroups that might be expected to differ on the attribute. And finally, the use of treatments, or experimental interventions, that might be expected to influence expression of the attribute.

Reliability

Reliability is concerned with the consistency, stability, and dependability (accuracy) with which an instrument measures a set of dimensions, characteristics, behaviors, etc. of research subjects. Reliability coefficients are **estimates** of the degree to which a scale score for each respondent represents either **true measurement**, or some degree of **measurement error**. For the purposes of instrumentation development, there are three types of reliability estimates discussed in the literature. These are the **coefficients of stability, equivalence**, and **internal consistency**. Each reliability

16

estimate serves a **distinct research purpose, and one procedure should not be used in place of the other.**

Coefficient of Stability

This procedure determines the reliability—the stability—of a test **over time.** The technique for establishing this type of reliability is referred to generally as the **test-retest method.** A correlation coefficient is computed between the first test administration with a second test administration with the same subjects, and with an approximately four to six week separation in time. The extent to which subjects' second test scores are similar to their first test scores determines the degree to which a large correlation coefficient is obtained between the two test administrations, and the extent to which the test is considered to be **stable.** This reliability procedure is most useful with pretest-posttest experimental research, where one should establish the stability of the pretest and posttest scores (over time). However, the procedure also suffers from a number of inherent weaknesses due to the necessity of establishing the reliability coefficient with human subjects over a prescribed time period. Internal validity factors such as history, maturation, and testing effect, to mention a few, often distort the reliability estimate obtained from the test-retest procedure.

Nunnally (1978) indicates that except for certain special instances, there are serious defects in using the retest method. The major problem is that experience in the first testing usually influences responses in the second testing. He recommends that this method generally not be used to estimate reliability.

Coefficient of Equivalence

This technique is referred to as **alternate forms,** and it is used to provide a reliability estimate between two parallel forms of the same test. A correlation coefficient is computed between Form A of a test with the alternate, or parallel, Form B of the same test across the same group of subjects. This reliability estimate is used primarily with the development of standardized tests, such as the GRE and SAT test batteries, where more than one form of the test is used. The **split-half** estimate corrected with the **Spearman-Brown Prophecy Formula** is a special case of the coefficient of equivalence. However, Nunnally (1978) suggested that the difficulty with the split-half method is that the correlation between halves will vary depending on how the items are divided, which raises questions regarding what the reliability is.

Coefficient of Internal Consistency

This reliability procedure provides an estimate of item to total scale homogeneity. Thorndike (1982) states that the analysis is built on the assumption that all items are measures of the same underlying attribute. That is, it is a test of the homogeneity of items in a scale. If the coefficient is low for a particular scale, the items in the scale are probably not measuring the same construct, behavior, or attribute. The internal consistency of items within a scale are evaluated from the **average correlation** among all items in the scale with **Coefficient Alpha** (Cronbach Alpha). Most measurement texts agree that this procedure provides the best method for determining estimates of internal consistency of tests. And, the internal consistency method of reporting reliability in most research situations is probably the more useful method. Nunnally (1978) states that even if other estimates of reliability are made for a particular measure, coefficient alpha should be obtained first. If it proves to be low, then there is no need to make other estimates of reliability because they will prove to be even lower (coefficient alpha sets an upper limit to the reliability of a test).

Although coefficient alpha is commonly used, there is considerable disagreement on what magnitudes of the coefficient are adequate for various types of measurement scales. Nunnally (1978) indicates that a satisfactory level of reliability depends greatly on how a measure is to be used. Exploratory, or preliminary, research may require less demanding levels of reliability estimates than basic research, or hypotheses testing. The magnitude of the coefficient is *directly related to the number of items* in a test. All things being equal, a short test (four or five items) should yield a lower alpha coefficient than a longer test (20 or 25 items). It is generally desirable that longer tests have alpha coefficients of at least 0.80, while shorter tests may be acceptable with coefficients in the high 0.60s or low 0.70s

Cronbach alpha is the generalized form of this test, and it is used with multiple choice, or Likert-type scales. The KR-20 and KR-21 formulas are special cases to be used with forced-choice (T-F) type scales.

Reliability of Raters

This reliability procedure (referred to also as **interrater reliability**) should be used in those cases where one's data gathering method employs raters, or judges, rather than some type of "paper and pencil test." There are two basic methods for estimating the reliability of ratings from a number of judges. The first is a method developed by Guilford (1954), and the second is an analysis of variance approach described by Ebel (1951). The Guilford formula requires that the k raters rank the N persons from high to low, and then the following formula may be used:

$$r = 1 - \frac{k(4N + 2)}{(k-1)(N-1)} + \frac{12S^2}{k(k-1)N(N^2-1)}$$

r = the average intercorrelation among individual judges and, more importantly, **the reliability of one judge**

k = the number of judges (raters)

N = the number of individuals (persons being rated)

S = the sum of ranks for any individual

It is important to note that this formula, when applied to a set of ratings, provides the reliability estimate for **one rater**. To determine the reliability estimate of an entire set of ratings (more than one judge), it is necessary to employ the Spearman-Brown Prophecy Formula with **n** in that formula equal to the **number of raters or judges**. The Spearman-Brown Formula is:

$$r = \frac{nr}{1+(n-1)r}$$

The data in Table 4 below demonstrate this reliability procedure using the rank-order ratings of four raters for nine individuals.

18

Table 4
DATA TABLE OF RANKINGS OF NINE INDIVIDUALS (N)
BY FOUR JUDGES (k)

JUDGES

Individual	S 1	2	S^2 3	4	Total Rating	$(Rating)^2$
1	7	9	6	8	30	900
2	3	1	1	2	7	49
3	2	2	5	1	10	100
4	8	8	9	7	32	1024
5	5	4	3	4	16	256
6	9	7	8	6	30	900
7	1	5	2	3	11	121
8	6	3	4	7	20	400
9	4	6	7	5	22	484

$$S^2 = 4234$$

By inserting data from the table above into the formula, we would obtain the following results:

$$r = 1 - \frac{(4)(38)}{(3)(8)} + \frac{(12)(4234)}{(4)(3)(9)(80)}$$

$$r = 1 - \frac{152}{24} + \frac{50,808}{8,640} = 1 - 6.333 + 5.881$$

$$r = .548$$

Note that the result, r = .548, is the reliability estimate for one rater. The Spearman-Brown formula must be used to determine the reliability estimate for the four judges in the example above. By inserting the data into the formula, we obtain the following:

$$r = \frac{(4)(.548)}{1+(3)(.548)} = \frac{2.192}{1 + 1.644} = \frac{2.192}{2.644} = .829$$

It has been shown that gains in interrater reliability may be made by adding raters when the initial reliability estimate is low. However, when the number of judges is greater than five or six, the increase in reliability is usually not justified by the addition of more raters. For example, one might perform a pilot study by having three judges rate student performance on a certain task. If the reliability estimate for the three judges is not sufficiently large, one could keep incrementing the value of n (number of raters) in the Spearman-Brown formula to determine the number of raters required until the desired reliability estimate is obtained.

Relation of Validity to Reliability

Both validity and reliability are highly interdependent mathematically. From a practical standpoint, Campbell (1976) has indicated that the concept of reliability becomes indistinguishable from that of validity. *The precision of the estimate of criterion validity is reduced as reliability is reduced.* Criterion validity of a test is affected by the reliability of a test. Thus, a test or measure may be reliable but not valid. **A test cannot be valid if it is not reliable.** An index of this relationship between reliability and validity is the **index of reliability**.

Index of Reliability

The validity of a test cannot exceed the square root of the reliability of the test. If test, X, is used to predict a criterion, Y, then P_{xy} is the validity coefficient. P_{xy} cannot be larger than the square root of P_{xx}—the reliability coefficient of test X.

The square root of the reliability of a measure provides an **upper bound** for its correlation with any other measure. For example, a measure with a reliability estimate of only .65 can never correlate greater with another test or variable than .81. This is referred to as the **index of reliability**.

That is: $r_{xy} = r_{xx} =$ Index of Reliability

This demonstrates the close relationship between reliability and criterion validity, as well as the importance of establishing the highest possible reliability estimates for all measures employed in a study when those measures will be correlated with other variables.

Attenuation

If scores obtained from two measures, a predictor X and a criterion Y, are unreliable, or found to have low reliability estimates, the correlation coefficient between the two measures will be reduced in value, or **attenuated**. When this occurs a correction for attenuation can be made. To correct for errors of measurement in both variables, the following formula may be used:

$$r_c = \frac{r_{xy}}{r_{xx}r_{yy}}$$

Where:

$r_c =$ the corrected correlation coefficient

r_{xx} and $r_{yy} =$ the reliability coefficients of the two measures

$r_{xy} =$ the correlation coefficient between the two measures

With this correction formula for attenuation, one might obtain the following results: If measure X has a reliability of .52 and measure Y has a reliability of .61, with a correlation coefficient of .43 between X and Y, the corrected correlation coefficient will be:

$$r_c = \frac{.43}{(.52)(.61)} = \frac{.43}{(.721)(.70)} = \frac{.43}{.505} = .85$$

The correlation coefficient is increased from .43 to .85 after being corrected for attenuation due to the low reliability of the two measures. Often test developers can only increase the reliability of an instrument by a small amount, and therefore, it is of interest to know the correlation between two measures if both were perfectly reliable.

Restriction of Range

If one uses a selected (homogeneous) subgroup of subjects with a limited range of scores on any measure, this will affect the outcome of correlation coefficients generally, and the computation of reliability and validity estimates specifically. When a range of scores is **restricted, the variance is also restricted**. The scores of a selected group of respondents between 95 and 100 on a test will have a lower correlation with a criterion (Y variable) than will those of the entire, more heterogeneous, group receiving scores across the entire range, i.e., 1 to 100. In the case with restricted scores, too little variation is present in the rawscore data.

Table 5 provides an example of the differences encountered when a total group is used, and when a group is restricted to one portion of the score range

Table 5
RESTRICTED RANGE OF SCORES

	Total Group	Total	Selected Group	Total
Test X	1 4 8 11 16 26 25	91	16 26 25	67
Test Y	5 6 7 8 9 10 11	56	9 10 11	30

Test X	Test Y	Test X	Test Y
N = 7	N = 7	N = 3	N = 3
X = 13	X = 8	X = 22.3	X = 10
sd^2 = 82.3	sd^2 = 4	sd^2 = 20.2	sd^2 = 0.667
sd = 9.1	sd = 2	sd = 4.5	sd = 0.82
r_{xy} =		r_{xy} =	

Test developers may encounter this problem, particularly in a pilot study, when one or more measures are used with a small and selected group of subjects. Both reliability and validity estimates may be lower than with a larger selection of subjects obtained from the final study.

Reliability of Difference, Change, or Growth Scores

In some studies dealing with students and classroom research, it is not uncommon that one may wish to compute scores on subjects from a pretest measure to posttest of the same measure. The purpose is to determine the amount of change, difference, or growth that may occur from pretest to posttest condition. Serious problems arise as to the reliability of difference, or change, scores between such measurement. Generally, *the difference between two scores is less reliable than the reliability of the individual scores*, even though the individual scores are quite reliable. Because these two scores measure essentially the same thing, they are, therefore, highly correlated. The high correlation between the two scores (pretest to posttest) tends to **reduce** the reliability of the difference, or change scores.

Although the computation of change scores is questionable and frequently difficult to properly interpret, Cronbach has provided a formula for estimating the reliability of a difference, or change, score between two standard scores:

$$r_{diff} = \frac{r_{aa} + r_{bb} - 2r_{ab}}{-2r_{ab}}$$

It should be noted that r_{aa} and r_{bb} are the reliabilities of the subtests and r_{ab} is the correlation between the scores on the two test.

Selected References

These references were used, in part, in developing this section.

Allen, M.J., and W.M. Yen. 1979. *Introduction to Measurement Theory*. Monterey, CA: Brooks-Cole.

Blood, D.F., and W.C. Budd. 1972. *Educational Measurement and Evaluation*. New York: Harper & Row.

Campbell, J.P. 1976. Psychometric theory. In P. Dunnette, ed. *Handbook of Industrial and Organizational Psychology*. Chicago: Rand-McNally.

Dick, W., and N. Hagerty. 1971. *Topics in Measurement: Reliability and Validity*. New York: McGraw-Hill.

Ebel, R.L. 1951. Estimation of the reliability of ratings. *Psychometrika* 16, 407-424.

Gorden, R.L. 1977. *Unidimensional Scaling of Social Variables*. New York: The Free Press.

Guilford, J.P. 1954. *Psychometric Methods* (2nd ed.). New York: McGraw- Hill.

Isaac, S. 1976. *Handbook in Research and Evaluation*. San Diego: Edits.

McIver, J.P., and E.G. Carmines. 1981. *Unidimensional Scaling* (#24). Beverly Hills: Sage.

Mitchell, T.R. 1985. An evaluation of the validity of correlational research conducted in organizations. *The Academy of Management Review* 10, 192-205.

Nunnally, J.P. 1978. *Psychometric Theory* (2nd ed.). New York: McGraw-Hill.

Osgood, C.E., G.J. Suci, and P.H. Tannenbaum. 1957. *The Measurement of Meaning*. Urbana, IL: University of Illinois Press.

Shaw, M.E., and J.M. Wright. 1967. *Scales for the Measurement of Attitudes*. New York: McGraw-Hill.

Smith, P.C., L.M. Kendall, and C.L. Hulin. 1969. *The Measurement of Satisfaction in Work and Retirement: A Strategy for the Study of Attitudes*. Chicago: Rand-McNally.

Snider, J.G., and C.E. Osgood, eds. 1969. *Semantic Differential Technique*. Chicago: Aldine.

Sullivan, J.L., and S. Feldman. 1979. *Multiple Indicators: An Introduction* (#15). Beverly Hills: Sage.

Thorndike, R.L. 1982. *Applied Psychometrics*. Boston: Houghton Mifflin.

Van de Ven, A.H., and D.L. Ferry. 1980. *Measuring and Assessing Organizations*. New York: Wiley.

Discussion and Examples of Psychometric Procedures: Reliability, Item Analysis, and Factor Analysis

This section provides an introduction with discussion and examples of three important psychometric procedures that are frequently used in the development of "good" measurement. These include the **Reliability** procedure with an explanation and interpretation of the Cronbach Alpha coefficient as an estimate of reliability. The **Item Analysis** techniques included in the reliability procedure are also discussed and interpreted. These are used when one wishes to analyze the effectiveness of individual items in a scale. Finally, a discussion of **Factor Analysis** with examples and explanations is included. The SPSS statistical program was used for all examples and data analysis. Actual data were taken from a sample of teachers in the New York metropolitan area.

These three techniques are discussed because they represent the minimum tests expected in the development of "good" measurement. At least one measure of reliability should be used. Techniques for evaluating the effectiveness of individual items in a scale are necessary. And most importantly, at least one method of obtaining construct validity should be documented. Factor Analysis is one procedure, among others, that is frequently used in evaluating instruments that are measuring complex, multidimensional concepts that have some type of subscale structure.

Reliability

One advantage of the SPSS reliability procedure is that it provides two separate techniques that may be used to analyze item-scale data when developing psychometrically sound instruments. It provides both reliability estimates (Alpha coefficient, KR-20, etc.) as well as some item analysis procedures ("corrected item-total correlations" and "Alpha if item deleted"). The reliability estimates are used to evaluate a **set of items in a scale** (their ability to work together as a set or composite) and item analysis procedures are used to evaluate the effectiveness of **each individual item** in conjunction with the other items in the scale. Information on each technique is obviously necessary if one wishes to develop a scale that is dependable and accurate. That is, the composite or total score for the scale assigned each respondent is reliable—the score represents as much as possible true or actual measurement and has as little error as possible. The reliability estimate provides this ratio of true measurement to measure error in the composite or total score.

Examples of these procedures are discussed below using actual and typical social science data taken from actual respondents.

Alpha Coefficient

The **Alpha coefficient** is the most commonly used reliability estimate and is a default procedure in SPSS. It should be used with all instruments that employ a Likert-type scale (Strongly Agree—Agree—Undecided—Disagree—Strongly Disagree). It is a test of the **internal consistency** of the items in the scale or the degree to which a scale score for each respondent represents either true measurement or measurement error (a test of **homogeneity** of items in the scale).

In Table 1 below, the Alpha coefficient computed for the ten-item scale is .8363. This can be rounded for discussion purposes to **.84**. This Alpha (measure of internal consistency or homogeneity of the items) was derived from a ten-item scale (instrument) designed to measure Burnout among teachers. The ratio of true measurement to measurement error can be determined by subtracting the estimate (.84) from one (1 - .84 = .16). Thus, the ten items account for 84% true measurement of Burnout among the respondents. They also contain about 16% measurement error. This error in measurement might be attributed to one or more items among the ten that do not belong to the set (not homogeneous or consistent with the other items), or a small amount of error may exist among all ten items. Nevertheless, the Alpha coefficient of .84 indicates that the ten items are contributing to a reasonable degree to the measurement of the same underlying attribute.

Thus, the Alpha coefficient provides a means of determining the extent to which any scale or instrument contains true measurement (consistency or homogeneity among the items) and the amount of error. **All measurement in the social sciences contain some amount of measurement error.** For a variety of reasons no instrument constructed to be used with live respondents can be totally error free. The issue is what amount of error can be tolerated in developing instruments for measurement purposes. This issue is somewhat subjective; however, we would hope for a reliability estimate as large as possible. That is, as close to 1.00 as possible. Therefore, it is clear that reliability estimates in the .90s are superior to those in the .80s and those in the .80s are superior to those in the .70s. As the reliability estimate gets closer to .50, then 50% of the items in the scale are measuring some attribute and the other 50% are contributing error to the measurement of that attribute.

The magnitude of the Alpha coefficient is also a **function of the length of the scale**. Instruments with a larger number of items (for example, 20 or more), if everything else is equal, will have a larger Alpha coefficient than a scale with only eight or ten items. Thus, an Alpha coefficient of .84 may be quite satisfactory for a ten-item scale, and it may not be as desirable with a 20-item or larger instrument.

Item Analysis

In those cases where the reliability estimate is lower than desired, two item analyses procedures are provided in SPSS that determine which items may be causing the measurement error. On the table below labeled "Item-Total Statistics," these procedures are the **Corrected Item-Total Correlation** and the **Alpha if Item Deleted.**

The Corrected Item-Total Correlation is a correlation coefficient (Pearson bivariate correlation) between each individual item in the scale and the composite or total score of the remaining items. In the example below of the ten items, var14 (item 14) has a correlation coefficient of .69 with the composite score of the other nine items (var5 through var13). This indicates that there is a reasonably close correspondence between item 14 and the remaining nine items. Thus, item 14 is not contributing sufficient measurement error that the item should be discarded. Var10 has a correlation coefficient of only .34 (the lowest of the ten items) indicating that this item is not contributing to, or has less to do with (is not as internally consistent), the total score computed from the other nine items. However, the magnitude of the correlation does not seem to be significantly serious to suggest discarding the item. To some extent this decision requires subjective judgment. Any individual constructing an instrument can determine the criterion level for including, discarding, or the necessity for rewriting items to be included in the final scale.

To help substantiate the above concern with item 14, the **Alpha if Item Deleted** procedure can be used. This column provides an Alpha coefficient associated with each item in the scale with that particular item removed from the Alpha calculation. For example, the Alpha associated with var5 (**.82**) was computed with item 5 removed from the calculation of the other nine items—var6 through var14. If the Alpha associated with a given item is larger than the Alpha computed for the total scale—all ten items (.84)—then this suggests that there would be an increase in the total Alpha coefficient if the particular item were deleted. The Alpha associated with var10 (.84) does not increase the overall Alpha for the total scale; therefore, there is no basis for discarding the item.

It should be noted that when one item (or more) has a very small correlation coefficient with the remaining items, indicating that the item might be removed, the Alpha coefficient associated with that item will only show **a very small increase.** Even if two or more items in the scale might be removed based on their correlation coefficients, the overall Alpha for the remaining items will not increase as much as one might expect. This is understandable if it is remembered that the computation of the Alpha coefficient is also a function of scale length—the number of items in the scale. As the number of items is reduced, the magnitude of the Alpha coefficient is also reduced even though items are removed that are contributing substantially to measurement error.

For example, assume that var10 below indicated a correlation coefficient on the Corrected Item-Total Correlation column of only .02. This would indicate that var10 had almost no correspondence, or relationship, with the other nine items. This would provide sufficient basis for removing the item. However, the Alpha coefficient would increase by only one, or at most, two points—Alpha would be .85 or .86. Again, this is the case because as one item is removed, the scale length is reduced from ten items to nine. This causes a reduction in the Alpha coefficient even though the removal of the one, noncorrelated, item also caused an increase. **The net result is never a large increase in the final Alpha coefficient.**

Table 1
Reliability Analysis—Alpha Coefficient
Item-total Statistics

	Scale Mean if Item Deleted	Scale Variance if Item Deleted	Corrected Item-Total Correlation	Alpha if Item Deleted
VAR5	21.00	34.71	.51	.82
VAR6	21.02	33.34	.63	.81
VAR7	22.14	35.41	.64	.81
VAR8	21.40	36.06	.37	.84
VAR9	21.00	34.82	.43	.83
VAR10	21.81	37.51	.34	.84
VAR11	22.07	33.53	.59	.81
VAR12	21.58	33.32	.59	.82
VAR13	22.37	35.84	.60	.82
VAR14	21.93	34.17	.69	.81

N of Cases = 57   N of Items = 10

Reliability Coefficient
Alpha = .8363

Factor Analysis

The object of factor analysis is to mathematically represent a set of variables in terms of a smaller number of hypothetical variables called **factors**. Its aim is the orderly simplification of a number of interrelated, or intercorrelated, measures. One of the most important uses of factor analysis is the identification of factors underlying a large set of variables, such as a number of items in an instrument. Clustering a large number of variables into a smaller number of homogeneous sets, and thereby creating a new variable can simplify large data sets. In each case, the subset of variables can be considered as a **manifestation of an abstract underlying dimension**—that is, a factor (or subscale). With factor analysis, one can systematically summarize large correlation matrices (Kachigan, 1982). Thus, factor analysis can be considered in at least three ways: 1) as a test of **parsimony**; 2) as a method of **data reduction**; and 3) as a test of **homogeneity** among multidimensional measures. These measures (variables) may be items in a test, multiple scores from several tests, or other multiple units of measurement.

When a group of variables, or a subset of variables within a larger data set (e.g., items in a test), has a great deal in common—high intercorrelations—a **factor may exist**. These related variables are discovered using basic techniques of correlation analysis, which underlies factor analysis. Thus, starting with a larger number of scores, which show correlation, one can end up with a few factors, or **dimensions**, which represent or account for the major variance among these scores. When this occurs, a **factor solution** has been derived.

Factor analysis has at least three general applications that are discussed in the literature. The first is an **exploratory** application. It is used to explore the underlying dimensions of a given data set. The minimum number of hypothetical factors that account for the observed (measured) covariation among a larger set of variables can be determined. Kachigan (1982) stated that one of the most important uses of factor analysis is in the identification of factors underlying a larger set of variables.

Second, it is used as a **confirmatory** procedure. This has to do primarily with hypotheses testing. One can hypothesize a smaller number of summarizing variables (factors) among a larger number of measures, and then use factor analysis to either confirm or deny the hypothesis. Factor analysis is useful because of its flexibility in being able to extract as few, or as many, factors as one desires, or as a particular conceptual framework may suggest (Kachigan, 1982).

Third, factor analysis is used more commonly as a **measurement and psychometric** procedure in the development and refinement of questionnaires and instruments. It has useful qualities that are very helpful in conducting item analyses. Although there is some disagreement, many measurement specialists consider factor analysis as a reasonable alternative in establishing **construct validity** (Kerlinger, 1975). Allen and Yen (1979) indicated that factor analysis can be used to examine the construct validity of a test, and that it can be used effectively in test development. Finally, factor analysis is important in the screening of variables for inclusion in subsequent statistical procedures such as regression or discriminant analysis. Since factor analysis identifies groupings of variables that are highly correlated, we can choose a single variable to represent a larger set for inclusion among a number of predictor variables, thereby avoiding the potential problem of multicollinearity.

Factor analysis is not one simple statistical procedure. But rather, the procedure represents a number of approaches to conceptualizing the grouping, or clustering, of variables into logical factors. Two researchers using the same data may arrive at quite different conclusions based on their past experience with factor analysis, the approach they use, and their ability to interpret the results. Factor analysis is not just a mathematical procedure, but it requires a good deal of intuitive and interpretive skill. Much of this skill may be developed only with time, experience, and some understanding of its basic underlying mathematical principles.

Nunnally (1978) pointed out that factor analysis has both a conceptual and a mathematical component. Although they are usually wedded in practice, one should maintain the distinction between factor analysis as a conceptual tool, and as a set of mathematical procedures. In the better factor analysis studies, the conceptual models and the mathematical models are both carefully considered and interwoven.

Steps in Conducting a Factor Analysis

An understanding of six major steps is necessary in order to correctly conduct a factor analysis. They are outlined below, and then some of these steps will be discussed in more detail in later sections along with actual data examples. Steps two, three, four, and six can be performed by SPSS with little, or no, intervention required of the user. **Default** procedures in the SPSS routines will be employed where the user does not make other requests. For example, the default values will provide a principal components extraction, employ the Kaiser Criterion (eigenvalues greater than one) to determine the number of factors to be extracted, and provide a varimax (orthogonal) rotation. Factor scores for each subject in the analysis can be automatically computed, if the appropriate request is included.

Data Collection

Variables should be selected that are appropriate to a factor analysis. Preferably, interval or ratio scored data provide the best input. The number of subjects (N of Cases) used for the analysis is very important. Most authorities suggest at least **ten subjects** for each variable in the analysis. Nunnally (1978) stated that frequently factor analyses of test items are undertaken with many fewer subjects than the minimum recommended of ten per item. There are some horrible examples in the literature where the number of subjects was approximately the same as the number of items. Unless the number of subjects is at least ten times as large as the number of items, factor analysis can take great advantage of chance. Then what appear to be factors are only artifacts because of sampling error.

Mathematically, one can perform the factor computations with **one subject** greater than the number of items. However, this may produce an unstable and uninterpretable factor solution. In practice, it has been found that at least five and, as stated above, preferably ten subjects per variable is recommended in order to obtain a meaningful and interpretable factor solution.

Preparation of the Correlation and Covariance Matrices

This step is totally computed by SPSS, and provides the foundation for the factor analysis. As mentioned previously, factor analysis is based on correlation procedures—on the analysis of the correlation matrix of variables included in the study. It is essentially an examination of the interrelationships among variables. The correlations within a subset (cluster) of variables will be greater than the relationship between the subsets of other variables. The within factor correlations of variables is greater than the correlations between the factors. Each factor is **extracted** from the matrix of correlations based on this principle.

Because of the importance of the correlation matrix of variables, which underlies the factoring process, SPSS provides several tests to evaluate the appropriateness of the factor model. These tests include Bartlett's test of sphericity, the anti-image correlation matrix (AIC), the Kaiser-Meyer-Olkin measure of sampling adequacy (KMO), the determinant of the correlation matrix (DET), and the reproduced correlation matrix (REPR). One should consult the SPSS manuals for information and guidance on the use of these tests.

Factor Extraction (Unrotated Factors)

Factors are extracted from the correlation matrix of variables until the number of factors needed to account for the variance among the variables is determined. That is, there is no appreciable variance left; the **residual** correlations among variables in the matrix are near zero.

Several factor extraction procedures are available in SPSS. The two major types are **principal component analysis** (default method) and **factor analysis**, sometimes called **principal axis** or **principal factors**. Other extraction procedures are maximum likelihood (Roa's canonical factoring), least squares method (minres), alpha factoring, and image factoring. Tabachnick and Fidell (1983) indicate that the differences between the solutions produced by these various extraction methods may be small with a good data set and similar communality estimates. In fact, one test of the stability of a factor solution is its similarity following different extraction procedures. **A stable solution usually tends to appear regardless of which extraction technique is employed.**

It is also necessary to establish the number of factors that one wishes to have extracted. The default procedure in SPSS, if the user does not indicate differently, is the Kaiser, **eigenvalue greater than one**, criterion. Factors are extracted from the matrix as long as the factors have an associated eigenvalue at least as great as, or greater than, **unity**. The user can override this default and establish the number of factors to be extracted (and concomitantly rotated). Other procedures used to determine the number of factors to be extracted are discussed below.

Factor Rotation

The purpose of factor rotation is to **redefine** the factors in order to make sharper distinctions in the meanings of the factors. This aids in the interpretation and definition of each factor by making the loadings either very high (1.0 or -1.0) or very low (near zero), eliminating as many medium-sized loadings as possible. There are two general types of rotations: **orthogonal** and **oblique**.

Orthogonal rotations create factors that are 90 degrees apart, **uncorrelated**, and independent. There are three types of orthogonal rotations: **varimax**, maximum variance distributed by columns; **quartimax**, maximum variance distributed by rows; and **equimax**, the variance is equalized by rows and columns. This is a compromise between varimax and quartimax. Varimax is the SPSS default rotation, and is more commonly used in many factor analysis studies.

Oblique rotations create factors where the angle between the factors is either less than, or greater than, 90 degrees. That is, the factors are intercorrelated either positively or negatively to some degree. The user in SPSS can set the degree of intercorrelation among the factors by using the **DELTA** specification. Tabachnick and Fidell (1983) indicate that when delta is less than zero, solutions are increasingly orthogonal. When delta is zero, solutions are allowed to be fairly highly correlated. Delta values near one can produce factors that are very highly correlated. Although there is a positive relationship between the size of delta and the size of the correlations among the factors, the exact amount of maximum correlation for various sizes of delta cannot be specified independent of a particular data set.

Factor Interpretation

The user is responsible for interpreting and defining the number of useful, or meaningful, factors. The mathematical, or statistical, aspects of factor analysis do not define or name the factors, nor indicate in any way which factors are meaningful and interpretable. This may be the most difficult step, which is totally dependent upon the researcher's background, intuition, and experience with factor analysis. Two individuals could interpret a rotated matrix of factor loadings and arrive at somewhat different conclusions, and interestingly, both may be "right." There are several procedures used as aids in the factor interpretation and definition process. These are Thurstone's concept of **simple structure**, the **magnitude** of the factor loadings, factor **pure** or factor **complex** variables, the **number** of variables on a factor with substantial loadings, and the **percent of variance** accounted for by a given factor.

Computation of Factor Scores (Total Scores)

There are several methods available for computing factor scores for each factor used in the final analysis for each respondent. Thus, one computes scores for each factor as a new variable to be used in subsequent data analyses. A **weighted standardized factor score** will be computed automatically by SPSS for each respondent, and these scores are included on the data matrix as new variables, or included in the existing data file, if the output specification is requested.

Factor Extraction

This section deals with two important aspects of the factor extraction process: criteria that are used to determine the number of factors to extract, including advantages and disadvantages of each; and types of factor extraction methods available with some of the major characteristics of each method. The three most frequently employed factor extraction methods are the Kaiser criterion (eigenvalue greater than one), the scree test as proposed by Cattell, and the amount of variance accounted for by the factor solution.

Kaiser Criterion

The Kaiser Criterion, also referred to as the **eigenvalue greater than one** criterion, is used to determine the number of factors that should be extracted during the initial factor extraction stage. Kaiser suggested that only those factors with eigenvalues greater than one (unity) be considered for rotation and for factor interpretation. As indicated, SPSS uses this as the **default** criterion during the factor extraction process.

Kachigan (1982) provides a useful interpretation of the utility of the eigenvalue. A factor associated with an eigenvalue of 3.69 indicates that the factor accounts for as much variance in the data as 3.69 variables, on an average. If one had factored a nine variable solution, each variable would account on an average for 11% of the total variance (100% divided by 9 = 11%). Thus, a factor with an eigenvalue of 3.69 would account for 3.69 X 11% = 41% of the total variance. Thus, the Kaiser criterion is simply suggesting that one not *retain factors that account for less variance than a typical variable*; that is, less than one eigenvalue.

Cattell (1947) suggested that the Kaiser Criterion is most reliable when the number of variables in the analysis is between 20 and 50. When the number of variables is less than 20, there is a tendency for this method to extract *too few factors*. When more than 50 variables are factored, the method typically extracts *too many factors*. **Residual factors** are extracted that in fact account for very little variance, and generally have few, if any, variables with substantial loadings. Or, several **unique factors** will be produced where only one variable has a substantial loading on the factor.

Scree Test

The scree test is a technique suggested by Cattell (1966) for determining the number of factors to extract. With this method, a graph is plotted of latent roots (eigenvalues) against the number of factors extracted in the order in which they are extracted. The shape of the resulting curve is used to determine the cut-off point (see Figure 1). The scree test can be obtained in SPSS by requesting the appropriate specification.

This test would be used after the initial factor extraction had been performed, generally, after the SPSS default procedure employing the Kaiser criterion is used. One should look for a point of diminishing returns, where inclusion of more factors adds very little to the variance accounted for by the solution. As illustrated in Figure 1, this point is reached after the third factor (eigenvalue equals 1.605), where the curve in the data points begins to flatten out. One may wish to experiment in future analyses by adding, or subtracting, one or two factors around the point of diminishing returns (Tabachnick and Fidell, 1983).

Figure 1
Scree Test for 16 Items from the Tolerance of Ambiguity Scale

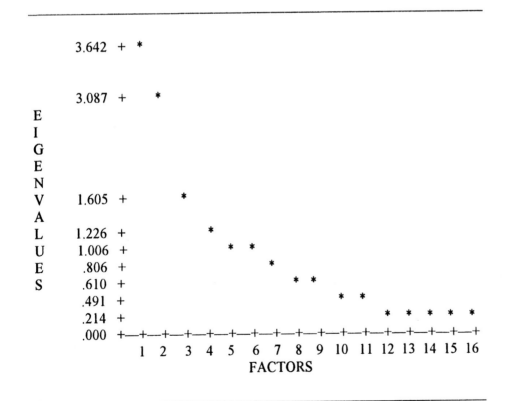

Variance Explained

A third method for determining the number of factors to extract and rotate is to consider the **total variance** accounted for, or explained, by the factors. Even though the objective is to account for as much variance as possible, this should be done with as few factors as possible. The compromise is frequently **between the amount of parsimony and the degree of comprehensiveness of the factor solution.** The final solution should also rest on the degree to which the analysis represents the conceptual framework that initiated the analysis in the first place.

Factor Extraction Methods

Several factor extraction methods are discussed in the literature. The two basic models are the **principal components analysis** and **factor analysis,** also referred to as either principal factors or principal axes. Additional extraction procedures are available, such as maximum likelihood including Roa's canonical factoring, least squares method (minres), alpha factoring, and image factoring. Each method deals with the variance accounted for in the correlation matrix, and deals with the estimation of orthogonal factors, in a slightly different way. As suggested earlier, the difference among the solutions may be small with a good data set and similar communality estimates.

Component Analysis vs. Factor Analysis

Technically, factor analysis extraction differs from principal components in that **estimates of communality,** instead of unity (ones), are inserted in the diagonal of the correlation matrix. In factor analysis, some account is taken of the presence of **unique variance,** whereas in principal component analysis, unique variance is ignored. In principal components, the unique variance is merged with the **common variance** to give hybrid common factors containing small proportions of unique variance.

The difference between the two models rests entirely on the assumptions one makes about the portions of the **unit variances** of each variable that appears in the common factors. These assumptions concerning the decomposition of the total variance is controlled by the value placed in the diagonal of the correlation matrix, because the diagonal value defines the total **common variance (communality)** of a variable to be distributed among the common factors. **Again, principal components inserts ones (unity), and factor analysis inserts an estimate of the communality.**

The exclusion of unique variance from the factor analysis model is based on the belief that this variability only confuses the structural picture that emerges from an analysis. Principal components may be thought of as analyzing variance and factor analysis as analyzing covariance (communality). If you are interested in an **inferred, hypothetical** solution uncontaminated by unique variance, factor analysis is the choice. If you desire an empirical summary of the data, principal components is the better choice (Tabachnick and Fidell, 1983).

If ones are used in the diagonal of the matrix (component analysis), in effect the assumption is made that the variable, or set of variables, is completely reliable and without error. With the factor loadings obtained from the analysis, there may be specific and error variance, but this is not accounted for in the procedure. However, if the common variance of a variable could be determined before commencing a factor solution and the common variance (communality) was inserted in the diagonal, specific and error variance would be eliminated from the model. This is the approach behind the factor analysis model. One of the dilemmas of this solution, however, is in computing the value of the communality before the analysis begins. The initial communality must be estimated, and through an iterative procedure, refined for the final solution. This simply means, starting from an informed guess as to the possible value of the communality, a more reliable value is calculated by repeated approximations until the final value alters very little with repeated calculations. Many of the differences among the various extraction methods are based on this approach to computing the value to be placed in the diagonal of the matrix.

Nunnally (1978) has pointed out that although there are numerous special approaches to common factoring, most of these boil down to what will be placed in the diagonal of the matrix—unities, reliability coefficients, squared multiple correlations, or some type of communality estimate. It is very safe to say that if there are as many as **20 variables** in the analysis, *then it does not matter what one puts in the diagonal.* The results from many studies could be cited to show that the only problem in employing unities in the diagonal come when the correlations in the matrix are small, and particularly, when the number of variables is small.

Other Extraction Methods

As suggested above, several additional extraction methods are discussed in the literature and available in SPSS. Each method, for the most part, deals with a different approach for determining the value to be placed in the diagonal of the correlation matrix. In brief, these are:

Image Factor Extraction: This provides a compromise between principal components and factor analysis. Like principal components it uses a fixed value in the matrix, but as with factor analysis a value that excludes specific and error variance. This solution employs the **squared multiple correlation** (SMC or R-square) of each variable with all other variables as the communality for that variable.

Maximum Likelihood Factor Extraction: Tabachnick and Fidell (1983) indicate that this method estimates population values for factor loadings by calculating a set of factor loadings that maximizes the probability of sampling the observed correlation matrix from a population. Population estimates for factor loadings are calculated that have the greatest probability of yielding a sample with the observed correlation matrix. This procedure is available through Roa's canonical factoring in SPSS, but as suggested by Tabachnick and Fidell, with an inefficient algorithm.

Alpha Factoring: In this method the concern is with the reliability of the common factors. Communalities are calculated using iterative procedures to maximize coefficient alpha for the factors.

Interpretation of the Rotated Factor Matrix

As stated previously, the purpose of the factor rotation is to redefine the factors in order to make sharper distinctions in the meanings of the factors. Generally, this aids in the interpretation and definition of each factor by maximizing the high loadings and minimizing the modest or low loadings. However, the mathematical, or statistical, process of executing a factor analysis does not provide an interpretation of any given solution. The user is totally responsible for the interpretation of the solution, and must understand acceptable procedures for making the factor identifications. This involves first determining how many meaningful (interpretable) factors explain a given data set, and how many factors should be rotated in a final solution. Finally, one must identify and name these factors.

To facilitate the factor interpretation and identification process, several procedures are suggested in the literature discussed briefly below.

Factor Loadings

In a rotated factor matrix the columns represent the derived factors, and the rows represent the original variables included in the analysis (see the Rotated Factor Matrix, page 43). The cell entries of the matrix are **factor loadings** (correlation coefficients of the factor on the variable) with values from -1.00 to +1.00. As with any correlation coefficient, this represents the **degree to which each variable correlates with each factor**. These factor loadings are correlation coefficients between the original variables (items in a test) and the newly derived factors, which are themselves **new variables** (Kachigan, 1982).

The higher the factor loading, the greater is the degree of overlapping variance between the variables and the factor, **and the more the factor represents a summary of the variables in question**. The **square of the loading** of the variable with the factor is a good indication of the extent of the overlap (amount of explained variance). Dividing the factor loading of a variable by the reliability estimate for the variable is sometimes helpful in order to get an indication of the correlation between the variable and the factor if the variable were perfectly reliable.

A frequent question is how large must the loading of the variable and a factor be to be regarded as "significant" or sufficiently substantial to be included in the factor matrix interpretation. There are no statistical standards to test a factor loading for statistical significance in the same manner in which we test other correlation coefficients. To some extent the interpretation of factor loadings is dependent on the overall configuration of loadings and the relationship among loadings.

Generally, a factor loading of **0.300** or lower is a commonly used cutoff for orthogonal factor loadings. However, a researcher may establish a higher cutoff, say 0.400, for a particular factor analytic study. In any case, no single criterion should be used alone, but several techniques should be used simultaneously in identifying and making judgments about any factor solution.

Factor Pure and Complex Variables

A **factor pure** variable is one that loads substantially on one factor and has near zero loadings on all other factors in the solution. A **factorially complex** variable is one that loads with near equal loadings on two or more factors. The more factor pure a variable, the easier it is to make inferences regarding the nature of the factor. These variables obviously aid in the interpretation of the factor. Variables that load on two or more factors with relatively high loadings (.50 or higher) are factorially complex variables. These variables are difficult to interpret in relation to a given factor, and may confuse the overall factor solution.

During the stages of instrumentation development and refinement, it is generally recommended that factorially complex variables be rejected, or, at least, revised. This is especially the case if one is working from the assumptions of Thurstone's **concept of simple structure**.

Concept of Simple Structure

Under ideal circumstances factor rotations should be performed so that each variable loads on **one and only one factor.** The rule need not require that there be the same number of pure variables for all factors, only that there be some pure variables for each factor (Nunnally, 1978). Attempts to approximate this ideal led to a set of rules referred to as Thurstone's (1947) concept of **simple structure**. This includes the following:

- Each row of the rotated factor matrix should have at least one zero (or near zero) loading.

- Each column of the rotated factor matrix will contain some zero (or near zero) loadings with some variables with high loadings.

- For every pair of columns, there should be several zero loadings in one column corresponding to nonzero (substantially higher) loadings in the other column. That is, between any pair of columns, the nonzero elements do not overlap—factor pure variables.

- When four or more common factors are obtained, each pair of columns should have a proportion of corresponding zero loadings. This requirement ensures that each reference axis is pertinent to only a few of the observed variables and, thus, guarantees a separation of the variables into distinct clusters.

With most social science data, one is not likely to see such simple structure. So the task becomes how to define factor structures that approximate simple structure. Thurstone's criteria only specify empirical conditions under which a simple structure can be identified unambiguously. A researcher will always need to compromise these rules in completing a meaningful factor interpretation.

Number of Variables per Factor

The greater the number of variables with substantial loadings on a factor (other things being equal) the easier it is to determine and isolate what the factor represents. While the authorities do not agree as to the number of variables a factor should have, they do generally agree that a factor that is defined by only **one or two variables (items)** is potentially unreliable and should be interpreted with great caution, or rejected.

Kim and Mueller (1978) suggested that there should be at least **three variables** that clearly load on a factor. Preferably these would be factor pure variables as well. Comrey (1973) indicated that there should be at least **five good marker variables** for each factor anticipated. It is clear that one needs to apply some degree of common sense and intuition. Absolute rules do not exist with many aspects of factor interpretation, and individual discretion within some logical boundaries must be exercised in the interpretation and definition of most factor solutions.

Factor Scores
Creating Composite (Total) Scores for Each Scale

One additional purpose for conducting a factor analysis, after the factor interpretation and identification stage are completed, is to obtain **factor scores** (composite scores) for each subject in the original data file for each factor retained. Each factor becomes a **new variable**, which, through the data reduction process, represents a large amount of information about a cluster of the original variables. If these factors as new variables are scored, they can be used for further data analysis. Most computer programs provide some technique for computing **factor scores**, such as the computation of factor scores provided in SPSS. Or, the researcher may wish to manually compute factor scores using some other procedure suggested in the literature. SPSS uses the **complete estimation method**. If one wishes to employ some other procedure, then these scores can be calculated using the SPSS COMPUTE statement.

Complete Estimation Method

With this method a factor-score coefficient is computed by SPSS that is used as a **weight** for each variable, or item, retained in the factor solution. It should be noted that with this procedure **all variables are scored on all factors**, not just the higher loaded variables, as is the case with other scoring methods. This allows for variables with small factor loadings to be used as **suppressor variables**. It is argued that this method provides the best estimate of the factor score. The weight for each variable on the factor is used to determine the contribution of that variable in computing the composite score for the factor. Obviously, variables with high factor loadings will have relatively higher weights than variables with low factor loadings, and thus, make a larger contribution to the factor score. In SPSS, a table of factor-score coefficients (weights) can be requested. This method produces a **weighted standardized factor score for each subject in the data file for each factor retained.**

Raw Factor Scores

This method computes factor scores based only on the highest loaded items on the factor. Generally, those items used during the factor interpretation and identification stage to name the factor are used to score the factor. The final composite score may be standardized but no weighting is used. Each variable contributes equally to the factor score regardless of its loading on the factor. To compute factor scores using this method with SPSS, the COMPUTE specification can be used.

Weighted Raw Factor Scores

This method is similar to the one above except the **factor loadings** of the variables are used as **weights** in the computation of the factor score. These scores may be standardized.

Weighted Factor Scores Using the Factor Coefficient

The factor-score coefficient produced by SPSS may be used as a weight instead of the factor loading. Again, the SPSS COMPUTE statement can be used to generate factor scores with this method.

In practice if the same data set is used, one would find very little difference in comparing the computations of factor scores across the four methods. One method will not enhance, or improve, a poor factor solution. On the other hand, a good factor solution will provide reasonably sound estimates of factor scores regardless of the method used.

Negative Factor Loadings

In computing factor scores a comment is in order concerning negative factor loadings. A negative correlation coefficient between two variables means that high scores on one tend to be associated with low scores on the other, and vice versa. The same thing is true with factor loadings, inasmuch as a factor loading is a correlation coefficient between a variable and an abstract factor. When a variable loads negatively on a factor, it simply means that a subject scoring high on the variable will score low on the factor, and vice versa. Or, a negatively loaded variable has **a meaning opposite to that of the factor** (Kachigan, 1982). In computing factor scores, the sign "+" or "−" will be used in the computation. Thus, the final factor score will be an algebraic sum of all positive and negative loaded items on the factor.

In computing factor scores for many instruments and questionnaires, it is common to find both positive and negative loaded items on each factor. This is the case where in the construction of the instrument, both positive and negative phrased statements (reversed items) are used, and these reversed statements are **not recoded** prior to data entry. Generally, the negatively phrased items will have a negative factor loading, and the positively phrased items a positive loading (although sometimes the two may be reversed). In practice, the important thing to remember, and a distinct advantage of computing factor scores with SPSS, is that one does not need to manually recode, or manually reverse, negatively phrased statements prior to data entry. Both positive and negative statements will be accommodated in the factor analysis process accordingly.

Common Errors in Using Factor Analysis

Some of the more common errors in the use of factor analysis are listed below. This list is a summary extracted, for the most part, from Comrey (1973) and from Guilford (1952).

❑ The use of variables in the analysis with bad distributions and inappropriate regression forms to include: badly skewed distributions; truncated distributions; bimodal distributions; distributions with a few extreme cases (outliers); extreme splits in dichotomized cases; and nonlinear regressions.

❑ The use of data variables that are not **experimentally independent** of each other to include: scoring the same item response on more than one variable; in a forced-choice item, scoring one response alternative on one variable and the other on a second variable; having one variable as a linear combination of other variables, for example, verbal, quantitative, and total score.

❑ Failure to **overdetermine** the factors. The number of variables should be several times as large as the number of factors. When designing the questionnaire, there should be at least **five good marker variables** for each factor anticipated.

❑ The use of too many **complex variables**. The best variables for defining factors are factor pure. Only a few multifactor variables should be used, and only if a larger number of factor pure variables are present.

❑ The failure to provide **good marker variables** for a factor that may be present in other factor-complex data variables. Without the markers (variables that are factor pure), the factor will be difficult to identify, even though variance for that factor will be interspersed among other factors.

❑ Poor **sampling procedures**, to include a sample of subjects too small to obtain stable correlations in the factor solution; combining two distinct groups with a different factor structure into the same sample; and loss of a factor because of biased sampling that restricts the range of variability on that factor.

❑ Not including **sufficient factors** in the solution. To have good hyperplanes for using simple structure as a guide in rotations, it is necessary to have a large number of points in the hyperplanes. Without **six or more factors** in the analysis that are relatively independent of each other, it is difficult to have good hyperplanes.

❑ The use of **inappropriate correlation coefficients**, such as the tetrachoric, in a situation that violates the assumptions underlying its use.

- The use of inappropriate **communality** estimates, for example, using ones in the diagonal of the matrix when the objective of the analysis is concerned with common-factor variance.

- Extracting **too few factors** by forcing a factor solution for several factors into a space of fewer dimensions with consequent distortion of the factor solution.

- The use of **poor rotation procedures**, such as a failure to rotate at all; using an orthogonal rotation when an oblique rotation would provide a clearer analysis; the use of rotational criteria that are not appropriate for the kind of data involved; and rotation of extra small factors that spreads the variance too much.

- The failure of interpreting the first extracted factor as a **general factor**.

- Leaping to a conclusion about the nature of a factor on the basis of insufficient evidence, for example, low loadings and lack of outside confirmation when identifying the factor. The interpretation of factors must be verified on the basis of evidence outside the factor analysis itself. Follow-up factor analyses and construct validation studies are an important part of this verification process. Again, a factor analytic study should be based on some conceptual framework, on a theory or, at least, on a sound taxonomy that can serve as a guide in the identification and verification of factors.

Reporting a Factor Analytic Study

A proper reporting of a factor analysis requires that the investigator provide the reader with enough information to permit the results to be independently verified. One should be able to gather similar data, and **replicate** the study from the information provided in the report. In order to verify the results, it is expected that the investigator make available the correlation matrix of data variables generated by the factor analysis. For a dissertation, this would probably be reported in the appendix. SPSS allows the use of a matrix of correlation coefficients as input to the FACTOR procedure. One does not need the original data file. Within the body of the document, the following should be reported:

Selection of Subjects: Information is required concerning the sample, or the method of selecting subjects, for the study. This should include the number of subjects (N of cases), and relevant personal and demographic data.

Data Variables: The data file (types of variables) should be described in sufficient detail to enable the reader to have an understanding of what is being measured. Again, appropriate variables could be items in a test, scores on a number of tests, or other similar units of measurement.

Matrix of Correlation Coefficients: Information should be provided concerning the level of measurement (scaling) of the variables, and the type of correlation coefficients computed. Violations of basic assumptions of correlational procedures should be noted.

Factor Extraction: The method of factor extraction should be provided, as well as the criterion, or criteria, used to determine the number of factors to extract and rotate.

Communalities: If a principal factor method is used, the type of communality estimates should be described, i.e., iteration of communalities, SMCs, reliability estimates, etc. The number of iterations required for the principal factor solution should be indicated.

Method of Rotation: The method of factor rotation and the evidence to support this as an appropriate procedure for the data should be provided. The theory, or conceptual framework, upon which the analysis is based should provide some evidence to the appropriateness of the type of factor rotation. The number of factors rotated and the extent to which the empirical data (factor structure) represents, or corresponds to, the theoretical and conceptual basis should be discussed.

One should provide information on the factor interpretation and identification stage of the analysis. Indicate the **cutoff** of factor loadings (.30) used to eliminate variables from the analysis. Report the number of factors from the initial solution with eigenvalues greater than one. If a smaller number is used in the final solution, indicate the reason for decreasing this number, i.e., several residual or unique factors were initially extracted. Indicate the percent of total variance accounted for by the final factor solution, as well as the percent of variance for each individual factor rotated in the final solution.

Table of Factor Results: A table should be provided listing each factor in the final solution, including the following information (see Table 2 as an example):

☐ A description and name of each factor should be provided. After naming the factors, **do not continue to refer to the factor by number,** but use the name of the factor throughout the report. Factor numbers are essentially meaningless and somewhat arbitrary based on the particular factor solution. A factor analysis based on similar data could have comparable factors in an entirely different numerical order.

☐ Provide a list of the original item numbers or, if appropriate, variable numbers. If one factor analyzes an instrument with a number of items, these item numbers should be tabled as a reference to the original variables within the instrument.

☐ The factor loading of each variable on the factor should be listed. The variables should be listed in **descending order** based on the size of the factor loadings, not in the order of the original variable or item number in the test.

☐ The **eigenvalue** associated with each factor, and the percent of variance accounted for, should be listed on the table for each factor.

☐ Finally, one should keep in mind that factor analysis merely provides the results of one investigator's way of interpreting the data. Any analysis is open to question and critique. Also, factor analysis, based on correlational statistics, is subject to considerable variation from population (or sample) to population. **Factor solutions can vary greatly from study to study.** One analysis based on one group of subjects may not be entirely replicated with a different selection of subjects, even though the variables and measurement remain the same.

Factor Analysis Examples and Explanation

The SPSS factor solution used in these examples employed the Tolerance-Intolerance of Ambiguity measure developed by Budner. The instrument contained 16 items anchored with a Likert-type scale. The examples and explanation below do not represent a complete computer printout of the factor analysis provided in SPSS. Rather, partial tables are used that provide a more basic and elementary analysis. As discussed above, there is no one best solution when conducting a factor analysis. The approach and analysis are often a matter of choice, or more appropriately, dictated by the outcome one is attempting to achieve.

In the examples below, the initial factor solution will employ the SPSS default procedures. In most cases for the beginning researcher, these are satisfactory and provide a reasonably good factor solution. Generally, more than one solution is required. Each should represent a different degree of refinement until the final factor solution is achieved (number of factors to be retained), at which time weighted factor scores can be computed for each factor.

Table 2
Varimax Rotated Factor Structure
Structural Properties Questionnaire (SPQ)
N = 1367

Factor Name: **Professional Latitude**

Factor Loading	Item Number	Item	h^2
.732	30	People here are allowed to do almost as they please.	.595
.718	26	Most people here make their own rules on the job.	.577
.616	13	Teaching in your school is a good job for someone who likes to be "his own boss."	.492
.567	20	How things are done is left up to the person doing the work.	.449
.485	35	A teacher can make his own decisions concerning instructional problems without checking with anybody else.	.408
.482	44	Teachers are allowed to violate minor rules and regulations.	.504

Eigenvalue = 3.60
Percent of Variance = 18.00%

The first example will use the SPSS default procedures, which includes a varimax (orthogonal) rotation, a principal components extraction method, and the Kaiser criterion (eigenvalue greater than one criterion) to determine the number of factors to be initially extracted.

The first analysis resulted in a six-factor solution. There were six eigenvalues greater than one; and thus, six factors were rotated. This initial solution needs to be interpreted in order to refine the analysis by reducing the number of factors rotated. The Kaiser criterion **over extracts** factors, which typically produce residual or unique factors that are generally not interpretable. Also, items must be analyzed that do not load above 0.30 on any factor. Items that have substantial loadings on two or more factors may be discarded. Finally, an initial factor interpretation and identification should be made. Each factor retained should be given a name. The arbitrary factor numbers assigned by SPSS should be discarded and not used in reporting the factor solution.

Basic Correlation Matrix

As discussed previously, the correlation matrix (see Table 3 below) forms the basis for the factor analysis, and can be studied and tested to determine the adequacy of the factor model. Items that do not appear to be related to other items can be identified. If the correlations between items are small (below .30), it is unlikely that they share a common factor. A number of tests are available in SPSS to determine the adequacy of the data associated with the matrix. These tests are more advanced and will not be discussed here.

Table 3
Correlation Matrix
(Partial Matrix)

	VAR1	VAR2	VAR3	VAR4	VAR5	VAR6	VAR7
VAR1	1.00						
VAR2	-.13	1.00					
VAR3	.23	.15	1.00				
VAR4	.16	.07	.23	1.00			
VAR5	.46	.20	.50	.33	1.00		
VAR6	.42	.13	.52	.44	.53	1.00	
VAR7	.09	.28	.13	.41	.37	.30	1.00
VAR8	.26	.15	.07	.12	.16	.22	.29
VAR9	.06	-.12	.38	.15	.28	.25	.07
VAR10	.05	-.17	.19	.05	.26	.21	-.09
VAR11	.10	-.29	.10	.05	.26	.09	-.13
VAR12	-.09	-.17	.15	.08	.10	.18	-.03
VAR13	.07	-.12	.00	-.27	-.04	-.03	-.11
VAR14	.13	.22	.06	.32	.01	-.16	.25
VAR15	.25	.00	-.06	-.19	-.01	.02	.08
VAR16	.07	-.14	-.05	.00	-.02	-.03	-.16

Partial matrix of correlation coefficients for the sixteen variables (items) in the questionnaire.

The **Initial Statistics** table (see Table 4) provides the basic statistics included in the factor analysis. These are **communalities, eigenvalues,** and **percent of variance** for each factor in the analysis. A principal components analysis always has communalities of one (unity)—ones are always inserted in the diagonal of the matrix. The magnitude of the eigenvalues indicates the number of factors that were extracted and rotated. Inasmuch as the default Kaiser criterion was used, six factors with eigenvalues greater than one were extracted. The cumulative percent of variance accounted for by the six factors is about 73%. That is, about 73% of the information contained in the 16 items of the instrument can be accounted for in the six "common" factors. The information not accounted for (about 27%) is either unique or error variance.

Table 4
Initial Statistics
Principal Components Analysis

Variable	Commun-ality	Factor	Eigenvalue	Percent Variance	Cumulative Percent
VAR1	1.000	1	3.642	22.8	22.8
VAR2	1.000	2	3.086	19.3	42.1
VAR3	1.000	3	1.605	10.0	52.1
VAR4	1.000	4	1.226	7.7	59.8
VAR5	1.000	5	1.066	6.7	66.4
VAR6	1.000	6	1.006	6.3	72.7
VAR7	1.000	7	.806	5.0	77.7
VAR8	1.000	8	.738	4.6	82.4
VAR9	1.000	9	.609	3.8	86.2
VAR10	1.000	10	.555	3.5	89.6
VAR11	1.000	11	.491	3.1	92.7
VAR12	1.000	12	.380	2.4	95.1
VAR13	1.000	13	.298	1.9	96.9
VAR14	1.000	14	.214	1.3	98.3
VAR15	1.000	15	.159	1.0	99.3
VAR16	1.000	16	.116	.7	100.0

Six Factors Extracted

Unrotated Factor Matrix

Table 5 provides an example of a partial unrotated factor matrix. This matrix can be difficult to interpret, and provides only tentative information concerning the most appropriate factor structure. For simplicity, only factor loadings of **0.300 or higher** have been included on the table.

Table 5
Unrotated Factor Matrix

Variable	Factor 1	Factor 2	Factor 3	Factor 4	Factor 5	Factor 6
VAR1		.421		-.757		
VAR2		.377	.377		.601	
VAR3	.369	.549				
VAR4		.631		.362	-.435	-.360
VAR5	.415	.672				
VAR6	.392	.700				
VAR7		.604	.367			
VAR8		.449		-.329	.327	.592
VAR9	.655		-.363			.325
VAR10	.648		-.323			
VAR11	.703					
VAR12	.763			.318		
VAR13	.695	-.440	.326			
VAR14		.301	.667		-.359	

42

Rotated Factor Matrix

In most cases, the **rotated factor matrix** is used to interpret the factors, to determine the number of factors to use, and to name the factors. Table 6 is an example of a complete rotated matrix (including all 16 variables and all loadings) based on the data from Table 5. Each value in the matrix is a factor loading, which is a correlation between the variable (item) and the factor. The magnitude of the loading indicates which factors have something in common with the items, and the items that should be considered in identifying and naming the factor. For example, Var13, Var12, Var15, and Var16 have a great deal to do with factor 1 (the loadings are all above 0.70). These items should be used in identifying and naming factor 1. Similarly, Var3, Var5, and Var6 should be used to identify and name factor 2. Factor 3 has only two highly loaded items (Var4 and Var14). Recall earlier in the discussion that a good, identifiable factor should have a minimum of three to five items. This third factor might be treated as a residual factor that could be dropped from the final solution. Factors 4, 5, and 6 are definitely residual or unique factors. Each has only one item loading on the factor. This suggests that the next factor analysis should be forced to **a maximum** of three factors to be rotated. The final factor solution would probably only retain two factors.

Table 6
Rotated Factor Matrix

Variables	Factor 1	Factor 2	Factor 3	Factor 4	Factor 5	Factor 6
VAR1	.032	.360	.070	-.203	.206	**.835**
VAR2	-.105	.168	.095	**.870**	.073	-.117
VAR3	-.016	**.799**	.015	.141	-.043	-.023
VAR4	-.135	.336	**.767**	-.214	.175	-.144
VAR5	.002	**.803**	.101	.063	.139	.210
VAR6	.009	**.705**	.330	.008	.140	.209
VAR7	-.027	.206	.505	.355	.409	.017
VAR8	-.121	.058	.037	.088	**.855**	.132
VAR9	.434	.487	-.126	-.237	.385	-.352
VAR10	.423	.486	-.132	-.258	-.144	-.227
VAR11	.546	.311	-.057	-.417	-.143	-.051
VAR12	**.785**	.171	.028	-.129	-.137	-.213
VAR13	**.878**	-.019	-.145	.049	-.120	.114
VAR14	.072	-.082	**.777**	.234	-.147	.180
VAR15	**.736**	-.086	.001	.210	-.100	.433
VAR16	**.730**	-.087	-.015	-.162	.177	-.042

Three Factor Solution

The factor matrix below (Table 7) is an example where a request is made to limit the number of factors extracted and rotated to **only three**. This solution can be controlled in SPSS by requesting that only three factors be rotated. In addition, the items loading on each factor are listed from the highest loading to the lowest, and only those loadings with values **above 0.300** are included. Lower values on each factor are excluded. This aids in the final interpretation of the factors to be retained. Note also that factor loadings for some items (Var13, Var15, and Var16) have decreased when compared to the six factor rotated solution in Table 6. This is normal and expected. Any change to a factor analysis (number of factors rotated, number of items included or excluded, size of the sample, etc.) will subsequently change the factor solution and subsequently the factor loadings.

This three factor analysis suggests also that the final solution should be forced to a two factor solution. Factor 3 is a residual factor. Two items on factor 3 (Var15 and Var7) also load on factors 1 and 2. In both cases, they have higher loadings on those factors. The only item unique to factor 3 is Var14, which constitutes a unique or residual factor that should be omitted from the final analysis. Note also that three items (Var1, Var2, and Var8) were not included in Table 7. This indicates that these items had loadings lower than **0.300** on all three factors. This indicates that only 13 items from the total of 16 items have measurement in common. Three items do not belong—are not correlated—with the other 13 items. The factor solution has discarded these items suggesting that they produce more measurement error than true measurement when used in conjunction with the other 13 items.

In summary, the three measurement techniques discussed in this section are very useful in evaluating existing measures or in developing new instruments. They are examples that provide the minimum required in analyzing the ability of any instrument to provide "good" measurement. They determine the extent to which the instrument provides true measurement and the degree to which the measurement is due to error. Individual items can be evaluated as to their contribution in the measurement of the given concept. Thus, these techniques provide at least one measure of reliability, a means of evaluating the contribution of individual items, and one measure of construct validity.

Table 7
Rotated Factor Matrix
Three Factor Solution

Variable	Factor 1	Factor 2	Factor 3
VAR12	.787		
VAR13	.706	-.495	
VAR11	.696		
VAR9	.668		
VAR10	.651		
VAR16	.597		
VAR15	.514		.482
VAR4		.694	
VAR6		.693	
VAR5		.658	
VAR3		.584	
VAR7		.577	.439
VAR14			.754

Selected References

Aldenderfer, M.S., and R.K. Blashfield, 1984. *Cluster Analysis* (#44). Beverly Hills: Sage.

Asher, H.B. 1976. *Causal Modeling* (#3). Beverly Hills: Sage.

Child, D. 1978. *The Essentials of Factor Analysis.* New York: Holt, Rinehart and Winston.

Comrey, A.L. 1973. *A First Course in Factor Analysis.* New York: Academic Press.

Gorsuch, R.L. 1974. *Factor Analysis.* Philadelphia: W.B. Saunders.

Harman, H.H. 1976. *Modern Factor Analysis* (3rd ed.). Chicago: The University of Chicago Press.

Kachigan, S.K. 1982. *Multivariate Statistical Analysis.* New York: Radius Press.

Kerlinger, F.N. 1979. *Behavioral Research: A Conceptual Approach.* New York: McGraw-Hill.

Kim, J., and C.W. Mueller. 1978. *Introduction to Factor Analysis* (#13). Beverly Hills: Sage.

Kim, J., and C.W. Mueller. 1978a. *Factor Analysis* (#14). Beverly Hills: Sage.

Kruskal, J.B., and M. Wish. 1978. *Multidimensional Scaling* (#11). Beverly Hills: Sage.

Long, J.S. 1983. *Confirmatory Factor Analysis* (#33). Beverly Hills: Sage.

Mulaik, S.A. 1972. *The Foundations of Factor Analysis.* New York: McGraw-Hill.

Nunnally, J.P. 1978. *Psychometric Theory* (2nd ed.). New York: McGraw-Hill.

Tabachnick, B.G., and L.S. Fidell. 1983. *Using Multivariate Statistics.* New York: Harper.

Thorndike, R.M. 1978. *Correlational Procedures for Research.* New York: Gardner Press.

Alienation

Alienation Scale

Dean, D.G. 1961. Alienation: Its meaning and measurement. *American Sociological Review* 26:753-758.

Comments: The 24-item AS assesses three aspects of alienation: powerlessness, normlessness, and social isolation. In addition, the AS has served as a model for the development of more recent instruments.

Scale Construction: This scale is based on the five meanings described by Seeman (powerlessness, normlessness, meaninglessness, isolation, and self-estrangement).

Sample: The original stratified sample consisted of 384 men from Columbus, Ohio in 1955. Additional samples consisted of 135 women from a Protestant liberal arts college in 1960; 121 women from a Catholic women's college in 1960; 75 women from a Protestant liberal arts college in 1955; and 65 women from a Catholic women's college.

Reliability: Corrected split-half correlation coefficients for the three scales were: 0.73 normlessness, 0.79 powerlessness, and 0.84 social isolation. The total reliability was 0.78.

Validity: Content validation was performed through a panel of seven judges. The Adorno F Scale was correlated with the Alienation Scale producing correlation coefficients ranging from 0.26 (alienation and authoritarianism) to 0.37 (powerlessness and authoritarianism).

Scales: There are three subscales. The powerlessness scale contains nine items: 2, 6, 9, 13, 15, 18, 20, 21, and 23; the normlessness scale contains six items: 4, 7, 10, 12, 16, 19; and the social isolation scale contains nine items: 1, 3, 5, 8, 11, 14, 17, 22, and 24.

References:
Calabrese, R.L., and J.E. Fisher. 1988. The effects of teaching experience on levels of alienation. *Journal of Psychology* 122:147-153.

Dean, D. 1956. Alienation and political apathy. Ph.D. dissertation, Ohio State University.

de Man, A.F. 1990. Repression-sensitization and measures of adjustment. *Social Behavior and Personality* 18:13-16.

Alienation Scale

1. Sometimes I feel all alone in the world.
2. I worry about the future facing today's children.
3. I don't get invited out by friends as often as I'd really like.
4. The end often justifies the means.
5. Most people today seldom feel lonely.
6. Sometimes I have the feeling that other people are using me.
7. People's ideas change so much that I wonder if we'll ever have anything to depend on.
8. Real friends are as easy as ever to find.
9. It is frightening to be responsible for the development of a little child.
10. Everything is relative, and there just aren't any rules to live by.
11. One can always find friends if he shows himself friendly.
12. I often wonder what the meaning of life really is.
13. There is little or nothing I can do towards preventing a major "shooting" war.
14. The world in which we live is basically a friendly place.
15. There are so many decisions that have to be made today that sometimes I could just "blow up."
16. The only thing one can be sure of today is that he can be sure of nothing.
17. There are few dependable ties between people any more.
18. There is little chance for promotion on the job unless a man gets a break.
19. With so many religions abroad, one doesn't really know which to believe.
20. We're so regimented today that there's not much room for choice even in personal matters.
21. We are just so many cogs in the machinery of life.
22. People are just naturally friendly and helpful.
23. The future looks very dismal.
24. I don't get to visit friends as often as I'd really like.

Scoring: Strongly Agree = 4; Agree = 3; Uncertain = 2; Disagree = 1; and Strongly Disagree = 0. The scoring is reversed for items: 5, 8, 11, 14, and 22. Scores range from a low of 0 to a high of 96.

Reprinted with permission of the American Sociological Association.

Pupil Attitude Questionnaire

Kolesar, H. 1967. An empirical study of client alienation in the bureaucratic organization. Ph.D. dissertation, University of Alberta, Edmonton, Canada.

Comments: The 60-item PAQ is based on Seeman's (1959) five alienation subscales: powerlessness, self-estrangement, normlessness, meaninglessness, and isolation.

Sample: As part of the pilot study, 163 high school students from Alberta, Canada responded to the PAQ. The original 164 items were reduced to 60 items based on three types of analysis. The revised PAQ was administered to 92 students over a one-week interval. Approximately 1,764 students in 20 high schools in Alberta, Canada completed the revised PAQ.

Reliability: Test-retest reliability for the entire PAQ with 92 students over a one-week period was 0.79.

Validity: Four kinds of validity were established: content, face, construct, and factorial validity. Content validity was established by using a large number of items representing various relationships between the student and the school. Face validity was established by using a panel of 14 judges who determined that the questionnaire measures what it purports to measure. Construct validity was established by correlating student scores on the PAQ with teacher ratings (significant at the 0.001 level). Factorial validity was established by performing several factor analyses.

Factor Analysis: A five-factor solution was accepted. The five factors are: 12 items on powerlessness (5, 7, 8, 13, 28, 29, 30, 34, 41, 51, 53, and 59); 12 on self-estrangement (10, 12, 16, 21, 26, 31, 32, 36, 40, 43, 44, and 54); 14 on normlessness (1, 2, 3, 11, 15, 18, 24, 27, 35, 42, 52, 56, 57, and 58); 12 on meaninglessness (6, 14, 17, 19, 33, 37, 38, 39, 45, 46, 47, and 60); and 10 on isolation (4, 9, 20, 22, 23, 25, 48, 49, 50, and 55).

Definition of Factors: Student *powerlessness* pertains to the student's sense of a lack of personal control over his/her state of affairs in school. *Meaninglessness* pertains to a sense of inability to predict outcomes. Student *normlessness* pertains to the belief that socially unapproved behaviors are required to achieve school goals. The *isolated student* is one who does not accept the goals of the school as his/her own. The *self-estranged student* is one who is unable to find school activities that are self-rewarding.

Data Analysis: Scores on each of the five scales were correlated with the scores on the other scales as well as with the total score. The results of all these correlations were all positive and significant, except the correlation between the meaninglessness and isolation scales.

Reference: Rafalides, M., and W.K. Hoy. 1971. Student sense of alienation and pupil control orientation of high schools. *High School Journal* 55:101-111.

Pupil Attitude Questionnaire

1. White lies are justified when they help to avoid punishment.
2. It is a good policy to tell teachers only what they want to hear.
3. In this school success is to be aimed for by any means that pupils can devise.
4. It is most important that right always be achieved even if it requires tremendous effort.
5. Schools are run by others and there is little that pupils can do about it.
6. I think that I can now predict what I can achieve in an occupation after graduation.
7. The school experiences of pupils are controlled by plans devised by others.
8. There really isn't much use complaining to the teachers about the school because it is impossible to influence them anyway.
9. The reason I endure some unpleasant things now is because I feel that it will benefit me later on.
10. Pupils should have most of their time free from study.
11. Sometimes it is necessary to make promises to school authorities which you don't intend to keep.
12. In order to get ahead in this school pupils are almost forced to do some things which are not right.
13. Pupils often are given the opportunity to express their ideas about how the school ought to be run.
14. It is possible on the basis of the level of my present school achievement, to predict with a high degree of accuracy, the level of achievement I can expect in adulthood.
15. It is very desirable that pupils learn to be good citizens
16. I think my teachers would have given me the same marks on the last report card no matter how well I really had done.
17. My school experiences will help me to become a good citizen.
18. It doesn't matter too much if what I am doing is right or wrong as long as it works.
19. At school we learn habits and attitudes which will guide us in the achievement of a good life.
20. I know that I will complete my high school education.
21. These days a pupil doesn't really know who he can count on.
22. I often worry about what my teachers think of me.
23. Pupils must try to develop an interest in their school subjects even when the content is dull.
24. It is more important to achieve enjoyment and personal satisfaction than to sacrifice yourself for others.
25. I study hard in school mainly because I want to get good grades.
26. I often read and study in my courses beyond what is required by my teachers.
27. Really, a pupil has done wrong only if he gets caught.
28. The school principal is really interested in all pupils in this school.
29. In discipline cases the pupil's explanation of the circumstances is carefully weighed by the school authorities before punishment is decided upon.
30. The teachers will not listen to pupil complaints about unfair school rules.
31. Usually, I would rather play hooky than come to school.
32. I would rather go to work now than go to school, but more education now will help me to get a better job later.
33. What I am doing at school will assist me to do what I want when I graduate.
34. Pupils have adequate opportunities to protect themselves when their interests conflict with the interests of those who run the school.
35. Copying parts of essays from books is justified if this results in good marks on the essays.
36. I get more satisfaction from doing an assignment well than from the marks which I receive on the assignment.
37. What we do at school will help us to affect the world in which we live.
38. Participation in student government activities will help me in anything I try to do in the future.
39. As a result of my school experiences I know what I will do when I graduate.
40. No matter how I try I don't seem to understand the content of my courses very well.
41. In this school the teachers are the rulers and the pupils are the slaves.

42. It is unlikely that in this school the pupils will achieve the goals in which they believe.
43. If homework assignments were not required, I would seldom do homework.
44. I like to do extra problems in mathematics for fun.
45. I understand how decisions are made regarding what we are to study in this school.
46. My school studies will help me to make predictions about the kind of world in which I will live in the future.
47. My present school studies will help me to understand others.
48. Pupils must be very careful to make the best possible impression with their teachers.
49. If I had my way, I'd close all schools.
50. Having lots of friends is more important than is getting ahead in school.
51. In this school pupils can complain to the principal and be given a fair hearing.
52. Copying another pupil's homework is justified if he agrees to let you do it.
53. Pupil's ideas about how the school should be run are often adopted in this school.
54. I find it easy to please my teachers.
55. I want to finish high school.
56. It is necessary to misbehave at school if you're going to have any fun.
57. Giving an answer to someone else during an examination is not really cheating.
58. Pupils must take advantage of every opportunity, fair or unfair, because good opportunities occur very infrequently at this school.
59. Pupils in this school are given considerable freedom in planning their own programs to meet their future needs.
60. Participation in student government activities will assist me to become a good citizen.

Scoring: Strongly Agree = 5; Agree = 4; Undecided = 3; Disagree = 2; Strongly Disagree = 1. The scoring is reversed for the following items: 4, 6, 13, 15, 20, 23, 26, 28, 29, 34, 36, 44, 45, 46, 51, 53, 54, 55, and 59. For the following items on the meaninglessness scale 14, 17, 19, 33, 37, 38, 39, 47, and 60 the scoring is as follows: SA = 1, A = 3, U = 5, D = 3, SD = 1.

Reprinted with permission of the author.

Alienation Scale

Pearlin, L.I. 1962. Alienation from work: A study of nursing personnel. *American Sociological Review* 4:466-479.

Comments: Although the original study was conducted in a mental hospital, the four-item questionnaire has recently been used in educational settings (urban and suburban school districts and universities). The instrument was designed to examine alienation in a bureaucratic setting. Alienation is defined as "a feeling of powerlessness over one's own affairs—a sense that the things that importantly affect one's activities and work are outside his control." Therefore, the relationships among responsibility, authority, and alienation were explored.

Sample: The original sample consisted of 1,138 nursing assistants, charge attendants, and registered nurses in a large mental hospital near Washington, D.C.

Reliability: A coefficient of reproducibility of 0.91 is reported for the four-item Guttman scale.

Data Analysis: Alienation is studied in terms of positional distance and status obeisance. A four-item Guttman scale assessing obeisance is included.

References:

Benson, N., and P. Malone. 1987. Teachers' beliefs about shared decision making and work alienation. *Education* 107:244-251.

Knoop, R. 1986. Causes of alienation among university professors. *Perceptual and Motor Skills* 63:677-678.

Pearlin, L.I., and M.L. Kohn. 1966. Social class, occupation and parental values: A cross-national study. *American Sociological Review* 4:466-479.

Alienation Scale

1. How often do you do things in your work that you wouldn't do if it were up to you? Never; Once in a while; Fairly often; *Very often.*
2. Around here it's not important how much you know; it's who you know that really counts. *Agree;* Disagree.
3. How much say or influence do people like you have on the way the hospital is run? A lot; Some; *Very little; None.*
4. How often do you tell (your superior) your own ideas about things you might do in your work? *Never; Once in a while;* Fairly often; Very often.

Scoring: The alienative answers are italicized.

Reprinted with permission of the American Sociological Association.

Anxiety/Frustration

Social Components of Retirement Anxiety Scale

Fletcher, W.L., and R.O. Hannson. 1991. Assessing the social components of retirement anxiety. *Psychology and Aging* 6:76-85.

Comments: The 23-item SCRAS examines the social aspects related to retirement anxiety.

Scale Construction: In order to develop and validate the SCRAS, four studies were conducted. In Study 1, a 30-item pilot scale was constructed and 56 workers participated. Based upon data analyses, the revised SCRAS contained 29 items. In Study 2, the construct validity of the scale was established with a sample of 175 workers from a restaurant chain, bank, and manufacturing company. Based on data analyses, the SCRAS was reduced to 23 items. In Study 3, discriminant and construct validity were examined further. In Study 4, the participants from Study 3 were combined with the participants from Study 4 in order to conduct factor analysis.

Sample: The sample for Study 3 consisted of 169 workers from a university and city government who were 50 years of age and older. The sample for Study 4 consisted of 292 workers from a manufacturing company, hospital, bank, oil company, and church groups who were 50 years of age and older. A combined sample of 461 people (Studies 3 and 4) was used for the factor analysis.

Reliability: For Study 1 the reliability was 0.90. For Study 2 the alpha coefficient was 0.87 and the Guttman split-half correlation was 0.82. For Study 3 the alpha coefficient was 0.87 and the Guttman split-half correlation was 0.82. For Study 4 the alpha coefficient was 0.84.

Validity: Study 1 and 2 established criterion, discriminant, and construct validity.

Factor Structure: A principal components factor analysis with a varimax rotation yielded four factors: Social Integration (1, 3, 4, 5, 7, 9, 10, 11, 13, and 20); Social Adjustment/Hardiness (6, 12, 14, 16, 17, and 21); Anticipated Social Exhaustion (2, 8, 15, and 19); and Lost Friendships (18, 22, and 23).

Data Analysis: Correlations with fear-of-retirement criterion items are presented for Studies 2 and 3. The results of additional correlational tests are also included as well as means and standard deviations.

References:
Braithwaite, V.A., et al. 1986. An exploratory study of poor adjustment styles among retirees. *Social Science and Medicine* 23:493-499.

Cook, J., and T.D. Wall. 1980. New work attitude measures of trust, organizational commitment and personal need non-fulfillment. *Journal of Occupational Psychology* 53:39-52.

Karp, D.A. 1989. The social construction of retirement among professionals 50-60 years old. *The Gerontologist* 29:750-760.

Russell, D., et al. 1980. The revised UCLA Loneliness Scale: Concurrent and discriminant validity. *Journal of Personality and Social Psychology* 39:472-480.

Watson, D., et al. 1988. Development and validation of brief measures of positive and negative affect: The PANAS scales. *Journal of Personality and Social Psychology* 54:1063-1070.

Social Components of Retirement Anxiety Scale

1. I can't imagine not working.
2. I am afraid I will lose all of my work friends as a retired person.
3. There really isn't much for a retired person to do.
4. I am afraid I will be a burden on my family as a retired person.
5. My job has always been a source of my identity. I hate to lose that.
6. Retirement will not bother me because I am sure I can make new friends no matter where I go.
7. I am afraid I will feel lonely after I retire.
8. Many of my colleagues will not have time for me after I retire.
9. After retirement I am not sure I will know how to stay involved.
10. I don't know what I am going to do without my job.
11. I worry that my family will not support me after I retire.
12. I have lots of friends I can depend on if I need them after I retire.
13. I will probably be sitting around alone after I retire.
14. I am too old to make new friends.
15. I won't have much in common with my co-workers anymore.
16. Retirement will allow me to do things with friends that I wasn't able to do while I was working.
17. I have already made plans for what I am going to do as soon as I retire.
18. It will be hard to replace my friends from work.
19. People will never call on me to do things with them after I retire.
20. My family does not want me to retire.
21. Retirement will give me new opportunities to make new friends.
22. Most of my friends have been my co-workers.
23. Keeping up with my friends will be difficult.

Scoring: A five-point Likert scale ranges from 1 = strongly disagree and 5 = strongly agree. The scoring is reversed for items 6, 12, 16, 17, and 21. Scores range from 23-115. The higher the score, the greater the retirement anxiety.

Reprinted with permission of the author.

Teaching Anxiety Scale

Parsons, J.S. 1973. Assessment of anxiety about teaching using the Teaching Anxiety Scale: Manual and research. Paper presented at American Educational Research Association. ERIC ED 079 330.

Comments: The 25-item TCHAS examines the relationship between teaching anxiety and acquiring teaching skills. In addition, the scale helps preservice teachers identify their strengths and weaknesses.

Scale Construction: The TCHAS was originally developed at Stanford University (two equivalent forms) to assess anxiety specifically related to the job of teaching. The scale was geared to preservice teachers. Revised forms are available with 24, 28, and 29 items for use with inservice teachers. About one-half of the items were written negatively.

Sample: Overall, six groups participated in the study. The four groups of preservice teachers consisted of 55 graduate preservice intern teachers (secondary); 79 undergraduate preservice teachers (secondary); 30 undergraduate preservice student teachers (elementary); and 36 undergraduate and graduate preservice elementary and secondary teachers. The two groups of inservice teachers consisted of 384 newly hired elementary and secondary teachers; and 23 elementary and junior high school teachers. A description of the samples is provided.

Reliability: Alpha coefficients for preservice teachers were 0.90 (undergraduate and graduate elementary and secondary preservice teachers); 0.92 (undergraduate preservice elementary student teachers; 0.92 (graduate preservice secondary intern teachers; and 0.88 (undergraduate secondary preservice teachers). Alpha coefficients for inservice teachers were: 0.87 (elementary and secondary teachers); and 0.93 (elementary and junior high school teachers). Test-retest correlations for four groups ranged from 0.60 to 0.95, indicating that the TCHAS is stable over short time periods. Detailed test-retest information is provided.

Validity: Component analysis, group differences, internal structure, and change over time are discussed as they establish the construct validity of the TCHAS. The TCHAS was positively correlated with the Taylor Manifest Anxiety Scale. In addition, most anxious and least anxious groups were used based on the opinion of 25 teaching supervisors. The most anxious group scored significantly higher on the TCHAS than the least anxious group. The high alpha coefficients present evidence that teaching anxiety is a single concept. Two factor analyses confirmed the single factor structure. The results of various studies show that teaching anxiety decreases over time for preservice teachers. Tables are presented to support construct validity.

Factor Analysis: The results of two factor analyses using the 25-item TCHAS confirmed a single factor solution with 22 of 25 items loading on one factor. The three items that failed to load on a single factor were 3, 17, and 22. Therefore, a new 22-item TCHAS was validated. On the 29-item TCHAS, items 26-29 failed to load on a single factor as well as three items from the 25-item TCHAS.

Data Analysis: Distribution statistics are provided for preservice and inservice teachers.

Reference:

Pigge, F.L., and R.N. Marso. 1994. Relationships of prospective teachers' personality type and locus of control orientation with changes in their attitude and anxiety about teaching. *Midwestern Educational Researcher* 7:2-7.

Teaching Anxiety Scale

1. I feel calm and collected when I think about holding parent-teacher conferences.   .
2. If I have trouble answering a student's question I (will find) find it difficult to concentrate on questions that follow.
3. I feel uncomfortable when I speak before a group.
4. I (would feel) feel calm (if I were) when I am preparing lessons.
5. I'm worried whether I can be a good teacher.
6. I feel sure I will find teaching a satisfying profession.
7. I would feel calm and collected if a student's parent observed in my classroom.
8. I feel inferior to other preservice teachers in my teacher preparation program.
9. I feel that students will follow my instructions.
10. I feel secure with regard to my ability to keep a class under control.
11. I'm less happy teaching than I thought I'd be.
12. I feel nervous when I am being observed by my college supervisor.
13. I feel confident about my ability to improvise in the classroom.
14. I feel other teachers (will think) think I'm very competent.
15. I (would feel) feel panicky when a student asks me a question I (couldn't) can't answer.
16. I feel anxious because I don't know yet whether I really want to be a teacher.
17. I feel better prepared for teaching than other preservice teachers in my teacher preparation program.
18. Lack of rapport with my students (will be) is one of my biggest worries.
19. I would feel anxious if the principal informed me he was coming to my class to observe.
20. I (would find) find it easy to speak up in the staff room.
21. I worry about being able to keep the students interested in what I (will teach) teach them.
22. I (would find) find it easy to admit to the class that I don't know the answer to a question a student asks.
23. Deciding how to present information in the classroom (would make) makes me feel uncertain.
24. I feel I will have good recall of the things I know when I am in front of the class.
25. I feel I (will be) am as competent in the classroom as other preservice teachers in my teacher preparation program.
26. I'm concerned about how to use my testing of students as a useful indication of how effectively I'm teaching them.
27. I'm worried that differences in background between my students and me (will prevent) prevent me from teaching effectively.
28. I am certain that my own personal "hang-ups" (will not) do not hinder my teaching effectiveness.
29. I'm uncertain whether I (will be able to) can tell the difference between really seriously disturbed students and those who are merely "goofing off" in class.

Scoring: Never = 1; Infrequently = 2; Occasionally = 3; Frequently = 4; and Always = 5. Scoring is reversed for the following items: 1, 4, 6, 7, 9, 10, 13, 14, 17, 20, 22, 24, 25, and 28.

Organizational Frustration Scale

Spector, P.E. 1975. Organizational Frustration Scale. Princeton, NJ: ETS Test Collection.

Comments: The 29-item OF Scale assesses organizational frustration. The original OF Scale consisted of 37 items based on the responses of 25 workers to the question "What is frustrating?" After an item analysis, only 29 items were retained that dealt with a job, a supervisor, and a job environment as they related to frustration ("the interference with an ongoing overt or covert response sequence"). The author has also developed the Work Locus of Control Scale (1988).

Sample: The sample consisted of 71 workers employed in a mental health institution and 10 additional workers including secretaries, nurses, custodians, clerical workers, and mental health aides.

Reliability: The alpha coefficient was 0.88 for the second sample of 50 workers.

Validity: Predicative validity was established through significant correlations between the OF Scale and the following worker behaviors: sabotage, hostility, and indirect aggression.

Factor Analysis: A principal components factor analysis with a varimax rotation yielded the following six factors: aggression against others, sabotage, wasting of time and materials, interpersonal hostility and complaining, interpersonal aggression, and apathy about the job.

Data Analysis: Scale means and standard deviations are reported. Norms are available from a psychiatric hospital (31 workers), general hospital (120 workers), county engineering department (44 workers), general hospital (140 workers), federal government (101 workers), and state research organizations (82 workers).

References:
Chen, P.Y., and P.E. Spector. 1992. Relationships of work stressors with aggression, withdrawal, theft and substance abuse: An exploratory study. *Journal of Occupational and Organizational Psychology* 65:177-184.

Fox, S., and P.E. Spector. In press. A model of work frustration–aggression. *Journal of Organizational Behavior* 19.

Spector, P.E. 1975. Relationships of organizational frustration with reported behavioral reactions of employees. *Journal of Applied Psychology* 60:635-637.

Spector, P.E. 1988. Development of the Work Locus of Control Scale. *Journal of Occupational Psychology* 61:335-340.

Organizational Frustration Scale

1. People act nasty toward me at work.
2. I find that every time I try to do something at work I run into obstacles.
3. There are a lot of petty and arbitrary rules at work.
4. I feel thwarted in my efforts to be creative.
5. My supervisor is always chewing me out.
6. My supervisor feels my performance is worse than it is.
7. I find it easy to talk to my supervisor.
8. I feel that I am accomplishing something worthwhile at work.
9. I enjoy my job.
10. The demands made of me at work are reasonable.
11. Policies at work are not fair.
12. My work area is a pleasant place to be.
13. I often feel that I am being run ragged.
14. I am given entirely to much work to do.
15. I find that some of the people I have to deal with are not competent.
16. I often have problems doing my job because of the incompetence of others.
17. My supervisor always seems to be looking over my shoulder.
18. My supervisor does not trust me.
19. I feel trapped in my job.
20. My job is not at all fulfilling.
21. I dread having to interact with my supervisor.
22. I do not like many of the tasks I have to do.
23. My job is boring and monotonous.
24. I get blamed for things that are not my fault.
25. I don't have the authority to do what I am supposed to do at work.
26. It seems that one person tells me to do one thing and another person tells me to do something else at work.
27. I am told to do things I don't think I should do at work.
28. I often have to waste time doing administrative tasks at work.
29. I often feel frustrated at work.

Scoring: Agree completely = +3; Agree pretty much = +2; Agree slightly = +1; Disagree completely = -3; Disagree pretty much = -2; and Disagree slightly = -1. Items 1-6, 11, and 13-29 are worded positively (+3 means maximum frustration and –3 means minimum frustration). Items 7-10 and 12 are worded negatively (+3 means minimum frustration and –3 means maximum frustration).

Reprinted with permission of Spector, P.E. (1975) Organizational Frustration Scale. University of South Florida, Tampa.

Change/Innovation

Institutional Renewal Scale

Crowley, R.J. 1976. The Institutional Renewal Scale: An instrument to measure attitudes toward educational innovation. ERIC ED 156 678.

Comments: The nine-item IRS assesses attitudes toward innovations in educational settings.

Scale Construction: A panel of 48 secondary teachers rated the 20 items that were developed to decide item appropriateness.

Sample: A sample of 126 secondary teachers responded to the 20-item IRS. Based upon their responses, individual phi coefficients were computed. Eight items were deleted. The revised form was administered to 378 secondary school teachers.

Reliability: The coefficient of internal consistency was 0.82, but increased to 0.88 when three items were deleted (2, 6, and 7).

Validity: Concurrent validity was established by correlating the IRS with the Minnesota Teacher Attitude Inventory (Cook, et al., 1951) and the Attitudes Toward Education Scale (Kerlinger, 1968). In addition, a known-groups technique was also employed.

Factor Analysis: A normalized varimax rotation yielded two factors.

Data Analysis: Distribution of responses, dichotomized response categories, and discriminating power of items are reported. The results of a chi-square test for item discrimination is provided.

References:
Cook, W.W., et al. 1951. Minnesota Teacher Attitude Inventory. New York, NY: Psychological Corporation.

Kerlinger, R.N. 1968. Attitude toward Education Scale, VII. Unpublished manuscript.

Institutional Renewal Scale

1. I think that too much money is being spent on educational innovations when compared with the benefit that is being derived.
2. I am indifferent to the pros and cons about educational innovations but would not like to see my attitude become general.
3. There is a need to innovate but I do not find what I want in most current educational innovations.
4. I believe that educational innovation keeps alive what is best in education.
5. Most school professionals should become much more enthusiastic about educational innovation than they presently are.
6. School-wide emphasis on trying educational innovations should be a prominent characteristic of a school.
7. The educational innovations that gain acceptance seem to me to do so at the expense of equally valid techniques.
8. Most educational innovations suggest unlimited possibilities for schools.
9. In my opinion most educational innovations are a hindrance to a sound education because so many of them depend on exaggerated claims.
10. The appeal for the use of more educational innovations that are currently in use appears to me to be a response to fashion rather than to sober judgement.
11. School professionals should be willing to revise their beliefs and attitudes in order to accommodate more educational innovations.
12. Experience with the process of innovating may well be worth the risks involved in innovating.

Scoring: Strongly Agree, Agree, Mildly Agree, Mildly Disagree, Disagree, and Strongly Disagree.

Reprinted with permission of the author.

Leadership Actions Survey

Goldstein, M.T. 1982. Using administrative tactics to introduce curriculum innovation. Paper presented at American Educational Research Association. ERIC ED 214 310.

Comments: The 24-item LAS identifies the tactics used by administrators in an attempt to influence the introduction of special education curriculum innovations. The survey was adapted from the work of Hull and others based on their theoretical framework of tactic types.

Sample: Surveys and interviews were obtained from administrators in 39 sites. These were administrators identified as advocates of a particular innovation.

Reliability: Although it was indicated that reliability estimates were obtained, actually, reliability values were not provided.

Validity: The categorizing of the initial item pool into tactic types was accomplished by a panel of six administrators serving as a panel of judges. Additional preliminary analyses were conducted to determine the content validity of the instrument.

Factor Analysis: A principal components, varimax rotation factor analysis was conducted, which yielded three factors that were named following Chin and Benne's conceptualization of strategies of changing.

Definition of Factors: The three factors are: *empirical-rational*, which involves the communication of information; *power coercive*, which involves the use of mandates or orders; and the *normative-reeducative*, which involves the creation of conditions within which teachers may innovate.

References:
Hull, W.L., et al. 1973. A conceptual framework for the diffusion of innovations in vocational and technical education. Columbus: Center for Vocational and Technical Education, Ohio State University.

Widmer, J.L. 1977. Innovation and bureaucracies: A reexamination of diffusion strategies for state and local systems. Paper presented at American Educational Research Association.

Leadership Actions Survey

1. Provided teachers with printed materials about the innovation.
2. Asked persons respected by the teachers to present the innovation to them.
3. Provided information about how the innovation has been used in other places.
4. Presented the innovation as unfinished to allow teachers to make it their own.
5. Emphasized aspects of the innovation that are consistent with what the teacher expects.
6. Answered questions about the innovation at meetings.
7. Gave recognition to teachers for trying the innovation.
8. Set a deadline for teachers to incorporate the innovation into their classroom activities.
9. Asked teachers to give their reasons for accepting or rejecting the innovation.
10. Observed the effectiveness of the innovation in classrooms.
11. Warned teachers of the consequences of resisting using the innovation.
12. Endorsed the innovation through persons perceived as highly credible by the teachers.
13. Provided explicit instructions by the developer on how to use the innovation.
14. Allowed the teachers to adapt the innovation to local conditions.
15. Explained the innovation through conferences with professional staff.
16. Visited a site which has installed the innovation.
17. Compelled teachers to use the innovation.
18. Conducted a pilot test of the innovation.
19. Gave pay to teachers for using the innovation.
20. Observed the innovation in operation.
21. Established program policies to insure the use of the innovation.
22. Informed teachers about the innovation at meetings.
23. Required teachers to use the innovation in their classrooms.
24. Tried the innovation on a small scale.

Scoring: A five-point Likert-type response set is labeled: All; Most; Half; Few; or None.

Reprinted with permission of the author.

Stages of Concern Questionnaire

Hall, G.E., et al. 1977. Measuring stages of concern about the innovation: A manual for the use of the SoC Questionnaire. ERIC ED 147 342.

Comments: The 35-item SoC measures current concerns about a specific innovation. The same 35 items may be used for any innovation. The only change that would need to be done would be to change the introductory page. No additional changes are necessary. Therefore, the SoC may be used in a wide variety of situations with numerous groups.

Scale Construction: The first pilot instrument that was developed to measure the concerns about a specific innovation used open-ended statements and a forced rank order. A Q-sort procedure was used by a panel of judges to group over 400 items into eight categories (the seven stages of concern and an unacceptable category). This procedure generated 195 items that were field tested by teachers and university faculty. The results of item correlations and factor analyses yielded seven factors. A panel of judges chose 35 items from each of the seven factors of the 195-item SoC. The new version of the SoC was given to 171 elementary teachers and college faculty to establish the test-retest reliability of the SoC over a one-week interval. Cross-sectional and longitudinal studies have been conducted. Detailed information about the development of the SoC is included.

Stages of Concern: There are seven stages of concern with five items for each stage. Stage 0 consists of items 3, 12, 21, 23, and 30. Stage 1 consists of items 6, 14, 15, 26, and 35. Stage 2 consists of items 7, 13, 17, 28, and 33. Stage 3 consists of items 4, 8, 16, 25, and 34. Stage 4 consists of items 1, 11, 19, 24, and 32. Stage 5 consists of items 5, 10, 18, 27, and 29. Stage 6 consists of items 2, 9, 20, 22, and 31. Definitions are provided for each of the seven stages.

Sample: In 1975, 646 people from elementary schools and universities who had experience with teaming or modules responded to the survey. Their responses were used to determine percentile scores.

Reliability: Alpha coefficients for a stratified sample of 830 teachers and professors were 0.64 for stage 0; 0.78 for stage 1; 0.83 for stage 2; 0.75 for stage 3; 0.76 for stage 4; 0.82 for stage 5; and 0.71 for stage 6. Test-retest reliability (Pearson) for 132 people over a two-week interval were 0.65 for stage 0; 0.86 for stage 1; 0.82 for stage 2; 0.81 for stage 3; 0.76 for stage 4; 0.84 for stage 5; and 0.71 for stage 6.

Validity: Information is provided about various validity studies that were conducted over several years. Intercorrelation matrices, information obtained using interview data, and predicted differences among groups support the validity of the SoC.

Factor Analysis: A principal components factor analysis with a varimax rotation yielded seven factors.

Data Analysis: Correlations between varimax factor scores and scale scores are reported as well as correlation of peak stage estimates and rank order of SoC percentile scores. Profile interpretation is provided for the typical nonuser and the single peak user.

References:

Fuller, F.F. 1969. Concerns of teachers: A developmental conceptualization. *American Educational Research Journal* 6:207-226.

Hall, G.E., et al. 1975. Levels of use of the innovation: A framework for analyzing innovation adoption. *Journal of Teacher Education* 26:52-56.

Wright, H.S. Jr. 1993. Analysis of changes in concerns of teachers, principals, and parents implementing school-based management in elementary schools. Ph.D. dissertation Virginia Commonwealth University.

SoC Questionnaire

1. I am concerned about students' attitudes toward this innovation.
2. I know of some other approaches that might work better.
3. I don't even know what innovation is.
4. I am concerned about not having enough time to organize myself each day.
5. I would like to help other faculty in their use of the innovation.
6. I have very limited knowledge about the innovation.
7. I would like to know the effect of reorganization on my professional status.
8. I am concerned about conflict between my interests and my responsibilities.
9. I am concerned about revising my use of the innovation.
10. I would like to develop working relationships with both our faculty and outside faculty using this innovation.
11. I am concerned about how the innovation affects students.
12. I am not concerned about this innovation.
13. I would like to know who will make the decisions in the new system.
14. I would like to discuss the possibility of using the innovation.
15. I would like to know what resources are available if we decide to adopt this innovation.
16. I am concerned about my inability to manage all the innovation requires.
17. I would like to know how my teaching or administration is supposed to change.
18. I would like to familiarize other departments or persons with the progress of this new approach.
19. I am concerned about evaluating my impact on students.
20. I would like to revise the innovation's instructional approach.
21. I am completely occupied with other things.
22. I would like to modify our use of the innovation based on the experiences of our students.
23. Although I don't know about this innovation, I am concerned about things in the area.
24. I would like to excite my students about their part in this approach.
25. I am concerned about time spent working with nonacademic problems related to this innovation.
26. I would like to know what the use of the innovation will require in the immediate future.
27. I would like to coordinate my effort with others to maximize the innovation's effects.
28. I would like to have more information on time and energy commitments required by this innovation.
29. I would like to know what other faculty are doing in this area.
30. At this time, I am not interested in learning about this innovation.
31. I would like to determine how to supplement, enhance or replace the innovation.
32. I would like to use feedback from students to change the program.
33. I would like to know how my role will change when I am using the innovation.
34. Coordination of tasks and people is taking too much of my time.
35. I would like to know how this innovation is better than what we have now.

Scoring: A seven-point scale is used. Not true of me now is 0 to1; Somewhat true of me now is 3 to 4; and 6 to 7 is Very true of me now. High numbers represent high concern, whereas low numbers represent low concern. Raw scores are converted into percentile scores. The SoC may be scored by a computer program. The easiest way to interpret the SoC is to find the highest (peak stage score) stage score. Profiles can be generated for individuals and groups. Guidelines for interpreting the SoC are included.

Climate

School Level Environment Questionnaire

Fisher, D.L., and B.J. Fraser. 1990. Validity and use of the School-Level Environment Questionnaire. Paper presented at American Educational Research Association. ERIC ED 318 757.

Comments: The 56-item SLEQ measures teachers' perceptions of the psychological environment of a school. The instrument has two answer forms—one measures the actual environment as seen by teachers, the other the preferred, or ideal, form.

Scale Construction: The scale development for this instrument was based on the Work Environment Scale (WES) designed by Moos. This WES has ten scales. These scales fall into three basic dimensions: relationship dimension, personal development dimension, and system maintenance and system change dimension. The three board dimensions were used for the SLEQ and include seven subscales.

Sample: Three different teacher samples were used in the development of the questionnaire. The largest sample was 109 teachers from ten elementary schools in Tasmania.

Reliability: Alpha coefficients as an estimate of each scale's internal consistency were provided. These ranged from a low of 0.70 to 0.91.

Subscales: The design of the instrument into seven subscales include: student support, affiliation, professional interest, staff freedom, participatory decision making, innovation, and resource adequacy. More recently, an eighth subscale, work pressure, has been added. Each subscale is assessed by seven items.

References:
Fisher, D.L., and B.J. Fraser. 1983. Use of WES to assess science teachers' perceptions of school environment of different types of schools. *European Journal of Science Education* 5: 231-233.

Fraser, B.J., and D.L. Fisher. 1986. Using short forms of classroom climate instruments to assess and improve classroom psychosocial environment. *Journal of Research in Science Teaching* 23:387-413.

Moos, R.H. 1979. *Evaluating educational environments*. San Francisco: Jossey-Bass.

School-Level Environment Questionnaire

1. There are many disruptive, difficult students in the school.
2. I seldom receive encouragement from colleagues.
3. Teachers frequently discuss teaching methods and strategies with each other.
4. I am often supervised to ensure that I follow directions carefully.
5. Decisions about the running of the school are usually made by the principal or a small group of teachers.
6. It is very difficult to change anything in this school.
7. The school or department library includes an adequate selection of books and periodicals.
8. There is constant pressure to keep working.
9. Most students are helpful and cooperative to teachers.
10. I feel accepted by other teachers.
11. Teachers avoid talking with each other about teaching and learning.
12. I am not expected to conform to a particular teaching style.
13. I have to refer even small matters to a senior member of staff for a final answer.
14. Teachers are encouraged to be innovative in this school.
15. The supply of equipment and resources is inadequate.
16. Teachers have to work long hours to complete all their work.
17. Most students are pleasant and friendly to teachers.
18. I am ignored by other teachers.
19. Professional matters are seldom discussed during staff meetings.
20. It is considered very important that I closely follow syllabuses and lesson plans.
21. Action can usually be taken without gaining the approval of the subject department head or senior member of staff.
22. There is a great deal of resistance to proposals for curriculum change.
23. Video equipment, tapes and films are readily available and accessible.
24. Teachers don't have to work very hard in this school.
25. There are many noisy, badly behaved students.
26. I feel that I could rely on my colleagues for assistance if I should need it.
27. Many teachers attend inservice and other professional development courses.
28. There are few rules and regulations that I am expected to follow.
29. Teachers are frequently asked to participate in decisions concerning administrative policies and procedures.
30. Most teachers like the idea of change.
31. Adequate duplicating facilities and services are available to teachers.
32. There is no time for teachers to relax.
33. Students get along well with teachers.
34. My colleagues seldom take notice of my professional views and opinions.
35. Teachers show little interest in what is happening in other schools.
36. I am allowed to do almost as I please in the classroom.
37. I am encouraged to make decisions without reference to a senior member or staff.
38. New courses or curriculum materials are seldom implemented in the school.
39. Tape recorders and cassettes are seldom available when needed.
40. You can take it easy and still get the work done.
41. Most students are well-mannered and respectful to the school staff.
42. I feel that I have many friends among my colleagues at this school.
43. Teachers are keen to learn from their colleagues.
44. My classes are expected to use prescribed textbooks and prescribed resource materials.

45. I must ask my subject department head or senior member of staff before I do most things.
46. There is much experimentation with different teaching approaches.
47. Facilities are inadequate for catering for a variety of classroom activities and learning groups of different sizes.
48. Seldom are there deadlines to be met.
49. Very strict discipline is needed to control many of the students.
50. I often feel lonely and left out of things in the staffroom.
51. Teachers show considerable interest in the professional activities of their colleagues.
52. I am expected to maintain very strict control in the classroom.
53. I have very little say in the running of the school.
54. New and different ideas are always being tried out in this school.
55. Projectors for filmstrips, transparencies and films are usually available when needed.
56. It is hard to keep up with your work load.

Scoring: SD = Strongly Disagree; D = Disagree; N = Neither agree or disagree; A = Agree; SA = Strongly Agree.

Reprinted with permission of the author.

Organizational Health Index-Elementary Schools
Organizational Health Index-Middle Schools
Organizational Health Index-Secondary Schools

Hoy, W.K., and C.J. Tarter. 1997. *The road to open and healthy schools: A handbook for change.* Thousand Oaks, CA: Corwin Press, Inc.

Comments: The 43-item OHI-E, the 45-item OHI-M, and the 44-item OHI-S assess the wellness or health of the school climate. Definitions for each aspect of school climate are included. Computer Scoring Programs are available through Arlington Writers Ltd.

Scale Construction: Several pilot studies were conducted in order to further examine the stability of the factor structures and the reliability of the subscales as well as to increase the sample of schools. Detailed information is provided.

Sample: The sample for the revised *OHI-E* consisted of 78 elementary schools in New Jersey. The sample for the revised *OHI-M* consisted of 86 middle schools in New Jersey. The sample for the revised *OHI-S* consisted of 78 secondary schools in New Jersey. Over 1,130 secondary teachers from 17 out of 21 counties in New Jersey participated.

Reliability: The alpha coefficients for the *OHI-E* were: 0.94 for teacher affiliation, 0.95 for collegial leadership, 0.89 for resource influence, 0.90 for institutional integrity, and 0.87 for academic emphasis. The alpha coefficients for the *OHI-M* were: 0.94 for teacher affiliation, 0.94 for collegial leadership, 0.96 for resource support, 0.93 for institutional integrity, 0.94 for academic emphasis, and 0.94 for principal influence. The alpha coefficients for the *OHI-S* were: 0.89 for resource support, 0.91 for institutional integrity, 0.93 for academic emphasis, 0.87 for principal influence, 0.90 for consideration, 0.89 for initiating structure, and 0.92 for morale.

Validity: Content validity was established by the procedures used to develop the survey. Factor analytic procedures were conducted to establish construct validity.

Factor Analysis: Five factors were identified for the *OHI-E* using a principal components factor analysis with a varimax rotation. The following five factors accounted for approximately 66% of the variance: teacher affiliation (nine items), collegial leadership (ten items), resource influence (seven items), institutional integrity (six items), and academic emphasis (five items). Six factors were identified for the *OHI-M* using a principal components factor analysis with a varimax rotation. The following six factors accounted for approximately 77% of the variance: teacher affiliation (eight items), collegial leadership (nine items), resource support (six items), institutional integrity (seven items), academic emphasis (nine items), and principal influence (six items). Seven factors were identified for the *OHI-S* using a principal components factor analysis with a varimax rotation. The following seven factors accounted for approximately 74% of the variance: resource support (five items), institutional integrity (seven items), academic emphasis (eight items), principal influence (five items), morale (nine items), consideration (five items), and initiating structure (five items).

Data Analysis: School means were computed for each item of the OHI-E, OHI-M, and OHI-S. Second-order factor analyses were conducted resulting in a one-factor solution, which was labeled General School Health. Detailed descriptions are presented.

References:

Barnes, K.M. 1994. The organizational health of middle schools, trust, and decision participation. Ed.D. dissertation. Rutgers University.

Feldman, J. 1985. The School Health Index: The development and test of an instrument using a Parsonian and Etzonian perspective. Ed.D. dissertation. Rutgers University.

Hoy, W.K., and J.W. Hannum. 1997. Middle school climate: An empirical assessment of organizational health and student achievement. *Educational Administration Quarterly* 33:290-311.

Podgurski, T. 1990. School effectiveness as it relates to group consensus and organizational health of middle schools. Ed.D. dissertation. Rutgers University.

OHI-E

1. The principal explores all sides of topics and admits that other opinions exist.
2. The principal gets what he or she asks for from superiors.
3. The principal discusses classroom issues with teachers.
4. The principal accepts questions without appearing to snub or quash the teacher.
5. Extra materials are available if requested.
6. Students neglect to complete homework.
7. Students are cooperative during classroom instruction.
8. The school is vulnerable to outside pressures.
9. The principal is able to influence the actions of his or her superiors.
10. The principal treats all faculty members as his or her equal.
11. The principal goes out of his or her way to show appreciation to teachers.
12. Teachers are provided with adequate materials for their classrooms.
13. Teachers in this school like each other.
14. Community demands are accepted even when they are not consistent with the educational program.
15. The principal lets faculty know what is expected of them.
16. Teachers receive necessary classroom supplies.
17. The principal conducts meaningful evaluations.
18. Students respect others who get good grades.
19. Teachers feel pressure from the community.
20. The principal's recommendations are given serious consideration by his or her superiors.
21. The principal maintains definite standards of performance.
22. Supplementary materials are available for classroom use.
23. Teachers exhibit friendliness to each other.
24. Students seek extra work so they can get good grades.
25. Select citizen groups are influential with the board.
26. The principal looks out for the personal welfare of faculty members.
27. Teachers express pride in their school.
28. Teachers identify with the school.
29. The school is open to the whims of the public.
30. A few vocal parents can change school policy.
31. Students try hard to improve on previous work.
32. Teachers accomplish their jobs with enthusiasm.
33. The learning environment is orderly and serious.
34. The principal is friendly and approachable.
35. There is a feeling of trust and confidence among the staff.
36. Teachers show commitment to their students.
37. Teachers are indifferent to each other.

OHI-M

1. The principal explores all sides of topics and admits that other options exist.
2. Students make provisions to acquire extra help from teachers.
3. The principal gets what he or she asks for from superiors.
4. The principal discusses classroom issues with teachers.
5. The principal accepts questions without appearing to snub or quash the teacher.

6. Extra materials are available if requested.
7. Students neglect to complete homework.
8. The school is vulnerable to outside pressures.
9. The principal is able to influence the actions of his or her superiors.
10. The principal treats all faculty members as his or her equal.
11. Teachers are provided with adequate materials for their classrooms.
12. Teachers in this school like each other.
13. Community demands are accepted even when they are not consistent with the educational program.
14. The principal lets faculty know what is expected of them.
15. Teachers receive necessary classroom supplies.
16. Students respect others who get good grades.
17. Good grades are important to the students of this school.
18. Teachers feel pressure from the community.
19. The principal's recommendations are given serious consideration by his or her superiors.
20. Supplementary materials are available for classroom use.
21. Teachers exhibit friendliness to each other.
22. Students seek extra work so they can get good grades.
23. Select citizen groups are influential with the board.
24. The principal looks out for the personal welfare of faculty members.
25. The school is open to the whims of the public.
26. A few vocal parents can change school policy.
27. Students try hard to improve on previous work.
28. Teachers accomplish their jobs with enthusiasm.
29. The learning environment is orderly and serious.
30. The principal is friendly and approachable.
31. Teachers show commitment to their students.
32. Teachers are indifferent to each other.
33. Teachers are protected from unreasonable community and parental demands.
34. The principal is able to work well with the superintendent.
35. The principal is willing to make changes.
36. Teachers have access to needed instructional material.
37. Teachers in this school are cool and aloof to each other.
38. Teachers in this school believe that their students have the ability to achieve academically.
39. The principal is understanding when personal concerns cause teachers to arrive late or leave early.
40. Our school gets its fair share of resources from the district.
41. The principal is rebuffed by the superintendent.
42. Teachers volunteer to help each other.
43. The principal is effective in securing the superintendent's approval for new programs or activities.
44. Academically oriented students in this school are ridiculed by their peers.
45. Teachers do favors for each other.

OHI-S

1. Teachers are protected from unreasonable community and parental demands.
2. The principal gets what he or she asks for from superiors.
3. The principal is friendly and approachable.

4. The principal asks that faculty members follow standard rules and regulations.
5. Extra materials are available if requested.
6. Teachers do favors for each other.
7. Students in this school can achieve the goals that have been set for them.
8. The school is vulnerable to outside pressures.
9. The principal is able to influence the actions of his or her superiors.
10. The principal treats all faculty members as his or her equal.
11. The principal makes his or her attitudes clear to the school.
12. Teachers are provided with adequate materials for their classrooms.
13. Teachers in this school like each other.
14. The school sets high standards for academic performance.
15. Community demands are accepted even when they are not consistent with the educational program.
16. The principal is able to work well with the superintendent.
17. The principal puts suggestions made by the faculty into operation.
18. The principal lets faculty know what is expected of them.
19. Teachers receive necessary classroom supplies.
20. Teachers are indifferent to each other.
21. Students respect others who get good grades.
22. Teachers feel pressure from the community.
23. The principal's recommendations are given serious consideration by his or her superiors.
24. The principal is willing to make changes.
25. The principal maintains definite standards of performance.
26. Supplementary materials are available for classroom use.
27. Teachers exhibit friendliness to each other.
28. Students seek extra work so they can get good grades.
29. Select citizen groups are influential with the board.
30. The principal is impeded by superiors.
31. The principal looks out for the personal welfare of faculty members.
32. The principal schedules the work to be done.
33. Teachers have access to needed instructional material.
34. Teachers in this school are cool and aloof to each other.
35. Teachers in this school believe that their students have the ability to achieve academically.
36. The school is open to the whims of the public.
37. The morale of teachers is high.
38. Academic achievement is recognized and acknowledged by the school.
39. A few vocal parents can change school policy.
40. There is a feeling of trust and confidence among the staff.
41. Students try hard to improve on previous work.
42. Teachers accomplish their jobs with enthusiasm.
43. The learning environment is orderly and serious.
44. Teachers identify with the school.

Scoring: RO = Rarely Occurs; SO = Sometimes Occurs; O = Often Occurs; and VFO = Very Frequently Occurs.

Reprinted with permission of the author. (Hoy, W.K., and C.J. Tarter. 1997. *The road to open and healthy schools: A handbook for change.* Thousand Oaks, CA: Corwin Press, Inc.)

Organizational Climate Index

Stern, G.G. 1970. *People in context: Measuring person-environment congruence in education and industry.* New York: Wiley.

Comments: The OCI is one of a set of indices (CCI, AI, HSCI) developed by George Stern and his associates. They were developed to measure both the personality needs of the individual and the psychological character of the environment (organization). The OCI is a measure of the environmental character of the organization. The Stern indices are based on the 30 Need-Press scales (model) of H.A. Murray, who stressed that explained behavior was a function of the relationship between an individual (personality needs) and the organization (environmental press). The OCI is a general instrument that can be used to characterize the psychological climate of a wide variety of organizations. According to Stern, needs are the tendencies that give unity and direction to an individual's behavior. Press describes the conditions that represent obstacles to the expression of a need or make such expression easier. Press can be further differentiated as either *beta press* or *consensual beta press.* Beta press is the private interpretation that each individual places on events around him. Consensual beta press recognizes that people who share a common ideology also tend to share a common interpretation of events. The OCI measures organizational members' interpretations of events, or beta press. When group scores (mean scores) are developed such scores provide a measure of consensual beta press.

Scale Construction: The OCI (long form) is a 300-item instrument, ten items for each of Murray's 30 need-press scales. The short form, which is included here, is an 80-item instrument.

Sample: The instrument was originally developed with college students and in five public schools in upstate New York. However, the instrument has been used extensively in research since the late 1950s.

Reliability: Reliability assessments are provided with KR-20 estimates of internal consistency. These estimates calculated on 931 public school teachers for the 30 press scales ranged from 0.23 to 0.87. The low estimates suggest that some scales should be treated with caution because of possible attenuation of relationships due to low reliability.

Validity: Primary validity information is in the form of significant differences among the average press scores from different organizational settings. Correlations of OCI factors or profiles with other criteria are also provided.

Factor Analysis: A principal component analysis with an equimax rotation yielded six first-order factors and two second-order factors. The second-order factors are Development Press and Control Press; the first-order are Intellectual Climate, Supportiveness, Orderliness, Achievement Standards, Practicalness, and Impulse Control.

References:
Frothingham, E.M. 1988. Teacher collegiality: Its relationship to professionalism and organizational climate in public and private schools. Ph.D. dissertation, New York University.

Meyer, D.E. 1988. The relationship of organizational climate to burnout among faculty in selected community colleges in the midwest. Ed.D. dissertation, Oklahoma State University.

Murray, H.A. 1938. *Explorations in personality*. New York: Oxford University. Press.

Stern, G.G., et al. 1970. The Organizational Climate Index. Syracuse, New York: Evaluation Research Association.

Taylor, J., and D.G. Bowers. 1972. The Survey of Organizations: A machine scored standardized questionnaire instrument. Ann Arbor, MI: Institute for Social Research.

Organizational Climate Index (Short Form)

1. Work programs are well organized and progress systematically from week to week.
2. People here express their feelings openly and enthusiastically.
3. Everyone here has a strong sense of being a member of the team.
4. There is a lot of group spirit.
5. Administrative policy, goals, and objectives are carefully explained to everyone.
6. When people here disagree with an administrative decision, they work to get it changed.
7. People here put a great deal of energy into everything they do.
8. Improving one's knowledge of important works of art, music, and drama is encouraged here.
9. One of the values most stressed here is open-mindedness.
10. Social events get a lot of enthusiasm and support.
11. People who have friends of the opposite sex show their affection openly.
12. People find others eager to help them get started.
13. People here spend a great deal of time thinking about and discussing complex problems.
14. The ability to plan ahead is highly valued here.
15. Many social activities are unplanned and spontaneous.
16. People are expected to have a great deal of social grace and polish.
17. Untidy reports or ones that depart from a specified style are almost certain to be returned unaccepted.
18. Most people here go to lots of parties and other social activities.
19. There are many facilities and opportunities for individual creative activity.
20. Most people here love to dance.
21. Personality and pull are more important than competence in getting ahead around here.
22. The administrative staff are often joked about or criticized.
23. Most activities here are planned carefully.
24. People here speak up openly and freely.
25. People here are not only expected to have ideas but to do something about them.
26. Good manners and making a good impression are important here.
27. The activities of charities and social agencies are strongly supported.
28. Criticism is taken as a personal affront in this organization.
29. Neatness in this place is the rule rather than the exception.
30. Male-female relationships sometimes become quite serious.
31. Many people here enjoy talking about poetry, philosophy, or religion.
32. Everyone is helped to get acquainted.
33. All work assignments are laid out well in advance, so that people can plan their own schedules accordingly.
34. People here thrive on difficulty—the tougher things get, the harder everyone works.
35. Individuals who are not properly groomed are likely to have this called to their attention.
36. Service to the community is regarded as a major responsibility of the institution.
37. People here are not really concerned with deep philosophical or ethical matters.
38. Good work is really recognized around here.
39. Work is checked to see if it is done properly and on time.
40. Administrators are practical and efficient in the way they dispatch their business.
41. There are no favorites in this place; everyone gets treated alike.
42. People here can get so absorbed in their work they often lose all sense of time or personal comfort.
43. People frequently do things on the spur of the moment.
44. Proper social forms and manners are not particularly important here.

45. Few people here are challenged by deep thinking.
46. People set high standards of achievement for themselves here.
47. New ideas are always being tried here.
48. People here tend to take the easy way out when things get tough.
49. Administrators put a lot of energy and enthusiasm into directing this program.
50. People here talk about their future imaginatively and with enthusiasm.
51. There is a general idea of appropriate dress which everyone follows.
52. There always seem to be a lot of little quarrels going on here.
53. It's easy to get a group together for games, Cokes, movies, etc.
54. The work atmosphere emphasizes efficiency and usefulness.
55. People spend a great deal of time together socially.
56. There is not wasted time here; everything has been planned right to the minute.
57. Discussions about improving society are common here.
58. Unusual or exciting plans are encouraged here.
59. People here feel free to express themselves impulsively.
60. People here expect to help out with fund drives, CARE, Red Cross, etc.
61. There is a specific place for everything and everyone here.
62. People here often get involved in long, serious intellectual discussions.
63. The administrative staff will go out of its way to help you with your work.
64. Many people here read magazines and books involving history, economics, or political science.
65. Looking and acting "right" is expected.
66. The people here are easily moved by the misfortunes or distress of others.
67. Everyone has the same opportunity to make good.
68. Communications within the organization is always carried on through formal channels.
69. Most activities here present a real personal challenge.
70. People ask permission before deviating from common policies or practices.
71. There is a recognized group of leaders who receive special privileges.
72. People here feel they must really work hared because of the important nature of their work.
73. Parties are colorful and lively here.
74. Programs here are quickly changed to meet new conditions.
75. People are always carefully dressed and neatly groomed.
76. "Lending a helping hand" could very well be the motto of this place.
77. There is considerable interest in the analysis of value systems and the relativity of societies and ethics.
78. There is a lot of interest in the philosophy and goals of science here.
79. Frank discussions about sec are not uncommon among people here.
80. People here are usually quick to help each other out.

Scoring: T-True. Generally true or characteristic of the organization, is something which occurs or might occur, is the way people tend to feel or act. F-False. Generally false or not characteristic of the organization, is something which is not likely to occur, is not the way people tend to feel or act.

Reprinted with permission of Carl R. Steinhoff.

Communication

Effects of Teacher Immediacy

Crump, C.A. 1996. Teacher immediacy: What students consider to be effective teacher behaviors. ERIC ED 390 099.

Comments: The 24-item ETIQ measures teachers' use of eight nonverbal and four verbal immediacy behaviors and the impact of these 12 immediacy behaviors on their students. There are two questions for each behavior. The questionnaire was developed as a result of the research examined by Gorham (1988).

Sample: The original sample consisted of 70 community college students taking communications courses who volunteered to participate in the study.

Reliability: The author states that the questionnaire has reliability.

Validity: The results of a review of the literature and prior studies with this questionnaire provide support for its face validity.

Data Analysis: The following 12 immediacy behaviors are presented in rank order in terms of the most motivating: humor, dynamic delivery, vocal variation, personal examples, friendly, eye contact, time outside of class, using "our" and "we," learn student names, physical distance, physical appearance, and appropriate touch. Means and standard deviations are reported.

References:
Christophel, D.M., and J. Gorham. 1995. A test-retest analysis of student motivation, teacher immediacy, and perceived sources of motivation and demotivation in college classes. *Communication Education* 44:292-305.

Gorham, J. 1988. The relationship between verbal teacher immediacy behaviors and student learning. *Communication Education* 37:40-53.

Sanders, J.A., and R.L. Wiseman. 1990. The effects of verbal and nonverbal teacher immediacy on perceived cognitive, affective, and behavioral learning in the multicultural classroom. *Communication Education* 39:341-353.

Effects of Teacher Immediacy

1. I tend to pay attention when an instructor makes eye contact with me.
2. I want to listen to instructors who use gestures, movement, and who have a dynamic delivery.
3. I lose interest in attending classes taught by instructors who are sloppy in their appearance.
4. I look forward to going to classes when the instructor uses humor frequently.
5. I feel comfortable in a class where the instructor smiles and is friendly.
6. It is hard for me to listen to an instructor in a monotone.
7. I tend to work harder in classes in which the instructor has learned my name.
8. I daydream in classes when an instructor fails to use good eye contact.
9. I get bored when an instructor lectures using few gestures or movements.
10. Vocal variation and vocal expressiveness in instructors aids in holding my attention.
11. When an instructor spends time with me outside of class (stays late and comes early), I tend to skip that class less than other classes.
12. I am more interested in what instructors say when they dress professionally.
13. I do not like it when an instructor uses humor in the classroom.
14. I feel a sense of belonging when an instructor uses the term "our class."
15. Instructors that pat me on the back or use touch appropriately make me feel comfortable.
16. I tend to pay attention when an instructor walks around the room and decreases the physical distance between himself/herself and the class.
17. I learn more when instructors give personal examples during class discussions.
18. Instructors that smile a lot and are friendly make me nervous.
19. I dislike instructors who do not learn my name.
20. I feel that it is inappropriate for instructors to use personal examples during class.
21. When an instructor touches me, I feel uncomfortable.
22. I think the instructor should keep a physical distance between themselves and their students.
23. I feel uncomfortable when instructors use words like "we" and "our" referring to the class.
24. I think that it is inappropriate for instructors to spend time with students before and after class.

Scoring: Strongly agree = 1; agree = 2; are undecided = 3; disagree = 4; and strongly disagree = 5.

Communication Training Impact Questionnaire

DeWine, S. 1987. Evaluation of organizational communication competency: The development of the Communication Training Impact Questionnaire. *Journal of Applied Communication Research* 15:113-127.

Comments: The 20-item CTIQ assesses behavioral changes and application in work situations of training impact. This questionnaire, which is based on the model of training impact developed by Kirkpatrick corresponds to level three in Kirkpatrick's research (improvements in job behavior). The other three levels that he examines are: general reaction; knowledge, attitudes or skills; and organizational results. In addition to the CTIQ, there is also a 13-item Supervisor's Training Impact Questionnaire that measures the impact of the training program on the worker's job.

Scale Construction: Based upon a review of the literature and topics recommended by Cornwell (1980), 31 items were written to fit into five categories. The results of factor analytic procedures reduced the total number of items to 20.

Sample: The original sample consisted of 267 people who were taking some kind of communication training program. The participants filled out the questionnaire between two and four weeks after finishing the training. The majority of the participants were middle managers (110), then college students enrolled in a leadership training program (63), 60 student doctors, and 34 workers in a financial organization.

Reliability: An alpha coefficient of 0.88 is reported for the entire sample. For middle managers the alpha coefficient was 0.87; 0.93 for college students; and 0.90 for student doctors and workers in a financial organization.

Validity: An oblique factor analysis and scree test yielded two factors: relationship of training to job and skilled performance. Relationship of training to the job consists of items 1-4, 10, 14, and 20-23; and skill performance consists of items 5-9, 11-13, 16, and 19. Evidence of predictive validity was also presented.

Data Analysis: Means and standard deviations are presented as well as the results of the factor analysis.

References:
Cornwall, J.B. 1980. Measuring back-on-the-job performance. *Training* 289-292.

DeWine, S., and J.S. Pearson. 1985. The most frequently used self-report instrument in communications. Paper presented at the International Communication Association.

Kirkpatrick, D.L. 1967. Evaluation of training. In R.L. Craig and L.R. Bittel (eds.), *Training and Development Handbook*. NY: McGraw-Hill.

Kirkpatrick, D.L. 1979. Techniques for evaluating training programs. *Training and Development Journal* 78-92.

Ledebur, G.W. 1982. Effects of interpersonal skill training upon the quality of parent-teacher conferences. Doctoral dissertation. Lehigh University.

Communication Training Impact Questionnaire

1. I use this skill regularly on the job.
2. After this training program I would perform this skill without practicing.
3. I didn't learn this skill in the training program, so I had to learn it on the job.
4. I perform the skill differently on the job because work conditions don't permit me to perform it the way I learned in the training program.
5. I perform the skills differently on the job because the skill doesn't work the way I learned it in training.
6. I perform the skill differently on the job because my supervisor told me to do it differently.
7. I never perform this skill on the job.
8. The skill isn't part of my job.
9. I get help to perform the skill because I didn't learn it in the training program.
10. I don't perform the skill on the job because the skill is too difficult for me.
11. I don't perform the skill on the job because the skill comes up so rarely that I forgot how to do it.
12. I don't perform the skill because I was assigned a different job.
13. I learned to perform the task well in the training program because the program was effective.
14. The skill could be learned from a manual or an instruction sheet as easily as in a training program.
15. I had trouble learning the skill because the training program was confusing.
16. The skill would have been easier to learn with more reference materials.
17. Because of learning this skill I feel more comfortable about doing my job.
18. Because of attending this training program, I feel better about the company.
19. After attending this training program, I am interested in attending other training programs.
20. I think my participation in this training program will help me to advance in the company.

Scoring: Strongly disagree = 1; disagree = 2; sometimes agree and sometimes disagree = 3; agree = 4; and strongly agree = 5. Scoring is reversed on the following items: 3-12, and 14-16.

Reprinted with permission of the author. (Taken from DeWine, S. 1987. Evaluation of organizational communication competency: The development of the Communication Training Impact Questionnaire. *Journal of Applied Communication Research* 15:113-127.)

Communication Relationships Scale
Receiver Information Scale

Goldhaber, G., et al. 1977. The ICA communication audit survey instrument. International Communication Association.

Comments: This survey is composed of two related questionnaires: the Communication Relationships Scale and the Receiver Information Scale. The Communication Relationships Scale is a 15-item questionnaire that measures communication skills between supervisor and subordinates. It taps behaviors applicable to an organizational setting. The Receiver Information Scale consists of 13 items focusing on organizational topic areas extracted from the Communications Relationships Scale.

Sample: One study used 300 faculty from a midwestern university.

Reliability: The Receiver Information Scale had coefficient alpha estimate of 0.88. The Communication Relationships Scale had four subscales (factors): immediate supervisor, 0.94; personal influence, 0.81; co-workers, 0.76; and top management, 0.88.

Validity: No validity studies were mentioned other than the factor analysis discussed below.

Factor Analysis: A principal component analysis produced four factors for the Communication Relationships Scale. The factor names are listed above under Reliability. The Receiver Information Scale is considered to be a unidimensional scale.

References:
Goldhaber, G., et al. 1977. The ICA Communication Audit Survey Instrument: 1977 Organizational Norms. Paper presented at the International Communication Association Convention.

Goldhaber, G., et al. 1978. Organizational communication. *Human Communication Research* 5:79-96.

McDowell, E.E. 1985. Faculty members' perceptions of information adequacy and communication relationships in their world of work. Paper presented at the Speech Communication Association. ERIC ED 263 638.

Communication Relationship Scale

1. My relationship with the chair/head of my department is satisfying.
2. I trust my chair/head.
3. My chair/head listens to me.
4. My chair/head is honest with me.
5. My chair/head is friendly with his/her faculty members.
6. I can tell my chair/head when things are going wrong.
7. My chair/head praises me for a good job.
8. I have a say in decisions that affect my job.
9. I influence operations in my department.
10. I have a part in accomplishing my organization's goals.
11. I trust my co-workers.
12. My co-workers get along with each other.
13. My relationship with my co-workers is satisfying.
14. I trust top management.
15. Top administrators are sincere in their efforts to communicate with faculty members.

Scoring: 1 = Strongly Agree; 2 = Agree; 3 = Uncertain; 4 = Disagree; and 5 = Strongly Disagree.

Reprinted with permission of the author.

Receiving Information Scale

1. How well I am doing in my position
2. My job duties
3. Department policies
4. Pay and benefits
5. How technical changes affect my position
6. Mistakes and failures of my department
7. How I am being judged
8. How my job related problems are being handled
9. How department decisions are made that affect my position
10. Promotion and advancement opportunities in my department
11. Important new program developments in my organization
12. How my job relates to the total department
13. Specific problems faced by administration

Scoring: 1 = Very Little; 2 = Little; 3 = Some; 4 = Great; and 5 = Very Great.

Reprinted with permission of the author.

Communicator Competence Questionnaire

Monge, P.R., et al. nd. Communicator competence in the workplace: Model testing and scale development. Communication Yearbook 5.

Comments: The 12-item CCQ was developed to measure communication competence in either supervisors or subordinates. Supervisors are asked to evaluate their subordinates and subordinates evaluate the supervisor.

Scale Construction: Items were developed to represent encoding and decoding skills appropriate for the workplace. Seven encoding items focus on specific behaviors such as being able to express one's ides clearly, having a good command of the language, and being easy to understand. Five decoding items focus on skills such as listening, responding to messages quickly, and attentiveness.

Sample: Samples were taken from two large firms in the same industry in the Midwest. One sample consisted of 220 respondents—supervisor-subordinate dyads. The second sample consisted of 60 staff people of manufacturing firm.

Validity: Convergent validity was assessed by correlating the competence scores on each factor with two global measures of competence. This analysis was conducted for both the supervisor and the subordinate data. The correlation between these measures was 0.74 offering reasonably good evidence for the convergent validity of the scales.

Factor Analysis: An oblique confirmatory factor analysis produced two factors—an encoding factor and a decoding factor. The two factors are free to covary and are significantly correlated.

References:
Level, D.A., and L. Johnson. 1978. Accuracy of information flows within the supervisor/subordinate relationship. *Journal of Business Communication* 15:13-22.

Wiemann, J.M. 1977. Explication and test of a model of communicative competence. *Human Communication Research* 3:195-213.

Communication Competence Questionnaire

1. My subordinate has a good command of the language.
2. My subordinate is sensitive to others' needs of the moment.
3. My subordinate typically gets right to the point.
4. My subordinate pays attention to what other people say to him or her.
5. My subordinate can deal with others effectively.
6. My subordinate is a good listener.
7. My subordinate's writing is difficult to understand.
8. My subordinate expresses his or her ideas clearly.
9. My subordinate is difficult to understand when he or she speaks.
10. My subordinate generally says the right thing at the right time.
11. My subordinate is easy to talk to.
12. My subordinate usually responds to messages (memos, phone calls, reports, etc.) quickly.

Scoring: *YES!* = very strong agreement; YES = strong agreement; yes = mild agreement; ? = neutral feelings of the language; *NO!* = very strong disagreement; NO = strong disagreement; no = mild disagreement.

Reprinted with permission of Sage Publications, Inc.

Communication Effectiveness Questionnaire

Viggiano, M.A. 1990. The relationship between the communicator style of the principal and the principal's effectiveness as a communicator in instructional matters. Ed.D. dissertation New York University.

Comments: This instrument is an adaptation, and refinement, of a questionnaire developed by the University of Washington for the Seattle Schools for use in their effective schools project. The instrument is designed to determine teachers' perceptions of the principal's effectiveness as a communicator. Communicator effectiveness is the ability of the principal to communicate clearly to teachers about instructional matters.

Sample: The initial sample was composed of 331 teachers and ten principals.

Reliability: The alpha coefficient for the scale is 0.90.

Validity: A panel of judges, teachers and principals, were used to establish the content validity of the instrument.

References:
DeVito, J.A. 1976. *The interpersonal communication book*. New York: Harper and Row Publishers.

Norton, R. 1983. *Communication style: Theory, applications and measures*. Beverly Hills: Sage Publications.

Communication Effectiveness Questionnaire

1. My principal provides a clear vision of what our school is all about.
2. My principal conducts formal discussions concerning the improvement of instruction.
3. My principal conducts formal discussions concerning student achievement.
4. Improved instructional practice results from discussion with my principal.
5. My principal provides me with information on current instructional topics.
6. My principal facilitates my participation in staff development opportunities.
7. My principal promotes an ongoing review of instructional materials.
8. My principal uses clearly established criteria for judging my performance in the classroom.
9. My principal provides frequent feedback concerning my classroom performance.
10. My principal is available to address my instructional concerns.

Scoring: A five-point Likert scale ranges from Little or None = 1 to Frequently or Always = 5.

Reprinted with permission from Martha Viggiano.

Conflict

Management of Differences Inventory

Kindler, H.S. 1981. Management of Differences Inventory. Pacific Palisades, CA: Center for Management Effectiveness.

Comments: The 36-item MODI measures the way employees handle differences. It provides the respondents with an analysis of their style for dealing with disagreement, managing differences, and conflict.

Sample: Over 200 managers were asked: "When your views on a work-related issue differ from the views of another person who also has a stake in the issue, how do you prepare to deal with the situation?" Based upon their responses, two dimensions emerged: viewpoint flexibility and interaction intensity.

Dimensions: *Viewpoint flexibility* reflects the importance and attainability of a person's position and what could be learned by listening to other points of view. *Interaction intensity* reflects the amount of involvement by the person and the type of relationship desired. Using these two dimensions, nine approaches for managing differences are identified. The nine approaches are: maintain, smooth, dominate, decide by rule, coexist, bargain, yield, release, and collaborate. For each of these approaches, intents, processes, applications, and examples are presented.

References:
Filley, A.C. 1978. Some normative issues in conflict management. *California Management Review* 63.

Pondy, L.R. 1967. Organizational conflict: Concepts and models. *Administrative Science Quarterly* 296-320.

Schmidt, W.H., and R. Tannenbaum. 1960. Management of differences. *Harvard Business Review* 107.

Management of Differences Inventory

1. A. I let emotions and tensions cool before taking decisive action.
   B. We find some formula or other criteria we both agree on.

2. A. I assert myself to gain what I'm after.
   B. We jointly develop a mutually agreeable plan that merges both views.

3. A. I follow my view, and the other person follows his or her view.
   B. I give in on some points to get my way on others.

4. A. I place more emphasis on similarities and less emphasis on differences.
   B. We find logical rules we both agree on as the basis for our decision.

5. A. We take action that lets both parties retain their positions, at least on an interim basis.
   B. Within agreed-upon limits, I give control to the other person.

6. A. I gain agreement for my position by avoiding detail on which we may disagree.
   B. I try solutions proposed by the other person.

7. A. I push to have my approach or my ideas prevail.
   B. I go along with the other person's view.

8. A. We work out a fair combination of gains and losses for both of us.
   B. I get both our concerns out in the open, and we problem-solve together.

9. A. I wait until I feel better prepared to take action.
   B. I let the other person come up with the plan.

10. A. I avoid unnecessary problems by delaying action.
    B. We agree to disagree, at least for a while or on an experimental basis.

11. A. I sell the person who disagrees with me on accepting my view by emphasizing its positive features.
    B. I fully express my ideas and feelings, and urge the other person to do the same.

12. A. We find some formula to resolve our differences.
    B. We find solutions in which gains balance out losses for both parties.

13. A. I do what it takes to get my ideas accepted.
    B. I allow the other person, within limits, to resolve our issue.

14. A. We mutually agree on rules or procedures to resolve our differences.
    B. I accommodate myself to the other person's view.

15. A. I gain compliance to my views.
    B. We acknowledge and allow each other's differences.

16. A. I go along with the views of the other person.
B. We work together to integrate ideas of both persons.

17. A. I minimize presenting information that makes my position less attractive.
B. Within a given framework, I let the other person handle the issue.

18. A. I wait until I have more information or emotions cool.
B. We find a mutually acceptable compromise by which to resolve our differences.

19. A. I delay suggesting changes until the timing feels right.
B. I don't resist the views of the other person.

20. A. We find mutually agreeable procedures (such as taking a vote or an appropriate test).
B. We find ways to jointly reframe our differences to satisfy both our needs.

21. A. I give in on some points if I believe the other person will reciprocate.
B. I state my expectation and concerns and let the other person work out a solution.

22. A. I show the other person that in the final analysis our views aren't very different.
B. I give the other person a turn or concession if I believe he or she will do the same for me.

23. A. We find ways that allow each of us to pursue our individual viewpoints.
B. We find solutions that take both our views into account.

24. A. I deal with differences only after waiting until I feel the time is right.
B. I act in ways that advance my position.

25. A. We mutually agree on a rule or procedure that will decide the issue.
B. We find ways in which we can both pursue our respective points of view.

26. A. I yield to the other person's views.
B. Given acceptable boundaries, I am willing to have the other person handle the issue.

27. A. I prevail on the other person to change his or her mind.
B. I establish an objective basis with the other person for resolving our differences.

28. A. I put off dealing with our differences until I have enough information.
B. I resolve our differences by emphasizing where we are not so far apart in our thinking.

29. A. We settle our differences by working out a compromise solution.
B. I accommodate myself to the other person's approach.

30. A. I point out that our differences aren't substantial enough to argue over.
B. I oppose the other person's view.

31. A. I defer making changes until I have adequate support.
B. We find new perspectives that satisfy both our needs.

32. A. I express some, but not all the negative aspects of my position.
    B. I get agreement from the other person to live with our differences, at least for a period of time.

33. A. We jointly agree to accept a criterion or the decision of a third party as the basis for resolving our differences.
    B. Within stated bounds, I encourage the other person to take the initiative.

34. A. I play to win.
    B. I make adjustments when the other person is willing to do the same.

35. A. I urge the other person to take the initiative within defined limits.
    B. We integrate the ideas expressed by both individuals.

36. A. We agree to follow our separate paths until joint action seems feasible.
    B. I go along with the other person's ideas.

Scoring: For every pair of items, 3 points are to be divided between the two alternatives to indicate frequency. Very often = 3; moderately often = 2; occasionally = 1; and rarely or never = 0. A profile that indicates management or differences/disagreement is included as part of the scoring. In addition, viewpoint flexibility/interaction intensity scoring is also provided. Finally, there is an explanation for each of the nine approaches.

Reprinted with permission of Herbert S. Kindler, Ph.D., Center for Management Effectiveness, P.O. Box 1202, Pacific Palisades, CA 90272.

Organizational Communication Conflict Instrument

Putnam, L., and C. Wilson. 1982 Communication strategies in organizational conflict: Reliability and validity of a measurement scale. In M. Burgoon, (ed.), *Communication Yearbook*. Beverly Hills, CA: Sage.

Comments: The authors contend that the OCCI is different from other conflict assessment instruments in that it focuses on behavioral choices that respondents make rather than a person's individual style of dealing with conflict.

Reliability: Internal consistency was assessed by the alpha coefficient. The three subscales were: nonconfrontation, 0.93; solution-orientation, 0.88, and control, 0.82.

Factor Analysis: Factor analysis produced three factors that account for 56% of the common variance. The nonconfrontation dimension consists of both smoothing and avoidance strategies; solution-orientation consists of compromise and collaborative strategies; and control refers to the polarized behaviors of the individual in group situations.

References:
Schuelke, D., and E. McDowell. 1990. A study of the relationship between willingness to communicate and preferred conflict strategy: Implications for teaching communication and conflict. Paper presented at International Communication Association. ERIC ED 322 561.

Wilson, C., and M. Waltman. 1988. Assessing the Putnam-Wilson Organizational Communication Conflict Instrument (OCCI). *Management Communication Quarterly* 1:367-388.

Organizational Communication Conflict Instrument

1.   I blend my ideas with others to create new alternatives for resolving conflict.
2.   I shy away from topics that are sources of disputes.
3.   I insist that my position be accepted during a conflict.
4.   I suggest solutions that combine a variety of viewpoints.
5.   I steer clear of disagreeable situations.
6.   I avoid a person I suspect of wanting to discuss a disagreement.
7.   I look for middle-of-the-road solutions.
8.   I give in a little on my ideas when the other person also gives in.
9.   I minimize the significance of conflict.
10. I integrate arguments into a solution from issues raised in a dispute.
11. I stress my point by hitting my fist on the table.
12. I will go fifty-fifty to reach a settlement.
13. I raise my voice when trying to get another person to accept my position.
14. I offer creative solutions in discussions of disagreement.
15. I keep quiet about views in order to avoid disagreements.
16. I frequently give in a little if the other person will meet me halfway.
17. I downplay the importance of a disagreement.
18. I reduce disagreements by saying they are insignificant.
19. I meet the opposition at the midpoint of our differences.
20. I assert my opinion forcefully.
21. I dominate arguments until the other person understands my position.
22. I suggest we work together to create solutions to disagreements.
23. I try to use everyone's ideas to generate solutions to problems.
24. I offer tradeoffs to reach solutions to problems.
25. I argue for my stance.
26. I withdraw when someone confronts me about a controversial issue.
27. I sidestep disagreements when they arise.
28. I try to smooth over disagreements by making them appear unimportant.
29. I stand firm in my views during a conflict.
30. I take a tough stand, refusing to retreat.

Scoring: Ranges from Strongly Agree = 1 to Strongly Disagree = 5.

Reprinted with permission of Earl E. McDowell.

Rahim Organizational Conflict Inventory II

Rahim, M.A., and C. Psenicka. 1984. Comparison of reliability and validity of unweighted and factor scales. *Psychological Reports* 55:439-445.

Comments: The 35-item ROCI II measures the degree of interpersonal conflict with superiors, subordinates, and peers.

Sample: Responses were received from 1,219 executives representing 25 different industries. The respondents represented top, middle, and lower management. The sample only included 50 women.

Reliability: The five scales obtained alpha coefficients ranging from 0.72 to 0.77.

Validity: Analysis of variance and discriminant functions analysis were used to determine whether the five conflict scales could discriminate how an executive handles conflict with boss, subordinates, or peers. An attempt was made to cross-validate the discriminant functions that correctly classified 52% of the cases into the three managerial groups.

Factor Analysis: Five factors were extracted with a principal factoring with a varimax rotation. The five factors accounted for 89% of the common variance. Only items with loadings greater than 0.40 were retained on the factor. The five scales (factors) are: integrating, obliging, dominating, avoiding, and compromising.

References:
Ashworth, M.A. 1989. A study of the conflict management styles of principals and superintendents in the public schools of Ohio. Ph.D. dissertation, Bowling Green State University.

Rahim, M.A. 1983. Rahim Organizational Conflict Inventory II. Palo Alto, CA: Consulting Psychologists Press.

Utley, M.E., et al. 1989. Personality and interpersonal conflict management. *Journal of Personality and Individual Differences* 10:287-293.

Rahim Organizational Conflict Inventory II

1. I try to investigate into an issue with my ___ to find a solution acceptable to us.
2. I generally try to satisfy the needs of my ___.
3. I attempt to avoid being "put on the spot" and try to keep my conflict with my ___ to myself.
4. I try to integrate my ideas with those of my ___ to come up with a decision jointly.
5. I give some to get some.
6. I try to work with my ___ to find solutions to a problem which satisfy our expectations.
7. I usually avoid open discussion of my differences with my ___.
8. I usually hold on to my solution to a problem.
9. I try to find a middle course to resolve an impasse.
10. I use my influence to get my ideas accepted.
11. I use my authority to make a decision in my favor.
12. I usually accommodate the wishes of my ___.
13. I give in to the wishes of my ___.
14. I win some and I lose some.
15. I exchange accurate information with my ___ to solve a problem together.
16. I sometimes help my ___ to make a decision in his favor.
17. I usually allow concessions to my ___.
18. I argue my case with my ___ to show the merits of my position.
19. I try to play down our differences to reach a compromise.
20. I usually propose a middle ground for breaking deadlocks.
21. I negotiate with my ___ so that a compromise can be reached.
22. I try to stay away from disagreement with my ___.
23. I avoid an encounter with my ___.
24. I use my expertise to make a decision in my favor.
25. I often go along with the suggestions of my ___.
26. I use "give and take" so that a compromise can be made.
27. I am generally firm in pursuing my side of the issue.
28. I try to bring all our concerns out in the open so that the issues can be resolved in the best possible way.
29. I collaborate with my ___ to come up with decisions acceptable to us.
30. I try to satisfy the expectations of my ___.
31. I sometimes use my power to win a competitive situation.
32. I try to keep my disagreement with my ___ to myself in order to avoid hard feelings.
33. I try to avoid unpleasant exchanges with my ___.
34. I generally avoid an argument with my ___.
35. I try to work with my ___ for a proper understanding of a problem.

Scoring: The word boss, subordinates, or peers appeared in each blank space in the instrument.

Reprinted with permission from C. Psenicka.

Culture

School Work Culture Profile

Snyder, K.J. 1988. *School Work Culture Profile*. Tampa, FL: School Management Institute.

Comments: The 60-item SWCP, which is based on systems theory, assesses the amount/type of involvement in decision making in four areas. There are ten dimensions that correspond to the each of the four subscales: organizational planning (school planning, team planning, and individual performance planning); staff development (staff development, clinical supervision, and work group development); program development (instructional management and resource development); and school assessment (quality control and assessing achievement). Definitions are provided for each of the work culture dimensions. Each of these four subscales contains 15 items. Another questionnaire, the Educational Quality Benchmark System, is also available. The EQBS assesses the following seven performance areas: visionary leadership, strategic planning, systems thinking and action, information systems, human resource development, quality services, and customer success and satisfaction.

Scale Construction: A 100-item questionnaire was developed based upon the research. The questionnaire was pilot tested for one year in workshops and a revised questionnaire was field tested in three states. Three years later, the questionnaire was revised and was sent to a national panel of 17 experts.

Sample: There were 925 participants (teachers and principals) from 112 schools in Florida.

Reliability: For the first sample (46 elementary school teachers), alpha coefficients ranged from 0.82 to 0.95 on the four subscales. The total reliability coefficient was 0.95. Test-retest reliability (50 elementary school teachers) over a two-week period was 0.78. The results of other reliability studies are reported.

Validity: Evidence of content and construct validity are provided.

Factor Analysis: Although a first-order principal components factor analysis originally yielded ten factors, additional factor analytic procedures were conducted. A second-order factor solution that yielded four factors (continuous improvement, human resource development and group planning, strategic planning and accountability, and collaboration) was accepted.

Data Analysis: The second-order factor loadings are presented.

References:
Acker-Hocevar, M. 1994. The content validation of standards, outcomes, and indicators for organizational development in region IV of Florida. Ph.D. dissertation. University of South Florida.

Johnson, W.L.,et al. 1997. Assessing school work culture. *Research in the Schools* 4:35-43.

School Work Culture Profile

Program Development Dimension

1. Instructional programs are guided by learning objectives.
2. Instructional programs facilitate student mastery of learning objectives.
3. Classroom organization and activities facilitate student learning.
4. Students are provided sufficient time to succeed in learning tasks.
5. Parents serve as a resource to the school's instructional program.
6. The school's leadership team helps work groups to succeed.

Staff Development Dimension

1. The staff development program builds the school's capacity to solve problems.
2. Staff development programs provide opportunities to learn new knowledge.
3. Staff development programs provide opportunities to practice newly learned skills.
4. Staff members have opportunities to develop skills for working successfully in a group or team.
5. Supervision of teaching is based on cooperatively identified goals and emerging needs.
6. Supervision builds and maintains professional self-esteem.

Program Development Dimension

1. Instructional programs are guided by learning objectives.
2. Instructional programs facilitate student mastery of learning objectives.
3. Classroom organization and activities facilitate student learning.
4. Students are provided sufficient time to succeed in learning tasks.
5. Parents serve as a resource to the school's instructional program.
6. The school's leadership team helps work groups to succeed.

School Assessment Dimension

1. Work groups of all types are assessed on their contribution to the achievement of school development goals.
2. School assessment is based on school development goals.
3. Work groups are assessed on the extent to which their goals are achieved, and the extent to which they respond to emerging challenges.
4. Individual staff members are assessed on their contribution to the school's development goals.
5. Periodic feedback from sources outside the school is used to modify work practices and programs.
6. Student achievement is assessed in relation to the school's development goals, and to emerging challenges and needs.

Scoring: Strongly disagree = 1; Disagree = 2; Undecided = 3; Agree = 4; and Strongly agree = 5.
Scores are obtained for each of the four subscales and can be plotted on a graph.

Reprinted with permission of the author.

Organizational Culture Assessment Inventory

Steinhoff, C.R., and R.G. Owens. 1988. The Organizational Culture Inventory: A metaphorical analysis of organizational culture in educational settings. Paper presented at American Educational Research Association.

Comments: This instrument was developed as an objective measure of organizational culture. Two major questions were of concern: (1) What are the essential factors that define the metaphor, Organizational Culture? and (2) How can these factors be evaluated objectively in a given organization? Organizational culture is a pattern of basic assumptions developed by a given group as it learns to cope with its problems of external adaptation and internal integration. The study of patterns of these assumptions has focused on control mechanisms, values, norms, history, traditions, ceremonies, rituals, heroes, symbols, and informal networks, as well as internalized solutions to internal and external problems.

Scale Construction: A taxonomy structure of organizational culture was developed from a review of the literature. This taxonomy has six dimensions that define the culture of a school: (1) the history of the organization; (2) values and beliefs of the organization; (3) myths and stories that explain the organization; (4) cultural norms of the organization; (5) traditions, rituals, and ceremonies; and (6) heroes and heroines of the organization.

Sample: The development of the instrument constituted two samples: (1) Several classes of graduate students provided 56 responses representing 47 individual schools. (2) Data were collected from eight elementary schools, which represented the major themes identified in the initial analysis.

Data Analysis: The analysis of the initial data produced descriptions of four cultural phenotypes that differentiate in terms of the metaphorical language recognized by respondents as characteristic of the schools in which they work.
1. The Family—Approximately one third of the respondents referred to their schools as the family, home, team, or womb. The principal was described as a parent (strong or weak), nurturer, friend, sibling, or coach.
2. Modern Times—Many respondents described their schools using the metaphor of the machine. They were described as well-oiled machines, political machines, beehives of activity, or rust machines.
3. The Cabaret—Some respondents described their schools as a circus, a broadway show, a banquet, or a well-choreographed ballet performed by well-appreciated artists.
4. The Little Shop of Horrors—A small percentage described their school as unpredictable, tension-filled nightmares having the characteristics of Paris during the French Revolution. Teachers in these schools lead isolated lives; there is little social activity.

Reference:
Owens, R.G., and C.R. Steinhoff. 1989. Towards a theory of organizational culture. *Journal of Educational Administration* 27:6-16.

Organizational Culture Assessment Inventory

1. Every school has a unique history all of its own. Teachers know something of that history even if they have not worked there for a long time, because people talk about things that went on in former times. Some of these events may have been powerful incidents in the community that affected the school, and others may be purely internal matters that might seem unimportant or even mundane to outsiders.

    Please describe in a brief paragraph some of the more important events or trends that helped to shape the character of your school as it is today.

2. Schools usually espouse some official, formal, public set of values and beliefs. Ordinarily these appear in handbooks, newsletters, speeches, and so on. But in day-to-day work, a school may sometimes seem to be operating from values and beliefs that are different from the official public statements. The latter values and beliefs are, of course, often implicitly understood but not often talked about.

    In a brief paragraph, please describe the actual, functional values and beliefs that are important in your school.

3. People who work in schools very often tell stories—perhaps mythical, or apocryphal, or humorous-that help to explain what life in them is really like.

    Briefly describe a common story that is likely to be told to a newcomer by an "old hand" in your school to impress upon the individual "how things are really done around here."

4. Every school has established but unwritten expectations for behavior on the job.

    In a brief paragraph, please describe some of the most important expectations that have to be met in your school in order to get along.

5. Schools often develop informal customs, or rituals, that are more or less unique. For example, in one school that we know of there is a bridge game going on in the teachers' lounge every day with different people sitting in as they come off of hall and cafeteria duty. In another school, the principal has an informal coffee klatch in the school kitchen every morning, and so on.

    In a brief paragraph, please describe any such rituals that are important in the daily life of your school.

6. Schools seem to have at least one person, either now or in the past, who is thought of with great respect (or even reverence) because he or she is/was so outstanding in the life of the school.

    If you can think of such an individual in the history of your school, please describe in a brief paragraph why it is that the individual is so well-regarded.

7. In responding to the previous questions, you have provided a rich description of important aspects of the culture of your school. But the culture of a school is a total entity, even greater than the sum of its parts. We now would like you to summarize the descriptions that you have

provided by using metaphors as a way to convey the essence of the culture of your school. A metaphor identifies one object with another and ascribes to the first object one or more qualities of the second. For example, some administrators speak of the school as a family.

People often use metaphors to succinctly describe complex ideas. For example, when we say that a school is a "well-oiled machine," that metaphor makes clear what that particular school is *really* like in the eyes of the people who work in it. For another example, for teachers to speak of a principal as being "Dr. Jekyll and Mr. Hyde" tells us a lot about the impact of the behavior of that individual principal on the teachers in that particular school.

In this sense, considering the descriptions that you have already written, what *one best* metaphor would you use to complete the following sentences:

   a. My school "is" a (an, the)
   b. Please explain why you chose this metaphor.
   c. The principal in my school "is" a (an, the)
   d. Please explain.
   e. The typical teacher in my school "is" a (an, the)
   f. Please explain why you chose this metaphor.
   g. The typical student in my school "is" a (an, the)
   h. Please explain why you chose this metaphor.
   I. The community in which my school is situated "is" a (an, the)
   j. Please explain.

8.   What, in your opinion, would be the metaphor for the ideal school?
9.   What, in your opinion, would be the metaphor for the ideal school principal?
10. What, in your opinion, would be the metaphor for the ideal teacher?
11. What, in your opinion, would be the metaphor for the ideal student?
12. What, in your opinion, would be the metaphor for the ideal school community?

Scoring: Responses are scored on the basis of school metaphor.

Reprinted with permission of the author.

Decision-Making

Decisional Participation Scale

Alutto, J.A., and J.A. Belasco. 1972. Patterns of teacher participation in school system decision making. *Educational Administration Quarterly* 9:27-41.

Comments: A 12-item instrument designed to measure a teacher's actual and desired rates of participation in decision-making. Individuals can be categorized as decisional deprived, at equilibrium, or saturated.

Sample: Teachers were taken from two school districts in western New York State, resulting in a sample of 454 teachers.

Reliability: Test-retest reliability estimates exceeded 0.80 for all sections of the questionnaire.

Validity: The Mohrman study cited below provides information on the validity and factor profile for the 12-item instrument. Three factors were found, one for actual participation and two for deprivation.

Definition of Factors: *Decisional deprivation* means current participation in decision-making less than preferred; *Decisional equilibrium* means current participation equal to preferred; and *Decisional saturation* means current participation greater than desired.

References:
Alutto, J.A., and J.A. Belasco. 1974. A typology for participation in organizational decision making. *Administrative Science Quarterly* 10:117-125.

Mohrman, A.M., et al. 1978. Participation in decision making: A multidimensional perspective. *Educational Administration Quarterly* 14:13-29.

Decisional Participation Scale

1. When a new faculty member is to be hired in your school or department, would you be involved in making such a decision?
   A. If yes, in what capacity?
   B. If you would be involved, with whom would you discuss this matter?
   C. Do you want to be involved in making such decisions?
   D. If you do, in what capacity?
   E. Who do you believe *presently* has the "final say" in deciding whether or not to hire a new faculty member in a given area?
   F. Who do you believe *should* have the "final say" in deciding whether or not to hire a new faculty member in a given area?

2. When school or department budgets are planned, would you be involved in their preparation?
   A. If yes, in what capacity?
   B. If you would be involved, with whom would you discuss this matter?
   C. Do you want to be involved in making such decisions?
   D. If you do, in what capacity?
   E. Who do you believe *presently* has the "final say" in deciding on departmental or school budgets?
   F. Who do you believe *should* have the "final say" in deciding on departmental or school budgets?

3. When a new textbook is needed for a course in your department of school, would you be involved in making such a decision?
   A. If yes, in what capacity?
   B. If you would be involved, with whom would you discuss this matter?
   C. Do you want to be involved in making such decisions?
   D. If you do, in what capacity?
   E. Who do you believe *presently* has the "final say" in selecting texts for courses?
   F. Who do you believe *should* have the "final say" in selecting texts for courses?

4. When one of your students becomes involved in academic or personal problems, would you be involved in deciding how to resolve the difficulties?
   A. If yes, in what capacity?
   B. If you would be involved, with whom would you discuss this matter?
   C. Do you want to be involved in making such decisions?
   D. If you do, in what capacity?
   E. Who do you believe *presently* has the "final say" in resolving such student problems?
   F. Who do you believe *should* have the "final say" in resolving such student problems?

5. When individual faculty assignments are considered, would you be involved in making such decisions?
   A. If yes, in what capacity?
   B. If you would be involved, with whom would you discuss this matter?
   C. Do you want to be involved in making such decisions?
   D. If you do, in what capacity?
   E. Who do you believe presently has the "final say" in designating faculty assignments?
   F. Who do you believe *should* have the "final say" in designating faculty assignments?

6. When a faculty member has a grievance, would you be involved in resolving the problem?
   A. If yes, in what capacity?
   B. If you would be involved, with whom would you discuss this matter?
   C. Do you want to be involved in making such decisions?
   D. If you do, in what capacity?
   E. Who do you feel *presently* has the "final say" in resolving faculty grievances?
   F. Who do you feel *should* have the "final say" in resolving faculty grievances?

7. When new instructional methods (e.g., team teaching) are suggested, would you be interested in making the decision whether to adopt them or not?
   A. If yes, in what capacity?
   B. If you would be involved, with whom would you discuss this matter?
   C. Do you want to be involved in making such decisions?
   D. If so, in what capacity?
   E. Who do you believe *presently* has the "final say" in deciding matters concerning new instructional methods?
   F. Who do you believe *should* have the "final say" in deciding matters concerning new instructional methods?

8. If new building facilities are needed, would you become involved in making such a decision?
   A. If so, in what capacity?
   B. If you would be involved, with whom would you discuss this matter?
   C. Do you want to be involved in making such decisions?
   D. If you do, in what capacity?
   E. Who do you believe *presently* has the "final say" concerning the construction of new facilities?
   F. Who do you believe *should* have the "final say" concerning the construction of new facilities?

9. When there are problems involving community groups (e.g., P.T.A., civil rights groups), would you become involved in eliminating the difficulties?
   A. If yes, in what capacity?
   B. If you would be involved, with whom would you discuss this matter?
   C. Do you want to be involved in making such decisions?
   D. If so, in what capacity?
   E. Who do you believe *presently* has the "final say" in determining how such difficulties are resolved?
   F. Who do you believe *should* have the "final say" in determining how such difficulties are resolved?

10. When there are problems with administrative services (clerks, typists, etc.), would you become involved in resolving such difficulties?
    A. If yes, in what capacity?
    B. If you would be involved, with whom would you discuss this matter?
    C. Do you want to be involved in making such decisions?
    D. If so, in what capacity?
    E. Who do you believe *presently* has the "final say" about how such problems are resolved?
    F. Who do you believe *should* have the "final say" about how such matters are resolved?

11. Would you be involved in any decisions concerning faculty members' salaries?
    A. If yes, in what capacity?
    B. If you would be involved, with whom would you discuss this matter?
    C. Do you want to be involved in making such decisions?
    D. If so, in what capacity?
    E. Who do you believe *presently* has the "final say" in such matters?
    F. Who do you believe *should* have the "final say" in such matters?

12. Would you be involved in decisions concerning general instructional policy?
    A. If yes, in what capacity?
    B. If you would be involved, with whom would you discuss this matter?
    C. Do you want to be involved in making such decisions?
    D. If so, in what capacity?
    E. Who do you believe *presently* has the "final say" about instructional policies?
    F. Who do you believe *should* have the "final say" about instructional policies?

Scoring: Responses are Yes or No for each of the general twelve questions and C; for A and D a brief explanation is required; for B, E and F the title of the appropriate person is required; and also for B the title of the appropriate person next to most often and often is required.

Reprinted with permission of the author.

Shared Decision-Making Survey

King, R.L., and E.J. Meshanko. 1992. Shared decision making in schools: The locus of control. Paper presented at Association of Teacher Educators. Mimeo.

Comments: The survey assesses the degree of involvement of teachers in shared decision-making within a school district. It is based on the question: Do teachers have a high personal stake in the decision? The assumption is made that if they have a personal involvement, interest in participation will be high. The survey is based on the literature, philosophy, and research that proposes that it is desirable for teacher participation in decision-making in education as well as the corporate world. Corollary terms upon which this survey is based are: school-site management, school-based management, decentralized management, and shared governance.

Sample: The study was based on a stratified random sample that selected nine school districts from 499 in the state of Pennsylvania. All teachers, principals, and school board members responded to the survey. This was 1,935 teachers, 77 principals, and 81 school board members.

Reliability: Reliability estimate was 0.87. Type of reliability was not indicated.

References:
Marcoline, J.F. 1990. A survey of shared decision-making in Pennsylvania: Comparing teacher and administrative perceptions. Ph.D. dissertation, Indiana University of Pennsylvania.

Meshanko, E. 1990. Teacher decision-making: An analysis of teachers, principals, and school board members perspectives. Ph.D. dissertation, Indiana University of Pennsylvania.

Shared Decision-Making Survey

Section I
1. Hiring a faculty member.
2. Selecting new textbooks.
3. Setting or revising school goals.
4. Determine faculty assignments.
5. Determine faculty evaluation procedures.
6. Determine classroom discipline policies.
7. Determine faculty schedules.
8. Determine budget priorities.
9. Determine staff development programs.
10. Determine grading policies.

Scoring: Indicate the extent that teachers in your school district actually participate in the above situations: Not participate = 1; Provide or gather information = 2; Suggest possible alternative decisions = 3; Recommend a decision = 4; and Make the decision = 5.

Section II

11. Hiring a new faculty member.
12. Selecting new textbooks.
13. Setting or revising school goals.
14. Determine faculty.
15. Determine faculty evaluation procedures.
16. Determine classroom discipline policies.
17. Determine faculty schedules.
18. Determine budgeting priorities.
19. Determine staff development programs.
20. Determine grading policies.

Scoring: Please indicate the extent that teachers in your school district would like to participate in the above situations: (see response scale above).

Section III

21. Hiring a new faculty member.
22. Selecting new textbooks.
23. Setting or revising school goals.
24. Determine faculty assignments.
25. Determine faculty evaluation procedures.
26. Determine classroom discipline policies.
27. Determine faculty schedules.
28. Determine budgeting priorities.
29. Determine staff development programs.
30. Determine grading policies.

Scoring: To the extent that teachers are involved in shared decision-making, it indicates the procedure that allows for this involvement: No involvement = 1; Informal discussions with administrators = 2; Formal committees organized as the need arises = 3; On-going formal committee structure without board policy = 4; and Board policy for shared decision-making = 5.

Reprinted with permission of the author.

Teacher Involvement and Participation Scale

Russell, J.J. 1992. Theory into practice: The realities of shared decision making. Ed.D. dissertation, Fordham University.

Comments: The 50-item TIPS 2 measures eight areas of teacher involvement in decision-making. TIPS can be used to determine areas for training. In addition, the responses of teachers and administrators can be compared. Sample items from each of the eight areas are provided.

Sample: The five schools in the sample were selected based upon their level of shared decision-making. Two schools were identified as having a high level of shared decision-making; two schools were identified as having a low level of shared decision-making; and one school was identified as having a moderate level of shared decision-making.

Reliability: Cronbach alpha, Spearman-Brown, and Guttman split-half techniques were used with 109 teachers from the five pilot schools to assess reliability. The alpha coefficient for the entire TIPS 2 was 0.96. The alpha coefficients ranged from 0.71 (goals/vision/mission) to 0.92 (staffing).

Validity: A thorough review of the literature on shared decision-making focused on eight areas. These eight areas formed the foundation for the TIPS. Content validity was established by using a panel of experts to match statements with subscales. In order for a statement to be included, it needed at least 80% agreement. Evidence of discriminant validity and construct validity were provided.

Subscales: The eight subscales/dimensions of the decision-making process that were identified were: nine items on goals/vision/mission (1-9); five items on standards (10-14); ten items on curriculum and instruction (15-24); six items on budget (25-30); four items on staffing (31-34); four items on operations (35-38); seven items on facilitating procedures/structures (39-45); and five items on staff development (46-50).

Data Analysis: Scale means and standard deviations are presented as well as the results of an analysis of variance. In addition, an analysis was conducted with each of the five schools in the sample.

References:
Conley, S.C., and S.B. Bachrach. 1990. From school-site management to participatory school-site management. *Phi Delta Kappan* 71:539-544.

David, J.L. 1989. Synthesis of research on school-based management. *Educational Leadership* 46:45-47, 50-53.

Russell, J.J., et al. 1992. How do you measure shared decision making? *Educational Leadership* 50:39-40

Sirotnik, K., and R. Clark. 1988. School centered decision making and renewal. *Phi Delta Kappan* 69:660-664.

Teacher Involvement and Participation Scale

1. The school's goals are consistent with my vision of this school.
2. Teachers contribute to the development of a plan to meet the school's goals.
3. Teachers play an active role in evaluating school goals.
4. Teachers contribute to the standards set for discipline in the school.
5. Teachers set standards for their student's work.
6. The school staff assumes responsibility for student performance.
7. Teachers participate in curricula development.
8. Teachers determine grouping for the purpose of instruction.
9. Teachers monitor the effectiveness of curricula.
10. Teachers contribute to the development of the school budget.
11. Teachers have a voice in the recruiting and selecting of teachers.
12. Teachers take part in staffing decisions including such tradeoffs as using instructional aids, or hiring vice-principals, counselors, and other special area staff.
13. Teachers have a voice in the recruiting and selecting of administrators.
14. Teachers play a part in determining how the school building is utilized.
15. Teachers are involved in the development of plans to improve building facilities.
16. Teachers play a role in establishing building maintenance priorities.
17. Teachers have access to the information they need to make school-wide decisions.
18. Teachers are represented on a council or committee that makes school-wide decisions.
19. Decisions are not made until everyone can accept the proposal to some extent.
20. Teachers have access to current research on effective programs and practices.
21. Teachers have opportunities to share their expert knowledge.
22. Teachers have access to special training when necessary.

Scoring: Almost Never = 1; Seldom = 2; Sometimes = 3; Frequently = 4; and Almost Always = 5.

Reprinted with permission of John J. Russell, RBG Associates, P.O. Box 182, New City, NY 10956.

Dogmatism

Dogmatism Scale (Form E)

Rokeach, M. 1960. *The open and closed mind.* New York: Basic Books.

Comments: This 40-item scale assesses individual differences in openness or closedness of belief systems. All the statements express an opinion and all statements are written in the negative. The items are based upon three dimensions of belief systems: belief-disbelief, central-peripheral, and time-perspective. The scale was refined through item analyses. Form E is the final version of the scale. In addition, the scale also assesses general authoritarianism and general intolerance. This is the most frequently cited instrument to measure dogmatism.

Scale Construction: Statements that reflected the characteristics of open and closed systems were written. Some of the items were the result of statements made by people who were considered to be closed-minded, while nine items came from the work of others. The scale went through five revisions. The initial scale contained 57 items; Form B had 43 items; Form C had 36 items; and Form D had 66 items. Forty items were taken from Form D and these became the final version, Form E.

Sample: Reliability data were gathered from samples of 959 university students attending Michigan State University, Ohio State University, and Purdue University in the Midwest; 207 university students attending New York University and Brooklyn College in New York; and 217 university students attending the University College in London as well as another British university. A group of 121 destitute veterans in New York and sample of 60 automobile factory workers participated in Great Britain.

Reliability: Corrected reliability for Form A was 0.70 and 0.75 for Form B. Form C had reliabilities lower than anticipated and, therefore, Form D contained 30 new items. The corrected reliability for Form D was 0.91. Twenty-six items were deleted in order to shorten the scale. Form E had a corrected reliability of 0.81 for the British college sample and 0.78 for the British automobile workers. Odd-even reliability coefficients corrected by the Spearman-Brown formula for six samples of American and British college students ranged from 0.68 (Ohio State University) to 0.85 (Ohio State University). Test-retest reliabilities over a five-to six-month period were 0.71 for 58 Ohio State University students, and over a one-month period 0.84 for 17 veterans. Overall, reliabilities ranged from 0.68 to 0.93.

Validity: Two construct validity studies were conducted using known high and low dogmatic groups. In the first study, no significant differences were found between graduate students selected by their college professors to be in one or the other group. However, in the second study, when psychology graduate students selected other students as most and least dogmatic, significant differences were found. Other researchers have conducted studies to establish construct, predictive, concurrent, and criterion validity.

Definition of Dimensions: The scale contains items involving the belief-disbelief dimension (4 items) and items involving the central-peripheral dimension (36 items). The belief-disbelief dimension consists of *isolation within and between belief*, which deals with the *accentuation of differences between the belief and the disbelief systems* (1) and *the coexistence of contradictions within the belief system* (2 and 3) as well as *relative amount of knowledge possessed* (4). The central-peripheral dimension consists of *specific content of primitive beliefs*, which deals with the *beliefs regarding the aloneness, isolation, and helplessness of man* (5, 6, 7, and 8), *beliefs regarding the uncertainty of the future* (9, 10, 11, 12, and 13), *beliefs about self-adequacy and inadequacy* (14), and *self-aggrandizement as a defense against self-inadequacy* (15, 16, and 17). *Formal content of the intermediate belief region* deals with *authoritarianism* (18 and 19), *belief in the cause* (20, 21, 22, 23, 24, 25, and 26), and *intolerance* (27, 28, 29, 30, 31, 32, and 33). *Interrelations among primitive, intermediate, and peripheral beliefs* deal with the *tendency to make a party-line change* (34 and 35), *narrowing* (36), *attitude toward the past, present, and future* (37), and *knowing the future* (38, 39, and 40).

Data Analysis: Means and standard deviations are reported as well as normative data for the original samples on all five forms of the scale.

References:
Esposito, J. 1974. Supervisor personality and task performance. *Journal of Experimental Education* 42:17-20.

Kleiber, D., et al. 1973. The multi-dimensionality of locus of control. *Journal of Clinical Psychology* 29:411-416.

McColskey, W., et al. 1985. Predictors of principals' reliance on formal and informal sources of information. *Evaluation and Policy Analysis* 7:427-436.

Spivey, J.R. 1975. Dogmatism and the secondary social studies teachers' perspective. *Illinois School Research* 11:26-31.

Ward, G. R., et al. 1978. Personality profiles and dogmatism in undergraduate teacher education students. *Psychology in the Schools* 15:33-36.

Dogmatism Scale

1. The United States and Russia have just about nothing in common.
2. The highest form of government is a democracy and the highest form of democracy is run by those who are most intelligent.
3. Even though freedom of speech for all groups is a worthwhile goal, it is unfortunately necessary to restrict the freedom of certain political groups.
4. It is only natural that a person would have a much better acquaintance with ideas he believes in than with ideas he opposes.
5. Man on his own is a helpless and miserable creature.
6. Fundamentally, the world we live in is a pretty lonesome place.
7. Most people just don't give a "damn" for others.
8. I'd like it if I could find someone who would tell me how to solve my personal problems.
9. It is only natural for a person to be rather fearful of the future.
10. There is so much to be done and so little time to do it in.
11. Once I get wound up in a heated discussion I just can't stop.
12. In a discussion I often find it necessary to repeat myself several times to make sure I am being understood.
13. In a heated discussion I generally become so absorbed in what I am going to say that I forget to listen to what the others are saying.
14. It is better to be a dead hero than to be a live coward.
15. While I don't like to admit this even to myself, my secret ambition is to become a great man, like Einstein, or Beethoven, or Shakespeare.
16. The main thing in life is for a person to want to do something important.
17. If given the chance I would do something of great benefit to the world.
18. In the history of mankind there have probably been just a handful of really great thinkers.
19. There are a number of people I have come to hate because of the things they stand for.
20. A man who does not believe in some great cause has not really lived.
21. It is only when a person devotes himself to an ideal or cause that life becomes meaningful.
22. Of all the different philosophies which exist in this world there is probably only one which is correct.
23. A person who gets enthusiastic about too many causes is likely to be a pretty "wishy-washy" sort of person.
24. To compromise with our political opponents is dangerous because it usually leads to the betrayal of our own side.
25. When it comes to differences of opinion in religion we must be careful not to compromise with those who believe differently from the way we do.
26. In times like these, a person must be pretty selfish if he considers primarily his own happiness.
27. The worst crime a person could commit is to attack publicly the people who believe in the same thing he does.
28. In times like these it is often necessary to be more on guard against ideas put out by people or groups in one's own camp than by those in the opposing camp.
29. A group which tolerates too much differences of opinion among its own members cannot exist for long.
30. There are two kinds of people in this world: those who are for the truth and those who are against the truth.
31. My blood boils whenever a person stubbornly refuses to admit he's wrong.
32. A person who thinks primarily of his own happiness is beneath contempt.
33. Most of the ideas which get printed nowadays aren't worth the paper they are printed on.
34. In this complicated world of ours the only way we can know what's going on is to rely on leaders or experts who can be trusted.
35. It is often desirable to reserve judgment about what's going on until one has had a chance to hear the opinions of those one respects.
36. In the long run the best way to live is to pick friends and associates whose tastes and beliefs are the same as one's own.

37. The present is all too often full of unhappiness. It is only the future that counts.
38. If a man is to accomplish his mission in life, it is sometimes necessary to gamble "all or nothing at all."
39. Unfortunately, a good many people with whom I have discussed important social and moral problems don't really understand what's going on.
40. Most people just don't know what's good for them.

Scoring: I agree a little = 1; I agree on the whole = 2; I agree very much = 3; I disagree a little = -1; I disagree on the whole = -2; and I disagree very much = -3. For scoring purposes, 4 is added to each item score, thus creating a 1-to-7 scale.

Ethics

Perceptions of Ethics Scale

Froelich, K.S., and J.L. Kottke. 1991. Measuring individual beliefs about organizational ethics. *Educational and Psychological Measurement* 51:377-383.

Comments: The ten-item scale measures workers' perceptions of suitable and unsuitable ethical behavior. It examines the differences between a person's ethical behavior and the interests of the organization. Several statements came from the work of Brenner and Molander (1977) and Clinard and Yeager (1980).

Sample: The pilot study consisted of 42 graduate and undergraduate students from a small state university in the southwest. Based on the results of the pilot study, a revised scale was developed and responses were received from 225 people from four small universities and businesses in southern California.

Reliability: The alpha coefficient for the original 21-item scale was 0.69, whereas the alpha coefficient for the revised 16-item scale was 0.85. The alphas for the final ten-item version is 0.84 for company support and 0.82 for lie to protect the company.

Validity: Construct validity was established by factor analytic procedures.

Factor Analysis: A varimax rotation yielded two factors. They are: company support (six items) and lie to protect the company (four items).

Data Analysis: Means and standard deviations are presented for the 16-item scale and for the ten-item scale.

References:
Brenner, S.N., and E.A. Molander. 1977. Is the ethics of business changing? *Harvard Business Review* 55:57-71.

Clinard, M.B., and P.C. Yaeger. 1980. *Corporate crime.* New York: The Free Press.

Perception of Ethics Scale

1. At work, employees can expect to experience a conflict between what is required of them as workers and what they believe is right as ethical people.
2. It is okay for a supervisor to ask an employee to support someone else's incorrect viewpoint.
3. An employee may need to lie to a customer/client to protect the company.
4. It is sometimes necessary for the company to engage in shady practices because the competition is doing so.
5. An employee should overlook someone else's wrongdoing if it is in the best interest of the company.
6. Organizations occasionally misrepresent products to make them look better to the consumer.
7. An employee should be asked to do business with a supervisor's friends.
8. A supervisor should not care how results are achieved as long as the desired outcome occurs.
9. There is nothing wrong with a supervisor asking an employee to falsify a document.
10. It is not unusual for employees to experience a conflict between their own beliefs of social responsibility and company requirements.
11. Pollution is a by-product of many companies' need to stay in business.
12. An employee may need to lie to a co-worker to protect the company.
13. Profits should be given a higher priority than the safety of a product.
14. An employee may need to lie to a supervisor/manager to protect the company.
15. Employees are entitled to receive gifts or kickbacks for doing their jobs.
16. An employee may need to lie to another company's representative to protect the company.

Scoring: A seven-point Likert scale was anchored with Strongly Agree = 1 and Strongly Disagree = 7.

Reprinted with permission of Janet Kottke. (Froelich, K.S., and J.L. Kottke. 1991. Measuring individual beliefs about organizational ethics. *Educational and Psychological Measurement* 51:377-383.)

Honesty/Trust

Applicant Review

Cherrington, D.J., and J.O. Cherrington. 1983. Applicant Review. Stanfordville, NY: CHC Forecast Inc.

Comments: The 102-item AR assesses honesty and aggressive tendencies. It has been used as a pre-employment screening device and has been revised in 1985, 1988, 1991, 1993, and 1996. A technical manual is available as well as computer scoring. The appendix contains an article on understanding honesty.

Sample: Over 33,330 people from ten organizations throughout the United States participated in this study. Some of the organizations sampled include employees from retail stores, convenience stores, electronic stores, specialty stores, grocery stores, small stores, hardware stores. In addition, validation studies included graduate students, students at an alternative high school, and store managers.

Validity: Face validity is established through the items that assess attitudes and behaviors of honesty. Construct validity is supported by the seven factors that were identified through factor analysis. Concurrent validity is described by using the known-group technique. Detailed information about the evidence based on test content, response processes, internal structure, and relations to other variables are presented in the technical manual. Results of validation studies are also included.

Reliability: Test-retest reliability for 30 college students over one week yielded correlations that ranged from 0.80 to 0.89 for five subscales. Another test-retest reliability for 44 students yielded a correlation of 0.83 for an overall honesty score. The alpha coefficients for the seven subscales with the original sample were: 0.73 (personal history and honesty of others), 0.66 (blame for dishonesty), 0.76 (definition/standards of honesty), 0.77 (punishment), 0.71 (moral reasoning), and 0.69 (past behavior).

Subscales: There are seven susbscales that comprise an honesty score (personal honesty, honesty of others, blame for dishonesty, definition and standards of honesty, punishment, moral reasoning, and past behavior). The first part of the review measures social attitudes (42 items). The second part measures personal behaviors (24 items). The third part measures past behaviors (11 items). The final part of the review measures future intentions (five items).

Data Analysis: Norms are provided for 33,332 people from ten organizations within the United States. Means and standard deviations are presented. Cumulative frequencies for the ten organizations are provided. Item analyses were conducted.

References:
Clark, J.P., and R.C. Hollinger. 1983. *Theft by employees in work organizations: Executive summary.* Washington, D.C.: National Institute of Justice, U.S. Government Printing Office.

Jones, J.W. 1991. *Preemployment honesty testing: Current research and future directions*. Westport, CT: Quorum Books.

Principles for the validation and use of personnel selection procedures. 1987. College Park, MD: Department of Psychology (Society for Industrial and Organizational Psychology), University of Maryland.

Rest, J.R., and D. Narvaez. 1994. *Moral development in the professions*. Hillsdale, NJ: Lawrence Erlbaum Associates.

Applicant Review

1. I dislike helping people who are intentionally rude and nasty.
2. I get bored very easily when I have to do the same thing over and over.
3. Most people usually tell the truth.
4. I often think it would be an exciting intellectual challenge to steal something just to see if I could get away with it.
5. Buying merchandise on sale is dishonest because stores don't receive a fair value for their merchandise.
6. Looking for ways to beat the system is just human nature.
7. A person who has taken company property should not be trusted in another job handling company money.
8. If an employee is caught stealing $600 from a company but promptly pays it back, he should not be fired and nothing should happen to him.
9. Most companies are not very concerned about honesty and do not care much about theft so long as the amounts are small.
10. Sales representatives who pad their expense accounts should be fired even if they only add an extra $10 or $15 per month.
11. Most customers are honest and if they receive too much change they will return it.
12. Nearly every worker has stolen something from his or her company at one time or another.

A long-term 50-year-old employee admitted that for 22 years he had stolen about $500 each year without being caught. He said he started stealing because he was underpaid and an examination revealed that he was only getting about ¾ of what others were getting for similar work. (Use this to answer statements 13-16.)

13. This man should be arrested.
14. Criminal charges should be placed against him, and he should receive a criminal record.
15. This man should be sent to jail.
16. This man is not a thief; the company is the thief and owes him back pay for cheating him.
17. In some situations there are good reasons why it is all right to cheat a company.
18. If I saw one of my co-workers take $5 from the cash register, I would report it to management.
19. The average employee will tell his boss about a fellow employee who is stealing company money.
20. I always drive legally and never exceed the speed limit.
21. It would really bother me if I knew someone I worked with was stealing little things now and then, even if I never saw it happen myself.
22. The average policeman would accept money to overlook a traffic violation if he thought he could avoid getting caught.
23. Everyone has a price and can be bribed if the conditions are right.
24. A supervisor knew that three of her subordinates had been stealing small amounts of merchandise from the company for five years, but did not report it. The supervisor should be fired even though she did not steal herself.
25. If all the people who stole things at work were fired, ¾ of the country would be out of work.
26. Most companies are unfair and try to cheat people working for them.
27. When an employee takes pens, paper, and envelopes from the company for her own personal use, she is stealing.
28. I have frequently associated with fellow employees who admitted they were stealing merchandise from the company.

29. If the manager of a theater offered to let me in without paying, I'd insist on paying anyway.
30. Most sales clerks deserve to steal a little now and then because they are so badly underpaid.
31. I am an honest person and would never steal or cheat.
32. I am always courteous even to people who are disagreeable.
33. If one of my friends was really broke and needed help, I would feel good about letting this friend use my employee discount.
34. Stores are primarily responsible for most of the shoplifting that occurs in them because of their carelessness.
35. If my co-workers violated company rules by taking small items, I would try to ignore it; it is better to get along with your co-worker than to hassle them about stealing.
36. A person who sees a fellow employee steal from the company but does nothing about it is also guilty of a dishonest act.
37. If I were a store owner and caught one of my employees stealing $50 from me, I would prosecute her.
38. There is nothing wrong with buying stolen merchandise as long as I have nothing to do with stealing it.
39. There is nothing wrong with taking damaged goods from the company without permission if they are just going to be thrown away.
40. Making personal long-distance phone calls on your employer's phone without permission is stealing.
41. The average sales clerk steals at least $10 each month from the company.
42. If a person took money from a company for a good cause and paid it back with interest six months later, he should tell his boss and take a chance of getting fired.

1. When things go wrong, I lose my temper.
2. If a pay phone gave me back my quarter after I finished my call, I would mail the quarter to the phone company.
3. If someone asks me how they look and I think they look awful, I will lie a little to avoid hurting their feelings.
4. When I get angry with my employer, I want to damage company property.
5. Salesmen who do not drink alcoholic beverages should feel free to add $60 to $75 to their monthly expense statements to make their expenses the same as others.
6. I have been completely honest in reporting my income taxes.
7. Supervisors who hassle employees deserved to be slapped or hit.
8. If I committed a crime with a friend and I got caught, I would take the blame myself and not tell on my friend.
9. If I mailed three cereal box tops to get a free baseball card and the company sent me two cards by mistake, I would immediately return the extra card.
10. When I am provoked, I get into fist fights.
11. If the conditions were right, I could be tempted to steal something from the company.
12. If I came home and found a sales clerk failed to add a $1.00 item to my bill, I would immediately return and pay the $1.00 to the store.
13. When people refuse to go along, I find it necessary to threaten them with physical force.
14. When I was in school, I used to cheat on exams.
15. If I stole little things from my employer, such as paper, pens, and envelopes, I would really feel guilty.
16. I shout at people when they do things wrong.
17. Even though I may not do it, I think about clever ways to steal without getting caught.
18. When vending machines give me too much change, I send the money to the vending machine company.

19. I will hit or slap people who really deserve it.
20. If a nine-year-old child asked my opinion of a picture she painted and I thought it was really ugly and sloppy, I would tell a lie; it's better to lie a little than tell the truth in this situation.
21. When I find money on the sidewalk, I take it to the police, even when it's less than one dollar.
22. I find myself in situations in which I am forced to physically defend myself.
23. When I read stories or see movies of famous outlaws, I usually find myself cheering for the outlaws and hoping they get away with it.
24. When customers accidentally receive too much change, I think "good for them; they deserve to win now and then."

Scoring: The honesty score has a range of 0 to 99 and may be interpreted like a percentile score. Section One: Strongly Disagree = 1; Disagree = 2; Agree =3; and Strongly Agree = 4. Section Two: Always = 1; Frequently = 2; Occasionally = 3; Seldom = 4; and Never = 5.

Group Openness/Trust Scale (GOTS)

Bulach, C. 1993. A measure of openness and trust. *People and Education* 1:382-392.

Comments: The 60-item GOTS measures group openness and group trust. The first 30 items are based on the individual's impression of what he/she is expected to do. The second 30 items are based on the individual's actual behavior. Trust is assessed by the following behaviors: character, truthfulness, ability, confidentiality, and predictability. Openness is assessed by the following behaviors: telling and listening.

Sample: The sample consisted of 525 persons from 24 elementary schools in Kentucky.

Reliability: Split-half reliability (Spearman-Brown) was 0.80 for group openness and 0.82 for group trust. Test-retest reliability over a period of one week using a sample of 50 graduate students was 0.78 for group openness and 0.80 for group trust.

Validity: Although the author examined the content, construct, and discriminant validity of the GOTS, the author makes a recommendation to conduct additional research to establish the validity of the GOTS.

References:
Bulach, C.R., and B. Malone. 1994. The relationship of school climate to the implementation of school reform. *ERS Spectrum: Journal of School Research and Information* 12:3-9.

Gurtman, M.B. 1992. Trust, distrust, and interpersonal problems: A circumplex analysis. *Journal of Personality and Social Psychology* 62:989-1002.

Pareek, U. 1989. Motivational analysis of organizations—climate (MAO-C). In J.W. Pfeiffer (ed.), *The 1989 annual developing human resources*. San Diego, CA: University Associates.

Rotter, J.B. 1991. A new scale for the measurement of interpersonal trust. In J.P. Robinson, et al. (eds.), *Measures of personality and psychological attitudes*. New York, NY: Academic Press.

Group Openness/Trust Scale

I have gotten the impression that they expect me to
1.   ..tell them what they think of the way they do things.
2.   ..tell them what I think of their ideas.
3.   ..tell them what I think of their educational values and beliefs.
4.   ..share my feelings with them.
5.   ..ask them what they think of the way I do things.
6.   ..ask them what they think of my ideas.
7.   ..ask them what they think of my beliefs and values.
8.   ..ask them about their feelings.
9.   ..accept their comments and reactions.
10. ..openly disagree with them if I don't agree with what is being said or done.
11. ..share positive thoughts with them instead of keeping them to myself.
12. ..share constructive criticism with them instead of keeping it to myself.
13. ..believe what I hear them say.
14. ..question their intentions and/or motives.
15. ..conceal my true feelings about what they do or say.
16. .."play it cool"—keep my distance.
17. ..count on them for assistance if I have a problem.
18. ..have faith in their ability.
19. ..believe that they care about me.
20. ..deal with them directly when there is a problem.
21. ..tell them interesting information I know about someone.
22. ..believe they will respond favorably in a given situation when my welfare is at stake.
23. ..rely on them to keep a confidence.
24. ..believe that they are honest.
25. ..count on them to do what they say they are going to do.
26. ..tell the truth when it needs to be told.
27. ..respect the opinions of my colleagues.
28. ..admit my mistakes and/or problems when necessary.
29. ..support their ideas, decisions, and actions.
30. ..believe that they will behave consistently regardless of the person or situation, or my level of stress.

31. I tell them what I think of the way they do things.
32. I tell them what I think of their ideas.
33. I tell them what I think of their educational values and beliefs.
34. I share my feelings with them.
35. I ask them what they think of the way I do things.
36. I ask them what they think of my ideas.
37. I ask them what they think of my educational beliefs and values.
38. I ask them about their feelings.
39. I accept their comments and reactions.
40. I openly disagree if I don't agree with what is being said or done.
41. I share positive thoughts with them instead of keeping them to myself.
42. I share constructive criticism with them instead of keeping it to myself.
43. I believe what I hear them say.
44. I question their intentions and/or motives.

45.   I conceal my true feelings to what they do or say.
46.   I "play it cool" —keep my distance from them.
47.   I count on them for assistance if I have a problem.
48.   I have faith in their ability to help me.
49.   I believe that they care about me.
50.   I deal with them directly when there is a problem.
51.   I tell them interesting information I know about someone.
52.   I expect them to respond favorably in a given situation when my welfare is at stake.
53.   I rely on them to keep a confidence.
54.   I believe that they are honest.
55.   I count on them to do what they say they are going to do.
56.   I tell the truth when it needs to be told.
57.   I respect the opinions of my colleagues.
58.   I admit my mistakes and/or problems when necessary.
59.   I support the ideas, decisions, and actions of my colleagues.
60.   I behave consistently regardless of the person or situation, or my level of stress.

Scoring: A five-point Likert scale ranges from strongly disagree to strongly agree. The higher the score, the higher the trust or openness (positive) and the lower the score, the lower the trust or openness (negative).

Reprinted with permission of the author.

Interpersonal Relations

Machiavellianism Scales (Mach Scales)

Christie, R., and F.L. Geis. 1970. *Studies in Machiavellianism.* New York: Academic Press.

Comments: The Mach IV examines how an individual deals with other individuals; specifically it assesses how manipulable an individual is in interpersonal relationships. A "Kiddie Mach" is also available. This is one of the most frequently used instruments to measure interpersonal relationships.

Scale Construction: Originally, 71 items were written based on the works of Machiavelli. These items fell into three categories: the nature of interpersonal tactics (32); views of human nature (28); and abstract or generalized morality (11). Sixty items correlated at the 0.05 level with a total Mach score. The ten highest items worded in the Machiavellian direction and the ten highest items worded in the opposite direction were selected for the Mach IV scale.

Sample: The original sample consisted of 1,196 university students in Iowa, New York, and North Carolina.

Reliability: Split-half reliabilities averaged 0.79. Average item-test correlation was 0.38.

Validity: Concurrent validation studies have been conducted using correlations between the Mach IV and the Mach V scales. Information is included about predictive validation studies.

Factor Analysis: Factor analysis yielded three factors: seven items on duplicity (2, 3, 6, 7, 9, 10, and 15); seven items on negativism (1, 5, 8, 12, 13, 18, and 20); and four items on distrust of people (4, 11, 14, and 16).

References:
Richford, M.L., and J.C. Fortune. 1984. The secondary principal's job satisfaction in relation to two personality constructs. *Education* 105:17-20.

Shea, M.T., and J.R. Beatty. 1983. Measuring Machiavellianism with Mach V: A psychometric investigation. *Journal of Personality Assessment* 47:509-513.

Machiavellianism Scales (Mach Scales)

1.   Never tell anyone the real reason you did something unless it is useful to do so.
2.   The best way to handle people is to tell them what they want to hear.
3.   One should take action only when sure it is morally right.
4.   Most people are basically good and kind.
5.   It is safest to assume that all people have a vicious streak and it will come out when they are given a chance.
6.   Honesty is the best policy in all cases.
7.   There is no excuse for lying to someone else.
8.   Generally speaking, men won't work hard unless they're forced to do so.
9.   All in all, it is better to be humble and honest than to be important and dishonest.
10. When you ask someone to do something for you, it is best to give the real reasons for wanting it rather than giving reasons which carry more weight.
11. Most people who get ahead in the world lead clean, moral lives.
12. Anyone who completely trusts anyone else is asking for trouble.
13. The biggest difference between most criminals and other people is that the criminals are stupid enough to get caught.
14. Most men are brave.
15. It is wise to flatter important people.
16. It is possible to be good in all respects.
17. Barnum was wrong when he said that there's a sucker born every minute.
18. It is hard to get ahead without cutting corners here and there.
19. People suffering from incurable diseases should have the choice of being put painlessly to death.
20. Most men forget more easily the death of their father than the loss of their property.

Scoring: Agree Strongly = 3; Agree Somewhat = 2; Agree Slightly = 1; Disagree Slightly = -1; Disagree Somewhat = -2; and Disagree Strongly = -3. Scoring is reversed for the following items: 3, 4, 6, 7, 9, 10, 11, 14, 16, and 17. For scoring purposes, Agree Strongly receives a score of 7; No Response receives a score of 4; and Disagree Strongly receives a score of 1. For reversed items, the scoring is reversed. Since a constant of 20 is added to all scores, scores range from a low of 40 to a high of 160 with 100 being a neutral score.

Reprinted with permission of Delores Kreisman, executor of the Estate of Richard Christie and Academic Press.

Quality of Relationships Inventory (QRI)

Pierce, G.R., et al. 1991. General and relationship-based perceptions of social support: Are two constructs better than one? *Journal of Personality and Social Psychology* 61:1028-1039.

Comments: The 29-item QRI measures three aspects of specific relationships: social support, conflict, and depth. Since the inventory measures relationships that are considered important, it might be useful to use the inventory within the educational system to discover positive as well as negative perceptions of the teacher-administrator relationship.

Sample: The original sample consisted of 116 undergraduate women and 94 undergraduate males. Participants were enrolled in an introductory course in psychology and earned extra credit for their taking part in this study.

Reliability: Internal reliability coefficients for friends were 0.85 (support), 0.91 (conflict), and 0.84 (depth). Alpha coefficients are also reported for mother and father. Based on the results of the most recent study by the authors, the three subscales of the QRI were stable over a period of one year.

Validity: Construct validity was established through factor analysis. Evidence for convergent and discriminant validity were included not only in the original article, but also in the follow-up study conducted by the authors.

Factor Analysis: An oblique rotation yielded three factors: seven items on social support; 12 items on conflict; and six items on depth. Four items failed to load significantly on one factor with minimum overlap on the other two factors.

Definition of Factors: *Social support* examines the ability to rely on others for help in various situations. *Depth* examines the usefulness of a relationship. *Conflict* examines anger or ambivalence toward the other participant in the relationship.

Data Analysis: Means, standard deviations, skewness, and range for each of the three factors (subscales) are presented.

References:
Cohen, S.R., et al. 1985. Measuring the functional components of social support. In I.G. Sarason and B.R. Sarason (eds.), *Social support: Theory, research and applications* (pp. 73-94). Dordrecht, The Netherlands: Martinus Nijhoff.

Cutrona, C.E., and D. Russell. 1987. The provisions of social relationships and adaptation to stress. In W.H. Jones and D. Perlman (eds.), *Advances in personal relationships* (Vol. 1, pp. 37-67). Greenwich, CT: JAI Press.

Pierce, G.R., I.G. Sarason, B.R. Sarason, J.A. Solky-Butzel, and L.C. Nagle. 1997. Assessing the quality of personal relationships. *Journal of Social and Personal Relationships* 14:339-356.

Sarason, I.G., H.M. Levine, R.B. Basham, and B.R. Sarason. 1983. Assessing social support: The Social Support Questionnaire. *Journal of Personality and Social Psychology* 44:127-139.

Quality of Relationships Inventory

1. To what extent can you count on this person to listen to you when you are very angry at someone else?
2. To what extent can you turn to this person for advice about problems?
3. To what extent can you really count on this person to distract you from your worries when you feel under stress?
4. To what extent could you count on this person for help with a problem?
5. If you wanted to go out and do something this evening, how confident are you that this person would be willing to do something with you.
6. To what extent could you count on this person to help you if a family member very close to you died?
7. To what extent can you count on this person to give you honest feedback, even if you might not want to hear it?
8. How angry does this person make you feel?
9. How upset does this person sometimes make you feel?
10. How often does this person make you feel angry?
11. How much do you argue with this person?
12. How often do you have to work hard to avoid conflict with this person?
13. How much would you like this person to change?
14. How much do you have to "give in" in this relationship?
15. How much does this person make you feel guilty?
16. How much does this person want you to change?
17. How often does this person try to control or influence your life?
18. How critical of you is this person?
19. How much more do you give than you get from this relationship?
20. To what extent can you trust this person not to hurt your feelings?
21. How often do problems that occur in this relationship get resolved?
22. How significant is this relationship in your life?
23. How much do you depend on this person?
24. How close will your relationship be with this person in 10 years?
25. How positive a role does this person play in your life?
26. How responsible do you feel for this person's well-being?
27. How much would you miss this person if the two of you could not see or talk with each other for a month?
28. If you could have only a small number of social relationships, how much would you want your contact with this person to be among them?
29. How considerate is this person to your needs?

Scoring: Not at all = 1; A little = 2; Quite a bit = 3; and Very much = 4.

Reprinted with permission of the author.

Fundamental Interpersonal Relationship Orientation (FIRO-B)

Schutz, W. 1978. *FIRO Awareness Scales Manual*. Palo Alto, CA: Consulting Psychologists Press.

Comments: FIRO-B refers to a theory of interpersonal relations that is helpful in predicting interaction between two individuals. The 54-item FIRO-B examines the behavior that a person exhibits to others and the behavior that a person desires from others in three categories: inclusion, control, and affection. Each of the six Guttman scales contains nine items. The FIRO-B has been replaced with Element B, which addresses concerns in the areas of response categories, item wording, and interpretation in scoring. This is one of the most frequently cited instruments to measure interpersonal relationships.

Sample: The original sample consisted of over 1,000 participants. The majority were university students and there was a small sample of air force personnel.

Reliability: The reproducibility coefficients for the six scales had a mean of 0.94. Reproducibility coefficients ranged from 0.93 to 0.94. Test-retest reliability coefficients (Harvard sample) over a one-month interval ranged from 0.71 to 0.82, with a mean of 0.76 for the six scales.

Validity: Information about content and concurrent validity is included in part I of the manual. In addition, FIRO-B scores are provided for 12 occupational groups. Part II contains a review of the research studies and various applications of the FIRO Awareness Scales from 1958-1977.

Definition of Scales: *Inclusion* is defined as the need to form and continue a satisfying relationship with people in terms of interaction and association. Positive inclusion refers to words such as mingle, communicate, companion, and togetherness. Negative inclusion refers to words such as outcast, lonely, withdrawn, and ignore. *Control* is defined as the need to form and continue a satisfying relationship with people in terms of control and power. Positive control refers to such words as power, authority, superior, and leader. Negative control refers to words such as resistance, anarchy, submissive, and follower. *Affection* is defined as the need to form and continue a satisfying relationship with people in terms of love and affection. Positive affection refers to words such as like, personal, intimate, and friend. Negative affection refers to words such as dislike, rejecting, hate, and cool.

References:
Fuqua, A.B. 1983. Professional attractiveness, inside sponsorship, and perceived paternalism as predictors of upward mobility of public school superintendents. Ed.D. dissertation, Virginia Polytechnic Institute and State University.

Lachiondo, D.K. 1985. The effects of selected personal and role variables of assistant principal-disciplinarians on the reported use of due process in student discipline. Ph.D. dissertation, University of Idaho.

Mulinaro, M.E. 1990. Relationship between the interpersonal relationship variables of inclusion, control and openness and self-perceived preferred leadership styles of deans and department chairpersons in the public and private colleges of West Virginia. Ed.D. dissertation, West Virginia University.

Phelps, H.A. 1989. A comparative investigation of the self-perceptions of the behavioral characteristics of principals of selected high schools. Ed.D. dissertation, Temple University.

Fundamental Interpersonal Relationship Orientation (FIRO-B)

1.   I try to be with people.
2.   I let other people decide what to do.
3.   I join social groups.
4.   I try to have close relationships with people.
5.   I tend to join social organizations when I have an opportunity.
6.   I let other people strongly influence my actions.
7.   I try to be included in informal social activities.
8.   I try to have close, personal relationships with people.
9.   I try to include other people in my plans.
10. I let other people control my actions.
11. I try to have people around me.
12. I try to get close and personal with people.
13. When people are doing things together I tend to join them.
14. I am easily led by people.
15. I try to avoid being alone.
16. I try to participate in group activities.
17. I try to be friendly to people.
18. I let other people decide what to do.
19. My personal relations with people are cool and distant.
20. I let other people take charge of things.
21. I try to have close relationships with people.
22. I let other people strongly influence my actions.
23. I try to get close and personal with people.
24. I let other people control my actions.
25. I act cool and distant with people.
26. I am easily led by people.
27. I try to have close, personal relationships with people.
28. I like people to invite me to things.
29. I like people to act close and personal with me.
30. I try to influence strongly other people's actions.
31. I like people to invite me to join in their activities.
32. I like people to act close toward me.
33. I try to take charge of things when I am with people.
34. I like people to include me in their activities.
35. I like people to act cool and distant toward me.
36. I try to have other people do things the way I want them done.
37. I like people to ask me to participate in their discussions.
38. I like people to act friendly toward me.
39. I like people to invite me to participate in their activities.
40. I like people to act distant toward me.
41. I try to be the dominant person when I am with people.
42. I like people to invite me to things.
43. I like people to act close toward me.
44. I try to have other people do things I want done.
45. I like people to invite me to join their activities.
46. I like people to act cool and distant toward me.
47. I try to influence strongly other people's actions.

48. I like people to include me in their activities.
49. I like people to act close and personal with me.
50. I try to take charge of things when I'm with people.
51. I like people to invite me to participate in their activities.
52. I like people to act distant toward me.
53. I try to have other people do things the way I want them done.
54. I take charge of things when I'm with people.

Scoring: Scoring for items 1-16 and 41-54 is: 1 = Never; 2 = Rarely; 3 = Occasionally; 4 = Sometimes; 5 = Often; and 6 = Usually. Scoring for items 17-40 is: 1 = Nobody; 2 = One or Two People; 3 = A Few People; 4 = Some People; 5 = Many People; and 6 = Most People. Scoring can also be relative or normative. More detailed information about scoring is covered in the manual. In addition, scoring templates are available.

Reprinted with permission of Will Schutz Associates.

Element B: Behavior

Schutz, W. 1992. Beyond FIRO-B. Three new theory-derived measures. Element B: Behavior, Element F: Feelings, Element S: Self. *Psychological Reports* 70:915-937.

Comments: Element B is the revised form of the FIRO-B. According to the author, it is a much stronger instrument both theoretically and psychometrically. Element B: Behavior measures three areas of interpersonal behavior: inclusion, control, and openness (openness replaces affection).

Sample: Fifty students in an adult education class participated in the development of Element B. In addition, 43 people from NASA, 23 from army intelligence, and 84 university students completed the instrument in order to obtain stable reproducibility coefficients.

Reliability: The reproducibility coefficients for the six scales had a mean of 0.92. Reproducibility coefficients ranged from 0.89 to 0.93. Since the test-retest reliability coefficient (over a three-week interval) for the FIRO-B had a mean of 0.76 for the six scales, this figure was used as an approximation of the stability of the scales of Element B.

Definition of Scales: *Inclusion* refers to reaching the correct amount of contact with individuals (do things with, share). *Control* refers to reaching the correct amount of control over individuals (take charge, influence). *Openness* refers to reaching the correct amount of openness (disclose, tell true feelings).

Data Analysis: Reproducibility and means for scales of Element B as well as mean scores based on age and sex are provided. Pearson intercorrelations of scales on Element B and FIRO-B are included.

Reference:
Schutz, W. 1987. *Guide to Element B.* Mill Valley, CA: Will Schutz Associates.

Element B

1. I seek out people to be with.
2. People decide what to do when we are together.
3. I am totally honest with my close friends.
4. People invite me to do things.
5. I am the dominant person when I am with people.
6. My close friends tell me their real feelings.
7. I join social groups.
8. People strongly influence my actions.
9. I confide in my close friends.
10. People invite me to join their activities.
11. I get other people to do things I want done.
12. My close friends tell me about private matters.
13. I join social organizations.
14. People control my actions.
15. I am more comfortable when people do not get too close.
16. People include me in their activities.
17. I strongly influence other people's actions.
18. My close friends do not tell me all about themselves.
19. I am included in informal social activities.
20. I am easily led by people.
21. People should keep their private feelings to themselves.
22. People invite me to participate in their activities.
23. I take charge when I am with people socially.
24. My close friends let me know their real feelings.
25. I include people in my plans.
26. People decide things for me.
27. There are some things I do not tell anyone.
28. People include me in their social affairs.
29. I get people to do things the way I want them done.
30. My closest friends keep secrets from me.
31. I have people around me.
32. People strongly influence my ideas.
33. There are some things I would not tell anyone.
34. People ask me to participate in their discussions.
35. I take charge when I am with people.
36. My friends confide in me.
37. When people are doing things together I join them.
38. I am strongly influenced by what people say.
39. I have at least one friend to whom I can tell anything.
40. People invite me to parties.
41. I strongly influence other people's ideas.
42. My close friends keep their feelings a secret from me.
43. I look for people to be with.
44. Other people take charge when we work together.
45. There is a part of myself I keep private.
46. People invite me to join them when we have free time.
47. I take charge when I work with people.
48. At least two of my friends tell me their true feelings.

49. I participate in group activities.
50. People often cause me to change my mind.
51. I have close relationships with few people.
52. People invite me to do things with them.
53. I see to it that people do things the way I want them to.
54. My friends tell me about their private lives.

Scoring: Respondents describe Expressed and Received behavior as well as Perceived (What I See) and Wanted (What I Want) behavior. What I See ranges from disagree to agree, while What I Want ranges from want to don't want. Each scale receives a score from 0 to 9. The higher the score, the greater the agreement. Dissatisfaction is the difference between the scores on What I Want and What I See. Information is provided to convert FIRO-B scores into Element B scores.

Reprinted with permission of Will Schutz Associates.

Questionnaire on Teacher Interaction

Wubbels, T., and J. Levy. 1989. A comparison of Dutch and American interpersonal teacher behavior. Paper presented at the American Educational Research Association. ERIC ED 307 311.

Comments: The 64-item QTI is based on Leary's model (1957) of interpersonal behavior that identifies two dimensions (dominance-submission and cooperation-opposition) that correspond to the following eight scales/types of interpersonal teacher behavior patterns: leadership, helpful/friendly, understanding, student responsibility/freedom, uncertain, dissatisfied, admonishing, and strict. The QTI was translated from Dutch to English in 1985. The original Dutch version has 77 items. The first version of the American OTI had 100 items, but after item analysis, 64 items were retained (59 items are translations from the Dutch OTI). According to the authors, the QTI is useful for pre- and in-service teacher education.

Sample: Thirty-one American teachers voluntarily used the OTI with two or more of their secondary school classes. A total of 1,606 students from 66 classes participated in this study. In addition, the 31 teachers completed the OTI.

Reliability: The alpha coefficients for the 66 classes were: 0.94 (leadership and understanding); 0.95 (helpful/friendly and strict); 0.86 (student responsibility/freedom); 0.96 (uncertain); 0.90 (dissatisfied); and 0.92 (admonishing). The alpha coefficients are also reported for the 1,606 students as well as for the teachers. In addition, the results of a comparable Dutch study are included.

Validity: The validity of the OTI was established by its ability to distinguish between classes.

Factor Analysis: A varimax orthogonal rotation confirmed the two factors: the cooperation-opposition dimension and the dominance-submission dimension. These results are similar to those obtained with the original Dutch version of the OTI. There are seven items on leadership (3, 31, 36, 40, 45, 52, and 62); eight items on helpful/friendly (5, 15, 29, 35, 37, 47, 50, and 60); eight items on understanding (4, 6, 11, 13, 17, 18, 32, and 56); eight items on student responsibility/freedom (8, 21, 25, 27, 33, 48, 49, and 64); seven items on uncertain (23, 34, 39, 42, 44, 46, and 55); nine items on dissatisfied (7, 10, 12, 19, 26, 28, 30, 54, and 58); eight items on admonishing (16, 24, 38, 41, 43, 51, 59, and 63); and nine items on strict (1, 2, 9, 14, 20, 22, 53, 57, and 61).

Data Analysis: Means are provided for each of the eight scales with the American and Dutch samples. The results of an analysis of variance with class as a variable are included.

References:
Leary, T. 1957. *An interpersonal diagnosis of personality.* New York, NY: Ronald Press Company.

Moos. R.H. 1974. The Social Climate Scales: An overview. Palo Alto, CA: Consulting Psychologists Press.

Wubbels, T., and J. Levy. 1991. A comparison of interpersonal behavior of Dutch and American teachers. *International Journal of Intercultural Relations* 15:1-18.

Questionnaire on Teacher Interaction

1. He/she is strict.
2. We have to be silent in his/her class.
3. He/she talks enthusiastically about his/her subject.
4. He/she trusts us.
5. He/she is concerned when we have not understood him/her.
6. If we don't agree with him/her we can talk about it.
7. He/she threatens to punish us.
8. We can decide some things in his/her class.
9. He/she is demanding.
10. He/she thinks we cheat.
11. He/she is willing to explain things again.
12. He/she thinks we don't know everything.
13. If we want something he/she is willing to cooperate.
14. His/her tests are hard.
15. He/she helps us with our work.
16. He/she gets angry unexpectedly.
17. If we have something to say he/she will listen.
18. He/she sympathizes with us.
19. He/she tries to make us look foolish.
20. His/her standards are very high.
21. We can influence him/her.
22. We need his/her permission before we speak.
23. He/she seems uncertain.
24. He/she looks down on us.
25. We have the opportunity to choose assignments which are most interesting to us.
26. He/she is unhappy.
27. He/she lets us fool around in class.
28. He/she puts us down.
29. He/she takes a personal interest in us.
30. He/she thinks we can't do things well.
31. He/she explains things clearly.
32. He/she realizes when we don't understand.
33. He/she lets us get away with a lot in class.
34. He/she is hesitant.
35. He/she is friendly.
36. We learn a lot from him/her.
37. He/she is someone we can depend on.
38. He/she gets angry quickly.
39. He/she acts as if he/she does not know what to do.
40. He/she holds our attention.
41. He's/she's too quick to correct us when we break a rule.
42. He/she lets us boss him/her around.
43. He/she is impatient.
44. He's/she's not sure what to do when we fool around.
45. He/she knows everything that goes on in the classroom.
46. It's easy to make a fool out of him/her.
47. He/she has a sense of humor.

48. He/she allows us a lot of choice in what we study.
49. He/she gives us a lot of free time in class.
50. He/she can take a joke.
51. He/she has a bad temper.
52. He/she is a good leader.
53. If we don't finish our homework we're scared to go to his/her class.
54. He/she seems dissatisfied.
55. He/she is timid.
56. He/she is patient.
57. He/she is severe when marking papers.
58. He/she is suspicious.
59. It is easy to pick a fight with him/her.
60. His/her class is pleasant.
61. We are afraid of him/her.
62. He/she acts confidently.
63. He/she is sarcastic.
64. He/she is lenient.

Scoring: 0 = A (never); 1 = B; 2 = C; 3 = D; and 4 = E (always). Item scores are summed to create a profile.

Reprinted with permission of the author.

Job Commitment

Work Commitment Index

Blau, G.J., et al. 1993. On developing a general index of work commitment. *Journal of Vocational Behavior.* 42:298-314.

Comments: The purpose of this research was to design a general work commitment index with distinct work commitment factors similar to the procedure used with job satisfaction to develop the Job Descriptive Index. This index demonstrates that employees view their job, organization, occupation, and work in general differently.

Scale Construction: Work commitment was measured across four facets: career (occupation), job, value, and organization. The 31 items measuring career came from four scales: Blau's (1988) career commitment scale; Gould's (1979) career involvement scale; Greenhaus's (1971) general attitude toward work subscale; and Sekaran's (1982) career salience measure. The ten items measuring job facet came from Kanungo's (1982) job involvement scale. The ten items measuring value facet came from Kanungo's measure of work involvement and Blood's (1969) Protestant work ethic scale. The eight items measuring organization facet came from Meyer and Allen's (1984) affective commitment scale.

Sample: The participants in the first study consisted of 407 part-time MBA students from three universities in the Philadelphia area and 383 part-time MBA students (seven weeks later). There were 328 students who completed the survey both times. The participants in the second study consisted of 339 full-time registered nurses from three hospitals in a large eastern city.

Reliability: The alpha coefficients (Cronbach) were 0.91 (occupational commitment), 0.81 (value of work), 0.82 (organizational commitment), and 0.83 (job involvement). Test-retest reliabilities were 0.90 (occupational commitment), 0.91 (job involvement), 0.92 (value of work), and 0.94 (organizational commitment).

Validity: Confirmatory factor analysis was used to test the discriminant validity of the four scales.

Factor Analysis: Although principal components analyses yielded five factors, only four factors were used to develop four separate scales. There were minor differences between the varimax rotation and the oblique rotation. Therefore, the results of the oblique rotation were reported. The four factors are: 11 items on occupational commitment (1-11); seven items on the value of work (12-18); six items on organizational commitment (19-25); and seven items on job involvement (26-31).

Data Analysis: Means, standard deviations, coefficient alpha, test-retest reliabilities, and correlations for the four factors are reported.

References:
Blau, G. 1988. Further exploring the meaning and measurement of career commitment. *Journal of Vocational Behavior* 32:284-297.

136

Blood, M. 1969. Work values and job satisfaction. *Journal of Applied Psychology* 53:456-459.

Gould, S. 1979. Characteristics of planners in upwardly mobile occupations. *Academy of Management Journal* 22:539-550.

Greenhaus, J. 1971. An investigation of the role of career salience in vocational behavior. *Journal of Vocational Behavior* 1:209-226.

Kanungo, R.N. 1982. Measurement of job and work involvement. *Journal of Applied Psychology* 3:341-349.

Meyer, J., and N. Allen. 1984. Testing the "side-bet theory" of organizational commitment: Some methodological considerations. *Journal of Applied Psychology* 69:372-378.

Sekaran, U. 1982. An investigation of the career salience in dual career families. *Journal of Vocational Behavior* 20:111-119.

Work Commitment Index

The following are not completed items. The respondent completes the statement with the personal pronoun or article as needed.

1. If could, would go into a different occupation
2. Can see self in occupation for many years
3. Occupation choice is a good decision
4. If could, would not choose occupation
5. No money need, still continue in occupation
6. Sometimes dissatisfied with occupation
7. Like occupation too well to give up
8. Education/training not for occupation
9. Have ideal occupation for life work
10. Wish chosen different occupation
11. Disappointed that entered occupation
12. Most important things involve job
13. Job only small part of who I am
14. Live, eat, and breathe my job
15. Most interests centered around my job
16. Most personal life goals are job-oriented
17. Job is very central to my existence
18. Like to be absorbed in job most of time
19. Hard work makes self a better person
20. Wasting time as bad as wasting money
21. Person's worth is how well does job
22. Better to have more responsible job
23. People should get involved in work
24. Work should be central to life
25. Life goals should be work-oriented
26. Don't feel like belong to organization
27. Not emotionally attached to organization
28. Organization has personal meaning for me
29. Do not feel like part of organization
30. Glad to spend rest of days with organization
31. Organization's problems are mine too

Scoring: Strongly Disagree = 1; Moderately Disagree = 2; Slightly Disagree = 3; Slightly Agree = 4; Moderately Agree = 5; and Strongly Agree = 6.

Reprinted with permission of the author.

Organizational Commitment Questionnaire

Mowday, R.T., et al. 1979. The measurement of organizational commitment. *Journal of Vocational Behavior* 14:224-247.

Comments: The 15-item OCQ measures organizational commitment, which is defined as "the relative strength of an individual's identification with and involvement in a particular organization." Commitment-related behaviors fall into three categories: belief and acceptance of organizational goals and values; willingness to exert effort for the organization; and a desire to continue membership in the organization. A nine-item OCQ is also available.

Sample: The original sample of the OCQ consisted of 2,563 workers from the following nine work organizations: public employees (569), classified university employees (243), hospital employees (382), bank employees (411), telephone company employees (605), scientists and engineers (119), auto company managers (115), psychiatric technicians (60), and retail management trainees (212).

Reliability: The alpha coefficients ranged from 0.82 to 0.93 for psychiatric technicians; 0.84 for scientists and engineers; 0.88 for hospital employees (short form) and bank employees; and 0.90 for public employees, classified university employees (short form), telephone company employees, and auto company managers. The median alpha is 0.90. Test-retest reliabilities for psychiatric technicians over a 2-month interval was 0.53; over a 3-month interval was 0.63; and over a 4-month interval was 0.75.

Validity: Factor analyses conducted on six samples yielded a single factor. Convergent validity was established by correlating the Sources of Organizational Attachment Questionnaire with the OCQ. Convergent validities ranged from 0.63 to 0.74. Discriminate validity was established by comparing the OCQ to one measure of job involvement, one measure of career satisfaction, and one measure of job satisfaction. Predictive validity was established by examining the relationship between performance and organizational commitment. Evidence is provided to support all three validity claims.

Factor Analysis: Factor analyses (varimax rotation) were conducted on the six samples. Each analysis yielded a one-factor solution.

Data Analysis: Means, standard deviations, item analyses correlations, and norms are reported.

References:
Dean, R., and J.P. Wanous. 1983. Reality shock and commitment: A study of new employees' expectations. Paper presented at American Psychological Association. ERIC ED 237 852.

Dornstein, M., and Y. Matalon. 1989. A comprehensive analysis of the predictors of organizational commitment: A study of voluntary army personnel in Israel. *Journal of Vocational Behavior* 34:192-203.

Porter, L.W., et al. 1976. Organizational commitment and managerial turnover: A longitudinal study. *Organizational Behavior and Human Performance* 15:87-98.

Organizational Commitment Questionnaire

1. I am willing to put a great deal of effort beyond that normally expected in order to help this organization be successful.
2. I talk up this organization to my friends as a great organization to work for.
3. I feel very little loyalty to this organization.
4. I would accept almost any type of job assignment in order to keep working for this organization.
5. I find that my values and the organization's values are very similar.
6. I am proud to tell others that I am part of this organization.
7. I could just as well be working for a different organization as long as the type of work was similar.
8. This organization really inspires the very best in me in the way of job performance.
9. It would take very little change in my present circumstances to cause me to leave this organization.
10. I am extremely glad that I chose this organization to work for over others I was considering at the time I joined.
11. There's not too much to be gained by sticking with this organization indefinitely.
12. Often, I find it difficult to agree with this organization's policies on important matters relating to its employees.
13. I really care about the fate of this organization.
14. For me this is the best of all possible organizations for which to work.
15. Deciding to work for this organization was a definite mistake on my part.

Scoring: Strongly Disagree = 1; Moderately Disagree = 2; Slightly Disagree = 3; Neither Disagree nor Agree = 4; Slightly Agree = 5; Moderately Agree = 6; and Strongly Agree = 7. The scoring is reversed for items 3, 7, 9, 11, 12, and 15. Responses are added and divided by 15 to reach an overall score.

Reprinted with permission of Lyman W. Porter.

Job Involvement

Job Involvement Scale

Lodahl, T., and M. Kejner. 1965. The definition and measurement of job involvement. *Journal of Applied Psychology* 49:24-33.

Comments: The 20-item JIS measures job involvement, which is defined as "the degree to which a person's work performance affects his self esteem." A six-item version consists of the following items: 3, 6, 8, 11, 15, and 18. The JIS is the most frequently cited instrument to measure job involvement. In addition, many instruments were based on their work.

Sample: The original samples consisted of 137 nursing personnel (head nurses, staff nurses, registered nurses, practical nurses, nurse aides, and orderlies), 70 engineers, and 46 graduate students studying business administration.

Reliability: Corrected split-half correlation coefficients were 0.72 for nurses, 0.80 for engineers, and 0.89 for graduate students.

Validity: Information about discriminant validity is provided. Four sets of data measured the relationship between job involvement and other variables.

Factor Analysis: Multiple factor analytic procedures were performed and a three-factor solution was accepted.

Data Analysis: Means and standard deviations are provided.

References:
Chadha, N.K., and R. Kaur. 1987. Correlational study of demographic variables with job involvement and job satisfaction in a public sector organization. *Perspectives in Psychological Researches* 10:11-18.

Chusmir, L.H. 1986. Gender differences in variables affecting job commitment among working men and women. *Journal of Social Psychology* 126:87-94.

Chusmir, L.H., and C.S. Koberg. 1986. Creativity differences among managers. *Journal of Vocational Behavior* 29:240-253.

Saal, F.E. 1978. Job involvement: A multivariate approach. *Journal of Applied Psychology* 63:53-61.

Job Involvement Scale

1. I'll stay overtime to finish a job, even if I'm not paid for it.
2. You can measure a person pretty well by how good a job he does.
3. The major satisfaction in my life comes from my job.
4. For me, mornings at work really fly by.
5. I usually show up for work a little early, to get things ready.
6. The most important things that happen to me involve my work.
7. Sometimes I lie awake at night thinking ahead to the next day's work.
8. I'm really a perfectionist about my work.
9. I feel depressed when I fail at something connected with my job.
10. I have other activities more important than my work.
11. I live, eat, and breathe my job.
12. I would probably keep working even if I didn't need the money.
13. Quite often I feel like staying home from work instead of coming in.
14. To me, my work is only a small part of who I am.
15. I am very much involved personally in my work.
16. I avoid taking on extra duties and responsibilities in my work.
17. I used to be more ambitious about my work than I am now.
18. Most things in life are more important than work.
19. I used to care more about my work, but now other things are more important to me.
20. Sometimes I'd like to kick myself for the mistakes I make in my work.

Scoring: Strongly Agree = 1; Agree = 2; Disagree = 3; and Strongly Disagree = 4. A high score represents low involvement.

Reprinted with permission of the author.

Job Satisfaction

Job Satisfaction Index

Brayfield, A.H., and H.F. Rothe. 1951. An index of job satisfaction. *Journal of Applied Psychology* 35:307-311.

Comments: The 18-item JSI provides an overall index of job satisfaction rather than measuring specific aspects.

Sample: Although different groups were used to develop the index, the final version of the index was given to two samples. The first sample consisted of 231 female office workers. The second sample consisted of 91 (49 men and 42 women) adult night school students attending classes in personnel psychology at the University of Minnesota.

Reliability: The scale was administered to 231 female office workers. The range of job satisfaction scores was 35-87. The mean score was 63.8 with a standard deviation of 9.4. The odd-even product moment reliability was 0.77, which was corrected by the Spearman-Brown formula to 0.87.

Validity: According to the authors, the individual items are evidence of face validity. In addition, 77 men who were members of an Army Specialized Training Program in personnel psychology at the University of Minnesota, were responsible for developing approximately 1,000 items. These items were edited and the remaining 246 items were sorted using the criteria established by Thurstone. The 77 adult judges agreed that the items expressed a feeling of satisfaction or dissatisfaction with a job and should therefore be included. An outside criterion was also used to establish validity. The scale was given to 91 adult night school students in classes in personnel psychology at the University of Minnesota. The 91 participants were then separated into two groups, personnel and non-personnel, based upon their employment. A comparison was made between the means of the two groups. Significant differences (0.05 level) were found between the two groups. Therefore, the evidence for the scale's validity is based upon the nature of the items, the method used to develop the scale, and its ability to differentiate between groups.

References:
Camp, W.G. 1987. Student misbehavior and job satisfaction of vocational agriculture teachers: A path analysis. ERIC ED 279 791.

Jones, J.J. 1983. The relationship between selected predictor variables and perceived job satisfaction of Oklahoma public school superintendents. Ed.D. Dissertation, Oklahoma State University

Tharrington, D.E. 1992. Perceived principal leadership behavior and reported teacher job satisfaction. Ed.D. dissertation, University of North Carolina, Chapel Hill.

Job Satisfaction Index

1. My job is like a hobby to me.
2. My job is usually interesting enough to keep me from getting bored.
3. It seems that my friends are more interested in their jobs.
4. I consider my job rather unpleasant.
5. I enjoy my work more than my leisure time.
6. I am often bored with my job.
7. I feel fairly well satisfied with my present job.
8. Most of the time I have to force myself to go to work.
9. I am satisfied with my job for the time being.
10. I feel that my job is no more interesting than others I could get.
11. I definitely dislike my work.
12. I feel that I am happier in my work than most other people.
13. Most days I am enthusiastic about my work.
14. Each day of work seems like it will never end.
15. I like my job better than the average worker does.
16. My job is pretty uninteresting.
17. I find real enjoyment in my work.
18. I am disappointed that I ever took this job.

Scoring: Strongly Agree = 1; Agree = 2; Undecided = 3; Disagree = 4; Strongly Disagree = 5. The scoring for items 1, 2, 5, 7, 9, 12, 13, 15, and 17 is reversed. The scores range from a low of 18 to a high of 90. The lower the score, the lower the level of job satisfaction.

Reprinted with permission of the author.

Academic Setting Evaluation Questionnaire

Fernandez, J., and M.A. Mateo. 1993. The development and factorial validation of the Academic Setting Evaluation Questionnaire. *Educational and Psychological Measurement* 53:425-435.

Comments: The 33-item ASEQ assesses faculty satisfaction with working conditions, social climate, and relationships with students.

Scale Construction: The original ASEQ contained 69 items and was validated with 800 university professors. Factor analytic procedures yielded six factors (dissatisfaction with the institution, social climate, student/faculty relationship, performance of center services, teaching autonomy, and faculty selection and evaluation) and a theta coefficient of 0.98 was obtained. The second version contained 59 items. The revised version, which is described below, contains 33 items based on the first three factors.

Sample: A random sample of 748 university professors from the Complutense University participated in this study. For purposes of data analysis, the sample was separated into two equal groups (cross-validation).

Reliability: The alpha coefficients were 0.89 (satisfaction with working conditions and social climate) and 0.87 (relationship with students). The total reliability was 0.90.

Factor Analysis: Principal component factor analysis with orthogonal and oblique rotations were conducted. A three-factor solution was accepted, which accounted for about 78% of the variance. There are 19 items on satisfaction with working conditions (1-4, 6, 9-20, 22, and 23); five items on social climate (5, 7, 8, 26, and 33); and seven items on relationship with students (21, 24, 25, 27-29, and 32.). Two items (30 and 31) failed to load on one of the three factors.

Data Analysis: Homogeneity and validity indices are provided. In addition, the results of a cross validation study are described.

References:
Fernandez, J., et al. 1995. Evaluation of the academic setting in Spain. *European Journal of Psychological Assessment* 11:133-137.

Fraser, B.J., and D.F. Treagust. 1986. Validity and use of an instrument for assessing classroom psychosocial environment in higher education. *Higher Education* 15:37-57.

Kremer, J.F. 1990. Construct validity of multiple measures in teaching, research, and service and reliability of peer ratings. *Journal of Educational Psychology* 82:213-218.

Mateo, M.A., and J. Fernandez. 1995. Evaluation of the setting in which university faculty carry out their teaching and research functions: The ASEQ. *Educational and Psychological Measurement* 55:329-334.

Academic Setting Evaluation Questionnaire

1.   The material conditions in which I carry out my work are satisfactory.
2.   Economically it is made possible for me to carry out my research.
3.   I am given institutional help to publish my studies.
4.   I consider my university teaching activities to be fairly paid.
5.   I feel supported by my colleagues in the activities I carry out as a faculty member.
6.   The academic context encourages my professional work.
7.   There is satisfactory academic communication among the members of my department.
8.   My human relationship with my departmental colleagues favours my academic/professional activity.
9.   Teacher selection systems are suitable.
10. Teaching activity control systems are appropriate.
11. There are clear criteria for evaluating research activities.
12. There is agreement between my expectations of what a faculty member should be and what s/he in fact is.
13. Society appreciates the work done by university faculty.
14. University institutions stimulate me to improve as a university faculty member.
15. Teacher promotion systems are appropriate.
16. I have been prepared institutionally to carry out my duties as a researcher suitably.
17. The prospects for my work as a faculty member are favorable.
18. Future prospects as a university researcher are favorable.
19. I find adequate institutional aid to solve my professional problems as a faculty member.
20. I have sufficient time to carry out my research duties.
21. Students show interest in the subject that I teach.
22. University institutions encourage my research activity.
23. The civil-service system is appropriate for carryout faculty's teaching and research functions.
24. Students ask about their doubts in the time set aside to receive them.
25. Students' opinions are taken into account with the aim of improving my teaching.
26. The faculty of the department cooperate in the preparation/execution of the department's research programs.
27. Each year I take students' opinions into account when working out my teaching methodology.
28. I adapt my teaching to the particular characteristics/demands of each group of students.
29. Students' work adapts easily to the demands of my subject.
30. Labor contracts would enable faculty duties to be carried out better.
31. Some "objective" system of evaluation of teach faculty member's research work is necessary.
32. Students show differential evaluation of each faculty member according to his/her teaching quality.
33. I feel supported by my departmental colleagues in my research.

Scoring: A seven-point Likert format ranges from 1 = the lowest level of agreement to 7 = the highest level of agreement.

Reprinted with permission of the author.

Teacher Job Satisfaction Questionnaire

Lester, P.E. 1984. Development of an instrument to measure teacher job satisfaction. Ph.D. dissertation, New York University.

Comments: The 77-item TJSQ is based on the work of Maslow and Herzberg. The TJSQ has been translated into Spanish, French, Arabic, and Mandarin. It has been used mainly in doctoral dissertations over the last decade.

Sample: A random sample of 620 teachers from elementary, junior high school, and senior high schools in New York City, Westchester, Nassau, and Suffolk Counties (New York) participated.

Reliability: The alpha coefficient (Cronbach) for the entire scale is 0.93. Coefficients of internal consistency are 0.92 (supervision), 0.82 (colleagues and work itself), 0.83 (working conditions), 0.80 (pay), 0.73 (responsibility), 0.81 (advancement), 0.71 (security), and 0.74 (recognition). Coefficients for scales range from 0.71 (security) to 0.92 (supervision). The alpha coefficient for each factor, means, standard deviations, and alpha, if item deleted are provided in tabular form.

Validity: Content validation was performed through a panel of judges reducing the original number of items from 120 to 77. Statements with less than 80% agreement were either rewritten or rejected. The items were edited into a form specifically geared to teachers in an educational setting. Vaguely defined words, words with double meanings, emotionally loaded words, double negatives, and unclear words were eliminated, resulting in clear, concise, and direct statements of no more than 20 words. Approximately 50% of the items were written in a positive form, and 50% in a negative form to avoid response set bias. The data were cross-validated using a split-sample technique. Construct validity was obtained through factor analysis.

Factor Analysis: A nine-factor orthogonal varimax solution was accepted using criterion of eigenvalues greater than or equal to unity. The nine factors are: 14 items on supervision (19, 73, 47, 11, 27, 71, 52, 34, 65, 70, 14, 62, 6, and 56); ten items on colleagues (22, 57, 77, 17, 48, 35, 43, 63, 60, and 45); seven items on working conditions 64, 20, 40, 18, 31, 29, and 10); seven items on pay (53, 2, 72, 42, 67, 5, and 76); eight items on responsibility (75, 69, 74, 44, 24, 39, 21, and 61); nine items on work itself (30, 28, 51, 33, 8, 3, 54, 13, and 55); five items on advancement (59, 37, 1, 23, and 9); three items on security (25, 15, and 32); and three items on recognition (16, 7, and 58). The following eleven items had factor loadings below 0.30 (4, 12, 26, 36, 38, 41, 46, 49, 50, 66, and 68) and therefore, were not included in any further statistical analysis. They are filler items. Factor loading, communalities, item reversals, eigenvalues, etc., are reported.

Definitions of Factors: *Supervision* refers to supervisory style, which may be defined in terms of task-oriented behavior and person-oriented behavior. Task-oriented behavior requires direction and coordination of group activities to achieve the goals of the organization. Person-oriented behavior requires trust, respect, support, friendship, openness, and attempts to improve the environment. *Colleagues* are the teaching work group and the social aspects of the school setting. The teachers in the work group give and receive support and seek cooperation in the achievement of a common purpose or goal. The similarity of attitudes, the performance of jobs, the formation of personal relationships among fellow teachers, and an increase in self esteem, are all aspects of social interaction. *Working Conditions* refer to the physical conditions of the work environment, as well as the overall aspects of the school organization as defined and communicated by its administrative policies. *Pay* refers to the annual income, which may serve as indicator of recognition and achievement, or of failure. *Respon-*

sibility is the desire to be accountable for one's own work, to help one's students learn, and the opportunity to take part in policy or decision-making activities. *Work Itself* is the job of teaching or the tasks related to the job. It involves the freedom to institute innovative materials and to utilize one's skills and abilities in designing one's work (creativity) as well as the freedom to experiment and to influence or control what goes on in the job (autonomy). *Advancement* or promotion refers to a change in status or position, which may be equated with greater wages and power. *Security* refers to the school's policies regarding tenure, seniority, layoffs, pension, retirement, and dismissal. *Recognition* involves the attention, appreciation, prestige, and esteem of supervisors, colleagues, students, and parents.

Data Analysis: The means and standard deviations for each of the nine factors of the TJSQ were analyzed by location (urban and suburban), size of district (small/large), county, school level, and school level within district. One-way analyses of variance were also performed with each of the personal and demographic variables and the nine factors of the TJSQ. The results of demographic analyses are provided.

References:
Coates, B.R. 1992. The effect of shared decision-making on teacher job satisfaction and teacher professionalism. Ed.D. dissertation, United States International University.

Ford, S.W. 1987. The relationship between expectations and realities of job satisfaction for elementary school teachers. Ed. D. dissertation, University of Colorado, Boulder.

Johnston, R.H. 1991. The relationship between job satisfaction of Colorado middle school teachers and selected school and teacher characteristics. Ph.D. dissertation, University of Southern Mississippi.

Raisnai, R.B. 1988. A study of relationship of organizational climate and teachers' and schools' selected demographic characteristics to teacher job satisfaction as perceived by the teachers in selected Michigan public secondary schools. Ph.D. dissertation, Michigan State University.

Rauch, L.E. 1990. The relationship between participative decision-making and job satisfaction of elementary, middle, and secondary public school teachers. Ed.D. dissertation, University of San Francisco.

Teacher Job Satisfaction Questionnaire

1. Teaching provides me with an opportunity to advance professionally.
2. Teacher income is adequate for normal expenses.
3. Teaching provides an opportunity to use a variety of skills.
4. When instructions are inadequate, I do what I think is best.
5. Insufficient income keeps me from living the way I want to live.
6. My immediate supervisor turns one teacher against another.
7. No one tells me that I am a good teacher.
8. The work of a teacher consists of routine activities.
9. I am not getting ahead in my present teaching position.
10. Working conditions in my school can be improved.
11. I receive recognition from my immediate supervisor.
12. If I could earn what I earn now, I would take any job.
13. I do not have the freedom to make my own decisions.
14. My immediate supervisor offers suggestions to improve my teaching.
15. Teaching provides for a secure future.
16. I receive full recognition for my successful teaching.
17. I get along well with my colleagues.
18. The administration in my school does not clearly define its policies.
19. My immediate supervisor gives me assistance when I need help.
20. Working conditions in my school are comfortable.
21. Teaching provides me the opportunity to help my students learn.
22. I like the people with whom I work.
23. Teaching provides limited opportunities for advancement.
24. My students respect me as a teacher.
25. I am afraid of losing my teaching job.
26. Teaching involves too many clerical tasks.
27. My immediate supervisor does not back me up.
28. Teaching is very interesting work.
29. Working conditions in my school could not be worse.
30. Teaching discourages originality.
31. The administration in my school communicates its policies well.
32. I never feel secure in my teaching job.
33. Teaching does not provide me the chance to develop new methods.
34. My immediate supervisor treats everyone equitably.
35. My colleagues stimulate me to do better work.
36. My students come to class inadequately prepared.
37. Teaching provides an opportunity for promotion.
38. My immediate supervisor watches me closely.
39. I am responsible for planning my daily lessons.
40. Physical surroundings in my school are unpleasant.
41. I do not have the freedom to use my judgment.
42. I am well paid in proportion to my ability.
43. My colleagues are highly critical of one another.
44. I do have responsibility for my teaching.
45. My colleagues provide me with suggestions or feedback about my teaching.
46. Teaching provides me an opportunity to be my own boss.
47. My immediate supervisor provides assistance for improving instruction.

48. I do not get cooperation from the people I work with.
49. My immediate supervisor is not afraid to delegate work to others.
50. Behavior problems interfere with my teaching.
51. Teaching encourages me to be creative.
52. My immediate supervisor is not willing to listen to suggestions.
53. Teacher income is barely enough to live on.
54. I am indifferent toward teaching.
55. The work of a teacher is very pleasant.
56. I receive too many meaningless instructions from my immediate supervisor.
57. I dislike the people with whom I work.
58. I receive too little recognition.
59. Teaching provides a good opportunity for advancement.
60. My interests are similar to those of my colleagues.
61. I am not responsible for my actions.
62. My immediate supervisor makes available the material I need to do my best.
63. I have made lasting friendships among my colleagues.
64. Working conditions in my school are good.
65. My immediate supervisor makes me feel uncomfortable.
66. I prefer to have others assume responsibility.
67. Teacher income is less than I deserve.
68. I go out of my way to help my colleagues.
69. I try to be aware of the policies of my school.
70. When I teach a good lesson, my immediate supervisor notices.
71. My immediate supervisor explains what is expected of me.
72. Teaching provides me with financial security.
73. My immediate supervisor praises good teaching.
74. I am not interested in the policies of my school.
75. I get along well with my students.
76. Pay compares with similar jobs in other school districts.
77. My colleagues seem unreasonable to me.

Scoring: Strongly Disagree = 1; Disagree = 2; Neutral (neither disagree or agree) = 3; Agree = 4; and Strongly Agree = 5. Scoring is reversed for the following 22 unfavorable items (27, 52, 65, 6, 56, 57, 77, 48, 43, 40, 18, 74, 61, 30, 33, 54, 13, 23, 9, 25, 32, and 58).

Reprinted with permission of the author.

Job Descriptive Index

Smith, P.C., et al. 1969. *The measurement of satisfaction in work and retirement.* Chicago: Rand McNally.

Comments: The original 72-item JDI contained five scales. The JDI was revised in 1985 by substituting several items. The revised JDI has a new scale that measures satisfaction with the job in general. The complete forms, scoring key, instructions, and norms can be obtained from Dr. Patricia C. Smith, Department of Psychology, Bowling Green State University, Bowling Green, OH 43403. Additional scales include the 18-item Job in General Scale, which assesses global job satisfaction and the 18-item Stress in General Scale, which measures overall job stress. An updated (1990) manual is available that explains the methodology in developing and revising the JDI and the JIG as well as the administration, scoring, and reporting results of the JDI, the revised JDI, and the JIG. The JDI is one of the most frequently used instruments to measure job satisfaction.

Sample: Although the original sample consisted of 988 people from seven different organizations, additional studies were conducted with 2,662 people from 21 different organizations.

Reliability: Corrected split-half correlations were 0.84 (work), 0.80 (pay), 0.86 (promotions), 0.87 (supervision), and 0.88 (co-workers). Means and standard deviations for male and female workers are also provided.

Validity: A multitrait-multimethod matrix assessed convergent and discriminant validity.

Scales: The original JDI contained the following five scales: co-workers (18), pay (9), supervision (18), work (18), and opportunities for promotion (9).

References:
Collier, D.O. 1992. Developmental changes in predictors of job satisfaction for female elementary school teachers. Ph.D. dissertation, Old Dominion University.

Glick, N.L. 1992. Job satisfaction among academic administrators. *Research in Higher Education* 33:625-639.

Secumski-Kiligian, E.A. 1993. The relationship between elementary school teachers' job satisfaction, principals' managerial styles and student achievement. Ed.D. dissertation, Wayne State University.

Warr, C.N. 1991. Job satisfaction and intent to leave present employment among secondary teachers in vocational/technical education in the United States. Ed.D. dissertation, University of Georgia.

Wilcox, H.D. 1992. The relationship between the teachers' perception of the high school principal's leadership style and the correlates job satisfaction and morale. Ed.D. dissertation, University of Akron.

Job Descriptive Index

Think of the work you do at present. How well does each of the following words or phrases describe your work? In the blank beside each word below, write

Y for "Yes" if it describes your work
N for "No" if it does NOT describe it
? if you cannot decide

WORK ON PRESENT JOB

Routine
Satisfying
Good

Think of the kind of supervision that you get on your job. How well does each of the following words or phrases describe this? In the blank beside each word below, write

Y for "Yes" if it describes the supervision you get on your job
N for "No" if it does NOT describe it
? if you cannot decide

SUPERVISION

Impolite
Praises good work
Doesn't supervise enough

Think of the pay you get now. How well does each of the following words or phrases describe your present pay? In the blank beside each word below, write

Y for "Yes" if it describes your pay
N for "No" if it does NOT describe it
? if you cannot decide

PRESENT PAY

Income adequate for normal expenses
Insecure
Less than I deserve

Think of the majority of the people that you work with now or the people you meet in connection with your work. How well does each of the following words or phrases describe these people? In the blank beside each word below, write

Y for "Yes" if it describes the people you work with
N for "No" if it does NOT describe them
? if you cannot decide

CO-WORKERS (PEOPLE)

Boring
Responsible
Intelligent

Think of the opportunities for promotion that you have now. How well does each of the following words or phrases describe these? In the blank beside each word below, write

Y for "Yes" if it describes your opportunities for promotion
N for "No" if it does NOT describe them
? if you cannot decide

OPPORTUNITIES FOR PROMOTION

Dead-end job
Unfair promotion policy
Regular promotions

Think of your job in general. All in all, what is it like most of the time? In the blank beside each word or phrase below, write

Y for "Yes" if it describes your job
N for "No" if it does NOT describe it
? if you cannot decide

JOB IN GENERAL

Undesirable
Better than most
Rotten

Scoring: Each scale is written on a separate page. For positive items, a Yes receives 3 points; ? receives 1 point; and No receives no points. For negative items the scoring system is reversed. The scores on each scale are tallied separately.

Reprinted with permission of Bowling Green State University, Department of Psychology, Bowling Green, OH 43403.

Minnesota Satisfaction Questionnaire

Weiss, D.J., et al. 1967. *Manual for the Minnesota Satisfaction Questionnaire*. Minneapolis, MN: Industrial Relations Center, University of Minnesota.

Comments: The 100-item MSQ measures actual satisfaction with intrinsic and extrinsic aspects of the work environment. In addition to the MSQ, the Minnesota Importance Questionnaire was developed to assess the importance of various aspects to potential satisfaction. A 20-item short form of the MSQ was created by taking one item (highest correlation) from each of the 20 scales. The MSQ is one of the most frequently used instruments to measure job satisfaction.

Scale Construction: The Work Adjustment Project used the Hoppock Job Satisfaction Blank, the 54-item Employee Attitude Scale created by the Industrial Relations Center, and 22 additional items to measure satisfaction. These 80 items were used to design various satisfaction instruments. However, these instruments focused primarily on extrinsic satisfaction. A new instrument, the MSQ, was developed to measure intrinsic and extrinsic aspects of job satisfaction. Each of the 20 scales contains five items.

Sample: The original samples consisted of 1,793 employees from 25 occupations. One hundred and ninety-one suburban elementary school teachers from kindergarten to grade six participated in the study.

Reliability: Hoyt reliability coefficients for 27 normative groups ranged from 0.93 (advancement and recognition) to 0.78 (responsibility). For the group of 191 teachers, the Hoyt reliability coefficients were 0.90 (ability utilization and recognition), 0.79 (achievement and social status), 0.85 (activity), 0.92 (advancement), 0.83 (authority), 0.90 (company policies/practices, compensation, and social service), 0.81 (co-workers, independence, and supervision-technical), 0.86 (creativity), 0.75 (moral values and responsibility), 0.74 (security), 0.84 (supervision-human relations), 0.76 (variety), 0.91 (working conditions), and 0.87 (general satisfaction). Test-retest correlation coefficients for a one-week interval ranged from 0.66 (co-workers) to 0.91 (working conditions) for 75 night school students. Test-retest correlation coefficients for a one-year interval ranged from 0.35 (independence) to 0.71 (ability utilization) for 115 workers.

Validity: Construct validity for the MSQ is supported by the validation studies of the Minnesota Importance Questionnaire, which is based on the Theory of Work Adjustment. A detailed description is provided in the Manual for the Minnesota Satisfaction Questionnaire. Concurrent validity was established by studying group differences in satisfaction. One-way analysis of variance and Bartlett's test of homogeneity of variance were performed on 25 occupational groups. Group differences were statistically significant at the 0.001 level for both means and variances on all 21 MSQ scales.

Scales: The 20 scales and their corresponding items are: ability utilization (7, 27, 47, 67, and 87); achievement (19, 39, 59, 79, and 99); activity (20, 40, 60, 80, and 100); advancement (14, 34, 54, 74, and 94); authority (6, 26, 46, 66, and 86); company policies and practices (9, 29, 49, 69, and 89); compensation (12, 32, 52, 72, and 92); co-workers (16, 36, 56, 76, and 96); creativity (2, 22, 42, 62, and 82); independence (4, 24, 44, 64, and 84); moral values (3, 23, 43, 63, and 83); recognition (18, 38, 58, 78, and 98); responsibility (17, 37, 57, 77, and 97); security (11, 31, 51, 71, and 91); social service (1, 21, 41, 61, and 81); social status (8, 28, 48, 68, and 88); supervision-human relations (10, 30, 50, 70, and 90); supervision-technical (15, 35, 55, 75, and 95); variety (5, 25, 45, 65, and 85); and working conditions (13, 33, 53, 73, and 93). It is also possible to include a general satisfaction scale. This scale consists of 20 items, one from each of the 20 scales (24, 25, 28, 30, 35, 43, 51, 61, 66, 67, 69, 72, 74, 77, 82, 93, 96, 98, 99, and 100).

Definition of Scales: *Ability utilization* refers to the chance to do something that makes use of my abilities. *Achievement* refers to the feeling of accomplishment I get from the job. *Activity* refers to being able to keep busy all the time. *Advancement* refers to the chances for advancement on this job. *Authority* refers to the chance to tell other people what to do. *Company policies and practices* refer to the way company policies are put into practice. *Compensation* refers to my pay and the amount of work I do. *Co-workers* refer to the way my co-workers get along with each other. *Creativity* refers to the chance to try my own methods of doing the job. *Independence* refers to the chance to work alone on the job. *Moral values* refers to being able to do things that don't go against my conscience. *Recognition* refers to the praise I get for doing a good job. *Responsibility* refers to the freedom to use my own judgment. *Security* refers to the way my job provides for steady employment. *Social service* refers to the chance to do things for other people. *Social status* refers to the chance to be "somebody" in the community. *Supervision-human relations* refers to the way my boss handles his men. *Supervision-technical* refers to the competence of my supervisor in making decisions. *Variety* refers to the chance to do different things from time to time. *Working conditions* refer to the actual working conditions. The short form of the MSQ is comprised of the 20 scale items listed above.

Factor Structure: Intercorrelations for 14 norm groups are presented. The intercorrelation matrices were factor analyzed using a principal factors solution. Two factors were extracted for the teacher group. The first factor was intrinsic satisfaction, which accounted for about two-thirds of the common variance. The second factor was extrinsic satisfaction (two supervision scales, co-workers, and recognition) and accounted for about one-third of the common variance.

Data Analysis: Means, standard deviations, standard errors of measurement, and normative data are presented for all groups. In addition, MSQ scale intercorrelations and factor analyses are reported.

References:
Bowers, B.L. 1991. The relationship of staff development/inservice education and teachers' job satisfaction in selected middle schools. Ph.D. dissertation, University of Minnesota.

Lawson, D.L. 1993. Job satisfaction and the Missouri career ladder program. Ph.D. dissertation, University of Mississippi.

Prest, G.S. 1993. A study of instructional assistants' job satisfaction and supervising teachers' leadership behavior. Ed.D. dissertation, University of Minnesota.

Thompson, J.M., and M.D. Blain. 1992. Presenting feedback on the Minnesota Importance Questionnaire and the Minnesota Satisfaction Questionnaire. *Career Development Quarterly* 41:62-66.

Wagner, C.R. 1991. Mentoring and job satisfaction in eleven northeast Minnesota school districts. Ph.D. dissertation, University of Minnesota.

Minnesota Satisfaction Questionnaire

On my present job, this is how I feel about:

1. The chance to be of service to others.
2. The chance to try out some of my own ideas.
3. Being able to do the job without feeling it is morally wrong.
4. The chance to work by myself.
5. The variety in my work.
6. The chance to have other workers look to me for direction.
7. The chance to do the kind of work that I do best.
8. The social position in the community that goes with the job.
9. The policies and practices toward employees of this company.
10. The way my supervisor and I understand each other.
11. My job security.
12. The amount of pay for the work I do.
13. The working conditions (heating, lighting, ventilation, etc.) on this job.
14. The opportunities for advancement on this job.
15. The technical "know-how" of my supervisor.
16. The spirit of cooperation among my co-workers.
17. The chance to be responsible for planning my work.
18. The way I am noticed when I do a good job.
19. Being able to see the results of the work I do.
20. The chance to be active much of the time.
21. The chance to be of service to people.
22. The chance to do new and original things on my own.
23. Being able to do things that don't go against my religious beliefs.
24. The chance to work alone on the job.
25. The chance to do different things from time to time.
26. The chance to tell other workers how to do things.
27. The chance to do work that is well suited to my abilities.
28. The chance to be "somebody" in the community.
29. Company policies and the way in which they are administered.
30. The way my boss handles his men.
31. The way my job provides for a secure future.
32. The chance to make as much money as my friends.
33. The physical surroundings where I work.
34. The chances of getting ahead on this job.
35. The competence of my supervisor in making decisions.
36. The chance to develop close friendships with my co-workers.
37. The chance to make decisions on my own.
38. The way I get full credit for the work I do.
39. Being able to take pride in a job well done.
40. Being able to do something much of the time.
41. The chance to help people.
42. The chance to try something different.
43. Being able to do things that don't go against my conscience.
44. The chance to be alone on the job.
45. The routine in my work.

46. The chance to supervise other people.
47. The chance to make use of my best abilities.
48. The chance to "rub elbows" with important people.
49. The way employees are informed about company policies.
50. The way my boss backs his men up (with top management).
51. The way my job provides for steady employment.
52. How my pay compares with that for similar jobs in other companies.
53. The pleasantness of the working conditions.
54. The way promotions are given out on this job.
55. The way my boss delegates work to others.
56. The friendliness of my co-workers.
57. The chance to be responsible for the work of others.
58. The recognition I get for the work I do.
59. Being able to do something worthwhile.
60. Being able to stay busy.
61. The chance to do things for other people.
62. The chance to develop new and better ways to do the job.
63. The chance to do things that don't harm other people.
64. The chance to work independently of others.
65. The chance to do something different every day.
66. The chance to tell people what to do.
67. The chance to do something that makes use of my abilities.
68. The chance to be important in the eyes of others.
69. The way company policies are put into practice.
70. The way my boss takes care of complaints brought to him by his men.
71. How steady my job is.
72. My pay and the amount of work I do.
73. The physical working conditions of the job.
74. The chances for advancement on this job.
75. The way my boss provides help on hard problems.
76. The way my co-workers are easy to make friends with.
77. The freedom to use my own judgment.
78. The way they usually tell me when I do my job well.
79. The chance to do my best at all times.
80. The chance to be "on the go" all the time.
81. The chance to be of some small service to other people.
82. The chance to try my own methods of doing the job.
83. The chance to do the job without feeling I am cheating anyone.
84. The chance to work away from others.
85. The chance to do many different things on the job.
86. The chance to tell others what to do.
87. The chance to make use of my abilities and skills.
88. The chance to have a definite place in the community.
89. The way the company treats its employees.
90. The personal relationship between my boss and his men.
91. The way layoffs and transfers are avoided in my job.
92. How my pay compares with that of other workers.
93. The working conditions.
94. My chances for advancement.
95. The way my boss trains his men.

96. The way my co-workers get along with each other.
97. The responsibility of my job.
98. The praise I get for doing a good job.
99. The feeling of accomplishment I get from the job.
100. Being able to keep busy all the time.

Scoring: I am not satisfied = 1; I am only slightly satisfied = 2; I am satisfied = 3; I am very satisfied = 4; and I am extremely satisfied = 5.

Reprinted with permission of Vocational Psychology Research, University of Minnesota.

Leadership

Least Preferred Co-worker

Fiedler, F.E. 1967. *A theory of leadership effectiveness*. New York: McGraw-Hill.

Comments: The 15-item LPC is a semantic differential instrument based on Fiedler's contingency theory of leadership effectiveness. It includes three dimensions: the quality of leader-member relations; degree of task structure; and a measure of leader-position power.

Scale Construction: The LPC is a brief and straightforward scale that uses a semantic differential format with 15 bipolar adjectives. In responding to the scale, individuals are instructed to think of a coworker with whom they **work least well**. It employees an eight-point Likert type response anchor. For each pair of bipolar adjectives (pleasant-unpleasant, friendly-unfriendly), the positive adjective receives the higher score. A person's LPC score is the sum of the ratings. Established norms indicate that a score of 63 or less constitutes a low LPC response, and a score of 73 or higher, a high LPC score. A high LPC score represents a more generalized interpersonally oriented leader style. The low LPC is considered to be a more task-oriented style.

Sample: The development of the LPC was based on large samples of adults (2,000 or more subjects) across a variety of adult populations.

Reliability: Split-half reliability estimates ranged from 0.86 to 0.92. Median test-retest reliability coefficients ranged from 0.67 to 0.81.

Validity: Extensive construct validity studies have documented that high LPC leaders are interpersonally oriented and that low LPC scores constitute a task-oriented leader style.

Factor Analysis: Fiedler employed a number of factor analytic studies in the development of the LPC. This information is documented in some detail in the references cited below.

References:
Fiedler, F.E., and M.M. Chemers. 1984. *Improving leadership effectiveness*. New York: Wiley.

Fiedler, F.E., and J.E. Garcia. 1987. *New approaches to effective leadership*. New York: Wiley.

Least Preferred Co-Worker Scale

1.	Pleasant	Unpleasant
2.	Friendly	Unfriendly
3.	Rejecting	Accepting
4.	Helpful	Frustrating
5.	Unenthusiastic	Enthusiastic
6.	Tense	Relaxed
7.	Distant	Close
8.	Cold	Warm
9.	Cooperative	Uncooperative
10.	Supportive	Hostile
11.	Quarrelsome	Harmonious
12.	Self-Assured	Hesitant
13.	Efficient	Inefficient
14.	Gloomy	Cheerful
15.	Open	Guarded

Scoring: See description above.

Reprinted with permission of the author.

Management Opinionnaire

Sistrunk, W.E., and E.R. Jenkins. 1980. The preferred leadership style of school superintendents. Paper presented at the Mid-South Educational Research Association. ERIC ED 197 430.

Comments: The 27-item opinionnaire focuses on three forces and seven styles of leadership. Two styles of management are rooted in McGregor's (1969) Theory X and Theory Y, while the remaining five styles of management are rooted in Blake and Mouton's (1964) Managerial Grid (Theory 1,1; Theory 1,9; Theory 9,1; Theory 5,5; and Theory 9,9).

Sample: The original sample consisted of 125 superintendents from Mississippi in 1980. Webb (1975) developed and validated the Management Opinionnaire using a sample of superintendents from North Carolina.

Reliability: The alpha coefficient for the opinionnaire was 0.80 using a pilot study with 30 educational administration students.

Scales: There are 12 items that relate to forces within the executive educational manager (1, 2, 7, 10, 11, 16, 20, 21, 23, 25, 26, and 27). These items deal with the values and beliefs that a manager has about him/herself. There are six items that relate to forces within the subordinate workers (8, 9, 14, 15, 19, and 24). These items deal with the values and beliefs that a manager believes that his/her subordinates ought to have about him/herself. There are nine items that relate to forces within the organization (3, 4, 5, 6, 12, 13, 17, 18, and 22). These items deal with the values and beliefs that a manager has for the organization in which he/she is employed.

Data Analysis: Percentages were computed for each response category. Chi square analysis was conducted to decide the effect that the three types of forces had on the superintendents' leadership style. Results of all data analysis are presented.

References:
Blake, R.R., and J.S. Mouton. 1964. *The managerial grid: Key orientation for achieving production through people*. Houston: Gulf Publishing Company.

McGregor, D. 1969. *The human side of enterprise*. New York: McGraw-Hill Book Company.

Webb, D.M. 1975. Modern management concepts and practices in North Carolina local school systems. Ed.D. dissertation, Duke University.

Management Opinionnaire

1. You consider that one of the most important job responsibilities of an executive educational manager is the stimulation of his subordinate workers to produce high standards of performance.
2. As an executive educational manager, you feel that those subordinate workers who are affected by the decisions made in a local school system should be allowed to participate in the decision-making process.
3. You feel that a more realistic fulfillment of objectives and attainment of goals can result if the organizational structure provides for a systematic, step-by-step procedure.
4. You feel that the organizational structure of a local school system should provide for the evaluation of executive educational managers on agreed upon competencies which have been stated in measurable terms.
5. You believe that a local system will meet with more success when the behaviors of the organization and the behaviors of the subordinate workers are developed and directed together.
6. You consider that the establishment of group-written organizational objectives and goals is an effective way for executive educational managers and subordinate workers to communicate.
7. You believe that an executive educational manager should be able to fulfill his responsibility without having to exert his authority.
8. As an executive educational manager, you believe that your subordinate workers are capable of providing self-control in their work.
9. You regard that subordinate workers should realize that certain unavoidable situations occur in any organization.
10. You feel that the subordinate workers in an organization should be evaluated on measurable competencies which they have helped to establish.
11. You regard that the personal satisfaction achieved from the fulfillment of objectives and the attainment of goals are all the rewards needed by an executive educational manager.
12. You believe that executive educational managers in a local school system perform best when they work under agreed upon job descriptions and organizational charts.
13. You believe that the potential needs of subordinates should be provided for by the organizational structure.
14. As an executive educational manager, you believe that your subordinate workers are capable of motivating themselves in their work.
15. As an executive educational manager, you feel that your subordinate workers will become committed to the purposes of a local school system if they can sense a realistic fulfillment of objectives and attainment of goals.
16. You feel that an executive educational manager should be a creative and imaginative person.
17. You believe that subordinate workers in a local school system can perform their best work when they are guided by job descriptions and organizational charts with which they agree.
18. You believe that positive results will occur in a local school system when the behaviors of the organization and the behaviors of executive educational managers are mutually developed and channeled in the same direction.
19. As an executive educational manager, you believe that your subordinate workers are capable of exercising self-direction in their work.
20. You regard that executive educational managers should acknowledge the fact that uncertainties arise in any organizational structure.
21. You believe that an executive educational manager should not only accept responsibility entrusted to him but that he should also seek responsibility.

22. You believe that the organizational structure of a local school system should be adaptable to the potential needs of executive educational managers.

23. You feel that an executive educational manager must be aware of the many ways to organize problems for solutions.

24. As an executive educational manager, you believe that your subordinate workers want to become involved in the activities of a local school system because they like their work.

25. You believe that the most effective communication in a local school system is that communication which flows from subordinate workers upward to executive educational managers.

26. You believe that an executive educational manager must individualize his methods when working with his subordinate workers.

27. You feel that an executive educational manager can only become effective through specific knowledge and experience.

Scoring: Strongly agree = 1; agree = 2; no opinion = 3; disagree = 4; and strongly disagree = 5.

Reprinted with permission of Walter E. Sistrunk, P.O. Box JG, MS State, MS 39762.

Locus of Control

Brown Locus of Control Scale

Brown, R. 1990. The construct and concurrent validity of the social dimension of the Brown Locus of Control Scale. *Educational and Psychological Measurement* 50:377-382.

Comments: The 25-item BLOCS assesses three aspects of control: internal (the person feels personal control), external social (the individual feels controlled by social interaction aspects, including social groups, work, and friends), and external other (the person feels controlled by chance, fate, or any other abstract authority).

Sample: The sample for the 1983 study consisted of 114 female graduate students. In addition, five additional samples from five other studies are presented.

Reliability: Alpha coefficients were 0.74 (internal), 0.71 (external social), and 0.66 (external other). Test-retest reliability over a two-week period with 92 students from the original sample was 0.88 (internal), 0.91 (external social), and 0.84 (external other).

Validity: Evidence for concurrent validity is provided in the numerous studies described that compared the results of the BLOCS with various psychological factors. The data reported in the 1990 study represents a compilation of various samples.

Factor Analysis: A three-factor solution was accepted. The factors are: internal (4, 9, 13, 16, 19, 20, 21, 22, and 25); external social (1, 6, 7, 8, 10, 11, 14, 15, and 23); and external others (2, 3, 5, 12, 17, 18, and 24).

Data Analysis: The means and standard deviations for the three BLOCS dimensions in five additional studies are presented.

References:
Brown, R. 1983. Locus of control and sex role orientation of women graduate students. *College Student Journal* 17:10-12.

Brown, R., and G.A. Marcoulides. 1996. A cross-cultural comparison of the Brown Locus of Control Scale. *Educational and Psychological Measurement* 56:858-863.

Levenson, H. 1974. Activism and powerful others: Distinctions within the concept of an internal-external control. *Journal of Personality Assessment* 38:377-383.

Rotter, J.B. 1966. Generalized expectancies for internal vs. external control of reinforcement. *Psychological Reports* 56:723-726.

Brown Locus of Control Scale

1.   My friendships depend on how well I relate to others.
2.   Accidental happenings have a lot to do with my life.
3.   Rules and practices that have been around for many years should determine what will happen to my life.
4.   I am fairly able to determine what will happen to my life.
5.   Religious faith will get me through hard times.
6.   The government will run whether I get involved or not.
7.   Getting ahead is a matter of pleasing people in power.
8.   Generally it's not what I know, but who I know.
9.   I make mistakes—accidents just don't happen.
10. Being in the right place at the right time is important for my success.
11. My friends often determine my actions.
12. The ideas about life that have been around since time began have an influence on my life.
13. Most of the time, I control what happens in my life.
14. Strong pressure groups determine my role in society.
15. My plans will not work unless they fit into the plans of those in power.
16. My close relationships with people don't just happen—they need to be worked on.
17. Some powerful force or person predetermined most of what happens in my life.
18. My life is often affected by fate.
19. My actions determine my life.
20. Hard work will get me where I want to go.
21. I can generally take care of my personal interests.
22. I have to work with others to get a job done.
23. My ability without pleasing people in power makes little difference.
24. My life is often affected by luck.
25. I can usually carry out plans that I make for myself.

Scoring: 6 = Very Strongly Agree; 5 = Strongly Agree; 4 = Agree; 3 = Disagree; 2 = Strongly Disagree; and 1 = Very Strongly Disagree. Each scale is scored separately by summing the responses for that scale. Comparisons can be made for each scale, but not across scales.

Reprinted with permission of the author.

Internal Control Index

Duttweiler, P.C. 1984. The Internal Control Scale: A newly developed measure of locus of control. *Educational and Psychological Measurement* 44:209-221.

Comments: The 28-item ICI was developed in four stages and was constantly revised based upon the results of each stage of development. It has two stable factors, internal consistency, norms for demographic categories from college students, and convergent validity.

Scale Construction: The pretesting stage consisted of identifying those aspects related to internal locus of control (autonomy, cognitive processing, delay of gratification, resistance to influence attempts, and self-confidence). Items were developed based on clarity and conciseness. The tryout test was administered to a sample of 548 junior college, continuing education, college, and university students. After item analysis and factor analyses, 28 items were selected for the field test administration, which included 684 people similar to the tryout sample. Analyses of variance, item analysis, and factor analyses were conducted to further refine the ICI.

Sample: The replication sample consisted of 133 students from Gainesville Junior College.

Reliability: Alpha coefficients of 0.84 for the field test and 0.85 for the Gainesville replication study were reported. Item total-score correlations for both samples are provided.

Validity: Convergent validity was established by correlating the ICI with Mirels' Factor I of Rotter's I-E Scale (significant at the 0.001 level).

Factor Analysis: A varimax rotation with both the field test sample and the Gainesville Junior College replication sample (133 students) resulted in a two-factor solution. The two factors are confidence in one's own ability and autonomous behavior. For the field test, 14 items loaded on confidence in one's own ability (3, 4, 5, 7, 9, 10, 13, 15, 16, 18, 20, 21, 25, and 28), whereas 13 items loaded on the same factor for the Gainesville replication sample (1, 3, 7, 9, 10, 12, 13, 15, 16, 19, 20, 23, and 28). For the field test, 13 items loaded on autonomous behavior (2, 6, 8, 11, 12, 14, 17, 19, 22, 23, 24, 26, and 27), whereas 14 items loaded on the same factor for the Gainesville replication sample (1, 2, 6, 8, 11, 14, 16, 18, 20, 21, 22, 24, 26, and 27).

Data Analysis: Field test means and standard deviations on the ICI are presented by age group, sex, race, educational level, and socioeconomic level.

References:
MacDonald, A.P., Jr. 1973. Measures of internal-external control. In J.P. Robinson and P.R. Shaver (eds.), *Measures of social psychological attitudes*. Ann Arbor: University of Michigan.

Mirels, H.L. 1970. Dimensions of internal versus external control. *Journal of Consulting and Clinical Psychology* 34:226-228.

Internal Control Index

1. When faced with a problem I try to forget it.
2. I need frequent encouragement from others to keep me working at a difficult task.
3. I like jobs where I can make decisions and be responsible for my own work.
4. I change my opinion when someone I admire disagrees with me.
5. If I want something I work hard to get it.
6. I prefer to learn the facts about something from someone else rather than have to dig them out for myself.
7. I will accept jobs that require me to supervise others.
8. I have a hard time saying "no" when someone tries to sell me something I don't want.
9. I like to have a say in any decisions made by any group I'm in.
10. I consider the different sides of an issue before making any decisions.
11. What other people think has a great influence on my behavior.
12. Whenever something good happens to me I feel it is because I've earned it.
13. I enjoy being in a position of leadership.
14. I need someone else to praise my work before I am satisfied with what I've done.
15. I am sure enough of my own opinions to try and influence others.
16. When something is going to affect me I learn as much about it as I can.
17. I decide to do things on the spur of the moment.
18. For me, knowing I've done something well is more important than being praised by someone else.
19. I let other peoples' demands keep me from doing things I want to do.
20. I stick to my opinions when someone disagrees with me.
21. I do what I feel like doing not what other people think I ought to do.
22. I get discouraged when doing something that takes a long time to achieve results.
23. When part of a group I prefer to let other people make all the decisions.
24. When I have a problem I follow the advice of friends or relatives.
25. I enjoy trying to do difficult tasks more than I enjoy trying to do easy tasks.
26. I prefer situations where I can depend on someone else's ability rather than just my own.
27. Having someone important tell me I did a good job is more important to me than feeling I've done a good job.
28. When I'm involved in something I try to find out all I can about what is going on even when someone else is in charge.

Scoring: Rarely = 5; Occasionally = 4; Sometimes = 3; Frequently = 2; and Usually = 1. The scoring is reversed for the following items: 3, 5, 7, 9, 10, 12, 13, 15, 16, 18, 20, 21, 25, and 28.

Reprinted with permission of the author.

Teacher Locus of Control

Rose, J.S., and F.J. Medway. 1981. Measurement of teachers' beliefs in their control over student outcome. *Journal of Educational Research* 74:185-189.

Comments: The 28-item TLC assesses teachers' perceptions about internal or external classroom control. The scale is internally consistent and has higher correlations with classroom teaching behaviors than Rotter's I-E scale.

Scale Construction: The original TLC contained 32 positive or success situations and 32 negative or failure situations. Three judges examined the items and categorized them as I+ or I-. They also looked at the clarity of the items. After each administration of the TLC, items were kept if they loaded on the appropriate scale, and if their biserial correlations with the total scale were significant at the 0.05 level. Out of the 28 items, 14 items describe positive (success) situations, while the other 14 describe negative (failure) situations.

Sample: Prior to the final version of the TLC, four samples that included 183 elementary school teachers completed three versions of the scale. The final sample consisted of 89 female teachers who taught the fourth grade.

Reliability: KR20 reliabilities were 0.71 (student success) and 0.81 (student failure).

Validity: One validation study examined the relationship between locus of control and the implementation of innovative educational practices. A second validation study looked at the relationship between the scores on the TLC and the classroom behavior of fourth grade teachers. The results of both validation studies demonstrated that the TLC was a better predictor of teacher and student behavior than Rotter's I-E scale (a more general assessment of control beliefs).

Factor Analysis: A principal factoring with a varimax rotation yielded two factors: student success (I+) and student failure (I-).

Data Analysis: Means and standard deviations are reported for the sample of 89 teachers. In addition, t-tests were performed to see if there were any significant differences related to teachers' race, socioeconomic level of the students, and the geographic location of the school. The only significant relationship was found on the I+ scale. Teachers in low SES schools scored significantly higher on the I+ scale than teachers in high SES schools.

References:
Rose, J.S. 1978. Relationships among teacher locus of control, teacher and student behavior, and student achievement. Ph.D. dissertation, University of South Carolina.

Thomson, J.R. Jr., and H.M. Handley. 1990. Relationship between teacher self-concept and teacher efficacy. Paper presented at Mid-South Educational Research Association. ERIC ED 327 508.

Teacher Locus of Control

1. When the grades of your students improve, it is more likely
    a. because you found ways to motivate the students, or
    b. because the students were trying harder to do well.

2. Suppose you had difficulties in setting up learning centers for students in your classroom. Would this probably happen
    a. because you lacked the appropriate materials, or
    b. because you didn't spend enough time in developing activities to go into the center?

3. Suppose your students did not appear to be benefiting from a more individualized method of instruction. The reason for this would probably be
    a. because you were having some problems managing this type of instruction, or
    b. because the students in your class were such that they needed a more traditional kind of approach.

4. When a student gets a better grade on his report card than he usually gets, is it
    a. because the student was putting more effort into his schoolwork, or
    b. because you found better ways of teaching that student?

5. If the students in your class became disruptive and noisy when you left them alone in the room for five minutes, would this happen
    a. because you didn't leave them interesting work to do while you were gone, or
    b. because the students were more noisy that day than they usually are?

6. When some of your students fail a math test, it is more likely
    a. because they weren't attending to the lesson, or
    b. because you didn't use enough examples to illustrate the concept.

7. Suppose you were successful at using learning centers with your class of 30 students. Would this occur
    a. because you worked hard at it, or
    b. because your students easily conformed to the new classroom procedure?

8. When a student pulls his or grade up from a "C" to a "B," it is more likely
    a. because you came up with an idea to motivate the student, or
    b. because the student was trying harder to do well.

9. Suppose you are teaching a student a particular concept in arithmetic or math and the student has trouble learning it. Would this happen
    a. because the student wasn't able to understand it, or
    b. because you couldn't explain it very well?

10. When a student does better in school than he usually does, is it more likely
    a. because the student was trying harder, or
    b. because you tried hard to encourage the student to do better?

11. If you couldn't keep your class quiet, it would probably be
    a. because the students came to school more rowdy than usual, or
    b. because you were so frustrated that you weren't able to settle them down.

12. Suppose a play put on by your class was voted the "Best Class Play of the Year" by students and faculty in your school. Would it be
    a. because you put in a lot of time and effort as the director, or
    b. because the students were cooperative.

13. Suppose it were the week before Easter vacation and you were having some trouble keeping order in your classroom. This would more likely happen
    a. because you weren't putting extra effort into keeping the students under control, or
    b. because the students were more uncontrollable than usual.

14. If one of your students couldn't do a class assignment, would it be
    a. because the student wasn't paying attention during the class lesson, or
    b. because you gave the student an assignment that wasn't on his or her level?

15. Suppose you wanted to teach a series of lessons on Mexico, but the lessons didn't turn out as well as you had expected. This would more likely happen
    a. because the students weren't that interested in learning about Mexico, or
    b. because you didn't put enough effort into developing the lessons.

16. Suppose a student who does not typically participate in class begins to volunteer his or her answers. This would more likely happen
    a. because the student finally encountered a topic of interest to him or her, or
    b. because you tried hard to encourage the student to volunteer his or her answers.

17. Suppose one of your students cannot remain on task for a particular assignment. Would this be more likely to happen
    a. because you gave the student a task that was somewhat less interesting than most tasks, or
    b. because the student was unable to concentrate on his or her schoolwork that day?

18. Suppose you were unable to devise an instructional system as requested by the principal, which would accommodate the "needs of individual students" in your class. This would most likely happen
    a. because there were too many students in your class, or
    b. because you didn't have enough knowledge or experience with individualized instructional programs.

19. If the students in your class perform better than they usually do on a test, would this happen
    a. because the students studied a lot for the test, or
    b. because you did a good job of teaching the subject area?

20. When the performance of a student in your class appears to be slowly deteriorating, it is usually
    a. because you weren't trying hard enough to motivate him or her, or
    b. because the student was putting less effort into his or her schoolwork.

21. Suppose a new student was assigned to your class, and this student had a difficult time making friends with his or her classmates. Would it be more likely
    a. that most of the other students did not make an effort to be friends with the new student, or
    b. that you were not trying hard enough to encourage the other students to be more friendly toward the newcomer?

22. If the students in your class performed better on a standardized achievement test given at the end of the year compared to students you had last year, it would probably be
    a. because you put more effort into teaching this year, or
    b. because this year's class of students were somewhat smarter than last year's.

23. Suppose, one day, you find yourself reprimanding one of your students more often than usual. Would this be more likely to happen
    a. because that student was misbehaving more than usual that day, or
    b. because you were somewhat less tolerant than you usually are?

24. Suppose one of your underachievers does his or her homework better than usual. This would probably happen
    a. because the student tried hard to do the assignment, or
    b. because you tried hard to explain how to do the assignment.

25. Suppose one of your students began to do better schoolwork than he usually does. Would this happen
    a. because you put much effort into helping the student do better, or
    b. because the student was trying harder to do well in school?

Scoring: The TLC uses a forced-choice format. Half of the items represent positive (success) situations, while the other half represent negative (failure) situations. Separate scores are obtained for student success (I+) and student failure (I-).

Reprinted with permission of the Helen Dwight Reid Educational Foundation. (Published by Heldref Publications, 1319 18th Street, NW. Washington, D.C. 20036-1802.)

Internal-External Locus of Control Scale

Rotter, J.B. 1966. Generalized expectancies for internal versus external control of reinforcement. *Psychological Monographs: General and Applied* 80 (Whole No. 609).

Comments: The 29-item I-E Scale assesses "generalized expectancies for internal versus external control of reinforcement." Item analysis, factor analysis, and reliability tests demonstrate the internal consistency of the scale. The I-E Scale has been used to develop validate other instruments. It is one of the most frequently used instruments to measure locus of control.

Scale Construction: The original I-E scale contained 100 forced-choice items, each one comparing an external belief with an internal one. Based upon item analysis and factor analysis, the revised scale contained 60 items. Item correlations with the Marlowe-Crowne Social Desirability Scale, validity data from two studies, and reliability data resulted in reducing the scale to 23 items. The final version of the scale contains 23 forced-choice items plus six filler items.

Sample: Biserial item correlations are reported for a sample of 200 men and 200 women enrolled in psychology courses at Ohio State University. In addition to students at Ohio State, other samples consisted of 10th, 11th, and 12th graders, a national stratified sample, prisoners at the Colorado Reformatory, elementary psychology students at Kansas State University, and Ohio Federal prisoners.

Reliability: The KR20 reliability coefficient was 0.70 for the sample of 200 men and 200 women. Test-retest reliability after one month was 0.72 and after two months was 0.55. Reliability data are provided for all of the samples.

Validity: Discriminant validity is supported by the low correlations with intelligence, social desirability, and political liberalness. Evidence of construct validity is found in the predicted differences in behavior for people above and below the median of the I-E Scale and from correlations with behavioral criteria. Numerous studies are discussed to support construct validity.

Factor Analysis: The two factor analyses that were performed support the unidimensionality of the scale.

Data Analysis: Biserial item correlations of each item with total score, excluding that item are presented. Means and standard deviations for various samples are also provided.

References:
Jones, B.J.W. 1993. Career socialization, locus-of-control and perceptions of sex role stereotypes among female administrators in Georgia's technical institutes. Ph.D. dissertation, Georgia State University.

Sillonis, R. 1991. The relationship between locus-of-control and self-esteem among K-12 public school principals and school effectiveness. Ed.D. dissertation, University of San Francisco.

Sims, B.J. 1992. Elementary school site implementation of centrally mandated policy: An interpretation of teacher locus-of-control, school climate, and principal leadership style. Ph.D. dissertation, University of California, Berkeley.

Internal-External Locus of Control Scale

1. a. Children get into trouble because their parents punish them too much.
    b. The trouble with most children nowadays is that their parents are too easy with them.

2. a. Many of the unhappy things in people's lives are partly due to bad luck.
    b. People's misfortunes result from the mistakes they make.

3. a. One of the major reasons why we have wars is because people don't take enough interest in politics.
    b. There will always be wars, no matter how hard people try to prevent them.

4. a. In the long run people get the respect they deserve in this world.
    b. Unfortunately, an individual's worth often passes unrecognized no matter how hard he tries.

5   a. The idea that teachers are unfair to students is nonsense.
    b. Most students don't realize the extent to which their grades are influenced by accidental happenings.

6. a. Without the right breaks one cannot be an effective leader.
    b. Capable people who fail to become leaders have not taken advantage of their opportunities.

7. a. No matter how hard you try some people just don't like you.
    b. People who can't get others to like them don't understand how to get along with others.

8. a. Heredity plays the major role in determining one's personality.
    b. It is one's experiences in life which determine what they're like.

9   a. I have often found that what is going to happen will happen.
    b. Trusting to fate has never turned out as well for me as making a decision to take a definite course of action.

10. a. In the case of the well-prepared student there is rarely if ever such a thing as an unfair test.
     b. Many times exam questions tend to be so unrelated to course work that studying is really useless.

11. a. Becoming a success is a matter of hard work; luck has little or nothing to do with it.
     b. Getting a good job depends mainly on being in the right place at the right time.

12. a. The average citizen can have an influence in government decisions.
     b. This world is run by the few people in power, and there is not much the little guy can do about it.

13. a. When I make plans, I am almost certain that I can make them work.
     b. It is not always wise to plan too far ahead because many things turn out to be a matter of good or bad fortune anyhow.

14. a. There are certain people who are just no good.
     b. There is some good in everybody.

15. a. In my case getting what I want has little or nothing to do with luck.
    b. Many times we might just as well decide what to do by flipping a coin.

16. a. Who gets to be the boss often depends on who was lucky enough to be in the right place first.
    b. Getting people to do the right thing depends upon ability, luck has little or nothing to do with it.

17. a. As far as world affairs are concerned, most of us are the victims of forces we can neither understand nor control.
    b. By taking an active part in political and social affairs, the people can control world events.

18. a. Most people don't realize the extent to which their lives are controlled by accidental happenings.
    b. There really is no such thing as "luck."

19. a. One should always be willing to admit mistakes.
    b. It is usually best to cover up one's mistakes.

20. a. It is hard to know whether or not a person really likes you.
    b. How many friends you have depends on how nice a person you are.

21. a. In the long run the bad things that happen to us are balanced by the good ones.
    b. Most misfortunes are the result of lack of ability, ignorance, laziness, or all three.

22. a. With enough effort we can wipe out political corruption.
    b. It is difficult for people to have much control over the things politicians do in office.

23. a. Sometimes I can't understand how teachers arrive at the grades they give.
    b. There is a direct connection between how hard I study and the grades I get.

24. a. A good leader expects people to decide for themselves what they should do.
    b. A good leader makes it clear to everybody what their jobs are.

25. a. Many times I feel that I have little influence over the things that happen to me.
    b. It is impossible for me to believe that chance or luck plays an important role in my life.

26. a. People are lonely because they don't try to be friendly.
    b. There's not much use in trying too hard to please people, if they like you, they like you.

27. a. There is too much emphasis on athletics in high school.
    b. Team sports are an excellent way to build character.

28. a. What happens to me is my own doing.
    b. Sometimes I feel that I don't have enough control over the direction my life is taking.

29. a. Most of the time I can't understand why politicians behave the way they do.
    b. In the long run the people are responsible for bad government on a national as well as on a local level.

Scoring: A forced-choice format is used. The total score is calculated by adding the number of external beliefs selected (2a, 3b, 4b, 5b, 6a, 7a, 9a, 10b, 11b, 12b, 13b, 15b, 16a, 17a, 18a, 20a, 21a, 22b, 23a, 25a, 26b, 28b, and 29a).

Perceived Control at School Scale

Adelman, H.S., et al. 1986. An instrument to assess students' perceived control at school. *Educational and Psychological Measurement* 46:1005-1017.

Comments: The 16-item PCSS measures students' perceived control at school. Data on reliability, validity, and factor structure are provided. Variations based upon sample characteristics have been found.

Scale Construction: Twelve items were written based on five areas of control in which schools are different. Four items were added as a reliability check to see if there were differences based on positively and negatively worded items. The pilot PCSS consisted of 16 items. Two forms of the PCSS were developed (one for the current school and one for the previous school).

Sample: Four samples were used. Two samples consisted of 107 special education students and the other two samples consisted of 113 regular education students. A description of the samples is provided.

Reliability: For the total special education samples the alpha coefficient was 0.80, while the alpha coefficient for the total regular education samples was 0.69. The alpha coefficient for all four samples was 0.65. Test-retest reliability over a two-week interval was 0.80 for special education students and 0.55 for regular education students.

Validity: To establish construct validity, the PCSS was correlated with the Nowicki-Strickland Locus of Control Scale. In addition, differences in group responses were used to further establish construct validity.

Factor Analysis: Principal components factor analysis with a varimax rotation yielded five factors for the special education samples and six factors for the regular education samples (there was overlapping). The five factors are: five items on personal power/decision-making (14, 12, 1, 15, and 3); four items on self-determination (8, 11, 7, and 10); four items on others interference with autonomy (2, 16, 5, and 13); two items on powerlessness (4 and 6); and two items on impersonal interference with autonomy (9 and 10). Factor loadings are presented.

References:
Nichols, B.K. 1985. Self-perceptions of control and esteem as related to participation in a leadership training program. Ph.D. dissertation. University of California, Los Angeles.

Taylor, L., H.S. Adelman, and N. Kaser-Boyd. 1984. Attitudes toward involving minors in decisions. *Professional Psychology: Research and Practice* 15:436-449.

Perceived Control at School Scale

At school, how much of the time do you feel...

1. you have a say in deciding about what the rules should be?
2. people don't let you be yourself and act the way you really are?
3. you have a say in deciding about what should happen to you if you break a rule?
4. you can't influence what is happening to you?
5. people want you to be yourself and to act the way you really are?
6. people don't let you take part in making decisions?
7. you have a choice about what you are doing or learning?
8. you can influence what is happening to you?
9. the rules make you do things you don't agree with?
10. no matter what you do you probably won't get what you want?
11. you have very little choice about what you are doing or learning?
12. you are able to change something if you don't like it?
13. others make your decisions for you?
14. you get to do things in the way you think is right for you?
15. people want you to take part in making decisions?
16. people don't treat you fairly?

Scoring: Never = 1; Not very often = 2; Slightly less than half the time = 3; Slightly more than half the time = 4; Very Often = 5; and Always = 6. Scoring is reversed on the following items: 2, 4, 6, 9, 10, 11, 13, and 16. Perceived control scores can range from 16 to 96.

Reprinted with permission of the author.

Mentoring

Questionnaire for Beginning Teachers
Questionnaire for Mentor Teachers

Reiman, A.J., and R.A. Edelfelt. 1991. The opinions of mentors and beginning teachers. Research Report, North Carolina State University. ERIC ED 329 519.

Comments: The questionnaires were designed to study beginning teachers and their mentors. They were developed to check the influence of long-term mentor training, with a focus on developmental supervision, and to examine the degree to which the intent of the North Carolina Certification Program was being carried out.

Scale Construction: Questionnaire items were created from an earlier study where ideas and themes were explored through interview techniques. Parallel forms of the instrument were developed for the mentor teacher and for the beginning teacher. The questionnaires employed a discrepancy model of investigation and scoring. The items with the largest discrepancy among respondents were critically analyzed. The respondents were instructed to indicate on a four-point scale the degree to which each condition in the questionnaire was operative in their situation.

Sample: Questionnaires were sent to 22 mentor teachers and 16 beginning teachers.

Reference:
School-based mentoring: Untangling the tensions between theory and practice. Research Report 90-7, North Carolina State University.

Questionnaire for Beginning Teachers

1. I have had adequate time to plan.
2. My mentor provided assistance with classroom management.
3. My mentor provided help with instructional concerns.
4. My mentor provided assistance with personal concerns.
5. I received help from the district office on salary and certification questions.
6. My mentor was in my classroom.
7. I was receptive to criticism.
8. Feedback from classroom observations was helpful.
9. My teaching assignment was realistic for a beginner.
10. I discussed all aspects of teaching with my mentor.
11. My mentor helped me keep current professionally.
12. I had opportunities to talk with other novice teachers.
13. I got help from colleagues.
14. I sought feedback from students.
15. There was time to reflect on my teaching.
16. I got adequate clerical support.
17. I found satisfaction in teaching.
18. Professional development opportunities were provided.
19. I have been helped to develop my own teaching style.
20. I followed the textbook in my teaching.
21. I have been helped to develop a repertoire of teaching strategies.
22. I felt a part of the school community.
23. Teaching included mundane duties.
24. The materials I needed for teaching were available.
25. I got help and encouragement from my principal.
26. I was assessed by administration on the Teacher Performance Appraisal Instrument.
27. The climate in my school supported a good learning environment for students.
28. The climate in our school supported a good learning environment for me as a beginning teacher.
29. I have thought that I would have liked to have been involved in the selection of my mentor.
30. I had opportunities to visit and observe exemplary teachers.
31. I had opportunities to read and to review educational research and theory with my mentor.
32. My mentor is empathic.
33. My mentor can describe teaching concepts in a way that is understandable.
34. My mentor has acted on my behalf.
35. I participated in decisions on school policy.
36. Teaching was what I thought it would be.
37. I think I will be teaching five years from now.
38. I felt pressured to teach in certain ways.
39. We used technology to great advantage in our school.
40. There were opportunities to exchange ideas with colleagues.
41. Students were responsive to the way I taught.
42. Motivating students was very difficult.
43. Classroom management was a problem for me.
44. I communicated with parents.
45. Our school functioned in an efficient and productive manner.
46. The rules and requirements in our school were reasonable.

Questionnaire for Mentor Teachers

I have enough time to work with my ICT.
I confer with my ICT.
I make formal observations of my ICT.
I make informal observations of my ICT.
I visit my ICT's classroom.
I consult with my ICT on

> discipline.
> classroom management.
> school routines.
> the content being taught.
> changing the way teachers and students work together.
> finding materials.
> selecting materials.
> making materials.
> developing curriculum.
> skills in questioning.
> cooperative learning.
> personal concerns.

I support my ICT in

> maintaining his or her well being.
> fostering self-evaluation.
> increasing student self-direction.
> and decision making.
> individualizing instruction.
> finding effective ways to group.
> students for learning.

I help my ICT understand

> the community.
> the goals of school.
> different cultures, races, and lifestyles.
> democratic values as they apply in school.
> instructional theory and research.
> dialects and language.
> usage.
> the issues in promotion and retention.
> the initial certification program.
> managing time.
> school policy.
> school district policy.

I assist my ICT with

> identifying student needs.
> identifying student interests.
> motivating students.
> teaching basic skills.
> planning lessons to achieve.

measurable learning outcomes.
working with the high-risk child.
working with exceptional children.
developing critical thinking.
employing democratic values.
fostering problem solving.
helping students help each other.
developing homework assignments.
evaluating student learning.
designing teacher-made tests.
interpreting standardized test scores.
reporting student achievement.
communicating with parents.
relating local issues to the curriculum.
planning professional development.

I challenge my ICT to
be an active listener.
employ positive reinforcement.
analyze his or her teaching.
reflect on teaching.
encourage original expression.
evaluate his or her teaching.
use technology.
use computers.
develop learning centers.
document student learning.
stay current professionally.
promote equal opportunity.

I encourage ICT reflection through
conferences.
journal writing.
audiotaping.
videotaping.

I have been able to use the knowledge and techniques learned in mentor training.
I do demonstration teaching.
I use developmental theory in my work with my ICT.
I use the research of Bruce Joyce in my work with my ICT.
I vary the amount of structure employed in working with my ICT.

Scoring: Scoring is identical for both questionnaires. Never or hardly ever = 1; Sometimes = 2; Frequently = 3; and Always or almost always = 4.

Reprinted with permission of the authors. (© Reiman and Edelfelt, 1990. Questionnaire for Beginning Teachers and Questionnaire for Mentor Teachers.)

Mentoring Function Scales

Tepper, K., et al. 1996. Latent structure of Mentoring Function Scales. *Educational and Psychological Measurement* 56:848-857.

Comments: The 16-item MFS consists of eight items that assess psychosocial mentoring functions and eight items that assess career-related mentoring functions.

Sample: The results of five samples are reported. Samples 1 and 2 were part of Tepper et al.'s (1993) study. Sample 1 consisted of 117 employees from a financial organization. Sample 2 consisted of 259 employees from banks, insurance, health, manufacturing, and educational organizations. Sample 3 consisted of 82 employees from a company that managed seafood restaurants. Sample 4 consisted of 65 employees from a soft drink manufacturer. Sample 5 consisted of 45 employees from an accounting and finance department.

Factor Structure: An oblique rotation using the total sample of 568 employees confirmed the original two factors: psychosocial mentoring functions (1, 3, 5, 7, 9, 11, 13, and 15); and career-related mentoring functions (2, 4, 6, 8, 10, 12, 14, and 16).

Data Analysis: Skewness and kurtosis for the 16 items are presented as well as the results of the factor analysis.

References:
Dreher, G.F., and R.A. Ash. 1990. A comparative study of mentoring among men and women in managerial, professional, and technical positions. *Journal of Applied Psychology* 75:539-546.

Noe, R. 1988. An investigation of the determinants of successful assigned mentoring relationships. *Personnel Psychology* 41:457-479.

Tepper, B.J. 1995. Upward maintenance tactics used in supervisory mentoring and nonmentoring relationships. *Academy of Management Journal* 38:1191-1205.

Tepper, B.J., et al. 1993. Strength of subordinates' upward influence tactics and gender congruency effects. *Journal of Applied Social Psychology* 23:1903-1919.

Mentoring Function Scales

1. Encouraged you to try new ways of behaving on the job.
2. Assigned responsibilities to you that have increased your contact with people who will judge your potential for future advancement.
3. Discussed your questions or concerns regarding feelings of competence, commitment to advancement, relationships with peers and supervisors or work/family conflicts.
4. Reduced unnecessary risks that could have threatened your opportunities for promotion.
5. Served as a role model.
6. Helped you meet new colleagues.
7. Demonstrated good listening skills in your conversations.
8. Given you assignments or tasks that have prepared you for higher positions.
9. Conveyed feelings of respect for you as an individual.
10. Helped you finish assignments or tasks or meet deadlines that otherwise would have been difficult to complete.
11. Encouraged you to talk openly about anxieties and fears that detract from your work.
12. Encouraged you to prepare for advancement.
13. Shared personal experiences as an alternative perspective to your problems.
14. Given you assignments that present opportunities to learn new skills.
15. Displayed attitudes and values similar to your own.
16. Given you assignments that have increased your contact with higher level managers.

Scoring: 5 = to a very large extent; 4 = to a large extent; 3 = to some extent; 2 = to a slight extent; and 1 = not at all.

Reprinted with permission of the author.

Morale

Purdue Teacher Opinionnaire

Bentley, R.R., and A.M. Rempel. 1970. *Purdue Teacher Opinionnaire*. Lafayette, IN: Purdue Research Foundation, Purdue University.

Comments: The 100-item PTO not only provides a total score that indicates a general level of teacher morale, but also ten subscale scores that provide meaningful information about the various components of teacher morale. The PTO is the most frequently cited instrument to measure morale.

Scale Construction: Originally, the 145-item PTO contained items in eight areas: teaching as an occupation; relationships with students; relationships with other teachers; administrative policies and procedures; relationships with community; curriculum factors; working conditions; and economic factors. KR reliability coefficients ranged from 0.79 to 0.98, with an overall reliability coefficient of 0.96.

Sample: The original sample of 3,023 consisted of high school teachers from 60 schools in Indiana (stratified random sample) and 16 schools in Oregon (eastern part of the state).

Reliability: The following test-retest correlations are reported: 0.88 (teacher rapport with principal); 0.84 (satisfaction with teaching); 0.80 (rapport among teachers); 0.81 (teacher salary); 0.77 (teacher load); 0.76 (curriculum issues); 0.81 (teacher status); 0.78 (community support of education); 0.80 (school facilities and services); and 0.62 (community pressures). The correlations range from 0.62 (community pressures) to 0.88 (teacher rapport with principal) with a median correlation of 0.87. In addition, norms are available for all school levels.

Validity: The PTO discriminates not only among different schools, but also among the individual teachers within a particular school. In addition, principals completed the PTO the way they thought their faculty would respond. Differences between the median scores for teachers and principals were not significant.

Factor Analysis: Originally, a principal components analysis and an oblique rotation of the extracted factors were performed (570 teachers). The results yielded eight factors. Then, additional factor analytic procedures were conducted to high, middle, and low teacher morale groups. Ten factors were identified instead of eight. The ten factors are: 20 items on teacher rapport with principal (2, 3, 5, 7, 12, 33, 38, 41, 43, 44, 61, 62, 69, 70, 72, 73, 74, 92, 93, and 95); 20 items on satisfaction with teaching (19, 24, 26, 27, 29, 30, 46, 47, 50, 51, 56, 58, 60, 76, 78, 82, 83, 86, 89, and 100); 14 items on rapport among teachers (18, 22, 23, 28, 48, 52, 53, 54, 55, 77, 80, 84, 87, and 90); seven items on teacher salary (4, 9, 32, 36, 39, 65, and 75); 11 items on teacher load (1, 6, 8, 10, 11, 14, 31, 34, 40, 42, and 45); five items on curriculum issues (17, 20, 25, 79, and 88); eight items on teacher status (13, 15, 35, 37, 63, 64, 68, and 71); five items on community support of education (66, 67, 94, 96, and 97); five items on school facilities and services (16, 21, 49, 57, 59); and five items on community pressures (81, 85, 91, 98, and 99). The PTO Supplement contains two new factors: teacher rapport with school board (ten items) and teacher rapport with superintendent (ten items).

Definition of Factors: *Teacher rapport with principal* deals with the teacher's feelings about the principal (his/her professional competency), his/her interest in teachers and their work, his/her ability to communicate, and his/her skill in human relations. *Satisfaction with teaching* deals with teacher relationships with students and feelings of satisfaction with teaching. *Rapport among teachers* deals with a teacher's relationships with other teachers. *Teacher salary* deals with the teacher's feelings about salary and salary policies. *Teacher load* deals with recordkeeping, clerical work, community demands on teacher time, extracurricular load, and keeping up-to-date professionally. *Curriculum issues* deal with teacher reactions to the adequacy of the school program in meeting student needs. *Teacher status* deals with the prestige, security, and benefits of teaching. *Community support of education* deals with the extent to which the community understands and is willing to support a sound educational program. *School facilities and services* deal with the adequacy of facilities, supplies, and equipment as well as the efficiency of the procedures for obtaining materials and services. *Community pressures* deal with community expectations with respect to the teacher's personal standards, his/her participation in outside-school activities, and his/her freedom to discuss controversial issues in the classroom.

Data Analysis: Test-retest correlations, frequency distribution of test-retest correlations for individual schools by factor and total scores, means and standard deviations, interfactor correlations, median scores by factors, percentile distribution of school medians by factors, and percentile distribution of school medians by items are reported.

References:
Carroll, D.F.O. 1992. Teacher morale as related to school leadership behavior. Ed.D. dissertation, East Tennessee State University.

Moyes, W.E. 1992. Career ladder participation and secondary school teacher morale. Ed.D. dissertation, University of Missouri, Columbia.

Pikos, S. 1993. Perceptions of building administrators and teachers at the secondary level on the role of the teacher in shared decision-making. Ed.D. dissertation, Wayne State University.

Podorf, F.M. 1992. The relationship between participatory management and teacher morale at the primary level in selected school districts in the state of New Jersey. Ed.D. dissertation, Seton Hall University, School of Education.

Zbikowski, L.G. 1992. A study of the relationship between elementary principal leadership behavior and teacher morale. Ph.D. dissertation, Michigan State University.

Purdue Teacher Opinionnaire

1. Details, "red tape," and required reports absorb too much of my time.
2. The work of individual faculty members is appreciated and commended by our principal.
3. Teachers feel free to criticize administrative policy at faculty meetings called by our principal.
4. The faculty feels that their salary suggestions are adequately transmitted by the administration to the school board.
5. Our principal shows favoritism in his relations with the teachers in our school.
6. Teachers in this school are expected to do an unreasonable amount of record-keeping and clerical work.
7. My principal makes a real effort to maintain close contact with the faculty.
8. Community demands upon the teacher's time are unreasonable.
9. I am satisfied with the policies under which pay raises are granted.
10. My teaching load is greater than that of most of the other teachers in our school.
11. The extracurricular load of the teachers in our school is unreasonable.
12. Our principal's leadership in faculty meetings challenges and stimulates our professional growth.
13. My teaching position gives me the social status in the community that I desire.
14. The number of hours a teacher must work is unreasonable.
15. Teaching enables me to enjoy many of the material and cultural things I like.
16. My school provides me with adequate classroom supplies and equipment.
17. Our school has a well-balanced curriculum.
18. There is a great deal of griping, arguing, taking sides, and feuding among our teachers.
19. Teaching gives me a great deal of personal satisfaction.
20. The curriculum of our school makes reasonable provision for student individual differences.
21. The procedures for obtaining materials and services are well defined and efficient.
22. Generally, teachers in our school do not take advantage of one another.
23. The teachers in our school cooperate with each other to achieve common, personal, and professional objectives.
24. Teaching enables me to make my greatest contribution to society.
25. The curriculum of our school is in need of major revisions.
26. I love to teach.
27. If I could plan my career again, I would choose teaching.
28. Experienced faculty members accept new and younger members as colleagues.
29. I would recommend teaching as an occupation to students of high scholastic ability.
30. If I could earn as much money in another occupation, I would stop teaching.
31. The school schedule places my classes at a disadvantage.
32. The school tries to follow a generous policy regarding fringe benefits, professional travel, professional study, etc.
33. My principal makes my work easier and more pleasant.
34. Keeping up professionally is too much of a burden.
35. Our community makes its teachers feel as though they are a real part of the community.
36. Salary policies are administered with fairness and justice.
37. Teaching affords me the security I want in a position.
38. My school principal understands and recognizes good teaching procedures.
39. Teachers clearly understand the policies governing salary increases.
40. My classes are used as a "dumping ground" for problem students.
41. The lines and methods of communication between teachers and the principal in our school are well developed and maintained.
42. My teaching load in this school is unreasonable.
43. My principal shows a real interest in my department.
44. Our principal promotes a sense of belonging among the teachers in our school.
45. My heavy teaching load unduly restricts my nonprofessional activities.
46. I find my contacts with students, for the most part, highly satisfying and rewarding.
47. I feel that I am an important part of this school system.

48. The competency of teachers in our school compares favorably with that of teachers in other schools that I know.
49. My school provides the teachers with adequate audiovisual aids and projection equipment.
50. I feel successful and competent in my present position.
51. I enjoy working with student organizations, clubs, and societies.
52. Our teaching staff is congenial to work with.
53. My teaching associates are well prepared for their jobs.
54. Our school faculty has a tendency to form into cliques.
55. The teachers in our school work well together.
56. I am at a disadvantage professionally because other teachers are better prepared to teach than I am.
57. Our school provides adequate clerical services for the teachers.
58. As far as I know, the other teachers think I am a good teacher.
59. Library facilities and resources are adequate for the grade or subject area which I teach.
60. The "stress and strain" resulting from teaching makes teaching undesirable for me.
61. My principal is concerned with the problems of the faculty and handles these problems sympathetically.
62. I do not hesitate to discuss any school problem with my principal.
63. Teaching gives me the prestige I desire.
64. My teaching job enables me to provide a satisfactory standard of living for my family.
65. The salary schedule in our school adequately recognizes teacher competency.
66. Most of the people in this community understand and appreciate good education.
67. In my judgment, this community is a good place to raise a family.
68. This community respects its teachers and treats them like professional persons.
69. My principal acts as though he is interested in me and my problems.
70. My school principal supervises rather than "snoopervises" the teachers in our school.
71. It is difficult for teachers to gain acceptance by the people in this community.
72. Teachers' meetings as now conducted by our principal waste the time and energy of the staff.
73. My principal has a reasonable understanding of the problems connected with my teaching assignment.
74. I feel that my work is judged fairly by my principal.
75. Salaries paid in this school system compare favorably with salaries in other systems with which I am familiar.
76. Most of the actions of students irritate me.
77. The cooperativeness of teachers in our school helps make my work more enjoyable.
78. My students regard me with respect and seem to have confidence in my professional ability.
79. The purposes and objectives of the school cannot be achieved by the present curriculum.
80. The teachers in our school have a desirable influence on the values and attitudes of their students.
81. This community expects its teachers to meet unreasonable personal standards.
82. My students appreciate the help I give them with their school work.
83. To me there is no more challenging work than teaching.
84. Other teachers in our school are appreciative of my work.
85. As a teacher in this community my nonprofessional activities outside of school are unduly restricted.
86. As a teacher, I think I am as competent as most other teachers.
87. The teachers with whom I work have high professional ethics.
88. Our school curriculum does a good job of preparing students to become enlightened and competent citizens.
89. I really enjoy working with my students.
90. The teachers in our school show a great deal of initiative and creativity in their teaching assignments.
91. Teachers in our community feel free to discuss controversial issues in their classes.
92. My principal tries to make me feel comfortable when he visits my classes.
93. My principal makes effective use of the individual teacher's capacity and talent.

94. The people in this community, generally, have a sincere and wholehearted interest in the school system.
95. Teachers feel free to go to the principal about problems of personal and group welfare.
96. This community supports ethical procedures regarding the appointment and reappointment of the teaching staff.
97. This community is willing to support a good program of education.
98. Our community expects the teachers to participate in too many social activities.
99. Community pressures prevent me from doing my best as a teacher.
100. I am well satisfied with my present teaching position.

Scoring: Agree = 4; Probably Agree = 3; Probably Disagree = 2; and Disagree = 1. The scoring is reversed for the following items: 1, 5, 6, 8, 10, 11, 14, 18, 25, 30, 31, 34, 40, 42, 45, 54, 56, 60, 71, 72, 76, 79, 81, 85, 98, and 99.

Reprinted with permission of the Purdue Research Foundation. West Lafayette, IN 47906.

Staff Morale Questionnaire

Smith, K.R. 1971. The validation of a morale measuring instrument. *Journal of Educational Administration* 9:32-37.

Comments: A new 72-item SMQ has been developed for teachers based on the three factors currently identified. The SMQ has been used in Great Britain, Australia, Indonesia, New Zealand, New Guinea, Canada, Israel, and the United States.

Scale Construction: The original 50-item SMQ based on the work of Cattell and Stice examined five areas: group cohesion; tenacity and fortitude; leadership synergy; adventurous striving; and personal reward. Originally, there were ten items in each category. When the 50-item questionnaire was factor analyzed, three factors emerged.

Sample: Teachers from six schools in Florida participated (four schools were identified as high morale schools and two schools were identified as low morale schools). Four hundred and fifteen secondary school teachers in Singapore completed the 24-item SMQ. Seven items from the original 50-item SMQ were added to the 24-item SMQ. Four months later, an additional 305 secondary school teachers in six schools in Singapore completed the SMQ.

Validity: The purpose of the Singapore study was to provide construct validation of the three factors in the SMQ. The factor loadings for the SMQ are provided.

Factor Analysis: A varimax rotation yielded seven factors. The first three factors are labeled as: leadership synergy, cohesive pride, and personal challenge. Ten items loaded on leadership synergy (9, 10, 11, 12, 13, 14, 15, 16, 26, and 29); nine items loaded on cohesive pride (1, 2, 3, 4, 8, 18, 20, 22, and 25), and five items loaded on personal challenge (23, 24, 27, 30, and 31). A second factor analysis was performed with the second sample. A varimax rotation yielded three factors: leadership synergy (1, 2, 7, 8, 9, 10, 11, 12, 13, 14, 18, 21, 22, 24, and 25); cohesive pride (3, 4, 5, 6, 15, and 17); and personal challenge (16, 19, 20, 23, 26, and 27).

Definition of Factors: *Cohesive pride* means that the staff works together to achieve the objectives of the school; it exemplifies cooperation. *Personal challenge* relates to the incentives that are received from job satisfaction; it assesses how a group uses its potentiality for freedom. *Leadership/synergy* describes the energy of the group and is viewed as the most important morale factor.

References:
Smith, K.R. 1976. Morale: A refinement of Stogdill's model. *Journal of Educational Administration* 14:87-93.

Smith, K.R. 1987. One hundred dissertations: A review of the University of New England Morale Research Project. *Journal of Educational Administration* 25:101-125.

Williams, K.W., and T.J. Lane. 1975. Construct validation of a Staff Morale Questionnaire. *Journal of Educational Administration* 13:90-97.

Wong, R.Y.L. 1991. Construct validation of the Staff Morale Questionnaire—The Singapore Scene. *Journal of Educational Administration* 29:71-80.

Staff Morale Questionnaire

1. I would rather teach with my present colleagues than with any other group of teachers in another school.
2. In this school teachers have a sense of belonging and of being needed.
3. The teachers in this school cooperate with each other to achieve common professional objectives.
4. Every teacher on this staff contributes toward the achievement of the school's aims.
5. I would perform my duties equally well and continuously under less pleasant conditions than I have at present.
6. I do school work beyond my normal working hours.
7. When I believe that suggestions made by my immediate supervisor are of little value, I ignore them.
8. Members of this staff can be relied upon to work with steady persistence.
9. On the whole, how much chance is given to you in this school to show what you can really do?
10. How well are you kept informed about what is going on in your school?
11. How do you feel after your immediate supervisor has talked to you about a mistake or weakness in your work?
12. How well are school policies and the reasons for them explained to you?
13. How well do you think your school is run?
14. The principal seems to want everything to depend solely on his judgment.
15. Our principal encourages teachers to participate in the formulating of major school projects.
16. Duties delegated to teachers are clearly and explicitly defined.
17. To what extent do teachers in your school pursue inservice or university courses?
18. In general, teachers on this staff show a great deal of originality and initiative in their teaching.
19. To me there is no more challenging profession than teaching.
20. Teachers in this school display confidence and keenness when called upon for a special effort.
21. In general, I have tried to be innovative in my teaching techniques on my own initiative.
22. Teachers in this school are convinced of the importance of the school's objectives.
23. The teaching I am doing at present gives me a feeling of success and pride.
24. I feel that I am an important part of my present school.
25. There is no complaining, arguing and taking of sides among my colleagues.
26. To what extent do you feel that your colleagues act as a unified staff rather than as a collection of independent individuals?
27. Keeping up to date professionally is too much of a burden.
28. Are you provided with the best possible equipment consistent with your school's aims and finances?
29. Would your immediate supervisor support you and back you up if something went wrong which was not your fault?
30. To what extent would you wish to share in the organization and running of your school?
31. To what extent do past successes in teaching cause you to strive for similar success in the future?

Scoring: A four-point scale is used ranging from 1 to 4.

Reprinted with permission of Kevin B. Smith, PO Box 440, Armidale NSW 2350, Australia.

Motivation/Money

Job Diagnostic Survey

Hackman, J.R., and G.R. Oldham. 1974. Job Diagnostic Survey. Tests in Microfiche, ETS Test Collection, Princeton, NJ.

Comments: The JDS has satisfactory psychometric characteristics. Internal consistency reliabilities are satisfactory and the scale items are able to discriminate. According to the authors, the JDS may be used to determine if motivation and satisfaction are really problematic; is the job low in motivation potential; what specific aspects of the job are causing the difficulty; how ready are the employees for change; and what special problems and opportunities are present in the existing work system? The JDS is the most frequently cited instrument to measure motivation.

Scale Construction: It took over two years to develop and refine the JDS, which is based on the work of Turner and Lawrence (1965) and Hackman and Lawler (1971). According to the theory, which is the basis for the JDS, positive personal and work outcomes are obtained when three critical psychological states exist. The three critical psychological states are created by the existence of five core dimensions. Using the theory, a motivating potential score can be computed. The JDS has been revised three times over the last two years.

Sample: The original sample consisted of 658 blue collar, white collar, and professional workers from seven industrial and service companies representing 62 distinct jobs. Demographic characteristics are included. Overall, over 1,500 employees from 15 distinct companies representing 100 jobs have participated.

Reliability: Internal consistency reliabilities were: 0.71 (skill variety, feedback from the job itself, and job choice format), 0.59 (task identity), 0.66 (task significance and autonomy), 0.78 (feedback from agents), 0.59 (dealing with others), 0.74 (experienced meaningfulness of the work), 0.72 (experienced responsibility for the work), 0.76 (knowledge of results, general satisfaction, and internal work motivation), 0.56 (social satisfaction), 0.79 (supervisory satisfaction), 0.84 (growth satisfaction), and 0.88 (would like format). Median off-diagonal correlations are also reported.

Validity: The substantive validity of the JDS is described in more detail in another report by Hackman and Oldham (1974). Overall, the variables assessed by the JDS relate to each other as predicted by the theory that is the foundation of the survey. In addition, the job dimensions are related to behavioral measures of absenteeism and supervisory ratings of performance effectiveness.

Job Measures: The JDS measures five core dimensions (skill variety, task identity, task significance, autonomy, and feedback from the job itself) and two additional dimensions (feedback from agents and dealing with others). Section one contains seven items, while Section two contains 14 items (two items for each dimension) The JDS also examines three psychological states (experienced meaningfulness of the work, experienced responsibilities for work outcomes, and knowledge of results) and three affective reactions to the job (general satisfaction, internal work motivation, and satisfaction with job security, pay and other compensation, peers and co-workers, supervision, and opportunities

191

for personal growth and development). Section three contains 15 items, while Section five contains ten items. Section four contains 14 items that relate to the five specific types of satisfaction. Finally, the JDS measures individual growth need strength. Section six contains 11 items in a would like format, while Section seven contains 12 items in a job choice format.

Data Analysis: Means, standard deviations, and the results of one-way analyses of variance are reported. Between-job differences are statistically significant for all of the JDS scale scores. Intercorrelations among the JDS scales are presented.

References:

Burk, M.P. 1991. A study of clinical supervision and the job satisfaction of elementary teachers in Oklahoma. Ed.D. dissertation, Oklahoma State University.

Dyer, L.S. 1992. A study relating job satisfaction, personal values, and personal characteristics to teacher absenteeism. Ed.D. dissertation, Oklahoma State University.

Hackman, J.R., and G.R. Oldham. 1974. Motivation through the design of work: Test of a theory (Technical Report No. 6). New Haven, CT: Yale University.

Matheson, R.R. 1992. A comparative study of the perceived job satisfaction of site administrators in San Diego city schools. Ed.D. dissertation, University of San Diego.

Morton, J.T. 1991. A test of the job characteristics model of motivation in public schools. Ed.D. dissertation, Rutgers University, State University of New Jersey, New Brunswick.

Job Diagnostic Survey Section One

1. To what extent does your job require you to *work closely with other people* (either clients, or people in related jobs in your organization)?

    1. Very little; dealing with other people is not at all necessary in doing the job.

    4. Moderately; some dealing with others is necessary.

    7. Very much; dealing with other people is an absolutely essential and crucial part of doing the job.

2. How much *autonomy* is there in your job? That is, to what extent does your job permit you to decide *on your own* how to go about doing the work?

    1. Very little; the job gives me almost no personal "say" about how and when the work is done.

    4. Moderate autonomy; many things are standardized and not under my control, but I can make some decisions about the work.

    7. Very much; the job gives me almost complete responsibility for deciding how and when the work is done.

3. To what extent does your job involve doing a *"whole" and identifiable piece of work*? That is, is the job a complete piece of work that has an obvious beginning and end? Or is it only a small *part* of the overall piece of work, which is finished by other people or by automatic machines?

    1. My job is only a tiny part of the overall piece of work; the results of my activities cannot be seen in the final product or service.

    4. My job is a moderate-sized "chunk" of the overall piece of work; my own contribution can be seen in the final outcome.

    7. My job involves doing the whole piece of work, from start to finish; the results of my activities are easily seen in the final product or service.

4. How much *variety* is there in your job? That is, to what extent does the job require you to do many different things at work, using a variety of your skills and talents?

    1. Very little; the job requires me to do the same routine things over and over again.

    4. Moderate variety.

    7. Very much; the job requires me to do many different things, using a number of different skills and talents.

5. In general, how *significant or important* is your job? That is, are the results of your work likely to significantly affect the lives or well-being of other people?

    1. Not very significant; the outcomes of my work are *not* likely to have important effects on other people.

    4. Moderately significant.

    7. Highly significant; the outcomes of my work can affect other people in very important ways.

6. To what extent do *managers or co-workers* let you know how well you are doing on your job?

    1. Very little; people almost never let me know how well I am doing.

    4. Moderately; sometimes people may give me "feedback"; other times they may not.

    7. Very much; managers or co-workers provide me with almost consistent "feedback" about how well I am doing.

7. To what extent does *doing the job* itself provide you with information about your work performance? That is, does the actual *work itself* provide clues about how well you are doing aside from any "feedback" co-workers or supervisors may provide?
    1. Very little; the job itself is set up so I could work forever without finding out how well I am doing.
    4. Moderately; sometimes doing the job provides "feedback" to me; sometimes it does not.
    7. Very much; the job is set up so that I get almost constant "feedback" as I work about how well I am doing.

Scoring: Various seven-point scales are used for the seven sections of the JDS. Section one of the JDS measures the seven job dimensions. Very Little: the job requires me to do the same routine things over and over again = 1; Moderate Variety = 4; and Very Much: the job requires me to do many different things, using a number of different skills and talents = 7.

Job Diagnostic Survey Section Two

1. The job requires me to use a number of complex or high-level skills.
2. The job requires a lot of cooperative work with other people.
3. The job is arranged so that I do *not* have the chance to do an entire piece of work from beginning to end.
4. Just doing the work required by the job provides many chances for me to figure out how well I am doing.
5. The job is quite simple and repetitive.
6. The job can be done adequately by a person working alone—without talking or checking with other people.
7. The supervisors and co-workers on this job almost *never* give me any "feedback" about how well I am doing in my work.
8. This job is one where a lot of other people can be affected by how well the work gets done.
9. The job denies me any chance to use my personal initiative or judgment in carrying out the work.
10. Supervisors often let me know how well they think I am performing the job.
11. The job provides me the chance to completely finish the pieces of work I begin.
12. The job itself provides very few clues about whether or not I am performing well.
13. The job gives me considerable opportunity for independence and freedom in how I do the work.
14. The job itself is *not* very significant or important in the broader scheme of things.

Scoring: Section two also measures the seven job dimensions. Very Inaccurate = 1; Mostly Inaccurate = 2; Slightly Inaccurate = 3; Uncertain = 4; Slightly Accurate = 5; Mostly Accurate = 6; and Very Accurate = 7.

Job Diagnostic Survey Section Three

1. It's hard, on this job, for me to care very much about whether or not the work gets done right.
2. My opinion of myself goes up when I do this job well.
3. Generally speaking, I am very satisfied with this job.
4. Most of the things I have to do on this job seem useless or trivial.
5. I usually know whether or not my work is satisfactory on this job.
6. I feel a great sense of personal satisfaction when I do this job well.
7. The work I do on this job is very meaningful to me.
8. I feel a very high degree of *personal* responsibility for the work I do on this job.
9. I frequently think of quitting this job.

10. I feel bad and unhappy when I discover that I have performed poorly on this job.
11. I often have trouble figuring out whether I'm doing well or poorly on this job.
12. I feel I should personally take the credit or blame for the results of my work on this job.
13. I am generally satisfied with the kind of work I do on this job.
14. My own feelings generally are *not* affected much one way or the other by how well I do on this job.
15. Whether or not this job gets done right is clearly *my* responsibility.

Scoring: Section three measures general satisfaction and internal work motivation. Disagree Strongly = 1; Disagree = 2; Disagree Slightly = 3; Neutral = 4; Agree Slightly = 5; Agree = 6; and Agree Strongly = 7.

Job Diagnostic Survey Section Four

1. The amount of job security I have.
2. The amount of pay and fringe benefits I receive.
3. The amount of personal growth and development I get in doing my job.
4. The people I talk to and work with on my job.
5. The degree of respect and fair treatment I receive from my boss.
6. The feeling of worthwhile accomplishment I get from doing my job.
7. The chance to get to know other people while on the job.
8. The amount of support and guidance I receive from my supervisor.
9. The degree to which I am fairly paid for what I contribute to this organization.
10. The amount of independent thought and action I can exercise in my job.
11. How secure things look for me in the future in this organization.
12. The chance to help other people while at work.
13. The amount of challenge in my job.
14. The overall quality of the supervision I receive in my work.

Scoring: Section four measures specific satisfactions. Extremely Dissatisfied = 1; Dissatisfied = 2; Slightly Dissatisfied = 3; Neutral = 4; Slightly Satisfied = 5; Satisfied = 6; and Extremely Satisfied = 7.

Job Diagnostic Survey Section Five

1. Most people on this job feel a great sense of personal satisfaction when they do the job well.
2. Most people on this job are very satisfied with the job.
3. Most people on this job feel that the work is useless or trivial.
4. Most people on this job feel a great deal of personal responsibility for the work they do.
5. Most people on this job have a pretty good idea of how well they are performing their job.
6. Most people on this job find the work very meaningful.
7. Most people on this job feel that whether or not the job gets done right is clearly their own responsibility.
8. People on this job often think of quitting.
9. Most people on this job feel bad or unhappy when they find that they have performed the work poorly.
10. Most people on this job have trouble figuring out whether they are doing a good or a bad job.

Scoring: Section five measures the three psychological states as well as general satisfaction and internal work motivation. It also measures general satisfaction and internal work motivation. Disagree Strongly = 1; Disagree = 2; Disagree Slightly = 3; Neutral = 4; Agree Slightly = 5; Agree = 6; and Agree Strongly = 7.

Job Diagnostic Survey Section Six

1.   High respect and fair treatment from my supervisor.
2.   Stimulating and challenging work.
3.   Chances to exercise independent thought and action in my job.
4.   Great job security.
5.   Very friendly co-workers.
6.   Opportunities to learn new things from my work.
7.   High salary and good fringe benefits.
8.   Opportunities to be creative and imaginative in my work.
9.   Quick promotions.
10.   Opportunities for personal growth and development in my job.
11.   A sense of worthwhile accomplishment in my work.

Scoring: Section six measures individual growth need strength. Would like having this only a moderate amount (or less) = 4; Would like having this very much = 7; and Would like having this extremely much = 10.

Job Diagnostic Survey Section Seven

1.   a. A job where the pay is very good.
     b. A job where there is considerable opportunity to be creative and innovative.

2.   a. A job where you are often required to make important decisions.
     b. A job with many pleasant people to work with.

3.   a. A job in which greater responsibility is given to those who do the best work.
     b. A job in which greater responsibility is given to loyal employees who have the most seniority.

4.   a. A job in an organization which is in financial trouble—and might have to close down within the year.
     b. A job in which you are not allowed to have any say whatever in how your work is scheduled, or in the procedures to be used in carrying it out.

5.   a. A very routine job.
     b. A job where your co-workers are not very friendly.

6.   a. A job with a supervisor who is often very critical of you and your work in front of other people.
     b. A job which prevents you from using a number of skills that you worked hard to develop.

7.   a. A job with a supervisor who respects you and treats you fairly.
     b. A job which provides constant opportunities for you to learn new and interesting things.

8. a. A job where there is a real chance you could be laid off.
    b. A job with very little chance to do challenging work.

9. a. A job in which there is a real chance for you to develop new skills and advance in the organization.
    b. A job which provides lots of vacation time and an excellent fringe benefit package.

10. a. A job with little freedom and independence to do your work in the way you think best.
    b. A job where the working conditions are poor.

11. a. A job with very satisfying team-work.
    b. A job which allows you to use your skills and abilities to the fullest extent.

12. a. A job which offers little or no challenge.
    b. A job which requires you to be completely isolated from co-workers.

Scoring: Section seven measures individual growth need strength. Strongly Prefer A = 1; Slightly Prefer A = 2; Neutral = 3; Slightly Prefer B = 4; and Strongly Prefer B = 5. A scoring key for the JDS is provided. In addition, a short form of the JDS is available.

Reprinted with permission of the author.

Teacher Motivation Diagnostic Questionnaire

Matthews, K.M., and C.T. Holmes. 1982. A method for assessing teacher motivation. *NASSP Bulletin* 66:22-28.

Comments: The 16-item TMDQ assesses the following four areas related to teacher motivation: attitude toward the principal (2, 6, 11, and 15), future utility (3, 7, 10, and 14), principal's expectations (1, 5, 12, and 16), and self-concept of ability (4, 8, 9, and 13). Each area contains four questions.

Reliability: Reliability estimates are provided in a study conducted by Matthews and Holmes (1982). Norms for the state of Georgia are presented in a study by Norton (1992). National norms are reported in a study by McDonough (1992).

Operational Definitions: *Attitude toward principal* is defined as the effective orientation of teachers toward their principals. *Future utility* is defined as the beliefs of teachers about the benefits to them personally of improving student achievement. *Principal's expectations* are defined as the beliefs of teachers about the expectations of their principals for improved student achievement. *Self-concept of ability* is defined as the beliefs of teachers about the probability that the academic achievement of their students could be improved.

Validity: Evidence of face validity was established by the teachers who responded to the questionnaire. Convergent construct validity was established by correlating the four areas of the TMDQ with a section of the Purdue Teacher Opinionaire.

References:
Callaway, C.A. 1994. The validity of the Teacher Motivation Diagnostic Questionnaire. Ed.D. dissertation, University of Georgia.

McDonough, M.L.B. 1992. Norms of the Teacher Motivation Diagnostic Questionnaire. Ed.D. dissertation, University of Georgia.

McNeely, C.A. 1996. Student achievement and teacher motivation in elementary schools. Ed.D. dissertation, University of Georgia.

Newman, P.P. 1993. A comparison of teachers' beliefs about principals' expectations and students' beliefs about teachers' expectations for improved student achievement. Ed.D. dissertation, University of Georgia.

Norton, N.B. 1992. Georgia norms for the Teacher Motivation Diagnostic Questionnaire. Ed.D. dissertation, University of Georgia.

Teacher Motivation Diagnostic Questionnaire

1. How much does your principal want test scores to improve?
2. How much do you want to please your principal?
3. How much would higher student achievement help you?
4. How much higher could your students' test scores be?
5. How much does your principal expect test scores to improve?
6. How much do you want to make your principal happy?
7. How much would higher achievement be to your advantage?
8. How good are you at helping students raise test scores?
9. How much could your students' achievement be raised?
10. How much would you benefit from higher achievement?
11. How much does your principal try to please you?
12. How important are high test scores to your principal?
13. How good could you be at improving students' achievement?
14. How much good would higher test scores do you?
15. How much do you like the way your principal works with you?
16. How much does your principal want higher test scores?

Scoring: The following semantic differential scoring technique is utilized: for items 1-2 (strong to weak) and it is reversed (weak to strong) for items 6 and 16; for items 3 and 7 (small to large) and it is reversed (large to small) for items 5, 10, 14, and 15; for item 4 (high to low) and it is reversed (low to high) for items 9, 11, and 12; and for item 8 (bad to good) and it is reversed (good to bad) for item 13.

Reprinted with permission of the author. (© Kenneth M. Matthews, 1985.)

Educational Works Components Study

Miskel, C.G., and L.E. Heller. 1973. The Educational Work Components Study: An adapted set of measures for work motivation. *Journal of Experimental Education* 42:45-50.

Comments: The Work Components Study was developed by Borgatta (1967) for industrial settings. Miskel and Heller modified the WCS for public schools. The theoretical foundation for the WCS is the two-factor theory of motivation (Herzberg, et al., 1959). The 56-item EWCS contains six factors.

Sample: The sample of 745 consisted of 153 seniors and 42 graduate students in a school of education as well as 118 administrators and 432 teachers from three public school districts. A stratified random sampling procedure was used.

Reliability: Alpha coefficients (Cronbach) for the WCS ranged from 0.68 to 0.83. For school personnel, alpha coefficients for the EWCS ranged from 0.73 to 0.83. The estimates of internal consistency were 0.80 (potential for personal challenge and development), 0.73 (competitiveness desirability), 0.79 (tolerance for work pressure), 0.81 (conservative security), 0.82 (willingness to seek reward in spite of uncertainty vs. avoidance), and 0.83 (surround concern).

Validity: Factor analysis was undertaken to determine the factorial stability of the EWCS.

Factor Analysis: Varimax orthogonal and maxplane oblique R-factor analysis procedures were performed, yielding six factors. The six factors are: eight items on potential for personal challenge and development (13, 24, 31, 34, 39, 42, 45, and 56); seven items on competitiveness desirability and reward of success (3, 11, 21, 35, 37, 49, and 52); nine items on tolerance for work pressure (7, 12, 18, 22, 27, 28, 43, 48, and 50); 11 items on conservative security (2, 10, 14, 15, 20, 26, 33, 36, 41, 47, and 54); ten items on willingness to seek reward in spite of uncertainty vs. avoidance of uncertainty (1, 4, 6, 9, 19, 25, 32, 40, 46, and 53); and 11 items on surround concern (5, 8, 16, 17, 23, 29, 30, 38, 44, 51, and 55).

Definition of Factors: Potential for personal challenge and development measures the desirability of a job that provides for creativity, responsibility, and measures personal ability. Competitiveness desirability and reward of success measure job situations where pay is based on merit, competition is keen, and accomplishment is emphasized. Tolerance for work pressure measures job situations where the work load may be excessive and the individual may have to take work home. Conservative security measures whether or not the person plays it safe and has job security. Willingness to seek reward in spite of uncertainty vs. avoidance of uncertainty measures the person's willingness to do interesting work although the person could lose his/her position. Surround concern measures the individual's concern for hygiene factors.

References:
Borgatta, E.F., et al. 1968. The Work Components Study: A revised set of measures for work motivation. *Multivariate Behavioral Research* 3:403-414.

Dunton, D.D. 1983. A study of demographic characteristics and stated attitudes towards work of new and re-entry teachers in selected Illinois districts. Ed.D. dissertation, University of Illinois, Urbana-Champaign.

Fuqua, A.B. 1983. Professional attractiveness, inside sponsorship, and perceived paternalism as predictors of upward mobility of public school superintendents. Ed.D. dissertation, Virginia Polytechnic Institute and State University.

Hatley, P.R. 1991. Work motivation and job satisfaction of principals and assistant principals in Missouri public high schools. Ed.D. dissertation, University of Missouri, Columbia.

Miskel, C. 1977. Principals' attitudes toward work and co-workers, situational factors, perceived effectiveness and innovation effort. *Educational Administration Quarterly* 13:51-70.

Educational Work Components Study Questionnaire

1. I could get fired easily, but the work would be very interesting.
2. The emphasis would be on carrying out clearly outlined school district policies.
3. Salary increases would be strictly a matter of how much you accomplished for the school district.
4. I could not be sure I could keep my job as long as I want it.
5. The lighting is good.
6. The school district is not stable.
7. Trouble might come up that I would have to take care of myself, even outside regular hours.
8. The community has good recreational facilities.
9. The school district has in the recent past been having a hard time holding its position.
10. The job is managing a small group of people doing routine jobs.
11. The school district is known to be involved in heavy competition.
12. The work might be excessive sometimes.
13. There is opportunity for creative work.
14. The work would be routine, but would not be hard to do.
15. I would work as a member of a more-or-less permanent group.
16. The climate would be pleasant.
17. The community would be a wonderful place to raise a family.
18. The schedule of hours might have to be flexible in response to the amount of work.
19. The work might run out, but it would be extremely interesting while it lasted.
20. The pay is not too high, but the job is secure.
21. Persons are supposed to "get the boot" if they don't make good and keep making good.
22. I might sometimes have to take work home with me.
23. The physical working conditions would be attractive.
24. I would have a chance to really accomplish something, even if others wouldn't know about it.
25. I could get fired easily.
26. The work is routine, but the initial salary is high.
27. The work might build up "pressures" on me.
28. The nature of the job changes because the school district changes.
29. The fringe benefits are very good.
30. The ventilation is modern.
31. There would be emphasis on individual ability.
32. There is little permanency of positions.
33. I would be under civil service.
34. The school district is located in a university center and would encourage further specialized work.

35.   There are opportunities to earn bonuses.
36.   Promotions come automatically.
37.   Competition would be open and encouraged.
38.   The community would have a good social and cultural life.
39.   I would have a chance to further my formal education.
40.   I could get fired easily, but the rewards would be high.
41.   The work is routine, but highly respected in the community.
42.   I would always have a chance to learn something new.
43.   There might occasionally be some physical danger.
44.   The supervisors are nice people.
45.   The work itself keeps changing and I need to change to keep up with it.
46.   The job is insecure.
47.   The salary increases are regularly scheduled.
48.   The work might come in big pushes.
49.   There is emphasis on the actual production record.
50.   I might be on call when there is pressure to get jobs done.
51.   The retirement plan is good.
52.   Salary increases would be a matter of how much effort you put in.
53.   Rewards are high, and the work interesting, but if one loses his job it is very difficult to get another one.
54.   There would be emphasis on satisfying superiors by carrying out school policy.
55.   I would have nice people for co-workers.
56.   There would be emphasis on originality.

Scoring: Respondents are asked "How desirable would you consider each of the following items in a job for you? A job in which..." Extremely Undesirable. Would never take the job = 1. Undesirable. Would avoid the job = 2. Neither Desirable or Undesirable = 3. Desirable. Would favor the job = 4. Extremely Desirable. Would favor job greatly = 5.

Reprinted with permission of the author.

Money Ethic Scale

Tang, T.L.P. 1990. The meaning of money revisited: Workers' view. Paper presented at the Southwestern Psychological Association. ERIC ED 318 984.

Comments: The original MES consisted of 50 items. There are several versions of the MES. The version referred to in this description has 30 items. Other versions contain six, 12, and 15 items.

Sample: The original sample consisted of 249 employees who were students and/or faculty from a state university in Tennessee who worked in schools, banks, churches, and other organizations.

Reliability: The Cronbach alpha for the six factors were: 0.81 (good); 0.69 (evil); 0.70 (achievement); 0.68 (respect/self esteem); 0.72 (budget); and 0.71 (freedom/power). Test-retest reliability over a four-week interval with 50 employees was: 0.67 (good); 0.56 (evil); 0.61 (achievement); 0.63 (respect/self esteem); 0.65 (budget); and 0.83 (freedom/power).

Validity: The author comments that additional research is necessary to establish construct validity.

Factor Structure: A principal components factor analysis yielded six factors that accounted for 42.8 percent of the variance. The six factors are: good (nine items), evil (six items), achievement (four items), respect/self esteem (four items), budget (three items), and freedom/power (four items).

Data Analysis: Means, standard deviations, and correlations of the MES and the nomological network (demographic variables, personality variables, the Protestant Ethic, the Leisure Ethic Scale, the JDI, and others) of the MES are reported.

References:
Campion, M.A. 1991. Meaning and measurement of turnover: Comparison of alternative measures and recommendations for research. *Journal of Applied Psychology* 76:199-212.

Furnham, A. 1996. Attitudinal correlates and demographic predictors of monetary beliefs and behaviors. *Journal of Organizational Behavior* 17:375-388.

Tang, T.L.P. 1995. The development of a short Money Ethic Scale: Attitudes toward money and pay satisfaction revisited. *Personality and Individual Differences* 19:809-817.

Tang, T.L.P., and P.R. Gilbert. 1995. Attitudes toward money as related to intrinsic and extrinsic job satisfaction, stress and work-related attitudes. *Personality and Individual Differences* 19:327-332.

Tang, T.L.P., and R. Luna-Arocas. 1997. Money as a motivator and the endorsement of the money ethic among university faculty in the USA and Spain: The development of a new Money Ethic Scale. Paper presented at the International Association for Research in Economic Psychology.

Money Ethic Scale

1. Money is an important factor in the lives of all of us.
2. Money is good.
3. Money can buy everything.
4. Money is evil.
5. Money represents one's achievement.
6. Money in the bank is a sign of security.
7. Money is a symbol of success.
8. Money is the most important thing (goal) in my life.
9. Money gives you autonomy and freedom.
10. Money can bring you many friends.
11. Money is attractive.
12. Money is the root of all evil.
13. Money is important.
14. Money is useless.
15. Money makes people respect you in the community.
16. Money spent is money lost (wasted).
17. Money is valuable.
18. Money will help you express your competence and abilities.
19. Money can buy you luxuries.
20. Money can give you the opportunity to be what you want to be.
21. Money means power.
22. Money is honorable.
23. Money is shameful.
24. Money does not grow on trees.
25. A penny saved is a penny earned.
26. I pay my bills immediately in order to avoid interest or penalties.
27. I think that it is very important to save some money.
28. I value money very highly.
29. I use my money very carefully.
30. I budget my money very well.

Scoring: A seven-point Likert type scale has the following anchors: disagree strongly = 1; neutral = 4; and agree strongly = 7.

Reprinted with permission of the author. (Tang, T.LP. 1990. The meaning of money revisited: Workers' view. ERIC ED 318 984.)

Work Domain Goal Orientation Instrument

VandeWalle, D. 1997. Development and validation of a Work Domain Goal Orientation Instrument. *Educational and Psychological Measurement* 57:995-1015.

Comments: The 16-item instrument measures the goal orientation of adults. An excellent summary of goal orientation instruments is included.

Scale Construction: Sample A completed the original pilot study that consisted of 50 items. Then based on the comments of focus groups and statistical analyses (reliability and exploratory factor analyses), Sample B completed the revised instrument. Factor analytic procedures were conducted and reliability estimates were obtained for Sample C. Test-retest reliability procedures were conducted for Sample D.

Sample: Four samples of volunteers were used. Sample A consisted of 66 college students from an undergraduate course in management. Sample B consisted of 198 college students from five sections of undergraduate courses in management. Sample C consisted of 239 community college students from 12 sections of courses in psychology and business management. Sample D consisted of 53 community college students from four sections of introductory courses in accounting.

Reliability: Reliability estimates (Cronbach alpha) for Sample C produced the following results for the three dimensions: 0.89 for learning; 0.85 for prove; and 0.88 for avoid. Test-retest reliability over three months were: 0.66 for learning; 0.60 for prove; and 0.57 for avoid.

Validity: Face validity was established through a panel of faculty and doctoral students in the area of management who reviewed the original 50 items based on the operational definitions of three goal orientations: learning, prove, and avoid. A principal components factor analysis was performed (Sample B). It yielded three factors: the learning scale (items 1 through 6); the prove scale (items 8 through 11); and the avoid scale (items 12 through 16). Additional reliability tests were performed and items 1 and 16 were deleted. The 13-item instrument (Sample B) was cross-validated with Sample C. An additional study was conducted to establish the construct validity of the instrument as well as its predictive validity.

Data Analysis: The results of the confirmatory factor analysis are presented (goodness-of-fit values for measurement models). In addition, the results of a hypothesized nomological network for goal orientation and correlations of goal orientations scales with other constructs are reported.

References:
Button, S., J. Mathieu, and D. Zajac. 1996. Goal orientation in organizational behavior research: A conceptual and empirical foundation. *Organizational Behavior and Human Decision Processes* 67:26-48.

Dweck, C.S., and E.L. Leggett. 1988. A social-cognitive approach to motivation and personality. *Psychological Review* 95:256-273.

Helmreich, R.L., and J.T. Spence. 1978. The Work and Family Orientation Questionnaire: An objective instrument to assess components of achievement motivation and attitudes toward family and career. *JSAS Catalog of Selected Documents in Psychology* 8:35.

Leary, M.R. 1983. A brief version of the Fear of Negative Evaluation Scale. *Personality and Social Psychology Bulletin* 9:371-376.

Schwab, D.P. 1980. Construct validity in organizational behavior. In B. Staw and L.L. Cummings (eds.), *Research in organizational behavior*. Greenwich, CT: JAI.

Work Domain Goal Orientation Instrument

1. I often read materials related to my work to improve my ability.
2. I am willing to select a challenging work assignment that I can learn a lot from.
3. I often look for opportunities to develop new skills and knowledge.
4. I enjoy challenging and difficult tasks at work where I'll learn new skills.
5. For me, development of my work ability is important enough to take risks.
6. I prefer to work in situations that require a high level of ability and talent.
7. I would rather prove my ability on a task that I can do well at than to try a new task.
8. I'm concerned with showing that I can perform better than my coworkers.
9. I try to figure out what it takes to prove my ability to others at work.
10. I enjoy it when others at work are aware of how well I'm doing.
11. I prefer to work on projects where I can prove my ability to others.
12. I would avoid taking on a new task if there was a chance that I would appear rather incompetent to others.
13. Avoiding a show of low ability is more important to me than learning a new skill.
14. I'm concerned about taking on a task at work if my performance would reveal that I had low ability.
15. I prefer to avoid situations at work where I might perform poorly.
16. When I don't understand something at work, I prefer to avoid asking what might appear to others to be "dumb questions" that I should know the answer to already.

Scoring: Strongly Agree = 6; Agree = 5; Agree Somewhat = 4; Disagree Somewhat = 3; Disagree = 2; Strongly Disagree = 1.

Reprinted with permission of the author.

Needs

Higher Order Need Strength Measure B

Hackman, J.R., and G.R. Oldham. 1974. *The Job Diagnostic Survey: An instrument for the diagnosis of jobs and the evaluation of job redesign projects.* New Haven, CT: Yale University, Department of Administrative Sciences, Technical Report No. 4.

Comments: This 12-item measure, part of the Job Diagnostic Survey (Section seven), assesses a worker's interest in getting "growth satisfaction" from work. Higher order needs include: participation in decision-making, the use of a variety of valued skills and abilities, freedom and independence, challenge, expression of creativity, and the opportunity for learning. Lower order needs include: high pay, fringe benefits, job security, friendly co-workers, and considerate supervision. Participants are asked to select between growth needs and other needs.

Scale Construction: See description of the Job Diagnostic Survey.

Sample: Overall, more than 1,500 people from 100 different jobs in 15 companies were surveyed. The respondents included blue-collar, white-collar, and professional workers.

Reliability: Internal consistency reliability for the "would like" format was 0.88 and 0.71 for the job choice format.

Validity: See description of the Job Diagnostic Survey.

Data Analysis: Means and variances of JDS scores for growth need strength are presented.

References:
Cameron, G.J. 1984. The effects of clinical and traditional supervision methods on the satisfaction levels of higher and lower-order need teachers. Ed.D. dissertation, University of San Diego.

Dunham, R.B. 1976. The measurement and dimensionality of job characteristics. *Journal of Applied Psychology* 61:404-409.

Katz, R. 1978. Job longevity as a situational factor in job satisfaction. *Administrative Science Quarterly* 23:204-223.

Pastor, M.C., and D.A. Erlandson. 1982. A study of higher order need strength and job satisfaction in secondary public school teachers. *Journal of Educational Administration* 20:172-183.

Higher Order Need Strength Measure B

1.   a. A job where the pay is very good.
        b. A job where there is considerable opportunity to be creative and innovative.

2.   a. A job where you are often required to make important decisions.
        b. A job with many pleasant people to work with.

3.   a. A job in which greater responsibility is given to those who do the best work.
        b. A job in which greater responsibility is given to loyal employees who have the most seniority.

4.   a. A job in an organization which is in financial trouble—and might have to close down within the year.
        b. A job in which you are not allowed to have any say whatever in how your work is scheduled, or in the procedures to be used in carrying it out.

5.   a. A very routine job.
        b. A job where your co-workers are not very friendly.

6.   a. A job with a supervisor who is often very critical of you and your work in front of other people.
        b. A job which prevents you from using a number of skills that you worked hard to develop.

7.   a. A job with a supervisor who respects you and treats you fairly.
        b. A job which provides constant opportunities for you to learn new and interesting things.

8.   a. A job where there is a real chance you could be laid off.
        b. A job with very little chance to do challenging work.

9.   a. A job in which there is a real chance for you to develop new skills and advance in the organization.
        b. A job which provides lots of vacation time and an excellent fringe benefit package.

10.   a. A job with little freedom and independence to do your work in the way you think best.
        b. A job where the working conditions are poor.

11.   a. A job with very satisfying teamwork.
        b. A job which allows you to use your skills and abilities to the fullest extent.

12.   a. A job which offers little or no challenge.
        b. A job which requires you to be completely isolated from co-workers.

Scoring: Strongly Prefer A = 1; Slightly Prefer A = 2; Neutral = 3; Slightly Prefer B = 4; and Strongly Prefer B = 5. A score over 3.00 signifies a predominance of higher order need choices, while a score under 3.00 signifies a predominance of lower order need choices.

Reprinted with permission of the author.

Management Position Questionnaire

Porter, L.W. 1961. A study of perceived need satisfactions in bottom and middle management jobs. *Journal of Applied Psychology* 45:1-10.

Comments: The MPQ contains 15 management position characteristics that relate to need satisfaction. Overall, these items correspond to Maslow's need hierarchy: security, social, esteem, autonomy, and self-actualization. No items related to physiological needs were included, and two other items related to pay and to the feeling of being-in-the-know were added. The MSQ examines the differences among needs within various levels of management. Several instruments grew out of the MPQ.

Sample: The original sample consisted of 64 bottom-level (lowest level of management in an organization) and 75 middle-level (above the first level of supervision) managers from three organizations. A description of the three organizations is provided.

Data Analysis: Data reflecting the differences between perceived amount of present fulfillment of needs and the amount of fulfillment believed should be available are reported for both bottom-level and middle-level positions. In addition, data reflecting the importance of these needs for both groups are also presented.

References:
Brown, F. 1973. The job satisfaction of administrators within a multi-ethnic setting. Paper presented at American Educational Research Association. ERIC ED 090 654.

Mitchell, V.F., and P. Moudgill. 1976. Measurement of Maslow's need hierarchy. *Organizational Behavior and Human Performance* 16:334-349.

Porter, L.W. 1962. Job attitudes in management: I. perceived deficiencies in need fulfillment as a function of job level. *Journal of Applied Psychology* 46:375-384.

Trusty, F.M., and T.J. Sergiovanni. 1966. Perceived need deficiencies of teachers and administrators: A proposal for restructuring teacher roles. *Educational Administration Quarterly* 2:168-180.

Van Maanen, J. 1975. Police socialization: A longitudinal examination of job attitudes in an urban police department. *Administrative Science Quarterly* 20:207-228.

Management Position Questionnaire

1. The *feeling of security* in my management position
2. The *opportunity*, in my management position, *to give help to other people*
3. The *opportunity to develop close friendships* in my management position
4. The *feeling of self-esteem* a person gets from being in my management position
5. The *prestige* of my management position *inside* the company (that is, the regard received from others in the company)
6. The *prestige* of my management position *outside* the company (that is, the regard received from others not in the company)
7. The *authority* connected with my management position
8. The *opportunity for independent thought and action* in my management position
9. The *opportunity*, in my management position, *for participation in the setting of goals*
10. The *opportunity*, in my management position, *for participation in the determination of methods and procedures*
11. The *opportunity for personal growth and development* in my management position
12. The *feeling of self-fulfillment* a person gets from being in my management position (that is, the feeling of being able to use one's own unique capabilities, realizing one's potentialities)
13. The *feeling of worthwhile accomplishment* in my management position
14. The *pay* for my management position
15. The feeling of *being-in-the-know* in my management position

Scoring: Each item is rated on a seven-point scale ranging from 1 (minimum) to 7 (maximum). Respondents are asked to give three ratings for each item in terms of: How much of the characteristic is there now connected with your management position? How much of the characteristic do you think should be connected with your management position? How important is this position characteristic to you?

Reprinted with permission of the author.

Manifest Needs Questionnaire

Steers, R.M., and D.N. Braunstein. 1976. A behaviorally-based measure of manifest needs in work settings. *Journal of Vocational Behavior* 9:251-266.

Comments: The MNQ, which measures four of Murray's needs, demonstrates evidence of convergent and discriminant validity. The authors cite the following as three limitations of the MNQ: additional organizations need to be surveyed; the MNQ is a research instrument and should not be used to make decisions about selection or placement; and the instrument only measures four needs.

Scale Construction: Items were written for four needs (achievement, affiliation, autonomy, and dominance) based upon the research of Murray (1938). Some items were worded negatively. A panel of judges examined the items for appropriateness, clarity, and content validity. Then, three studies were conducted to validate the MNQ. The first study was a pilot study. The 20-item MNQ contains five statements for each need.

Sample: The original sample consisted of 96 management students who were working in business, government, and education.

Reliability: Alpha coefficients (Cronbach) were 0.66 (achievement), 0.56 (affiliation), 0.61 (autonomy), and 0.83 (dominance). Test-retest reliabilities over a two-week interval with 41 people were 0.72 (achievement), 0.75 (affiliation), 0.77 (autonomy), and 0.86 (dominance).

Validity: The scores on the MNQ were compared with the scores on the Personality Research Form (Jackson, 1967) to establish convergent and discriminant validity. In addition, four independent judges rated 49 participants to establish discriminant validity. The MNQ was also used to predict work group preferences.

Data Analysis: Means, standard deviations, and off-diagonal correlations are reported for the four scales. Point biserial correlations between MNQ scores and eight work group preferences are provided.

References:
Chusmir, L.H. 1988. An update on the internal consistency of the Manifest Needs Questionnaire. *Psychology: A Journal of Human Behavior* 25:14-18.

Chusmir, L.H., and J.N. Hood. 1986. Relationship between Type A behavior pattern and motivational needs. *Psychological Reports* 58:783-794.

Dreher, G.F., and R.R. Mai-Dalton. 1983. A note on the internal consistency of the Manifest Needs Questionnaire. *Journal of Applied Psychology* 68:194-196.

Mowday, R.T., and D.G. Spencer. 1981. The influence of task and personality characteristics on employee turnover and absenteeism incidents. *Academy of Management Journal* 24:634-642.

Steers, R.M., and D.G. Spencer. 1977. The role of achievement motivation in job design. *Journal of Applied Psychology* 62:472-479.

Manifest Needs Questionnaire

1. I do my best work when my job assignments are fairly difficult.
2. When I have a choice, I try to work in a group instead of by myself.
3. In my work assignments, I try to be my own boss.
4. I seek an active role in the leadership of a group.
5. I try very hard to improve on my past performance at work.
6. I pay a good deal of attention to the feelings of others at work.
7. I go my own way at work, regardless of the opinions of others.
8. I avoid trying to influence those around me to see things my way.
9. I take moderate risks and stick my neck out to get ahead at work.
10. I prefer to do my own work and let others do theirs.
11. I disregard rules and regulations that hamper my personal freedom.
12. I find myself organizing and directing the activities of others.
13. I try to avoid any added responsibilities on my job.
14. I express my disagreements with others openly.
15. I consider myself a "team player" at work.
16. I strive to gain more control over the events around me at work.
17. I try to perform better than my co-workers.
18. I find myself talking to those around me about non-business related matters.
19. I try my best to work alone on a job.
20. I strive to be "in command" when I am working in a group.

Scoring: Always, Almost Always, Usually, Sometimes, Seldom, Almost Never, and Never. Scoring is reversed for items 8, 10, 13, 14, and 15.

Reprinted with permission of the author.

Organizational Assessment/Effectiveness

Effective School Function Inventory

Carter, J., and W.B. Michael. 1995. The development and validation of an inventory of effective school function. *Educational and Psychological Measurement* 55:811-817.

Comments: The 39-item inventory examines teachers' perceptions about the effectiveness of various school operations. The works of Miller (1992), Brown (1971), and Stoddard (1992) served as the conceptual basis for the inventory.

Scale Construction: A pilot study using a sample of 101 teachers who were not in the Distinguished Schools Group was conducted. Based on the results of item analyses, teachers' comments, and recommendations from an expert in educational measurement, the inventory was revised Based on the conceptual model, three broad categories were identified: framework for administrative leadership, teacher behaviors associated with significant learning outcomes, and critical commonalities contributing to broad community involvement. Each broad category contained three subcategories.

Sample: The original sample consisted of 124 teachers from 18 schools in California that were part of the Distinguished Schools Group.

Reliability: Coefficients of internal consistency ranged from about 0.60 to 0.75 for the nine subcategories.

Validity: Although there is only modest support for the construct validity of the inventory with the current sample, the use of additional samples within different settings could help to establish its construct validity.

Factor Analysis: Orthogonal varimax rotations yielded four, five, six, seven, and eight factors. Although a six-factor varimax solution was accepted, only the first four factors were easily identifiable. The six factors are: 12 items on supportive-collegial interaction (1, 2, 4, 16, 17, 20, 23, 25, 28, 31, 32, and 35); eight items on cooperative facilitation of goal attainment in the teaching-learning process (8, 10, 21, 22, 26, 27, 30, and 37); seven items on morally oriented leadership (3, 7, 9, 11, 14, 36, and 39); five items on instructional strategy sharing by teachers (6, 15, 18, 19, and 38); four items on teacher readiness for innovation facilitated by leadership and teacher attitude toward instruction (12, 13, 24, and 29); and three items on facilitation of professionalism (5, 33, and 34).

References:
Brown, G.I. 1971. *Human teaching for human learning: An introduction to confluent education.* NY: Viking Press.

Carter, J.W. 1994. The development of a conceptual model for effective school function and the construct validation of an inventory to represent it. Ed.D. dissertation, University of Southern California.

Miller, R. 1992. *What are schools for? Holistic education in American culture*. Brandon, VT: Holistic Education Press.

Mitchell, D.E., and S. Tucker. 1992. Leadership as a way of thinking. *Educational Leadership* 49:30-35.

Stoddard, L. 1992. *Redesigning education: A guide for developing human greatness*. Tucson, AZ: Zephyr Press.

Effective School Function Inventory

1. Once an initiative or curriculum project gets started, the efforts of the principal are sustained by staff and teachers.
2. Teachers are generally motivated to follow through on curriculum projects with little coercion because of the interpersonal leadership of the principal.
3. Improvement strategies tend to change the way things look, but not the way they work.
4. A widely shared philosophy exists at my school.
5. When major curriculum changes are required for improving student outcomes, small, focused efforts rather than large-scale efforts are most effective.
6. Professional standards are a part of the principal's leadership practice.
7. At this school the moral dimension in leadership is a powerful factor as a basis for school leadership practices.
8. Our school is more of a community than an organization.
9. Leadership is an attitude that informs or directs behavior, rather than a set of discrete leadership skills or qualities, whether innate or acquired.
10. My principal's leadership is based on an understanding of how children and adults learn and keep learning and the ability to build communities of learners.
11. My principal believes that leadership should be shared with everyone: teachers, students, parents and community members.
12. There is an important distinction between leadership attitude and leadership skill.
13. Our school leadership is less theory and more successful practice.
14. In my school, leadership behavior focuses on quality rather than quantity outcomes.
15. Teachers who feel good about themselves and their abilities generally are those who experience success with students.
16. In our school there is a comprehensive staff development plan that gives teachers new to the system confidence and validity in their purpose.
17. At our school there is an on-site support mechanism that keeps new teachers from feeling isolated.
18. The most successful approach to learning new teaching strategies is through teacher demonstrations and sharing.
19. Teachers helping one another is the strength of new teacher survival.
20. The principal provides an opportunity for teachers to observe each other in the classroom setting.
21. The role of our principal is to build a shared understanding of the school goals so that the group will take responsibility.
22. Teachers are taught different techniques and strategies to widen their repertoires of teaching skills as a part of the principal's staff development plan.
23. Cooperative learning is widely practiced at my school.
24. There is a direct correlation between the amount of inservice training that new teachers receive and the effectiveness of student learning.
25. Staff development at my site includes theory, demonstration, practice, feedback, and classroom application.
26. Teachers have input into what skills are part of their training plan.
27. The training provided by my school/district is the kind that could be used immediately in the classroom.
28. Implementation in the classroom of many new skills that appear worthwhile have been difficult.

29. If I do not understand and believe in the new approaches, I cannot achieve success by trying them.
30. The strongest feature of this school is a student-centered system that stimulates growth.
31. In this school teachers organize into groups to provide collegial interaction and engage in positive inquiry.
32. Groups in our school meet to share understandings, implement curriculum innovations, and collaboratively plan for school improvement.
33. Study groups contribute toward the professionalism of teachers.
34. Research forms the basis for our current school changes.
35. The principal has strong expectations for students, teachers and himself/herself which are conveyed through frequent communications.
36. Moral standards are part of the principal's leadership practice.
37. A contributing factor to school improvement is a sense of community.
38. An important role of the principal is to cultivate the leadership potential of every single employee.
39. My perception of the test scores in this school is that they have improved over the past three years.

Scoring: Strongly disagree = 1; disagree = 2; agree = 3; and strongly agree = 4.

Reprinted with permission of the author.

School Effectiveness Questionnaire

Detroit Public Schools Research and Evaluation Department. 1990. School Effectiveness Questionnaire, Elementary/Middle School Edition, Fifth Revised Edition. Detroit, MI.

Comments: The SEQ is based on the questionnaire developed by the Connecticut State Education Department to measure school effectiveness. The SEQ has been modified four times. This version of the SEQ has retained five categories from the original questionnaire. Modifications were made based upon the literature on school and instructional effectiveness, items from other school effectiveness questionnaires, and the development of new items specific to the Detroit Public Schools. There is one edition for elementary and middle schools and one edition for high schools.

Categories: The eight effectiveness categories are: school learning climate; clear school mission; instructional leadership; high expectations; effective instruction; frequent monitoring of student progress; home-school relations; and rewards and praise.

Definitions: Definitions/descriptions are provided for each of the eight categories.

Data Analysis: For each category, there is an average score as well as the average percentage of positive responses.

School Effectiveness Questionnaire

1. Teachers and parents are aware of the homework policy in this school.
2. A variety of teaching strategies (e.g., lecture, discussion, cooperative/team learning) are used in classrooms.
3. Vandalism or destruction of school property is *not* a problem.
4. Teachers review and analyze test results to plan instructional program modification.
5. There are few interruptions during class time.
6. The Chapter 1/Article III program curriculum is congruent with the regular school curriculum.
7. Most students are eager and enthusiastic about learning.
8. Students are acknowledged and rewarded for academic improvements and achievements in this school.
9. Teachers believe that they make a difference in improving student achievement.
10. The principal encourages and facilitates staff working together to improve instruction.
11. This school has a strong feeling of, "Let's get things done."
12. Students treat each other with respect.
13. There is an active parent group in this school.
14. Students are offered multiple opportunities to practice new skills in group and individual settings.
15. Daily lessons in classrooms typically follow this sequence: student focus on the intended learning, teacher presentation, guided practice, specific feedback, independent work, and evaluation of achievement.
16. Parent-teacher conferences result in specific plans for home-school cooperation aimed at improving student achievement.
17. Staff spend more time communicating with parents about the good things students do than about the bad.
18. Multiple assessment methods are used to assess student progress (e.g., criterion-referenced tests, work samples, and mastery checklists).
19. Students not achieving identified standards are given additional help until standards are achieved.
20. This school's School Improvement Plan focuses on student learning and achievement as the school's major responsibility.
21. Students receive more praise than criticism.
22. Parents make sure that students complete assigned homework.
23. Special attention is focused on building good continuity across grade levels and programs.
24. Students who achieve identified standards do so regardless of home background.
25. Students receive immediate and specific feedback on homework assignments.
26. Students abide by school rules.
27. The principal uses test results to recommend modifications in classroom instruction.
28. Teachers in this school believe they are responsible for all students mastering basic skills at each grade level.
29. The principal (or other school administrators) makes several formal classroom observations each year.
30. Most homework assigned to students is related to what has already been learned in class.
31. Chapter 1/Article III programs are effective in helping low-achieving students attain reading and mathematics skills.
32. Formal observations by the principal (or other school administrators) are regularly followed by a post-observation conference.

33. The effective teachers in this building receive both praise and recognition from their colleagues.
34. Administrators support teachers in dealing with student discipline matters.
35. This school is a safe and secure place to work.
36. The mission of this school is clearly communicated to staff and parents and serves as a framework for making decisions.
37. Most parents would rate this school as an effective school.
38. The counseling program is effective in modifying student behavior.
39. The principal puts much emphasis on the meaning and use of standardized test results.
40. Students generally believe that school rules are reasonable and appropriate.
41. There are provisions for coordination between teachers in Chapter 1/Article III programs and teachers in regular classrooms.
42. The students in this school are told what objectives they are expected to learn.
43. Generally, discipline is *not* a problem in this school.
44. Low-achieving students usually answer classroom questions as often as other students.
45. The principle is highly visible throughout the school.
46. During parent teacher conferences, there is a focus on student achievement and basic skills mastery.
47. Students and staff take pride in the school and help keep the building and grounds clean and attractive.
48. Teachers believe that a student's home background is not the primary factor that determines individual student achievement.
49. As a regular practice, teachers talk with each other about the academic work of students for whom they share responsibility.
50. Parents actively support the learning objectives of this school.
51. The principal frequently communicates to teachers their responsibilities in relation to student achievement.
52. Parents know and reinforce school rules.
53. The principal actively promotes inservice training for staff.
54. The principal is an important instructional resource person.
55. Many parents are involved in home-school support activities.
56. Low-achieving students receive frequent rewards, praise and/or recognition.
57. There is systematic, regular assessment of students' basic skills in most classrooms.
58. A positive feeling permeates the school.
59. Students are praised for specific behavior immediately after the behavior occurs.
60. Teachers are encouraged to visit other classrooms to observe the other instructional activities of their colleagues.
61. Teachers provide activities that develop student thinking skills.
62. Students' academic work is publicly displayed or featured.
63. All staff in this school clearly understood their responsibility for basic skills achievement.
64. Collaborative school planning and decision making are typical at this school.
65. Students receive immediate and specific feedback on classroom work.
66. Discussions with the principal (or other school administrators) often result in improved instructional practices.
67. During instructional time, students are actively engaged in learning tasks most of the time.
68. The principal emphasizes staff development training and teacher skill building.
69. The principal conducts frequent meetings concerning instruction and student achievement.
70. There is an identified set of objectives or skills that all students are expected to master at each grade level.

71. Students are often given the grades A,B,C, D, or E to describe the quality of their work. Suppose your school was "graded" in the same way. What grade would you give your school?
72. Students are often given the grades A,B,C, D, or E to describe the quality of their work. Suppose the Detroit Public Schools were "graded" in the same way. What grade would you give the Detroit Public School system?

Scoring: Strongly Disagree, Disagree, Undecided or Does Not Apply, Agree, and Strongly Agree.

Reprinted with permission of Linda Leddick, Director, Detroit Public Schools, Office of Research, Evaluation and Assessment.

Quality of School Life Scale

Epstein, J.L., and J.M. McPartland. 1977. Administration and technical manual for the Quality of School Life Scale. The Johns Hopkins University, Baltimore. Mimeo.

Comments: The 27-item QSL is a multidimensional measure of student reactions to school in general, to their classwork, and to their teachers. It is designed for use with students in grades 4-12. It will help teachers, administrators, and researchers measure students' reactions, to describe and monitor the conditions of school life, and to make decisions about the success of school programs.

Scale Construction: The instrument uses multiple choice, true-false, and Likert-type formats, alternately, in order (according to the authors) to minimize response set. Of the 27 items that make up the instrument, 14 items use a true-false response, nine items use multiple choice, and four items use a Likert response.

Sample: The sample consisted of 1,060 elementary students and 3,206 secondary students from one school district in Maryland.

Reliability: Reliability estimates for the total instrument and for the subscales ranged between 0.80 and 0.89 for the various student groups.

Validity: Evidence for concurrent and discriminate validity was obtained from questionnaire items, open-ended written comments, peer and teacher nominations (known group method) and achievement tests. Correlations are provided of the QSL with school performance and participation, family background variables, and educational and occupational plans. In general, students who report high satisfaction with the quality of their school experience are those who are comfortable with the demands and opportunities of the school setting, are industrious and ambitious, have more positive self-evaluations, and receive positive evaluation from teachers and parents.

Factor Analysis: A principal components analysis with a varimax rotation was performed to check the dimensionality among the 27 items. Four interpretable factors emerged. Two of these correspond to the SAT and COM subscales, two other factors divided the TCH subscale into two parts. However, after several statistical tests and comparisons, the TCH subscale was retained as a single dimension.

Definition of Subscales: Three subscales were derived: *Satisfaction with School* (SAT) subscale examines students' general reactions to school. Students who are positive in their evaluation of school life may be more likely to experience feelings of general well-being. *Commitment to Classwork* (COM) subscale deals with the level of student interest in classwork. *Reactions to Teachers* (TCH) subscale examines student evaluations of instructional and personal interactions with teacher. Overall the quality of school experiences may influence student behavior and attitudes.

References:

Epstein, J.L., and J.M. McPartland. 1976. Quality of School Life Scale. Chicago, IL: Riverside Publishing Company.

Epstein, J.L., and J.M. McPartland. 1976. The concept and measurement of the Quality of School Life. *American Educational Research Journal* 13:15-30.

Quality of School Life Scale

Sample Items:

1. I like school very much.
2. Most of the time I do not want to go to school.
3. The school and I are like : Good Friends; Friends; Distant Relatives; Strangers; Enemies.
4. Work in class is just buys work and a waste of time.
5. In class, I often count the minutes till it ends.
6. In my classes I get so interested in an assignment or project that I don't want to stop work. Everyday; quite often; hardly ever; never.
7. The things I get to work on in most of my classes are: Great stuff—really interesting to me; Good stuff—pretty interesting to me; OK—school work is school work; Dull stuff—not very interesting to me; Trash—a total loss for me.
8. I wish I could have the same teachers next year.
9. Most of my teachers want me to do things their way and not my own way.
10. Teachers here have a way with students that makes us like them.
11. Thinking of my teachers this term, I really like: All of them; Most of them; Half of them; One or two of them; None of them.

Scoring: The SAT subscale score is the sum of the points received for items 3, 7, 11, 19, 24; COM subscale is items 1, 5, 9, 13, 15, 17, 20, 22, 23, 25, 27; and TCH subscale is items 2, 4, 6, 8, 10, 12, 14, 16, 18, 21, 26.

Reprinted with permission of the authors. (Scale available from Riverside Publishing Company, 8420 Bryn Mawr Avenue, Chicago, IL 60631.)

Profile of a School
Profile of Organizational Characteristics

Likert, R. 1980. Survey of Organizations. Rensis Likert Associates, Inc. San Diego, CA: University Associates.

Comments: Likert developed three instruments designed to evaluate various aspects of organizations. The three instruments are based on his Systems Four concept of organizational/administrative behavior. System One is characterized as exploitive-authoritative organizational behavior; System Two benevolent authoritative; System Three consultative; and System Four allows for group participation in decision making and organizational activities.

Scale Construction: The *Profile of a School* is a 64-item instrument with parallel forms designed to be used with students, teachers, administrators, central office staff, and school board members. Its greatest value is the ability to compare scores and responses, one-on-one, across all members of a school system concerning their perceptions of the organizational functioning of a school district.

The *Profile of Organizational Characteristics* is a 43-item inventory that covers eight organizational variables: the leadership process used; the character of motivational forces; the character of the communication process; the character of the interaction-influence process; aspects of the decision-making process; the nature of goal setting or ordering; aspects of organizational control; and the performance goals and training practices. This profile is intended to describe the nature of managerial systems used in industrial organizations. Sample items from this instrument are provided below.

Reliability: The testing (technical) manuals associated with each instrument provide ample information on the development of each scale. They also provide reliabilities, validity information, and other psychometric qualities of each scale. All reliability estimates ranged in the low to mid 90s.

References:
Barney, D.G. 1990. An integrative assessment of department head supervisory system-teacher conflict-teacher job satisfaction. Ph.D. dissertation, Marquette University.

Likert, R. 1967. *The human organization.* New York: McGraw Hill.

McGarry, G.T. 1980. Impact of a training program in a state agency. Ed.D. dissertation, Boston University School of Education.

Peoples, P.J. 1990. The relationship among school context factors and leadership style factors of principals of effective and other high schools in Southern California. Ed.D. dissertation, University of Southern California.

Tomlin, M.E. 1988. A study to determine if secondary school teachers trained in "teacher expectations and student achievement" have a different perception of the organizational climate of their schools than teachers not so trained. Ed.D. dissertation, University of Wyoming.

Vizzini, C.T. Jr. 1989. The relationship of role conflict and ambiguity as a function of organizational characteristics: A study of curriculum supervisors in the public schools of North Carolina. Ed.D. dissertation, University of North Carolina, Chapel Hill.

Profile of a School

1. How often is your behavior seen by your students as friendly and supportive?
2. How often do you seek to be friendly and supportive to your students?
3. How much confidence and trust do you have in your students?
4. How much trust and confidence do your students have in you?
5. How much interest do your students feel you have in their success as students?
6. How free do your students feel to talk to you about academic matters such as their work, course content, teaching plans, and methods?
7. How free do your students feel to talk to you about non-academic school matters such as student activities, rules of conduct, and discipline?
8. How often do you seek and use your students' ideas about academic matters?
9. How often do you seek and use your students' ideas about non-academic school matters?
10. How much do your students feel that you are trying to help them with their problems?
11. How much influence do you think students have on academic matters?
12. How much influence do you think students have on non-academic matters?
13. How much influence do you think students should have on academic matters?
14. How much influence do you think students should have on non-academic matters?
15. To what extent are students involved in major decisions affecting them?
16. What is the general attitude of your students concerning class, school or personal matters?
17. How accurate is information given to you by your students concerning class, school, or personal matters?
18. How do students view communications from you?
19. How do students view communications from the principal?
20. How well do you know the problems faced by your students in their school work?
21. What is the character and amount of interaction in your classroom?
22. To what extent do your students help each other when they want to get something done?
23. To what extent do your students look with pleasure on coming to school?
24. To what extent do you look forward to your teaching day?
25. To what extent do your students feel excited about learning?
26. How often do you see your principal's behavior as friendly and supportive?
27. How much confidence and trust does your principal have in you?
28. How much confidence and trust do you have in your principal?
29. How free do you feel to talk to your principal about academic and non-academic school matters?
30. How often do you try to be friendly and supportive to your principal?
31. How often do you try to be friendly and supportive to other teachers?
32. How often are your ideas sought and used by the principal about academic and non-academic school matters?
33. In your job, how often is it worthwhile or a waste of time for you to do your very best?
34. How much influence do you think teachers have on academic and non-academic school matters?
35. How much influence do you think teachers should have on academic and non-academic school matters?
36. How much influence do you think principals have on academic and non-academic school matters?
37. How much influence do you think principals should have on academic and non-academic school matters?

38. How much influence do you think central office staff has on academic and non-academic school matters?
39. How much influence do you think central office staff should have on academic and non-academic school matters?
40. How often are students' ideas sought and used by the principal about academic matters?
41. How often are students' ideas sought and used by the principal about non-academic school matters?
42. How much do you feel that your principal is interested in your success?
43. How often does your principal use group meetings to solve school problems?
44. To what extent does your principal make sure that planning and the setting of priorities are well done?
45. To what extent does your principal try to provide you with the materials and space you need to do your job well?
46. To what extent does your principal give you useful information and ideas?
47. To what extent are you encouraged to be innovative in developing better educational practices and course content?
48. What is your general attitude toward your school?
49. What is the direction of the flow of information about academic and non-academic school matters?
50. How do you view communications from the principal?
51. How accurate is upward communication to the principal?
52. How well does your principal know the problems faced by teachers?
53. What is the character and amount of interaction in your school between the principal and teachers?
54. What is the character and amount of interaction in your school among teachers?
55. In your school, it is "every man for himself" or do principal, teachers, and students work as a team?
56. How are decisions made in your school system?
57. At what level are decisions made about academic matters?
58. To what extent are you involved in major decisions related to your work?
59. How much does your principal try to help you with your problems?
60. How much help do you get from the central staff?
61. To what extent are decision-makers aware of problems, particularly at lower levels?
62. How high are your principal's goals for educational performance?
63. Who holds high performance goals for your school?
64. Who feels responsible for achieving high performance goals in your school?
65. To what extent is there student resistance to high performance goals in your school?

Scoring: A series of descriptive terms is used to define, broadly, four positions along the continuum. For example: Very Little (1 and 2); Some (3 and 4); Considerable (5 and 6); and Very Great (7 and 8).

Reprinted with permission of Jane Gibson Likert.

Profile of Organizational Characteristics

Sample Items:

1. How much confidence and trust is shown in subordinates?
2. How free do they feel to talk to superiors about job?
3. How often are subordinates' ideas sought and used constructively?
4. Is predominant use made of 1 fear, 2 threats, 3 punishment, 4 rewards, 5 involvement?
5. Where is responsibility felt for achieving organization's goals?
6. How much cooperative teamwork exists?
7. What is the usual direction of informational flow?
8. How is downward communication accepted?
9. How accurate is upward communication?
10. How well do superiors know problems faced by subordinates?
11. At what level are decisions made?
12. Are subordinates involved in decisions related to their work?
13. What does the decision-making process contribute to motivation?
14. How are organizational goals established?
15. How much covert resistance to goals is present?
16. How concentrated are review and control functions?
17. Is there an informal organization resisting the formal one?
18. What are cost, productivity and other control data used for?

Scoring: A series of descriptive terms is used to define four positions along the continuum. For example: System 1 (Virtually None); System 2 (Some); System 3 (Substantial amount); and System 4 (A Great Deal).

Reprinted with permission of Jane Gibson Likert.

Position Analysis Questionnaire

Mecham, R.C., et al. 1969. Users manual for the Position Analysis Questionnaire. University Book Store, 360 W. State St., Lafayette, IN 47906.

Comments: According to the authors, the PAQ is a structured job analysis questionnaire that provides quantified information about the nature of jobs. It differs from most checklist instruments in that the items describe job characteristics, or job contexts, which may be found in a wide variety of occupational areas. The instrument generates data that may be applied in employee selection and placement, job evaluation and classification, performance appraisal, determining the similarity of jobs, and the like. The analysis is carried out by numerically rating the degree to which each of 194 job elements (items) applies to the job or position being rated. Based on this rating, it is possible to compare jobs, quantitatively, in terms of similarities, or differences, as to their job dimension profiles.

Reliability: The PAQ has extensive manuals and technical documentation that provide complete and detailed information on the development of the scales and the approach, or application, in utilizing the questionnaire. In addition, complete information is provided on reliability and validity of the scales.

Questionnaire Divisions: The questionnaire is divided into six major divisions. (1) Information input: Where and how does the worker get the information that he uses in performing the job? (2) Mental processes: What reasoning, decision-making, planning, and information processing activities are involved in performing the job? (3) Work output: What physical activities does the worker perform and what tools are required in performing the job? (4) Relationships with other persons: What relationships with other people are required in performing the job? (5) Job Context: In what physical and social contexts is the work performed? (6) Other job characteristics: What activities, conditions, or characteristics other than those described above are relevant to the job?

These six divisions are further divided into sections and subsections. Each is composed of a group of related job elements (items within the questionnaire).

Reference:
Mecham, R.C. 1974. Comparison of job evaluation methods. *Journal of Applied Psychology* 59:633-637.

Position Analysis Questionnaire

Sample Items:

1. Reasoning in problem solving
2. Amount of planning/scheduling
3. Advising
4. Negotiating
5. Persuading
6. Instructing
7. Interviewing
8. Routine information exchange
9. Nonroutine information exchange
10. Public speaking
11. Job-required personal contact
12. Supervision of nonsupervisory personnel
13. Direction of supervisory personnel
14. Coordinates activities
15. Staff functions
16. Supervision received
17. Frustrating situations
18. Strained personal contacts
19. Personal sacrifice
20. Interpersonal conflict situations
21. Non-job-required social contact
22. Updating job knowledge
23. Working under distractions.
24. Recognition
25. Attention to detail
26. Time pressure of situation
27. Following set procedures
28. Repetitive activities

Scoring: Each category contains a six-point rating scale that measures importance to this job. N = Does Not Apply; 1 = Very Minor; 2 = Low; 3 = Average; 4 = High; and 5 = Extreme.

Staff Assessment Questionnaire

Seattle School District and the University of Washington. 1984. The School Self-Assessment Service.

Comments: The 94-item Staff Assessment Questionnaire measures the responses of the staff to the following nine areas: strong leadership, dedicated staff, high expectations, frequent monitoring, early identification, positive learning climate, curriculum continuity, multicultural education, and sex equity. Additional instruments include: School Goals Survey, School Assessment Questionnaire (grades 1-3), Intermediate Student Assessment Questionnaire (grades 4-6), the Secondary Student School Assessment Questionnaire (grades 7-12), and a Parent Survey.

Scale Construction: Instruments were developed based on operational definitions for the 12 characteristics of effective schools. Nine of these characteristics are addressed in the Staff Assessment Questionnaire. The remaining three are: clear goals, which is examined in the School Goals Survey; Communication and Parent/Community, which are studied in the Parent Survey. The surveys were examined by several professional groups including representatives from the Seattle Teachers' Association as well as the Principals' Association of Seattle Schools. A random sample of principals, teachers, students, and parents completed a pilot study.

Sample: The first random group consisted of 125 teachers. The second group consisted of 2,145 teachers from 99 schools. The final group consisted of 2,774 teachers from urban, suburban, and rural school districts.

Reliability: Alpha coefficients are reported for four samples. For the first sample they range from 0.97 (strong leadership) to 0.70 (early identification problems); for the second and third samples the results are almost identical. However, for the fourth sample, although strong leadership still has the highest coefficient (0.92), the lowest coefficient changes to curriculum (0.74). In addition, test-retest reliability with a sample of 32 teachers over a period of two weeks produces a range from 0.91 (frequent monitoring of student progress) to 0.70 (early identification of student learning problems).

Validity: Content validity was established by the construction of the instrument. Predictive validity examined the relationship to student achievement in mathematics and reading.

Data Analysis: Means, standard deviations, and reliability estimates are reported. The results of regression analysis and analysis of variance have been included.

Staff Assessment Questionnaire

1. District-adopted textbooks guide my planning of instruction.
2. Our school provides its students with a strong multiethnic-multicultural education.
3. I teach basically the same content that is taught in other classes at the same grade or same course in my school.
4. Staff members of our school are sensitive to the needs and concern of both sexes.
5. Staff at our school have the same expectations of academic achievement for both female and male students.
6. Criterion-referenced tests are used to assess basic skills throughout the school.
7. The curriculum of our school is multiethnic and multicultural.
8. Student assessment information (such as criterion-referenced tests, skill checklists, etc.) is used regularly to give specific student feedback and plan appropriate instruction.
9. My school has effective programs for students who are in need of remediation.
10. Our school's staff examines instructional materials for ethnic and racial bias.
11. Assemblies and special activities at our school reflect the ethnic and cultural diversity in the community.
12. The principal uses test results to recommend changes in the instructional program.
13. My school has effective procedures for identifying students with special learning needs.
14. The teaching styles in our school are sensitive to the needs and concerns of both sexes.
15. Multiple assessment methods are used to assess student progress in basic skills (e.g. criterion-referenced tests, work samples, mastery checklists, etc.).
16. Teachers in my school frequently assess the progress of students in basic skills.
17. The principal in my school is aware of student progress in relation to instructional objectives.
18. What I teach in my class contributes to the content of the grade or course that follows it.
19. Our school's curriculum helps students view ideas from diverse ethnic perspectives and points of view.
20. Staff members of our school are sensitive to ethnic and cultural differences.
21. My school is responsive to students with special learning needs.
22. Staff review and analyze test results to plan instructional program changes.
23. Students with special learning needs in my class are not receiving the instructional program they need.
24. The teaching styles in our school are sensitive to the ethnic and cultural diversity of our students.
25. District curriculum documents guide my planning of instruction.
26. The atmosphere of our school is responsive to cultural, ethnic, and language differences.
27. Procedures used to motivate students are fair to both sexes.
28. What I teach in my class builds upon the content of the grade or course that precedes it.
29. Bulletin boards and other displays in our school reflect ethnic and cultural pluralism.
30. People in my school are willing to listen to the ideas and feelings of others, even when they disagree.
31. Most students in my school will perform at about the national average in academic achievement.
32. Students cut a lot of classes.
33. No challenge is too tough for our staff.
34. My principal leads formal discussions concerning instruction and student achievement.
35. Many of my students will probably leave school before high school graduation.
36. Most students in my school are capable of mastering grade-level academic objectives.
37. Vandalism is a problem in my school.

38. People in our building seek out training experiences that increase their ability to educate students.
39. Teachers in my school turn to the principal with instructional concerns or problems.
40. Teachers know and treat students as individuals.
41. I would transfer to another school if I could.
42. My principal provides frequent feedback regarding my classroom performance.
43. Teachers in my school generally believe most students are able to master the basic reading/math skills.
44. I expect that most students in my school will perform above the national average in academic achievement.
45. Our staff holds itself to the highest professional standards.
46. My principal assists faculty in interpreting test results.
47. We are committed to working together as a faculty.
48. Nearly all of my students will be at or above grade level by the end of this year.
49. Drug and alcohol abuse are problems in this school.
50. My principal is an effective disciplinarian.
51. People in our building work hard to maintain good relations with parents.
52. Discipline is fair and related to violations of agreed-upon rules.
53. Teachers in other schools would rate my school's level of academic achievement as good.
54. Stealing is a problem in this school.
55. My principal is an important instructional resource in our school.
56. A positive feeling permeates this school.
57. I am satisfied with the variety of extracurricular activities at this school.
58. My principal promotes staff development activities for faculty.
59. My principal communicates clearly to me regarding instructional matters.
60. Teachers and staff members take a real interest in their students' future.
61. Staff in our building have a great deal of trust.
62. My principal is accessible to discuss matters dealing with instruction.
63. My principal encourages the use of different instructional strategies.
64. I enjoy working at this school.
65. Student behavior is generally positive at my school.
66. Most of my students will show at least one year's growth in academic achievement this year.
67. My principal mobilizes support to help achieve academic goals.
68. Discussions with my principal result in improved instructional practice.
69. If a person in the building runs into trouble, someone helps him or her out.
70. The academic ability of students in my school compares favorably with students in other schools.
71. I expect most students in my school will perform below the national average in academic achievement.
72. My principal makes frequent classroom observations.
73. Most of the students in my school will ultimately graduate from high school.
74. My principal is knowledgeable about instructional resources.
75. Students can count on staff members to listen to their side of the story and be fair.
76. The district can count on us to give our best.
77. My principal's evaluation of my performance helps me improve my teaching.
78. Students in my school abide by school rules.
79. My principal is a strong instructional leader.
80. My school building is neat, bright, clean and comfortable.
81. Staff in our school are proud of what they do.
82. My principal is an active participant in staff development.

83. We are ready to learn to do our jobs in a new way if it will meet the needs of students.
84. Staff and students do not view security as an issue in my school.
85. Staff in this school really care about how much students learn.
86. This school makes students enthusiastic about learning.
87. My principal is a "visible presence" in our building to both staff and students.
88. Whatever it takes, people in our building solve problems.
89. I feel there are procedures open to me to go to a higher authority if a decision has been made that seems unfair.
90. My principal uses clearly communicated criteria for judging my performance.
91. My principal provides a clear vision of what our school is all about.
92. The physical condition of my school is generally pleasant and well-kept.
93. Problems in this school are recognized and worked on.
94. People in this building are willing to help out wherever they are needed.

Scoring: Strongly Agree, Agree, Undecided, Disagree, and Strongly Disagree.

Reprinted with permission from Jerry Bamburg, Director, Center for Effective Schools College of Education, University of Washington.

School Quality Satisfaction Survey

Suba, K. 1997. School Quality Satisfaction Survey: Assessing expectation for and satisfaction with quality of education provided by elementary schools. Ph.D. Dissertation, Pennsylvania State University.

Comments: The 44-item survey assesses the opinions of parents, teachers, and administrators regarding the delivery of an excellent quality education. It examines the characteristics of an excellent elementary school and their perceptions about the absence or presence of these characteristics in their current school situation.

Sample: The League for Educational Advancement, which is comprised of a group of seven Pennsylvania school districts, selected the pilot school districts for the sample. Three school districts, representing eight elementary schools, agreed to take part in the study. They represented urban, suburban, and rural districts.

Reliability: The following alpha coefficients were obtained with a pilot study using three elementary schools: parents—excellent school (0.92) and parents—your school (0.92); teacher—excellent school (0.91) and teacher—your school (0.84); and administrators—excellent school (0.93) and administrators—your school (0.84). In addition, alpha coefficients are reported for each of the three groups by category.

Factor Analysis: Although a principal components factor analysis yielded one interpretable factor, school quality satisfaction, the author breaks down the items into the following five categories: physical attributes (1-4); attention to individual needs (5-24); instructional leadership (25-32); community involvement (33-38); and learning outcomes (39-44).

Data Analysis: Aggregated mean scores are reported for each of the 44 items as well as for each of the five categories. In addition, gap analysis provides information about differences among the three groups.

References:
Babakus, E., and W.G. Mangold. 1992. Adapting the SERVQUAL scale to hospital services: Empirical investigation. *HSR: Health Services Research* 26:767-786.

Hartman, W.T. 1994. *TQM goes to school*. University Park, PA: The Center for Total Quality Schools.

Jacobson, L. 1997. PTA issues parent involvement standards for schools. *Education Week* 16:8.

National Institute of Standards and Technology. 1996. The Malcolm Baldrige national quality award: 1996 award criteria. Gaithersburg, MD: United States Department of Commerce Technology Administration.

School Quality Satisfaction Survey

Physical Attributes

1. Schools have modern-looking equipment.
2. The school's physical facilities appear to be safe and in compliance with building code regulations.
3. Teachers and staff are neat in appearance.
4. The school's physical facilities provide a neat and clean educational environment.

Attention to Needs of Individuals

5. The school staff carries out promised actions such as educational activities, by the time agreed upon.
6. The school responds correctly to the needs of a parent or student the first time.
7. Teachers and staff inform students and parents of the date and time of educational activities.
8. Teachers and staff give prompt and accurate information to students and parents.
9. Teachers and staff are respectful with the students.
10. Teachers and staff are respectful with their student's parents.
11. Informational materials associated with the education (such as pamphlets and letters) received by parents are visually appealing, grammatically correct, and factual.
12. The school gives students individual attention.
13. The school gives parents individual attention.
14. The school and school activity hours are convenient for their students.
15. The school and school activity hours are convenient for the parents.
16. The teachers and staff understand the specific needs of their students.
17. The teachers and staff understand the specific needs of parents.
18. The teachers and staff are helpful to their students.
19. The teachers and staff are helpful to parents.
20. Teachers and staff respond to parent questions in a timely manner.
21. Students feel safe in their interactions with the school staff.
22. Parents feel safe in their interactions with the school staff.
23. When a student has a problem, the school shows a sincere interest in solving it.
24. When a parent has a problem, the school shows a sincere interest in solving it.

Instructional Leadership

25. The school has a curriculum that is meaningful and relevant to the students and to the community.
26. The school has a curriculum that encourages the students becoming involved in their education.
27. Homework is required to be performed by the students on a regular basis.
28. Homework is assigned as a review of the instructional activity in the classroom.
29. Homework is assigned which may require further guidance and assistance from the parent.
30. The behavior of teachers and staff instills confidence in students.
31. The behavior of teachers and staff instills confidence in the parents.
32. Teachers and staff have knowledge to answer parents' educational questions.

Community Involvement

33. The school includes the community in the development of the curriculum.
34. The school works with the community as equal partners to set and meet goals for the students.
35. The school works with the students and their parents as equal partners to set and meet goals for the students.
36. The school has individuals in leadership positions who invest time to develop a common sense of purpose in the school community.
37. The school promotes parental involvement in the education of their child (for example by volunteering).
38. The school offers parenting skills classes to the parents on a voluntary basis.

Learning Outcomes

39. The school maintains accurate and up-to-date student performance records (for example assessment tests and report cards).
40. The school's primary purpose is to assist the students in achieving the district's academic goals.
41. The school promotes methods that focus on teaching the basic content areas (for example reading, math, science, and social studies).
42. Teaching methods are utilized to foster creative thinking skills.
43. Student achievement results are used to assess the overall academic performance of the school.
44. Students achieve at or above an average level in their academic subjects.

Scoring: For Excellent Schools: 1 = Not Essential; 2 = Slightly Essential; 3 = Neutral; 4 = Essential; and 5 = Absolutely Essential. For Your School: 1 = Not at All; 2 = Rarely; 3 = Sometimes; 4 = Almost Always; 5 = Always; and 6 = Don't Know.

Reprinted with permission of the author.

Connecticut School Effectiveness Interview and Questionnaire

Villanova, R.M., et al. 1984. Handbook for the Use of the Connecticut School Effectiveness Interview and Questionnaire. Hartford, CT: Connecticut Department of Education.

Comments: The 97-item CSEQ measures seven characteristics of effective schools. Information about the development and validity of the questionnaire and interview are included in the handbook. A summary profile and an integrated item profile were generated.

Reliability: The alpha coefficients for 423 teachers were 0.87 (safe and orderly environment); 0.90 (clear school mission); 0.93 (instructional leadership); 0.55 (expectations); 0.66 (opportunity to learn); 0.77 (monitoring student progress); and 0.89 (home/school relations). Test-retest reliabilities for 60 elementary teachers over a ten-day period were 0.85 (safe and orderly environment); 0.90 (clear school mission); 0.83 (instructional leadership); 0.69 (expectations); 0.74 (opportunity to learn); 0.67 (monitoring student progress); and 0.82 (home/school relations).

Validity: Content validity was established from the far-right descriptors in the Interview items. A panel of experts sorted items into the various categories. At least 80 percent agreement was required before an item was included. To further refine the questionnaire, a pilot study was conducted with six teachers. Construct validity was achieved by a multitrait-multimethod analysis. Support is provided for convergent validity and discriminant validity. Results of factor analytic procedures were not available.

Definitions: Definitions are provided for each of the seven effective school characteristics.

Characteristics: The seven effective school characteristics are: safe and orderly environment (1-9), clear school mission (10-25), instructional leadership (26-49), high expectations (50-63), opportunity to learn and time-on-task (64-73), frequent monitoring of student progress (74-82), and home-school relations (83-91).

Data Analysis: Means, standard deviations, and a rank order for the seven characteristics are reported for ten schools. The results of the multitrait-multimethod analysis is reported for 247 educators.

References:
Edmonds, R. 1979. A discussion of the literature and issues related to effective schooling. Cambridge, MA: Center for Urban Studies, Harvard Graduate School of Education.

Proctor, C.P. 1984. Teacher expectations: A model for school improvement. *Elementary School Journal* 84:469-481.

Purkey, S.C., and M.S. Smith. 1983. Effective schools: A review. *Elementary School Journal* 83:427-452.

Connecticut School Effectiveness Questionnaire

SAFE AND ORDERLY ENVIRONMENT

1. This school is a safe and secure place to work.
2. The school building is neat, bright, clean and comfortable.
3. A positive feeling permeates the school.
4. Most students in this school are eager and enthusiastic about learning.
5. Student behavior is generally positive in this school.
6. Teachers, administrators, and parents work cooperatively to support the discipline policy in this school.
7. The discipline policy is consistently enforced by all staff in this school.
8. Students in this school abide by school rules.
9. Class atmosphere in this school is generally very conducive to learning for all students.

CLEAR SCHOOL MISSION

10. This school has a written statement of purpose that is the driving force behind most important decisions.
11. In this school, the primary emphasis is on teaching and learning.
12. All materials and supplies necessary for instruction are available.
13. In reading, written, sequential objectives exist in all grades.
14. Reading objectives are coordinated and monitored in all grades.
15. In reading, there is an identified set of objectives that all students must master in all grades.
16. In reading, curriculum objectives are the focus of instruction in this school.
17. In language arts, written, sequential objectives exist in all grades.
18. Language arts objectives are coordinated and monitored in all grades.
19. In language arts, there is an identified set of objectives that all students must master in all grades.
20. In language arts, curriculum objectives are the focus of instruction in this school.
21. In mathematics, written, sequential objectives exist in all grades.
22. Mathematics objectives are coordinated and monitored in all grades.
23. In mathematics, there is an identified set of objectives that all students must master in all grades.
24. In mathematics, curriculum objectives are the focus of instruction in this school.
25. Almost all the students in this school try hard to get good grades.

INSTRUCTIONAL LEADERSHIP

26. There is clear, strong, centralized instructional leadership from the principal in this school.
27. Most problems facing this school can be solved by the principal and faculty without a great deal of outside help.
28. The principal is very active in securing resources, arranging opportunities and promoting staff development activities for the faculty.
29. The principal is highly visible throughout the school.
30. The principal is accessible to discuss matters dealing with instruction.
31. The principal is an important instructional resource person in this school.
32. Teachers in this school turn to the principal with instructional concerns or problems.
33. The principal makes informal contacts with students and teachers around the school.

34. Discussions with the principal often result in some aspect of improved instructional practice.
35. The principal leads frequent formal discussions concerning instruction and student achievement.
36. The principal regularly brings instructional issues to the faculty for discussion.
37. The principal reviews and interprets test results with the faculty.
38. The principal emphasizes the meaning and the use of test results.
39. The principal frequently communicates to teachers their responsibility in relation to student achievement.
40. The principal uses test results to recommend modifications or changes in the instructional program.
41. At the principal's initiative, teachers work together to coordinate the instructional program within and between grades.
42. The principal requires and regularly reviews lesson plans.
43. The principal regularly gives feedback to teachers concerning lesson plans.
44. Supervision is directed at instruction.
45. The principal makes formal classroom observations.
46. Individual teachers and the principal meet regularly to discuss what the principal will observe during a classroom observation.
47. Formal observations by the principal are regularly followed by a postobservation conference.
48. During follow-up to formal observations, a plan for improvement frequently results.
49. During follow-up to formal observations, the principal's main emphasis is on instructional issues.

HIGH EXPECTATIONS

50. Ninety-five to one hundred percent of the students in this school can be expected to complete high school.
51. All teachers in this school hold consistently high expectations for all students.
52. Teachers believe that a student's home background is *not* the primary factor that determines individual student achievement in this school.
53. In this school low-achieving students are as well behaved as other students.
54. Teachers in this school believe they are responsible for all students mastering basic skills at each grade level.
55. Teachers believe that all students in this school can master basic skills as a direct result of the instructional program.
56. This school has successful preventive strategies for helping students at risk of school failure.
57. In this school, remedial programs are a last resort.
58. The number of low-income children promoted is proportionately equivalent to all other children promoted.
59. In this school, there are clear guidelines for grouping students for instruction.
60. In reading, instruction is often presented to a heterogeneous ability group of students.
61. In mathematics, instruction is often presented to a heterogeneous ability group of students.
62. In language arts, instruction is often presented to a heterogeneous ability group of students.
63. Within the classroom, students are assigned to groups for extra help on a temporary basis only.

OPPORTUNITY TO LEARN AND TIME-ON-TASK

64. The school's daily schedule supports the goals of the instructional program.
65. Two hours or more are allocated for reading/language arts each day throughout this school.

66. Fifty minutes or more are allocated for mathematics each day throughout this school.
67. Pull-out programs (e.g., Chapter 1, special ed., instrumental music, etc.) do not disrupt or interfere with basic skills instruction.
68. Special instructional programs for individual students are integrated with classroom instruction and the school curriculum.
69. Teachers implement the homework policy in this school.
70. Factors outside the classroom rarely interfere with instruction in this school.
71. There are few interruptions due to discipline problems during class time.
72. During classroom instruction students do not work independently on seatwork for the majority of the allocated time.
73. Students are absent from school only for good reasons.

FREQUENT MONITORING OF STUDENT PROGRESS

74. Multiple indicators are used regularly to assess student progress (e.g., grades, tests, discipline referrals, extracurricular, etc.).
75. The testing program is an accurate and valid measure of the curriculum in this school.
76. Criterion-referenced tests are used to assess instruction throughout the school.
77. Achievement test scores are analyzed separately for subgroups of students (e.g., gender, race, ethnicity, social class, etc.) to assure that all students are achieving.
78. Teachers and the principal thoroughly review and analyze test results to plan instructional program modifications.
79. Many students receive honor and recognition for academic performance.
80. Students have many opportunities to demonstrate leadership skill.
81. Students have many opportunities to demonstrate talents in art, music, drama, dance and athletics.
82. In this school, all teachers apply consistent criteria to assigning course grades.

HOME-SCHOOL RELATIONS

83. There is an active parent/school group in this school.
84. Many parents are involved in school activities.
85. Many parents initiate contacts with the school each month.
86. Most parents understand and promote the school's instructional program.
87. Parents support the school in matters of student discipline.
88. Parents support the homework policy in this school.
89. There is cooperation with regard to homework between parents and teachers in this school.
90. Almost all students complete assigned homework before coming to school.
91. Ninety to one hundred percent of your students' parents attend scheduled parent-teacher conferences.
92. During parent-teacher conferences there is a focus on factors directly related to student achievement.
93. Parent-teacher conferences result in specific plans for home-school cooperation aimed at improving student classroom achievement.
94. Beyond parent conferences and report cards, teachers in this school use other ways of communicating student progress to parents (e.g., home visits, phone calls, newsletters, regular notes).
95. Parents of students in your class have regular opportunities to observe the instructional program.
96. Parents of students in your class have a significant, rather than a superficial, role in the educational program.

97.   Most parents would rate this school as excellent.

Scoring: Strongly Disagree = 1; Disagree = 2; Undecided = 3; Agree = 4; and Strongly Agree = 5.

Reprinted with permission of Richard E. Lappert, Bureau of Certification and Professional Development, Connecticut State Department of Education, Revised 1989.

Organizational Structure

Structural Properties Questionnaire

Bishop, L.K., and J.R. George. 1973. Organizational structure: A factor analysis of structural characteristics of public elementary and secondary schools. *Educational Administration Quarterly* 9:66-80.

Comments: The 45-item SPQ was designed to measure the structural (bureaucratic) characteristics of elementary and secondary schools based on three conceptual areas proposed by Hage—*complexity, centralization, and formalization*. A prerequisite of structure is the need to have policies, programs, standing orders, procedures, and operating instructions that enable organizational members to behave in a prescribed manner. It includes the following factors: faculty involvement in decision-making, the degree of administrative control, the uniform adherence to rules and regulations, the exercise of professional latitude, or restrictions applied to various modes of organizational interactions.

Scale Construction: An original 350-item pool was developed based on the operational definition associated with the three structural properties and appropriate to an educational setting. Through a variety of psychometric procedures, the instrument has undergone four major revisions. It uses a modified four-category Likert response scale.

Sample: The final version (Form Four) of the instrument was based on a sample of 1,367 teachers located in 45 schools including elementary and secondary. The sample included rural, suburban, and urban areas from states in the Midwest and Northeast. The size and regional diversity of the sample further enhances the representatives of the data, and supports the stability of the factor structure and factor scores associated with the instrument.

Reliability: The Cronbach coefficient alpha for the entire scale was 0.94. Individual coefficients for the 12 subscales ranged from 0.74 to 0.85.

Validity: Several panels of judges were used to determine the content validity of the final 45-item instrument. In each case, 100% agreement was necessary in order for an item to be retained. A criterion-related validity study was conducted by comparing two school districts (known-groups method)—one considered to be highly structured (bureaucratic), the other significantly less structured. Comparisons of average responses of teachers on all 12 scales indicated the ability of the test to discriminate without exception between the two types of organizational structures (all tests of statistical significance for t-tests of comparisons on all scales were 0.05 or smaller). In the development of the 45-item instrument a number of factor analytic solutions were explored, including principal components, principal axes, and image factoring in conjunction with varimax and oblique rotations. Each solution yielded substantial congruence in the item loadings.

Factor Analysis and Scoring: A 12-factor orthogonal (varimax) principal component analysis was selected for the final solution and for scoring. This factor solution accounted for 57% of the common variance. The scoring program used factor score coefficient weighted Z scores, which facilitates comparisons between groups on the various factors. Using a linear coefficient weighted equation (factor loadings are used as weights) to calculate factor scores allows for supressor effects of certain variables to enter into the factor estimation.

Definition of Factors: The 12 factors derived from the analysis can be unambiguously assigned to one of the three structural characteristics proposed by Hage. *Centralization* (how power is distributed among organizational positions): Participation in Decision-Making I & II and Hierarchy of Authority I & II; *Formalization* (how rules are used in an organization): Role Specificity and Standardization I, II, & III and Rule Observation-Professional Latitude I & II; *Complexity* (the degree of professional activity required and supported): Specialization, Professional Activity and Professional Training.

Data Analysis: Means, standard deviations, and comparative data among the 45 school districts and 1,376 teachers are provided.

References:
Bishop, L.K., et al. 1967. Structural Properties Questionnaire—Form 1. Claremont Graduate School, California. Working paper.

Bishop, L.K., and J.R. George. 1971. Relationship of organizational structure and teacher personality characteristics to organizational climate. *Administrative Science Quarterly* 16:467-475.

Murphy, M.J. 1979. Structural characteristics and organizational design decision. Paper presented at American Educational Research Association. ERIC ED 170 937.

Murphy, M.J., and L.K. Bishop. 1975. Defining organizational properties of schools: A focus on structure. Paper presented at American Educational Research Association.

Structural Properties Questionnaire
Form 4

Who has the greatest influence in decisions about:

1.	The instructional program?	1. Teachers
2.	Teaching methods?	2. Department or Grade Chairmen
3.	Textbook selection?	3. Consultants or Specialists
4.	Curricular offerings?	4. Administrators

1. Rarely
2. Sometimes
3. Often
4. Very Frequently

5. Teachers are required to follow suggested instructional sequences and unit plans as closely as possible.
6. Principals in your district must refer most non-routine decisions to someone higher up for the final O.K.
7. Rules and regulations concerning teacher behavior are uniformly applied.
8. Days in the school calendar are allotted exclusively to teachers for professional activities.
9. Academic degrees are an important consideration in recruitment of administrative staff.
10. Teachers are required to follow an adopted course of study.
11. Vice-principals and department chairmen in your school must refer most non-routine decisions to someone higher up for a final O.K.
12. Teachers' responsibilities and lines of authority within the school are well-defined.
13. Teaching in your school is a good job for someone who likes to be "his own boss."
14. Teachers receive help from an instructional media specialist in the use of audiovisual equipment.
15. Teachers make visitations to schools outside of the district.
16. Advanced degrees are an important consideration in promotion.
17. Teachers are evaluated according to a formalized procedure.
18. Even small matters often have to be referred to someone higher up for a final answer.
19. At this school, procedures for disciplining students are well-defined.
20. How things are done is left up to the person doing the work.
21. Teachers attend professional conferences during the school year.
22. Academic degrees are an important consideration in recruitment of instructional staff.
23. Teachers are allowed to teach only those subjects which are included in the course of study.
24. There can be little action taken here until a superior approves decision.
25. Teachers' activities are governed by written rules and regulations.
26. Most people here make their own rules on the job.
27. Teachers are required to do paper work which could be done by a school office staff.
28. Teachers are allowed to teach outside of their major areas of study.
29. Teachers are required to maintain lesson plans.
30. People here are allowed to do almost as they please.
31. Teachers are allowed to teach outside of their major and minor area of study.
32. Teachers in our school must refer most non-routine decisions to someone higher up for a final O.K.

33. Administrators strictly follow established rules and regulations in dealing with the teaching staff.
34. The Principal's activities are governed by written rules and regulations.
35. A teacher can make his own decisions concerning instructional problems without checking with anybody else.
36. Teachers here teach out of their field of specialization.
37. Any decision I make has to have my superior's approval.
38. Teachers are required to submit lesson plans.
39. The Principal is willing to by-pass regulations to help teachers.
40. Teachers are required to go through channels (chain of command) for routine decisions.
41. The Principal is willing to by-pass regulations to help pupils.
42. Teachers' daily activities must have the approval of a superior.
43. Teachers in this school are closely supervised.
44. Teachers are allowed to violate minor rules and regulations.
45. Rules requiring teachers to sign in and out are strictly followed.

Scoring: Very frequently = 4; Often = 3; Sometimes = 2; Rarely = 1.

Reprinted with permission of the author.

Politics

Perceptions of Organizational Politics Scale

Kacmar, K.M., and D.W. Carlson. 1997. Further validation of the Perceptions of Politics (POPS): A multiple sample investigation. *Journal of Management* 23:627-658.

Comments: The revised 15-item POPS assesses the following three areas that were identified in the original study: general political behavior, go along to get ahead, and pay and promotion policies. A brief description about the development and construct validation of the original 12-item POPS is included. The results of three additional studies are presented.

Scale Construction: The first study examined the dimensionality of the POPS. The second study focused on an analysis of each individual item through factor analyses and mean scores. The third study consisted of developing new items and then examining them in terms of content adequacy, content analysis, and factor analysis.

Sample: There were 749 respondents from a large state agency in Study 1. The sample for Study 2 consisted of: 466 workers from an electronic cooperative; 581 human resource professionals; 220 nonfaculty workers; and an additional 320 workers. The sample for Study 3 consisted of 123 members of the Society for Human Resource Management and 182 college students.

Reliability: The internal reliability for the original 12-item POPS in Study 1 was 0.87. The internal reliability for the original 12-item POPS in Study 2 for the four samples ranged from 0.86 to 0.89. The internal reliability for the 20-item POPS in Study 3 was 0.81.

Validity: Study 2 provides evidence for convergent and discriminant validity.

Factor Analysis: A principal components factor analysis with an oblimin rotation was conducted on all four groups in Study 2. Although the results of the factor analysis yielded a three-factor solution that was consistent with the original study, only two items loaded sufficiently on each of the three factors. Another principal components factor analysis with an oblimin rotation was conducted in Study 3 to determine which of the 14 new items would be included. The following three-factor solution was accepted: general political behavior (1 and 2); go along to get ahead (3 through 9); and pay and promotion policies (10 through 15).

Data Analysis: Means and standard deviations are presented. Item loadings, squared multiple correlations, chi-square, goodness-of-fit, normed fit index, comparative fit index, and parsimony fit index are reported for Study 1 and Study 3. Item analysis, content adequacy, and means are included for Study 2.

References:
Kacmar, K.M., and G.R. Ferris. 1991. Perceptions of Organizational Politics Scale (POPS): Development and construct validation. *Educational and Psychological Measurement* 51:193-205.

Medsker, G.J., et al. 1994. A review of current practices for evaluating causal models in organizational behavior and human resources management research. *Journal of Management* 20:439-464.

Nye, L.G., and L.A. Witt. 1993. Dimensionality and construct validity of the perceptions of politics scales (POPS). *Educational and Psychological Measurement* 53:821-829.

Perceptions of Politics Survey

1. People in this organization attempt to build themselves up by tearing others down.
2. There has always been an influential group in this department that no one ever crosses.
3. Employees are encouraged to speak out frankly even when they are critical of well-established ideas.
4. There is no place for yes-men around here; good ideas are desired even if it means disagreeing with superiors.
5. Agreeing with powerful others is the best alternative in this organization.
6. It is best not to rock the boat in this organization.
7. Sometimes it is easier to remain quiet than to fight the system.
8. Telling others what they want to hear is sometimes better than telling the truth.
9. It is safer to think what you are told than to make up your own mind.
10. Since I have worked in this department, I have never seen the pay and promotion policies applied politically.
11. I can't remember when a person received a pay increase or promotion that was inconsistent with the published policies.
12. None of the raises I have received are consistent with the policies on how raises should be determined.
13. The stated pay and promotion policies have nothing to do with how pay raises and promotions are determined.
14. When it comes to pay raise and promotion decisions, policies are irrelevant.
15. Promotions around here are not valued much because how they are determined is so political.

Scoring: A five-point scale ranges from Strongly Disagree (1) to Strongly Agree (5).

Reprinted with permission of the author.

Power

School Participant Empowerment Scale

Short, P.M., and J.S. Rinehart. 1992. School Participant Empowerment Scale. Auburn University. Mimeo.

Comments: The SPES, a refined 38-item instrument, was developed to measure school participant (teacher) empowerment. It was designed to measure several themes such as trust, communication, structures for involvement, risk taking, and critical incidents. In addition, such themes as opportunities for decision-making, control over daily schedule, opportunities for growth and development can be empowering aspects of a teacher's job.

Scale Construction: To generate items for the original instrument, teachers were asked to list ways in which they felt empowered in the schools in which they taught. This process yielded 110 items of which 75 were judged to represent empowerment components based on the literature and past research of empowerment.

Sample: The sample consisted of 211 secondary teachers from high schools in three geographic regions—south, southwest, and the midwest. Schools ranged in size from 70 teachers to 125 teachers.

Reliability: The total scale (38 items) alpha coefficient was 0.94. Coefficients for each of the subscales were decision-making 0.89; professional growth 0.83; status 0.86; self efficacy 0.84; autonomy 0.81; and impact 0.82.

Validity: Content validity was determined by a panel of four judges that rated the overall representativeness of each item. From this analysis, 68 items reached general agreement. The 68-item instrument was submitted to a factor analysis from which a final 38 items were retained on six factors.

Factor Analysis: A principal component analysis followed by an oblique rotation was used. Only those items with a factor loading of 0.600 or higher were retained on the factor. This yielded six factors, which accounted for about 51% of the common variance. The six dimensions produced by the factor analysis are decision-making (ten items); professional growth (six items); status (six items); self efficacy (six items); autonomy (four items); and impact (six items).

References:
Short, P.M., and J.T. Greer. 1989. Increasing teacher autonomy through shared governance: Effects on policy making and student outcomes. Paper presented at American Educational Research Association.

Short, P.M., J.T. Greer, and R. Michael. 1991. Restructuring schools through empowerment. *Journal of School Leadership* 1:5-25.

School Empowerment Survey

1. I am given the responsibility to monitor programs.
2. I function in a professional environment.
3. I believe that I have earned respect.
4. I believe that I am helping kids become independent learners.
5. I have control over daily schedules.
6. I believe that I have the ability to get things done.
7. I make decisions about the implementation of new programs in the school.
8. I am treated as a professional.
9. I believe that I am very effective.
10. I believe that I am empowering students.
11. I am able to teach as I choose.
12. I participate in staff development.
13. I make decisions about the selection of other teachers for my school.
14. I have the opportunity for professional growth.
15. I have the respect of my colleagues.
16. I feel that I am involved in an important program for children.
17. I have the freedom to make decisions on what is taught.
18. I believe that I am having an impact.
19. I am involved in school budget decisions.
20. I work at a school where kids come first.
21. I have the support and respect of my colleagues.
22. I see students learn.
23. I make decisions about curriculum.
24. I am a decision maker.
25. I am given the opportunity to teach other teachers.
26. I am given the opportunity to continue learning.
27. I have a strong knowledge base in the areas in which I teach.
28. I believe that I have the opportunity to grow by working daily with students.
29. I perceive that I have the opportunity to influence others.
30. I can determine my own schedule.
31. I have the opportunity to collaborate with other teachers in my school.
32. I perceive that I am making a difference.
33. Principals, other teachers, and school personnel solicit my advice.
34. I believe that I am good at what I do.
35. I can plan my own schedule.
36. I perceive that I have an impact on other teachers and students.
37. My advice is solicited by others.
38. I have an opportunity to teach other teachers about innovative ideas.

Scoring: 1 = Strongly Disagree; 2 = Disagree; 3 = Neutral; 4 = Agree; 5 = Strongly Agree.

Reprinted with permission of the author.

Zones of Indifference Instrument

Wilkes, S.T., and J.M. Blackbourn. 1981. The design of an instrument to measure zones of indifference of teachers to directives issued by administrators. Mississippi State University. ERIC ED 212 063.

Comments: The 78-item instrument measures the zones of indifference of teachers to directives issued by administrators. Zones of indifference describe the extent to which people will respond to orders or directives issued by authority figures. It suggests that some orders are clearly unacceptable, while some are neutral, and others are unquestionably acceptable. It is also suggested that this "zone of indifference" will be wider or narrower with different organizational members. The difference in the size of the zone is created by the degree to which inducements exceed consequences that determine the individual's adhesion to the organization.

Scale Construction: One hundred twenty-five teachers submitted items, which eventually were categorized into two sets of items. One set explained variables describing teacher-determined practices, while the other dealt with administrator-determined policy. This produced an initial instrument of 134 items.

Sample: The initial instrument of 134 items was field tested with 104 teachers in four states. Through a variety of factor analytic procedures, the 134 items were reduced to a final 78-item instrument comprising a two-factor solution.

Reliability: Alpha coefficient for the total instrument was 0.95. The two subscales (factors) were 0.92 for each subscale.

Validity: Other than the factor analyses conducted, no other information on obtaining validity of the instrument was reported.

Factor Analysis: Responses to the 134-item instrument were submitted to several principal component analyses, which reduced the instrument to 80 items and three factors. Only items with loadings of 0.40 or higher were retained. With the use of image analysis and orthogonal rotation the instrument was reduced to two factors: factor 1 deals with teacher determined practices and factor 2 deals with administrator determined policy. Examples of items with high loadings on the two factors are as follows: teacher determined practices (45, 126, 128, 46, 57) and administrator determined policy (121, 102, 97, 123, 114).

References:
Barnard, C.I. 1948. *The functions of the executive*. MA: Harvard University Press.

Kunz, D.W. 1973. Leader behavior of principals and the professional zone of acceptance of teachers. Ed.D. dissertation, Rutgers University.

Zones of Indifference

Indicate how you would respond to the following directives issued by an administrator that would:

1. Provide for the enforcement by teachers of general rules governing student conduct at school.
2. Attempt to structure discussion of school policy, problems or procedure by teachers with members of the community unless a positive approach is evident.
3. Establish heating and cooling regulations for the classroom.
4. Establish a procedure for teachers to "sign-in" and "sign-out" for the school day.
5. Give directions to advance a student to another level when the present progress of the student is not satisfactory.
6. Prescribe procedure for the conduct of club activities.
7. Require attendance at staff-development activities.
8. Instruct teachers to attend open house activities.
9. Establish grading procedures to be used by teachers.
10. Give directions for the changing of classroom bulletin boards at regular intervals.
11. Structure a daily morning devotional activity in the classroom.
12. Require supervision of students after school hours for those students who have to stay after school to make up assignments.
13. Require participation in the teacher evaluation program.
14. Designate specific topics to be taught at specific times.
15. Require teachers to have students recite "The Lord's Prayer" in the homeroom or classroom.
16. Make assignment to study committees of the school.
17. Require attendance at P.T.A. meetings.
18. Require participation in a curriculum study group.
19. Require a six week grade report to the administration.
20. Question non-attendance of teachers at professional meetings.
21. Provide additional time for student classroom assignment conferences.
22. Structure seating arrangement of students in assemblies.
23. Insist upon personal comments on grade sheets in each instance of a decline in student achievement.
24. Require ability grouping of students.
25. Dictate the use of only adopted textbooks in the classroom.
26. Be related to membership in professional organizations.
27. Place ultimate concern on the student.
28. Determine method to be used in the handling of classroom discipline problems.
29. Prohibit students from using the library during class time without teacher supervision.
30. Require the grading of English usage in all subjects taught.
31. Direct teachers to alter records to indicate accreditation compliance.
32. Require a written proposal for all planned field trips.
33. Require written goals and objectives of teachers.
34. Prescribe testing schedules and procedures.
35. Specify methods to be used in teacher-parent relations.
36. Require maintenance of accurate school classroom records.
37. Suggest the use of a teacher's name to order supplies for other teachers.
38. Schedule the use of planning time for supervising another teacher's class who is out on some school activity.
39. Establish a policy of student grade reduction for unexcused absences and tardiness.
40. Forbid the use of tobacco by teachers at school.

41. Determine the time of the teachers' workday.
42. Direct teachers to meet the parents for conference.
43. Require extra assignments that would reduce time for classroom instruction.
44. Require long-range lesson plans.
45. Select teaching procedures to be utilized in the classroom.
46. Structure the standardization of classroom furniture arrangement.
47. Provide for the monitoring of student behavior on the way to school and from school by teachers.
48. Prohibit the consumption of refreshment by teachers in the classroom.
49. Instruct teachers to teach content without regard to student acquisition level.
50. Require attendance at faculty meetings.
51. Prevent teachers from leaving school.
52. Require teacher participation in a census of school age children during or after school hours.
53. Question student religious beliefs and home life.
54. Establish directives requiring teachers to supervise school bus loading/unloading of students.
55. Establish a bimonthly teaching meeting practice.
56. Provide a list of discipline cases handled by the teacher in the classroom.
57. Require teachers to perform tasks that maintenance or custodial personnel are hired to do.
58. Schedule male/female teacher supervision of restrooms.
59. Require teachers to purchase season football tickets.
60. Establish conditions under which corporal punishment could be administered.
61. Determine the test exemption policy.
62. Excuse students from classes to attend other school sponsored activities.
63. Allow the expenditure of school funds for extracurricular activities.
64. Provide guidelines outlining student assignment requirements for classroom work.
65. Direct teachers to escort sick students home.
66. Involve altering a student's grade.
67. Be related to teacher involvement in political activities.
68. Direct all teachers to be on duty in the halls during the changing of classes.
69. Determine the amount of planning time per week.
70. Notify teachers of grade/subject assignments.
71. Establish the practice of planning individual student lesson prescriptions.
72. Require a teacher to supervise two classes in the same period in separate rooms.
73. Constitute running errands for the administration which are unrelated to the school program.
74. Assign school related duties outside the classroom involving no students.
75. Attempt to restrict topics that could be discussed in the lounge area.
76. Outline the policy concerning attendance at work.
77. Require a very low noise level to be maintained in the classroom.
78. Instruct teachers to accept a student into class after the suspension of a student.
79. Prohibit the keeping of report cards in the classroom.
80. Establish the policy of paying substitute teachers for sponsoring club activities or other extracurricular activities.
81. Limit the number of graduate courses a teacher could be enrolled in after school hours.
82. Schedule duty assignments at times other than the required school day.
83. Allow the public to use classroom after hours.
84. Instruct each class to contribute a specified amount of money to the school activity fund.
85. Assign a student with the disciplinary record to your instructional group.
86. Prevent the early dismissal of classes by teachers.
87. Instruct teachers to monitor student classroom appearance in keeping with the school dress code.

88. Assign selected teachers to duties that are not assigned to the entire faculty.
89. Restrict students from restraining students from participation in the activity period.
90. Not allow athletes to participate in sports due to academic problems.
91. Require submission of lesson plans weekly by teachers.
92. Require strict adherence to the curriculum guide and/or daily lesson plan.
93. Structure teacher dress practices.
94. Direct all teachers to attend all school functions.
95. Structure student dress practices.
96. Require the issuance of student failure reports by teachers.
97. Require a standing position while teaching class.
98. Schedule teachers to supervise school-related meetings at school.
99. Provide the procedure for recording student absences.
100. Require attendance at an administrator/teacher conference.
101. Require the submission of absentee and tardy reports every period of the school day.
102. Make assignments of teachers as sponsors to student club activities.
103. Require teachers to use the school cafeteria for lunch.
104. Provide guidelines determining advancement and retention practices.
105. Require the use of a teaching syllabus.
106. Provide guidelines concerning the manner by which sick leave should be utilized by teachers.
107. Schedule teacher to supervise P.E. classes during an unassigned period.
108. Schedule the utilization of teacher aids in the classroom instead of substitute teachers when the regular teacher is not present.
109. Establish the format for written lesson plans.
110. Schedule teachers to move to different rooms for instructional purposes.
111. Direct a teacher to alter attendance reports of students.
112. Determine specific staff development activities.
113. Require teachers to perform information gathering that other professionals are employed to do.
114. Prohibit teachers from leaving the school during school hours.
115. Schedule work days prior to the commencement of school without pay and not specified by contract.
116. Require the keeping of an extensive record of library books that are issued to students.
117. Result in the lowering of grades for poor conduct by students.
118. Establish written job descriptions for teachers.
119. Indicate that classroom materials had been selected by the administration.
120. Require teacher direction of a staff development activity.
121. Direct teachers to refrain from expressing opinions about community problems.
122. Require an instant gathering of data for office purposes.
123. Prohibit the use of corporal punishment as a method of punishment.
124. Determine the length of exams to be administered.
125. Require the maintenance of discipline of students at all times in the classroom.
126. Establish the practice for teachers to collect student activity fees.
127. Structure teacher arrival at school prior to the designated time for the beginning of the school day.
128. Schedule classroom activities by the principal.
129. Prohibit the wearing of jeans by teachers.
130. Involve a teacher administering corporal punishment to another teacher's student.
131. Require the presence of teachers with students in the cafeteria.
132. Prohibit a teacher from being employed in another job.
133. Provide an individual teacher personnel file in the office.
134. Suggest an explanation by the teacher of personal life activities.

Scoring: 1 = A directive you would comply with without question; 2 = A directive you would comply with but mentally question the authority of the administrator to issue; 3 = A directive issued by the administrator that you mentally question the authority of, but alter the application more in keeping with what you think should be done; and 4 = A directive issued by the administrator that you question mentally and refuse compliance with unless forced to do so.

Reprinted with permission of the author.

Professional Performance

Professional Orientation Scale

Corwin, R.G. 1963. The development of an instrument for examining staff conflicts in the public schools. U.S. Office of Education, Dept. of Health Education and Welfare, Contract No. 1934.

Comments: The scale originally contained 45 items as developed by Corwin. Corwin's scales were designed to analyze staff conflict in public schools. Later work by Kuhlman modified the original Corwin 45-item scale into a 24-item instrument. Fifteen items comprise the *Bureaucratic Orientation Scale* and nine items comprise the *Professional Orientation Scale.*

Sample: The scale was administered to a sample of 322 prospective elementary and secondary school teachers from four New Jersey colleges in spring of the year at the completion of their undergraduate teacher preparation training. A follow-up of the same sample was made one year later after they completed their first year of teaching.

Reliability: A split-half reliability estimate for the entire scale was 0.83. Individual subscale reliabilities for the five factors are not provided.

Factor Analysis: The 15-item BOS scale was factor analyzed, yielding a five-factor solution that measures five aspects of bureaucratic orientation. The factors were named organizational control, subordination-standardization, rule orientation, community orientation, and organizational loyalty. The author indicates that a total BOS score, across the 15 Likert-type items, provides an overall index of bureaucratic orientation.

References:
Corwin, R.G. 1970. *Militant professionalism.* New York: Appleton.

Kuhlman, E.L., and H.K. Hoy. 1974. The socialization of professionals into bureaucracies. *Journal of Educational Administration* 2:18-27.

Bureaucratic and Professional Orientation Scales
Form B-P

1. Teachers should subscribe to and diligently read the standard professional journals.
2. Rules stating when the teachers should arrive and depart from the building should be strictly enforced.
3. Unless he/she is satisfied that it is best for the student, a teacher should *not* do what he/she is told to do.
4. Personnel who openly criticize the administration should be encouraged to go elsewhere.
5. Teachers should be active members of at least one professional teaching association and should attend most conferences and meetings of the association.
6. Teachers should be obedient, respectful and loyal to the principal.
7. Teachers should be completely familiar with the written descriptions of the rules, procedures, manuals and other standard operating procedures for running the class.
8. The criterion of a good school should be one that serves the needs of the local community.
9. A teacher should consistently practice her ideas of the best educational practices even though the administration prefers other views.
10. There should be definite rules specifying the topics that are not appropriate for discussion in a classroom.
11. It should be permissible for the teacher to violate a rule if he/she is sure that the best interests of the students will be served in doing so.
12. Teachers should not publicly advocate a position on the place of religion in the school which differs greatly from the majority of the community.
13. A good teacher should not do anything that he/she believes may jeopardize the interests of the students regardless of who tells him or what the rule states.
14. In case of a dispute in the community over whether a controversial textbook or controversial speaker should be permitted in the school, the teacher should look primarily to the judgment of the administration for guidance.
15. A good teacher should put the interests of his/her school above everything else.
16. Teachers should not attempt to discuss any controversial issue (such as abolishing the House Un-American Activities Committee) which may jeopardize the school's public relations.
17. Schools should hire no one to teach unless he/she holds at least a 4-year bachelor's degree.
18. Teachers of the same subject throughout the system should follow the same kind of lesson plan.
19. The ultimate authority over the major educational decisions should be exercised by professional teachers.
20. Teachers should take into account the opinions of their community in guiding what they say in class and in their choice of teaching materials.
21. It should be permissible to hire teachers trained at non-accredited colleges.
22. When a controversy arises about the interpretation of school rules, a teacher should not "stick her neck out" by taking a definite position.
23. The school should have a manual of rules and regulations which are actually followed.
24. Teachers should not allow themselves to be influenced by other teachers whose opinions and thinking are different than the administration's.

Scoring: SA = Strongly Agree; A = Agree; U = Undecided; D = Disagree; SD = Strongly Disagree
Items 1, 3, 5, 9, 11, 13, 17, 19, 21 are reverse scored.

Reprinted with permission of the author.

Diagnostic Assessment of School and Principal Effectiveness

Ebmeier, H. 1988. Reference Manual for the Diagnostic Assessment of School and Principal Effectiveness. Topeka, KS: KanLEAD Educational Consortium.

Comments: There are five instruments that were designed to assess school and principal effectiveness. In each instrument, some of the questions are identical, while others are specific to each of the following five groups: the principal, the principal's supervisor, teachers, students, and parents. The staff instrument examines the staff's view of himself or herself (morale scale, commitment scale, and job satisfaction scale); the staffs' view of the school (maintenance scale, adaptation scale, goal attainment scale, and integration scale); and the staffs' view of the principal (principal maintenance behaviors scale, principal adaptation behaviors scale, principal goal attainment behaviors scale, and principal integration behaviors scale). The principal instrument examines the principal's view of the school (same as above, except principal's perception instead of the teachers' perception) and the principal's view of himself or herself (same as above, except principal's perception instead of the staffs' perception).

Scale Construction: The instruments for the staff, principal, and principal's supervisor are almost identical except for small changes in wording for each of the groups. Each instrument contains three sections (one section requests demographic information). The other two sections are described above. In order to develop these instruments, over 1,500 articles were reviewed by graduate students, university professors, and school administrators in an attempt to identify the attitudes, behaviors, and skills that are associated with effective leadership. The 150 competencies that were agreed upon were then examined by state and national experts who further reduced the list to 60 competencies. These competencies comprise the view of the school section of the instrument. Detailed information about instrument development.

Sample: The original sample consisted of 23 schools in Kansas.

Reliability: The alpha coefficients for the eleven scales of the staffs' instrument (423 teachers) ranged from 0.76 (staff satisfaction) to 0.97 (principal behavior-maintenance, principal behavior-adaptation, principal behavior-goal attainment, and principal behavior-integration). The alpha coefficients for the eight scales of the principal's instrument (23 principals) ranged from 0.73 (building integration) to 0.92 (principal behavior-adaptation). In addition, the alpha coefficients are presented for the parents, students, and supervisors.

Validity: Content validity was established through the procedure for identifying items. Construct validity for the staff instrument was determined by means of an oblique factor analysis. Interscale and intrascale correlations were also examined. Predictive validity was established by using the known-groups technique. Evidence for all three forms of validity is presented.

Factor Analysis: An oblique factor analysis of the staff instrument confirmed three factors: principal behavior-goal attainment, principal behavior-adaptation, and principal behavior-integration.

Data Analysis: A reference manual is available that includes detailed information about the technical development of the instruments, the administration of the instruments, understanding the results (comparing scores between groups and comparing to other schools using percentile ranks), and planning for improvement.

References:

Ebmeier, H. 1991. The development and field test of an instrument for client-based principal formative evaluation. *Journal of Personnel Evaluation in Education* 4:245-278.

Levine, D., and L. Lezotte. 1990. *Unusually effective schools.* Madison, WI: National Center for Effective School Research and Development.

Rosenholtz, S.J. 1989. Workplace conditions that affect teacher quality and commitment: Implications for teacher induction programs. *Elementary School Journal* 89:421-439.

Toll, M.M. 1990. Conflict management and school administrators. Ed.D. dissertation, Kansas State University.

Wilson, A., et al. 1988. Documents for Discovery III: A Working Bibliography of Resources Used to Identify Traits, Generic Skills and Specific Skill of Administrators. Topeka, KS: KAN-LEAD and United School Administrators of Kansas.

Diagnostic Assessment of School and Principal Effectiveness
Principal Version

School Effectiveness

1. I am concerned with faculty working conditions.
2. Teachers at this school do not have a great deal of confidence in each other's abilities.
3. Teachers in this school are encouraged to implement new teaching techniques.
4. As students move from one grade level to the next or from one course to another, teachers generally can be assured that the students were soundly prepared in the previous course.
5. Teachers in this school are open to changes that will improve the school.
6. Student achievement is rewarded in this school.
7. The workload is adequately balanced among the faculty members of this school.
8. Teachers in my school have respect for professional competence of other teachers, departments, or levels.
9. Student creativity is encouraged and rewarded in this school.
10. I am not proud of this school.
11. In spite of limited financial resources, this school is able to get the money and equipment we need to conduct an effective educational program.
12. Teachers have a pretty good idea how the various departments or grade levels within our school function.
13. Teachers in this school work closely with the community.
14. Teachers derive professional satisfaction from their jobs in this school.
15. This school seems to be more effective than other schools in our district in obtaining adequate resources to support the educational program.
16. The development of student self-confidence is stressed at this school.
17. It is not clear to teachers what each department or level is supposed to do.
18. There are open lines of communication between faculty and the building administrators.
19. This school is an excellent organization.
20. The development of individual student self-concept is not emphasized in this school.
21. Before a decision is made in my school, there is a good deal of communication between teachers.
22. Teachers are satisfied with the amount of work they are expected to do.
23. Administrative policies are available to the faculty in printed form.
24. Before a decision which would affect everyone is made in my school, there is a good deal of communication between grade levels or departments.
25. Teachers in this school are trying hard to promote student achievement.
26. Some teachers would leave this school for any other.
27. Our school staff works together to jointly write grants or requests to secure resources from outside agencies.
28. The quality of teaching in my school is very high.
29. The staff in my school respect each other and work well together.
30. Teachers are not satisfied with the amount of money they make.
31. There is general faculty confidence in the building administrators.
32. There are often conflicts between teachers in this school.
33. Teachers tell their friends that I would stay in this school for many years to come.
34. Teachers are satisfied with the fringe benefits in this school district.
35. There are sufficient social activities for the faculty.
36. Productivity is high in this school.
37. If offered a better salary, most teachers would move to another school.

38. Teachers are satisfied with the trust they have in building administrators.
39. This school is effective in gaining community support for our programs.
40. The social contact between students and faculty is adequate.
41. Conflict between staff members in this school is rare.
42. Teachers at this school are not very loyal to the school and staff.
43. Teachers believe in the goals and objectives of this school.
44. In this school, the workload among teachers is pretty evenly distributed.
45. This school has activities to help us keep in touch with the wants and desires of the community.
46. In this school, all students are treated with respect—even those from poor backgrounds or those of limited intellectual ability.
47. Teachers are satisfied with the professional competence and leadership of their building administrator.
48. In this school, everything is arranged to facilitate the achievement of our goals.
49. Most of my teachers' interests lie outside their job at school.
50. The size of classes is satisfactory.
51. Teachers at this school respect parents and attempt to work with them whenever possible.
52. Each year in this school we make an extra effort to identify problems and set school-wide improvement goals.
53. Unlike this school, most of the teachers would like to work in a school that holds the same values as they do.
54. This school seems especially effective in adopting new and innovative instructional techniques.
55. Teachers in this school do not hold each other in high regard.
56. Teachers are satisfied with the opportunities provided to discuss problems with building administrators.
57. This school uses pretty standard curriculum material and does not generally seek out new or updated material on a systematic basis.
58. This school has a clear mission.
59. Faculty members are friendly to one another.
60. The values of this school are inconsistent with my own values.
61. This school is especially effective in seeking out new programs or practices in response to changes in the community or the pedagogical knowledge.
62. Teachers are not satisfied with the goals and objectives emphasized by this school.
63. The building administrators encourage suggestions from their faculty.
64. This school is efficient in how it uses material and how it organizes the staff.
65. Teachers in this school work closely with parents.
66. This school seems to be very innovative in comparison to other schools.
67. Teachers feel that others in this school value their ideas and suggestions.
68. Many teachers at this school are actively experimenting with new teaching methods or curriculum material.
69. Administrators and teachers in this school work together toward making the school run effectively.
70. There is a systematic effort in this school for teachers to share new curriculum material.
71. The climate in this school is poor.
72. Teachers tend to identify with this school and strongly support it when it is attacked.
73. The staff of this school can easily handle unusual or non-routine problems that may come up.
74. The communications in this school are good.
75. Teachers enjoy their school work very much.
76. The staff of this school are very supportive of each other in their attempt to try new techniques or methods.

77. The staff of this school are very interested in trying new teaching techniques or curriculum material.
78. I have a lot of very good friends at this school.
79. The staff at this school is not very interested in promoting their own professional development.
80. The staff at this school engage in peer observations and peer study groups to improve their own instruction and try new techniques.
81. This school is especially good in efficiently organizing students into groups that maximize learning.
82. Supplies and equipment are readily available when needed.
83. This school is especially good at anticipating problems with parents or students and preventing them before they become major problems.
84. The goals of this school are not clearly spelled out and communicated to all parties.
85. The staff at this school are well informed about educational issues that could affect their work.
86. Teachers sometimes are not sure what this school expects—one time the administration says one thing, the next time a different goal is emphasized.
87. When changes are made at this school, the faculty adjusts quickly.
88. Teachers in this school are given the freedom to make professional decisions.
89. Teachers in this school actively seek grants and other resources.
90. Teachers in this school are flexible and can change easily when necessary.
91. Teachers are expected to grow as professional staff members in this school.
92. Teachers in this school stay abreast of current technology in the classroom.
93. In this school, attention is focused on improvement of instruction.
94. Teachers in this school are unwilling to share ideas and techniques.
95. Professional development in this school is designed to meet the needs of the community.
96. Teachers in this school work harmoniously with community health and social agencies.
97. Teachers in this school encourage each other to try new techniques and strategies.
98. Teachers in this school provide training for other teachers when they have a successful program to share.
99. Teachers in this school have difficulty getting the necessary resources to successfully implement new programs.
100. Professional development activities in this school are oriented toward meeting future needs of the school.

Principal Behavior
To what extent do you...
1. demonstrate understanding of the staff's desires.
2. keep abreast of current technology.
3. work to establish peer improvement groups.
4. provide sound internal communications.
5. effectively deal with political changes that impact the building.
6. effectively diagnose and prioritize needs to achieve goals.
7. recognize the needs and concerns of parents.
8. engage in activities to promote staff development.
9. make yourself accessible to others.
10. provide continuous development opportunities for others.
11. participate in professional associations and community groups.
12. promote discussions of issues, problems, and recommendations pertaining to education.
13. articulate the school's mission to the community.
14. describe the school's mission to the school's staff and students.
15. cooperate with community agencies.

16. involve the community in school affairs.
17. maintain a good public relations program.
18. garner resources from the community.
19. effectively cope with disruptions in the normal school routine.
20. support new and innovative projects.
21. encourage the staff to assume new roles and responsibilities.
22. effectively utilize the existing skills of the staff.
23. alleviate difficult conflicts among the staff.
24. promote staff cohesion.
25. actively encourage the staff to use different institutional techniques.
26. entrust and support others.
27. understand how the school really works.
28. engage in coaching of teachers.
29. model different instructional techniques for the staff.
30. anticipate and react to community problems as they influence the school.
31. consider how your decisions might affect the school as a whole.
32. appropriately allocate time and resources.
33. protect the instructional time from interruptions.
34. appropriately delegate responsibility.
35. urge group involvement in decision making.
36. efficiently use the school facilities.
37. acquire outside funding to support innovative projects.
38. understand and respect employee rights typically found in the teacher-board contract.
39. explain to the staff why each part of the school organization is important and how they work together.
40. distribute workloads appropriately.
41. use different techniques and methods when working with individual staff members to help them improve their instruction.
42. hold high performance expectations for the staff.
43. conduct effective evaluation conferences.
44. show consideration for the students and staff.
45. actively promote school spirit and morale.
46. conduct frequent evaluation conferences.
47. provide useful feedback that can be used to improve instruction.
48. select quality new teachers to fill vacancies.
49. effectively deal with societal changes that impact the building.
50. share decision making with others.
51. schedule appropriate and meaningful meetings.
52. recognize the needs and concerns of students.
53. actively coordinate the curricular program.
54. display a detailed understanding of the instructional program in your school.
55. provide appropriate structure within the school organization.
56. support high professional standards.
57. set improvement goals.
58. systematically evaluate the educational program.
59. encourage cooperation rather than competition among the staff.
60. emphasize the importance of each part of the school organization.
61. maintain a high visibility in the building.
62. clearly understand what are important school problems.
63. place a high priority on student academic achievement.

64. make decisions based on information rather than personal opinion.
65. place a high priority on student emotional development.
66. support the staff.
67. write concisely and correctly.
68. emphasize production and getting things done on time.
69. demonstrate skills in problem resolution and decision making.
70. use effective oral communication skills.
71. support non-conventional activities.
72. assist the staff with personal and professional concerns.
73. understand diverse ethnic and multicultural backgrounds of staff and students.
74. actively help the staff achieve their goals.
75. place a high priority on student social development.
76. provide positive reinforcement to students and staff.
77. provide sound leadership.
78. provide social leadership within the building.
79. show an employee centered orientation.
80. expect staff loyalty to the school.
81. serve as a symbol of the building.
82. assign staff to positions in which they are most comfortable.
83. arrange the school to promote employee job satisfaction.

Diagnostic Assessment of School and Principal Effectiveness
Staff Version

School Effectiveness
1. The principal is concerned with faculty working conditions.
2. Teachers at this school do not have a great deal of confidence in each other's abilities.
3. Teachers in this school are encouraged to implement new teaching techniques.
4. As students move from one grade level to the next or from one course to another, teachers generally can be assured that the students were soundly prepared in the previous course.
5. Teachers in this school are open to changes that will improve the school.
6. Student achievement is rewarded in this school.
7. The workload is adequately balanced among the faculty members of this school.
8. Teachers in this school have respect for the professional competence of other teachers, departments, or levels.
9. Student creativity is encouraged and rewarded in this school.
10. I am not proud of this school.
11. In spite of limited financial resources, this school is able to get the money and equipment we need to conduct an effective educational program.
12. I have a pretty good idea how the various departments or grade levels within this school function.
13. Teachers in this school work closely with the community.
14. My job gives me professional satisfaction.
15. This school seems to be less effective than other schools in our district in obtaining adequate resources to support the educational program.
16. The development of student self-confidence is stressed at this school.
17. It is not clear to me what each department or level is supposed to do.
18. There are open lines of communication between the faculty and the building administrators.
19. This school is an excellent organization.

20. The development of individual student self-concept is not emphasized in this school.
21. Before a decision is made in this school, there is a good deal of communication among teachers.
22. I am satisfied with the amount of work I am expected to do.
23. Administrative policies are available to faculty in printed form.
24. Before a decision which would affect everyone is made in this school, there is a good deal of communication among grade levels or departments.
25. Teachers in this school are trying hard to promote student achievement.
26. I would leave this school for any other.
27. Our school staff works together to jointly write grants or requests to secure resources from outside agencies.
28. The quality of teaching in this school is very high.
29. The staff in this school respects each other and work well together.
30. I am not satisfied with the amount of money I make.
31. There is general faculty confidence in the building administrators.
32. There are often conflicts between teachers in this school.
33. I tell my friends that I will stay at this school for many years to come.
34. I am satisfied with the fringe benefits in this school district.
35. There are sufficient social activities for the faculty.
36. Productivity is high in this school.
37. If offered a better salary, I would move to another school.
38. I am satisfied with the trust I have in building administrators.
39. Our school is not very effective in gaining community support for our programs.
40. The social contact between students and faculty is friendly.
41. Conflict between staff members in this school is rare.
42. Teachers at this school are not very loyal to the school and staff.
43. I believe in the goals and objectives of this school.
44. In this school, the workload among teachers is pretty evenly distributed.
45. This school has activities to help us keep in touch with the wants and desires of the community.
46. In this school, all students are treated with respect—even those from poor backgrounds or those of limited intellectual ability.
47. I am satisfied with the professional competence and leadership of my building administrator.
48. In this school, everyone is arranged to facilitate the achievement of our goals.
49. Most of my interests lie outside my job at school.
50. The size of classes is satisfactory.
51. Teachers at this school respect parents and attempt to work with them whenever possible.
52. Each year in this school we make an effort to identify problems and set school-wide improvement goals.
53. Unlike this school, I would like to work in a school that holds the same values I do.
54. This school seems especially effective in adopting new and innovative instructional techniques.
55. Teachers in this school do not hold each other in high regard.
56. I am satisfied with the opportunities provided to discuss problems with building administrators.
57. This school uses standard curriculum material and does not generally seek out new or updated material on a systematic basis.
58. This school has a clear mission.
59. Faculty members are friendly to one another.
60. The values of this school are inconsistent with my own values.

61. This school is especially effective in seeking out new programs or practices in response to changes in the community or the pedagogical knowledge.
62. I am not satisfied with the goals and objectives emphasized by this school.
63. The building administrators encourage suggestions from the faculty.
64. This school is efficient in how it uses materials and how it organizes the staff.
65. Teachers in this school work closely with parents.
66. This school seems to be more innovative than other schools.
67. I feel that others in this school value my ideas and suggestions.
68. Few teachers at this school are actively experimenting with new teaching methods or curriculum material.
69. Administrators and teachers in this school work together to make the school run effectively.
70. There is a systematic effort in this school for teachers to share new curriculum material.
71. The climate in this school is poor.
72. I tend to identify with this school and strongly support it when it is attacked.
73. The staff of this school could easily handle unusual or non-routine problems that may come up.
74. The communications in this school are good.
75. I enjoy my school work very much.
76. The staff of this school is very supportive of each other in their attempts to try new techniques or methods.
77. The staff at this school is very interested in trying new teaching techniques or curriculum material.
78. I have a lot of very good friends at this school.
79. The staff at this school is not very interested in promoting their own professional development.
80. The staff at this school engage in peer observations and peer study groups to improve their own instruction and try new techniques.
81. This school is especially good in efficiently organizing students into groups that maximize learning.
82. Supplies and equipment are rarely available when needed.
83. This school is especially good at anticipating problems with parents or students and preventing them before they become major problems.
84. The goals of this school are not clearly spelled out and communicated to all parties.
85. The staff at this school are well informed about educational issues that could effect their work.
86. I sometimes am not sure what this school expects of me—one time they say one thing, the next time a different goal is emphasized.
87. When changes are made at this school, the faculty adjusts very slowly.
88. As a teacher in this school, I am given the freedom to make professional decisions.
89. Teachers in this school actively seek grants and other resources.
90. Teachers in this school are flexible and can change easily when necessary.
91. I am expected to grow as a professional staff member at this school.
92. Teachers in this school stay abreast of current technology in the classroom.
93. In this school, attention is focused on improvement of instruction.
94. Teachers in this school are unwilling to share ideas and techniques.
95. Professional development in this school is designed to meet the needs of the community.
96. Teachers in this school work harmoniously with community health and social agencies.
97. Teachers in this school encourage each other to try new techniques and strategies.
98. Teachers in this school provide training for other teachers when they have a successful program to share.
99. Teachers in this school have difficulty getting the necessary resources to successfully implement new programs.

100. Professional development activities in this school are oriented toward meeting future needs of the school.

Principal Behavior

To what extent does your principal...

1. demonstrate understanding of the staff's desires.
2. keep abreast of current technology.
3. work to establish peer improvement groups.
4. provide sound internal communications.
5. effectively deal with political changes that "impact" the building.
6. effectively diagnose and prioritize needs to achieve goals.
7. recognize the needs and concerns of parents.
8. engage in activities to promote your development.
9. make himself/herself accessible to others.
10. provide continuous development opportunities for others.
11. participate in professional associations.
12. promote discussions of issues, problems, and recommendations pertaining to education.
13. articulate the school's mission to the community.
14. describe the school's mission to the school's staff and students.
15. cooperate with community agencies.
16. involve the community in school affairs.
17. maintain a good public relations program.
18. garner resources from the community.
19. effectively cope with disruptions in the normal school routine.
20. support new and innovative projects.
21. encourage the staff to assume new roles and responsibilities.
22. effectively utilize the existing skills of the staff.
23. resolve difficult conflicts among the staff.
24. promote staff cohesion.
25. actively encourage the staff to use different instructional techniques.
26. entrust and support others.
27. understand the informal structure and operations of the school.
28. engage in coaching of teachers.
29. model different instructional techniques for the staff.
30. anticipate and react to community problems as they influence the school.
31. consider how his/her decisions might affect the school as a whole.
32. appropriately allocate time and resources.
33. protect the instructional time from interruptions.
34. appropriately delegate responsibility.
35. involve the school staff in decision making.
36. efficiently use the school facilities.
37. acquire outside funding to support innovative projects.
38. understand and respect employee rights typically found in the teacher-board contract.
39. explain to the staff why each part of the school organization is important and how they work together.
40. distribute workloads appropriately.
41. use individualized techniques and methods when working with different staff members to help them improve their instruction.
42. hold high performance expectations for the staff.
43. conduct effective evaluation conferences.

44. show consideration for the students and staff.
45. actively promote school spirit and morale.
46. conduct frequent evaluation conferences.
47. provide useful feedback that can be used to improve instruction.
48. select quality new teachers to fill vacancies.
49. effectively deal with societal changes that "impact" the building.
50. share decision making with others.
51. schedule appropriate and meaningful meetings.
52. recognize the needs and concerns of students.
53. actively coordinate the curricular program.
54. display a detailed understanding of the instructional program in your school.
55. provide appropriate structure within the school organization.
56. support high professional standards.
57. set improvement goals.
58. systematically evaluate the educational program.
59. encourage cooperation rather than competing among the staff.
60. emphasize the importance of each part of the school organization.
61. maintain high visibility in the building.
62. clearly understand what are important school problems.
63. place a high priority on student academic achievement.
64. make decisions based on information rather than personal opinion.
65. place a high priority on student emotional development.
66. support the staff.
67. write concisely and correctly.
68. emphasize production and getting things done on time.
69. demonstrate skill in problem resolution and decision making.
70. use effective oral communication skills.
71. support unconventional activities.
72. assist the staff with personal and professional concerns.
73. understand diverse ethnic and multi-cultural backgrounds of staff and students.
74. actively help the staff achieve their goals.
75. place a high priority on student social development.
76. provide positive reinforcement to students and the staff.
77. provide sound leadership.
78. provide social leadership within the building.
79. show an employee-centered orientation.
80. expect staff loyalty to the school.
81. serve as a symbol of the building.
82. assign staff to positions in which they are most comfortable.
83. arrange the school to promote employee job satisfaction.
84. participate in community groups.

Scoring: For school effectiveness: Strongly Agree = A; Agree = B; Neutral = C; Disagree = D; and Strongly Disagree = E. For principal behavior: Never = A; Almost Never = B; Sometimes = C; Often = D; Almost Always = E; and Always = F.

Reprinted with the permission of M. Katherine Weickert, Director of Administrator Services. (© United School Administrators of Kansas.)

Principal Performance Rating Scale

Weiss, K. 1989. Evaluating principal performance. Ph.D. dissertation, New York University.

Comments: The instrument was developed to assess a principal's performance, as well as to be utilized by a principal in self-improvement. The assessment tool is based on basic administrative competencies such as organizational skills, leadership, decision-making, staffing, staff evaluation, and the like. The instrument can be used to determine areas of strength and weakness in a principal's performance. The information obtained can be used as the basis of an administrative appraisal process in which goals and objectives can be cooperatively established by the superintendent, or some other supervisor, and the principal.

Scale Construction: The initial item pool consisted of 229 items. These were submitted to a panel of judges for clarification and content analysis. Seventy-nine items survived this process.

Sample: Thirty-seven principals (19 elementary, nine middle, and nine high school) from eight school districts in Nassau and Suffolk Counties in New York participated in the initial study. These districts were chosen because the principals had diversified characteristics in years of service as administrators, degrees earned, sex, and age.

Reliability: Alpha coefficients were obtained for the total instrument of 0.98 and for each subscale, which ranged from 0.89 to 0.96.

Validity: Content, criterion-related, and construct validity are provided for the instrument, and five factors were produced from this process: educational, leadership, interpersonal, professional, and managerial.

Factor Analysis: A known-groups techniques was used for determining criterion and construct validity.

References:
Baehr, M. 1975. A national occupational analysis of the school principalship. Chicago, IL: Industrial Relations Center and Consortium for Educational Leadership. ERIC ED 116 340.

Human Synergistics. 1982. Educational Administrator Effectiveness Profile. Plymouth, MI: Author.

Principal Performance Rating Scale

Leadership
1. Encourages and emphasizes team work and staff participation.
2. Encourages staff to use their own.
3. Effectively shares decision making responsibilities with staff when appropriate.
4. Develops and disseminates goals and objectives of the school.
5. Seeks relevant input from staff in the planning process.
6. Shares responsibilities and authority with other staff members.
7. Is able to inspire and challenge staff.
8. Encourages staff initiative and innovation.
9. Delegates authority effectively.
10. Delegates tasks in order to assist staff in improving their skills.
11. Provides clear and consistent direction.
12. Utilizes committees in sharing responsibility for certain policy decisions.
13. Ensures that the authority and responsibility of each subordinate are clearly understood.
14. Uses appropriate support personnel effectively.

Educational
1. Works toward articulation between grades and school.
2. Observes and evaluates all members of the teaching staff on a regular basis.
3. Systematically evaluates the instructional program and uses the results for continuous program improvement.
4. Actively evaluates curriculum.
5. Supervises the instructional staff in the development and implementation of curriculum.
6. Seeks way to support and strengthen the teaching/learning process.
7. Initiates instructional improvement efforts based on educational research and proven methods.
8. Visits classrooms regularly to supervise and evaluate the instructional program.
9. Establishes and maintains expectations for student achievement.
10. Provides systematic and effective supervision to improve instruction.
11. Ensures that curriculum content is related to established goals and objectives.
12. Monitors effective use of classroom time.
13. Is actively involved in the development of curricula.
14. Provides for organizing, collecting and analyzing data to be used to identify curriculum needs.
15. Is continuously involved with the evaluation of the curriculum.

Interpersonal
1. Counsels teachers regarding their personal problems.
2. Works with the community to determine its expectations for the school.
3. Establishes good working relationships with members of the school board.
4. Establishes good working relationships with local news media.
5. Encourages members of the community to participate in school activities.
6. Effectively gives and receives cues to/from the staff and school community.
7. Effectively counsels and advises students and parents.
8. Works supportively with the board of education in recommending and implementing policy.
9. Uses effective techniques in establishing and maintaining good relations with the students.
10. Uses effective techniques in establishing and maintaining good relations with the community.
11. Demonstrates concerns and openness in the consideration of teacher and/or student problems.
12. Has the ability to listen, understand and appreciate others.

Professional

1. Views keeping up with new techniques and developments as important.
2. Attends professional meetings and seminars outside of the school district.
3. Behaves in an appropriate manner.
4. Keeps abreast of current and innovative trends in education.
5. Keeps informed and up-to-date regarding new developments in curriculum and instruction.
6. Participates in activities to improve personal knowledge and skills.
7. Maintains a regular program of reading and study in the professional field.
8. Achieves success and honors in the areas of scholarship or other areas relevant to the job.
9. Belongs to and participates in professional organizations directly related to job tasks.
10. Pursues a planned program of professional growth.
11. Creates a favorable impression by dressing and grooming appropriately.
12. Sets personal professional goals on a yearly basis.
13. Is punctual to work, meetings and appointments.
14. Participates actively in workshops and conferences.

Managerial

1. Efficiently prepares, monitors and implements budget requests.
2. Demonstrates knowledge of finance and budget.
3. Schedules instructional space to provide for maximum utilization and minimum disruption.
4. Accounts for budget expenditures.
5. Effectively plans and implements transportation procedures and resolves related problems.
6. Establishes procedures for maintenance and accountability of facilities, equipment and inventory.
7. Plans for beautification of building and grounds.
8. Maintains and monitors records required by law.
9. Provides for availability of supplies and equipment.
10. Supervises cafeteria programs.
11. Inspects physical plant on a regular basis.
12. Ensures that student records are systematically and accurately maintained.
13. Allocates funds based upon fair, predetermined and well understood criteria.
14. Effectively schedules and utilizes school facilities.
15. Establishes a system of control for the inventory of materials and supplies.
16. Identifies, proposes and plans construction needs.
17. Develops and implements fiscal procedures with input from staff members.
18. Develops master schedule to optimize utilization of personnel and facilities.
19. Ensures the safety of the physical plant and of the personnel.

Scoring: Unsatisfactory Performance = 1; Marginal Performance = 2; Satisfactory Performance = 3; Above Average = 4; and Outstanding = 5.

Reprinted with permission of the author.

Role

Teacher Role Survey

Maes, W.R., and D.E. Anderson. 1985. A measure of teacher locus of control. *Journal of Educational Research* 79:27-32.

Comments: The revised 24-item Teacher Role Survey (TRS) assesses control expectancies for elementary and secondary school teachers' roles.

Scale Construction: The original item pool consisted of 75 items in 14 categories. There were eight items in each of the following primary categories: work with students; relations with teachers; sense of achievement; curriculum and program freedom; responsibility; recognition; and attitudes of society and parents. One to five items were written for each of the following remaining categories: administration, personnel policies, salary, working conditions, workload, security, and social service. Each item consisted of two statements. One statement represented an external belief and the other an internal belief. Five forms of the TRS were constructed, by positioning the items in various sequences. The original results indicated that item position influenced responses. Thirty-two items were retained based on item correlations that ranged from 0.30 to 0.50.

Sample: The original sample consisted of 321 teacher volunteers who were enrolled in graduate education courses or who were teaching.

Reliability: The alpha coefficient for the 32-item TRS was 0.86 (with a cross-validation sample of 166 teachers). Test-retest reliability over a two-week period was 0.75 (43 graduate students) and 0.62 over a three-week period (34 student teachers and student teacher supervisors).

Validity: Content validity was established by the procedures used to develop the survey. Factor analytic procedures were conducted to establish construct validity.

Factor Analysis: Twelve factors were identified using a principal components factor analysis with a varimax rotation. However, only the first four factors had factor loadings of at least 0.35 or higher and fit within the logical framework for the construction of the survey. The four factors are recognition, teaching/learning process, relations with teachers, and attitudes of parents and society.

References:
Anderson, D.E., and W.R. Maes. 1986. Teacher locus of control and teacher characteristics. Unpublished manuscript.

Guskey, T.R. 1981. Measurement of the responsibility teachers assume for academic successes and failures in the classroom. *Journal of Teacher Education* 32:44-51.

Maes, W.R., and D.E. Anderson. 1983. The Teacher Role Survey: A measure of teacher locus of control. ERIC ED 240 153.

Teacher Role Survey

1. a. Teachers will never be able to negotiate for satisfactory personnel policies.
    b. It appears that teachers are just now on the brink of a period of improved negotiations over personnel policies.

2. a. Teachers are given recognition in proportion to the quality of their performance.
    b. Given society's attitude toward teaching, there is really very little a teacher can do to gain the recognition deserved.

3. a. If I work hard and perform effectively, administrators are very supportive of my work.
    b. I find that principals and superintendents base their support of a teacher more on whim and hearsay than on quality of work.

4. a. Parents will cooperate with teachers if teachers put forth skillful effort.
    b. Teachers have reason to be pessimistic about getting parents "on their side."

5. a. One of the rewards of teaching is the chance to put one's abilities to work.
    b. School systems seem to invent obstacles to keep teachers from doing their best.

6. a. In this day and age, teachers are deprived of a strong sense of personal responsibility.
    b. Teaching is a profession that enables one to develop a strong sense of personal responsibility.

7. a. The more one teaches effectively, the more one is delegated responsibility for classroom management.
    b. With all the "snoopervisors" in schools, teachers are watched over regardless of their competence level.

8. a. To get duly recognized, a teacher needs only exert the effort to perform well.
    b. One of the problems with teaching is that there is little recognition even when it is earned.

9. a. Teachers touch the lives of pupils and parents in effective ways, and a natural by-product is personal and professional recognition.
    b. One certainly does not choose teaching for the professional recognition it offers.

10. a. It is clear that a teacher can take delight in creative development of learning experiences.
    b. More and more learning experiences are "canned" and mandated for the teacher.

11. a. Schools have been and perhaps always will be rather uninteresting, oppressive places in which to work.
    b. The fact that teachers are so influential at the building level enables them to greatly affect their working conditions.

12. a. All about that is required of a teacher is the ability to follow directions from above.
    b. The longer I stay in teaching, the more I feel that my presence in the classroom makes a difference.

13. a. The long-term negative attitude of our society towards teachers need not persist into the future.
    b. The negative attitude of society towards teaching is something that just has to be endured.

14. a. Students are becoming increasingly independent and unruly.
    b. If teachers really put themselves into the task, it is possible for them to exert meaningful influence on students.

15. a. There is always more work to be done by a teacher than can possibly be finished.
    b. Careful planning and scheduling of time makes the job of teaching more manageable.

16. a. I feel that I am delegated the responsibility to do my job as I see fit.
    b. I feel that my responsibility as a teacher is eroded by too many guidelines and supervisors.

17. a. Because a teacher's best efforts go unobserved behind closed doors, it is natural that due recognition is not received.
    b. In spite of the criticism leveled at schools, effective teachers receive due recognition from within and outside of schools.

18. a. Teachers will be treated as responsible professionals to the degree that they earn such treatment.
    b. There is too great a tendency to treat teachers like children.

19. a. Teaching is a profession in which a sense of achievement is often missing because it is difficult to know the effect of one's work.
    b. One of the advantages of teaching is that one is the "manager of the classroom" and thus can arrange things so as to get a clear sense of what has been accomplished.

20. a. Being "a part of the group" of teachers in a building depends on one's behavior.
    b. Every school has its pecking order which determines those teachers who are accepted and those who are not.

21. a. Teaching is one of the last remaining job fields that permits genuine giving to others.
    b. It is increasingly difficult for teachers to realize the joy of giving to others when they receive so little in return.

22. a. Parents are easily incited to discontent toward teachers.
    b. I have never met a parent who couldn't be won over by a sincere approach.

23. a. It seems inevitable that parents are quick to give negative feedback to teachers, but reluctant to dispense praise.
    b. Parents appreciate teachers for work well done.

25. a. School administrators are highly responsive to directives "from above" but not very responsive to influence from teachers.
    b. Teachers are heard and responded to by administrators to the degree that they effectively plead their case.

Scoring: Each of the following statements receives a score of one: 1a, 2b, 3b, 4b, 5b, 6a, 7b, 8b, 9b, 10b, 11a, 12a, 13b, 14a, 15a, 16b, 17a, 18b, 19a, 20b, 21b, 22a, 23a, 24a. Scores range from 0 to 24.

Reprinted with permission of the author.

Role Conflict/Role Ambiguity Questionnaire

Rizzo, R.J., et al. 1970. Role conflict and ambiguity in complex organizations. *Administrative Science Quarterly* 15:150-163.

Comments: The role conflict scale was designed to measure the role ambiguity and role conflict of individuals within an organization. Role ambiguity is defined as the extent to which an individual is unclear about the role expectations of others, as well as the degree of uncertainty associated with one's role performance. It is often noted in the literature that role ambiguity leads to role conflict. Role conflict is the degree to which expectations of a role are incompatible, or incongruent, with the reality of the role. This incompatibility may be due to conflicts between organizational demands and one's own values, problems of personal resource allocation, or conflicts between obligations to several different people.

Scale Construction: The questionnaire originally consisted of 30 items, 15 dealt with role ambiguity and 15 with role conflict. Of the role conflict items, ten were stress worded and five were comfort worded. The role ambiguity items consisted of six that were stress worded and nine were comfort worded.

Reliability: The six items of the role ambiguity scale had an alpha coefficient of 0.73, and the eight items on the role conflict scale was 0.88.

Factor Analysis: The 30 items were factor analyzed using an image covariance method with a varimax rotation. Only 14 items were retained on two factors, which accounted for 56% of the common variance. A high score on role ambiguity indicates feelings of comfort with a role; however, scoring on these items is usually done in the reverse to indicate ambiguity or discomfort with the role. Items 1, 3, 5, 8, 10, 13 provide a measure of role ambiguity (RA), while the remaining items are used to score role conflict (RC).

References:
Lane, T., and T.W. Johnson. 1981. What do role conflict and role ambiguity scales measure? *Journal* of *Applied Psychology* 66:464-469.

Wilson, S.M. 1979. Role conflict, role ambiguity, and job satisfaction among full-time principals and teaching principals in Maine. Ed.D. dissertation, George Peabody College.

Role Conflict/Role Ambiguity

1. I have clear, planned goals and objectives for my job.
2. I have to do things that should be done differently.
3. I know I have divided my time properly.
4. I receive an assignment without the assistance to complete it.
5. I know what my responsibilities are.
6. I have to buck a rule or policy in order to carry out an assignment.
7. I work with two or more groups who operate quite differently.
8. I know exactly what is expected of me.
9. I receive incompatible requests from two or more people.
10. I feel certain about how much authority I have.
11. I do things that are apt to be accepted by one person and not by others.
12. I receive an assignment without adequate resources and materials to complete it.
13. Explanation is clear of what has to be done.
14. I work on unnecessary things.

Scoring: A Likert-type scale was used ranging from Definitely not true of my job = 1 to Extremely true of my job = 7.

Reprinted with permission from R.J. House.

Parent-School Communities Questionnaire

Wiener, W.K. 1975. Measuring school boundary permeability. Paper presented at the New England Educational Research Association. ERIC ED 125 052.

Comments: The 50-item PSCQ was designed to measure the permeability of school boundaries. The concept of permeability assumes that any social system, such as a school, is surrounded by a psychological boundary that insulates it from its environment. The degree to which this boundary is permeable to input from outside the system is directly proportional to the openness of the system.

Scale Construction: Originally, the PSCQ consisted of 50 descriptive statements that respondents were asked to rate on a five-point Likert scale. The original factor analysis yielded dimensions dealing with the process parents used to contact school personnel; attempts by school personnel to contact parents; parental perceptions of the character of the school organization; and a dimension relevant to the quality and nature of parent-teacher interactions.

Sample: The first analysis was based on a sample of 500 parents taken from three elementary schools. The feedback from this study prompted a second factor analysis with 278 parent responses.

Validity: Interviews were conducted with a known-group of parents to determine the degree of correspondence between the parents interview comments and those items coded on the questionnaire.

Factor Analysis: The result of the second factor analysis—a principal axis analysis with a varimax rotation—produced three interpretable factors. The criterion for acceptance of items on a given factor was 0.500.

Definition of Factors: The three factors are: *Teacher-parent* interactions, which deals with the quality of interactions between parent and teacher; *Parent-principal interactions*, which is concerned with the quality of interactions between the parent and the school administration; and *Accessibility*, which refers to parents perceptions of the mechanics involved in making contact with the school.

Reference:
Wiener, W.K., and A. Blumberg. 1973. The Parent School Communications Questionnaire: A measure of school boundary permeability. Paper presented at American Educational Research Association. ERIC ED 075 916.

The Parent-School Communications Questionnaire:
A Measure of School Boundary Permeability

Factor I: Mechanical:
1. If my youngster is having a problem in school, the best way to contact the teacher is in writing rather than by phone.
2. Before talking with a teacher, I feel that I must first contact the principal.
3. It is difficult to get in touch with a teacher on the phone.
4. It is difficult to get in touch with the principal on the phone.
5. In order for me to see my youngster's teacher, I need only stop in at the school office without prior contact and ask.
6. In order for me to see the principal, I need only stop in at the school office without prior contact and ask.
7. The school secretary will forward my message to the principal or the teacher.

Factor II: Outreach:
8. My youngster's teacher contacts me personally when something goes wrong with his work.
9. My youngster's teacher contacts me personally when his work has been progressing particularly well.
10. The principal takes initiative in contacting parents about school matters.
11. The principal encourages parents to contact teachers about their children's school activities.
12. Teachers resist attending parent-teacher functions.
13. Teachers cooperate willingly with the parent group in discussing school issues.
14. Parent nights at school are events which I feel are useful and instructive.
15. Parents have a standing invitation to visit their youngster's classes with a few days notice.
16. After I have met with my youngster's teacher concerning a problem, the teacher contacts me with the follow-up information about the situation.
17. Ample notice is given by the school to inform me about parent organizational functions.
18. Most communications from the school are impersonal in tone.

Factor III: Organizational Climate:
19. Teachers see parents as a nuisance.
20. Teachers seem threatened by parents who ask questions.
21. Teachers are friendly and warm in their communications with parents.
22. When I walk into my youngster's classroom, I feel uncomfortable.
23. When I walk into the school, I sense a friendly warm atmosphere.
24. Teachers in the school like parents to contact them about their child.
25. Teachers do not think highly of the parent organization of the school.
26. The atmosphere at parent-teacher gatherings is strained and tense.
27. Teachers in the school are willing to listen to negative things I have to say about what is going on in school.
28. The principal is a limiting force on parent organization activities.
29. The principal actively supports the parent organization.

Factor IV: Interpersonal Climate:
30. I like to talk about my youngster's work with his teacher.
31. My youngster likes me to see his teacher on his behalf.
32. The principal sees parents as being a nuisance.
33. When I get a notice from a teacher that he wants to see me about my youngster, I feel tense.

34. When I talk with my youngster's teacher, I feel he is holding back information I would like to have.
35. When I talk to the principal, I feel that he is evasive.
36. I have no hesitancy at all about contacting a teacher about my youngster's work in school.
37. The principal is willing to listen to negative things I have to say about what's going on in the school.
38. If I complain to a teacher about my youngster's negative reaction to his teaching, I am afraid that teacher will act negatively toward my youngster.
39. The principal sees parents as a source to help him.
40. I feel free to stop and chat with teachers in the school.
41. The school secretary is helpful to me when I visit the school.

Factor V: Influences
42. Parent groups have no real influence on the school.
43. I feel that when I talk with the principal, I make an impact on him.
44. I feel that when I talk with my youngster's teacher, it makes an impression on him.
45. I trust the principal to communicate parental concerns to the teachers.
46. The principal only responds to pressure from a group of parents, not individuals.
47. Teachers seem to pay attention to parents.
48. The principal pays attention to parents.
49. The principal actively uses the parent organization to help in solving school problems.
50. I am made to feel that I as a parent, and not the school, must make all the changes to solve a problem.

Scoring: A five-point Likert scale ranging from "this is always true" = 5, to "this is never true" = 1.

Reprinted with permission of the author.

Self-Actualization

Index of Self-Actualization

Jones, A., and R. Crandall. 1986. Validation of a short Index of Self-Actualization. *Personality and Social Psychology Bulletin* 12:63-73.

Comments: The 15-item ISA discriminates between self-actualizing and non-self-actualizing individuals. Evidence of its reliability and validity are provided in the research.

Scale Development: The basis for this index was the Personal Orientation Inventory (Shostrom, 1964). Half of each of the 150 two-choice POI items were rewritten using an agree-disagree format. These new items as well as the POI were given to 73 college students. The ten items that had the highest item-total correlation with the total score (one from each of the ten subscales) on the POI were selected. Four additional items from the POI were selected (highest correlation without regard to subscale) as well as five items (highest factor loadings on various subscales) from the Personal Orientation Dimensions (Shostrom, 1975). The original 19-item index was reduced to 15 items based on Cronbach's alpha.

Sample: Approximately 500 people took part in validating the index. In general, classes of students in psychology, sociology, and business programs in two senior and three junior colleges in Texas participated. In addition, 73 college students from Illinois and 22 people from North Carolina participated.

Reliability: Test-retest reliability for a 12-day interval (67 students) was 0.69 using the original four-point scale. Test-retest reliability for a two-week interval (67 students) was 0.81 using a six-point scale. The correlation between the original four-point scale and the six-point scale was 0.91 (84 students). The coefficient alpha for the index with a four-point scale was 0.65. The new alpha was 0.72 (274 students).

Validity: The index was correlated with Eysenck's Personality Inventory (Eysenck & Eysenck, 1968); the Rational Behavior Inventory (Whiteman & Shorkey, 1978); Rosenberg's Self-Esteem Scale (Rosenberg, 1965); Budner's Tolerance of Ambiguity Scale (Budner, 1962); Slivken and Crandall's Leisure Ethic Scale (Crandall & Slivken, 1980); and the Personal Orientation Inventory (Shostrom, 1964).

Factor Analysis: A principal components factor analysis with a varimax rotation yielded five factors. The five factors are five items on autonomy or self-direction (2, 5, 9, 10, and 11); three items on self-acceptance and self esteem (6, 8, and 14); two items on acceptance of emotions and freedom of expression of emotions (1 and 4); three items on trust and responsibility in interpersonal relations (3, 13, and 15); and two items on the ability to deal with undesirable aspects of like rather than avoiding them (7 and 12).

References:

Flett, G.L., et al. Factor structure of the Short Index of Self-Actualization. In A. Jones and R. Crandall, eds. 1991. Handbook of self-actualization. *Journal of Social Behavior and Personality* 6:321-329.

Richard, R.L., and S.M. Jex. Further evidence for the validity of the Short Index of Self-Actualization. In A. Jones and R. Crandall, eds. 1991. Handbook of self-actualization. *Journal of Social Behavior and Personality* 6:331-338.

Shostrom, E.L. 1975. *Personal Orientation Dimensions.* San Diego, CA: Educational and Industrial Testing Service.

Tucker, R.K., and D.R. Weber. 1988. Factorial validity of Jones and Crandall's Short Index of Self-Actualization. *Psychological Reports* 63:39-45.

Weiss, A.S. The measurement of self-actualization: The quest for the test may be as challenging as the search for the self. In A. Jones and R. Crandall, eds. 1991. Handbook of self-actualization. *Journal of Social Behavior and Personality* 6:265-290.

Short Index of Self-Actualization

1.   I do not feel ashamed of any of my emotions.
2.   I feel I must do what others expect of me.
3.   I believe that people are essentially good and can be trusted.
4.   I feel free to be angry at those I love.
5.   It is always necessary that others approve what I do.
6.   I don't accept my own weaknesses.
7.   I can like people without having to approve of them.
8.   I fear failure.
9.   I avoid attempts to analyze and simplify complex domains.
10.   It is better to be yourself than to be popular.
11.   I have no mission in life to which I feel especially dedicated.
12.   I can express my feelings even when they may result in undesirable consequences.
13.   I do not feel responsible to help anybody.
14.   I am bothered by fears of being inadequate.
15.   I am loved because I give love.

Scoring: Strongly Agree = 6; Agree = 5; Somewhat Agree = 4; Somewhat Disagree = 3; Disagree = 2; and Strongly Disagree = 1. For items 2, 5, 6, 8, 9, 11, 13, and 14 the scoring is reversed. Self-actualizing responses receive a score of 6, while non-self-actualizing responses receive a score of 1.

Reprinted with permission of the author.

Personal Orientation Inventory

Shostrom, E.L. 1966. *Manual for the Personal Orientation Inventory*. San Diego, CA: Educational and Industrial Testing Service.

Comments: The 150-item POI discriminates among self-actualized, normal, and non-self-actualized individuals.

Scale Construction: Although the POI is based on Maslow's theory of self-actualization, items were also taken from the following humanistic, existential, or gestalt therapy writers Perls, May, Angel, Ellenberger, Fromm, Horney, Rogers, Riesman, Watts, and Ellis. Items were also chosen from observed value judgments of clinically healthy and troubled patients. Scores of relative time competence and relative inner—and other—directedness.

Sample: One validation study was conducted using 650 freshmen at Los Angeles State College, 150 patients in therapy, 75 members on the Sensitivity Training Program at UCLA, and 15 school psychologists.

Reliability: Test-retest reliability coefficients of 0.91 and 0.93 were reported. Coefficients of reliability ranged from 0.55 (acceptance of aggression) to 0.85 (existentiality), with a median of 0.74.

Validity: The POI and the MMPI were correlated in one validation study. Significant relationships (0.01 level) between two groups were found on four of the MMPI scales (D, Pd, Pt, and Sc) and all 12 POI scales. The POI and the Eysenck Personality Inventory were correlated in another study. Significant relationships were found. The POI possesses predictive validity because it is able to differentiate between healthy and unhealthy groups. The POI is also able to differentiate between self-actualized, normal, and non-self-actualized groups.

Scales: The POI contains ten subscales: 26 items on self-actualizing values, 32 items on existentiality, 23 items on feeling reactivity, 17 items on spontaneity, 26 items on self-acceptance, 16 items on nature of man, 16 items on self-regard, nine items on synergy, 25 items on acceptance of aggression, and 28 items on capacity for intimate contact.

Definitions of Subscales: *Self-actualizing values* refer to values held by self-actualizing people. *Existentiality* refers to the ability to react to situations without rigid adherence to principles. *Feeling reactivity* refers to the sensitivity of responsiveness to one's own needs and feelings. *Spontaneity* refers to the ability to be oneself or react spontaneously. *Self-acceptance* refers to acceptance of oneself in spite of weaknesses. *Nature of man* refers to the view of man, masculinity and femininity. *Self-regard* refers to self-worth. *Synergy* refers to the ability to surpass dichotomies. *Acceptance of aggression* refers to the ability to tolerate aggression. *Capacity for intimate contact* refers to the ability to cultivate intimate relationships.

References:
Doyle, J.A. 1976. Self-actualization, neuroticism, and extraversion revisited. *Psychological Reports* 39:1081-1082.

Margulies, N. 1969. Organizational culture and psychological growth. *Journal of Applied Behavioral Science* 5:491-508.

Scoring: A forced-choice format is used so that each item is written twice (items represent both ends of the continuum).

Sample Items:

39. a. I trust my ability to size up a situation.
    b. I do not trust my ability to size up a situation.
60. a. It is important that others accept my point of view.
    b. It is not necessary for others to accept my point of view.
80. a. For me, work and play are the same.
    b. For me, work and play are opposites.
127. a. I like to participate actively in intense discussions.
    b. I do not like to participate actively in intense discussions.
150. a. I can overcome any obstacles as long as I believe in myself.
    b. I cannot overcome every obstacle even if I believe in myself.

Personal Orientation Dimensions

Shostrom, E.L. 1977. *Manual for the Personal Orientation Dimensions*. San Diego, CA: Educational and Industrial Testing Service.

Comments: The 260-item POD is a refinement and extension of the Personal Orientation Inventory. It contains 13 scales with 20 items in each scale that represent an aspect in the actualizing individual.

Scale Construction: The POD is based on item analyses and construct validation studies that were conducted on the POI. Items were written based on the development of the POI and the theoretical model of the actualizing individual. An item pool of 370 items was created and several samples participated in the development of the POD. Items are stated both in the positive and in the negative. Scales from the POI that had predictive and factorial validity were utilized by either adding new items or rewriting old items.

Sample: The original sample consisted of 402 college freshmen.

Reliability: Test-retest reliability coefficients over a one-week period ranged from 0.53 (weakness) to 0.79 (potentiation), and over a three-month period ranged from 0.55 (strength) to 0.72 (weakness).

Validity: In order to establish the predictive validity of the POD, it was administered to a group of actualizing individuals and a group of non-actualizing individuals. Significant differences were found for all scales. Concurrent validity was established by correlating the POD with the Eysenck Personality Questionnaire and the Clinical Analysis Questionnaire.

Factor Analysis: First order and second order analyses were performed. The POI scale of Time Competence became the POD scale of Time Orientation; Self-Regard became Strength; Self-Acceptance became Weakness; Existentiality became Potentiation; Nature of Man-Constructive became Trust in Humanity; Synergy became Synergistic Integration; and Acceptance of Aggression became Anger. The POD scales of Creative Living, Mission, and Manipulation Awareness are new scales.

Definition of Scales: *Time Orientation* refers to living in the present instead of blaming the past or relying on the future. *Core Centeredness* refers to believing in one's feelings. *Strength* refers to power, security, worth, adequacy, or competence. *Weakness* refers to humanness, vulnerability, hurt or helplessness. *Anger* refers to feelings and experiences of anger. *Love* refers to feelings and experiences of warmth, tenderness, or affection. *Synergistic Integration* demonstrates that opposites or polarities are not necessarily opposites. *Potentiation* views life as a gestalt. *Being* refers to expressing feelings or thoughts. *Trust in Humanity* refers to viewing human nature as basically good. *Creative Living* refers to effectiveness and innovation. *Mission* refers to commitment to a life task. *Manipulation Awareness* refers to manipulative or controlling actions.

Data Analysis: Intercorrelations among the POD scales are reported as well as intercorrelations between the POD and the POI, and between the POD, the Eysenck Personality Questionnaire, and the Myer Briggs Type Indicator. Scale means, standard deviations, and reliabilities are presented. In addition, significant relationships between the POD and the Clinical Analysis Questionnaire are documented.

References:
Knapp, R.R., and L. Knapp. 1978. Conceptual and statistical refinement and extension of the measurement of actualizing: Concurrent validity of the Personal Orientation Dimensions (POD). *Educational and Psychological Measurement* 38:523-26.

Lerner, D.L. 1977. Self-actualizing profiles of scientists and actors as described by the Personal Orientation Dimensions. Ph.D. dissertation, United States International University.

Maslow, A.H. 1971. *The further reaches of human nature.* New York: Viking.

Rofsky, M., et al. 1977. Assessing the level of actualizing of psychiatric in-patients: Validity of the Personal Orientation Dimensions. *Educational and Psychological Measurement* 37:1075-79.

Shostrom, E.L., et al. 1976. Validation of the Personal Orientation Dimensions: An inventory for the dimensions of actualizing. *Educational and Psychological Measurement* 36:391-494.

Scoring: A forced-choice format is used so that each item is written twice (items represent both ends of the continuum). Machine scoring is available.

Sample Items: (not actual item numbers)
1.   a. I feel that I have a right to expect others to do what I want of them.
   b. I do not feel that I have a right to expect others to do what I want of them.
2.   a. I fear failure.
   b. I don't fear failure.
3.   a. I follow diligently the motto, "Don't waste your time."
   b. I do not feel bound by the motto, "Don't waste your time."
4.   a. I feel that people are more basically good than bad.
   b. I feel that people are more basically bad than good.
5.   a. I feel dedicated to my work.
   b. I do not feel dedicated to my work.

Self Concept

Tennessee Self-Concept Scale

Fitts, W.H. 1965. *Manual: Tennessee Self-Concept Scale.* Los Angeles, CA: Western Psychological Services.

Comment: The 100-item TSCS examines self concept as a multidimensional construct that measures internal and external aspects of self concept. Western Psychological Services provides a detailed Test Report for the TSCS. A revised manual (1988) includes information on administration, scoring, norms, psychometric properties, and a review of the literature that includes references to studies using the TSCS. Although questions have been raised about the factor structure of the TSCS, it is the most frequently cited instrument to measure self concept.

Scale Construction: A large pool of items from other self-concept instruments and self-descriptions was the basis for the internal/external categories of the TSCS. Seven clinical psychologists matched items into each of 15 areas. When all the psychologists agreed on an item, it was included in the appropriate category. There were six items selected for each of the 15 areas. Ten items were selected from the L-Scale of the MMPI.

Sample: The original sample consisted of 626 individuals ranging in age from 12 to 68 and from diverse economic, social, and educational levels.

Reliability: The split-half reliability for the total score on the TSCS was 0.91. The results of additional reliability studies are presented in the manual. Test-retest reliabilities ranged from 0.60 (row variability) to 0.92 (total score and psychosis) over a two-week interval with a sample of 60 university students. Test-retest reliability of the major TSCS scores are provided.

Factor Analysis: Numerous factor analytic studies have been conducted on the TSCS. A detailed description and summary is presented. Overall, factor analysis yielded eight factors: three internal self (row) subscales (identity, behavior, and self-satisfaction) and five external self (column) subscales (moral-ethical, social, personal, physical, and family). Factor loadings from the confirmatory rotation of internal (row) and external (column) factors are reported.

Validity: Content validity was established by the representativeness of the TSCS items and the use of facet-design. In order to establish its convergent and discriminant validity, the TSCS has been correlated with the MMPI, the Edwards Personal Preference Schedule, and other personality scales. The results of the correlations are reported in the manual. Statistically significant correlations are highlighted. Although factor analytic studies support the internal and external aspects of self concept, the 15 facets of self concept are not supported. Several studies examined the relationship between the TSCS and various outcome variables to establish criterion validity.

Definition of Scales: *Physical Self* refers to body, health, physical appearance, skills, and sexuality. *Moral-Ethical Self* refers to moral worth, relationship to God, satisfaction with religion, and feelings of being a good or bad individual. *Personal Self* refers to personal worth, feelings of adequacy, and self-evaluation of the personality. *Family Self* refers to worth and value as a member of a family. *Social Self* refers to adequacy and worth with others in social interactions. In addition to these five external aspects of self concept, the TSCS also provides scores on six empirical scales: *Defensive Positive* (29 items); *General Maladjustment* (24 items); *Psychosis* (23 items); *Personality Disorder* (27 items); *Neurosis* (27 items); and *Personality Integration* (25 items). In addition, scores are obtained for *Total Conflict*, and *Number of Deviant Signs*. The *Total Score* is considered to be the most important score because it represents overall self esteem.

Data Analysis: Means, standard deviations, and internal consistency reliability for the WPS Test Report Sample are provided.

References:
Amundson, M.E. 1993. A study of the professional characteristics of juvenile court school educators in California and the self concept of juvenile court school educators in Southern California. Ed.D. dissertation, University of LaVerne.

Greenan, J.P., et al. 1994. Relationship between self-concept and self-ratings of students in vocational programs. *Journal of Industrial Teacher Education* 31:94-110.

Meyer, M.M. 1991. The effects of assertion training on assertive behaviors, self-acceptance, self-concept, and locus of control. Ph.D. dissertation, University of Missouri, Kansas City.

Myers, L.C. 1992. Self-concepts of career level II and III teachers and career ladder eligible teachers in the public schools of Tennessee. Ed.D. dissertation, East Tennessee State University.

Scoring: Completely False = 1; Mostly False = 2; Partly False and Partly True = 3; Mostly True = 4; and Completely True = 5. The TSCS has two scoring modes: the Counseling mode, which includes 14 scores and the Clinical Research mode, which includes 20 scores. Computer scoring is available as well as profiles.

Sample Items:

8. I am a calm and easygoing person.
24. I have a lot of self-control.
48. I try to please others, but I don't overdo it.
60. I wish I didn't give up as easily as I do.
64. I am satisfied with the way I treat other people.
66. I ought to get along better with other people.
73. I try to change when I know I'm doing things that are wrong.
76. I take the blame for things without getting mad.
81. I try to understand the other fellow's point of view.
89. I sometimes use unfair means to get ahead.

(Items from the *Tennessee Self-Concept Scale* copyright © 1983 by Western Psychological Services, copyright © 1964 by William H. Fitts. Reprinted with permission of the publisher, Western Psychological Services, 12031 Wilshire Boulevard, Los Angeles, California 90025. No additional reproduction may be made without the expressed, written consent of Western Psychological Services. All rights reserved.)

Wallace Self-Concept Scale

Wallace, G.R. 1980. *WSCS technical manual.* St. Louis, MO: University of Missouri, St. Louis, Dept. of Behavioral Studies.

Comments: The WSCS is a 15-item bipolar adjective scale that measures an individual's perception of "Myself as a Person." It is a global measure of the self. There are two forms (A and B) in English and one form (A) in Spanish.

Scale Development: Based upon a review of the literature, an initial item pool consisting of 75 bipolar adjectives was developed. A panel of three judges rated the adjectives using a three-point scale. Thirty-four items were retained and administered to the original sample. The 15 items that were included in the final version of the WSCS met the following criteria: the item scores correlated equal to or greater than 0.40 with the total WSCS and the item scores correlated equal to or less than 0.23 with the Marlowe-Crowne Social Desirability Scale. Form B was constructed by making the top half of Form A the bottom of Form B and vice versa. All the bipolar items were also reversed. Forms A and B are considered alternate forms.

Sample: The original sample consisted of 100 people (teachers, college students, and businessmen). Descriptive statistics are provided for four groups: adults (1,257), adolescents (771), college students (287), and a total sample (2,301). Normative data (raw scores, frequencies, cumulative frequencies, NCEs, standardized T scores, and the normalized Z scores) are included for each of the four groups.

Validity: Two types of validity are reported for Form A. Convergent validity is reported between the WSCS and the Tennessee Self-Concept Scale (0.45), the Rosenberg Self-Esteem Scale (0.60), the Personal Orientation Inventory (0.51), and the Piers-Harris Self-Esteem Concept Scale (0.64). Discriminant validity with the Marlowe-Crowne Social Desirability Scale is 0.23.

Reliability: Three types of reliability estimates are reported for Form A. Coefficient alpha for Form A was 0.81. Test-retest reliabilities ranged from 0.72 to 0.81 over a two-week period. Alternate form reliabilities between Form A and B ranged from 0.71 to 0.80 over a three-week period.

References:
Wallace, G.R., and S.P. Walker. 1990. Self-concept, vocational interests, and choice of academic major in college students. *College Student Journal* 23:361-367.

Wallace, G.R., et al. 1984. Factorial comparison of the Wallace Self-Concept Scale between special education teachers and regular classroom teachers. *Educational and Psychological Measurement* 44:199-207.

Wallace Self-Concept Scale (Form A)

1. Eager   Indifferent
2. Passive   Active
3. Rigid   Flexible
4. Participating   Avoiding
5. Lethargic   Energetic
6. Powerful   Powerless
7. Negative   Positive
8. Hardworking   Lazy
9. Repulsive   Attractive
10. Sharp   Dull
11. Unpleasant   Pleasant
12. Useless   Useful
13. Happy   Sad
14. Pessimistic   Optimistic
15. Ugly   Beautiful

Scoring: Each bipolar adjective item is scored on a scale from 1 to 7. The six reverse scored adjectives are: eager, participating, powerful, hardworking, sharp, and happy.

Reprinted with permission of Gaylen R. Wallace, Ed.D. Department of Behavioral Studies, University of Missouri at St. Louis, St. Louis, MO 63121.

Teacher Self-Concept Inventory

Zinnerstrom, K.H. 1988. The development and validation of a teaching self-concept inventory for student teachers. Ph.D. dissertation, State University of New York at Buffalo.

Comments: The 50-item TSCI assesses the self concept of student teachers in relation to their teaching performance. There are 15 items on the role of planner, nine items on the role of instructor, 11 items on the role of administrator/manager, and 15 items on the role of evaluator.

Scale Construction: In order to develop the TSCI, four major roles (planner, instructor, administrator/manager, and evaluator) connected with teaching were identified by looking at several competency-based teacher preparation programs. Then each of these roles was studied in terms of the tasks, skills, and knowledge associated with teaching. As a result, about 100 items were written. Teachers and professors evaluated these items. Based upon the comments of the teachers and professors, 50 items were retained. A pilot study was conducted with nine student teachers. A shortened form of the TSCI (20 items) was distributed to student teachers, cooperating teachers, and university supervisors. Minor revisions were made after analyzing the results of the pilot study. Once again, the TSCI was evaluated by a panel of experts.

Sample: A total of 82 student teachers from the State University responded to the inventory over a two-year period.

Reliability: The alpha coefficient for the inventory (82 student teachers) was 0.90.

Validity: Content validity was established by the steps taken to develop the inventory. Evidence is provided to support the construct validity of the TSCI.

Data Analysis: Means and standard deviations are reported.

References:
Borich, G.D. 1980. A needs assessment model for conducting follow-up studies. *Journal of Teacher Education* 31:39-42.

Middleton, E.J., and S. Cohen. 1979. Evaluating a teacher education program. *Journal of Teacher Education* 30:42-44.

Moxley, R.A. Jr. 1978. Teacher evaluation: Images and analysis. *Journal of Teacher Education* 29:61-66.

Zahorik, J.A. 1980. Teacher experiential knowledge about verbal behavior. *Journal of Teacher Education* 31:44-49.

Teacher Self-Concept Inventory (TSCI)

1. Construct instructional objectives appropriate to specific topics within the course of study.
2. Utilize a variety of learning activities such as games, demonstrations, reading materials, student activities, audiovisual materials, etc.
3. Understand the formal chain of communication and , authority within the district.
4. Select objectives consistent with state and local syllabi.
5. Interpret the purpose and goals of the curriculum to students, administrators and the community.
6. Coordinate aims and goals of lesson for long range objectives of the course.
7. Give specific feedback to a student regarding performance.
8. Sequence instructional activities according to content, learning and skill considerations.
9. Select goals and objectives which will help students plan for careers and the future.
10. Encourage students to ask questions.
11. Diagnose students for their incoming abilities and basic skills.
12. Utilize other teachers and school personnel *in* planning for instruction.
13. Ask clear questions with a specific response expected of students.
14. Assess individual students for learning problems (e.g., visual, motor, speech, etc.).
15. Construct lessons compatible with ability levels of students.
16. Sequence questions from factual to higher levels of thinking.
17. Assess handicapped students' instructional levels and learning needs.
18. Analyze instructional materials for concepts and values appropriate for use in the classroom.
19. Provide experiences conducive to developing a positive attitude towards the content area.
20. Develop or select test questions that are related to specific instructional objectives.
21. Arrange objectives and learning experiences based on the major topics of the content.
22. Cultivate social skills of cooperation and self-evaluation.
23. Evaluate student achievement on levels higher than recall when consistent with instructional objectives.
24. Provide an appropriate information base for higher levels of cognitive learning.
25. Establish an efficient system to maximize student instructional time on task.
26. Utilize a variety of modes (e.g., projects, oral presentations, papers, etc.) to assess student achievement.
27. Develop the overall goals, specific objectives and requirements of the course.
28. Establish clear but flexible rules for classroom management.
29. Assess students at the end of a unit of study for appropriate skills and attitudes.
30. Utilize learning activities that maintain student attention and motivation.
31. Consistently follow the discipline code established by the school.
32. Evaluate students during a unit of study for progress.
33. Plan learning activities that relate previous experiences to the specific lesson.
34. Guide students toward self-discipline and respect for others.
35. Communicate to parents their child's academic performance.
36. Relate subsequent work and assignments to the present activity.
37. Recognize that discipline problems might arise because of inappropriate learning experiences.
38. Record, interpret and report student performance.
39. Utilize student's out of school experiences and learning in lesson planning.
40. Recognize that discipline problems might arise because of the pupil's out of school situation.
41. Modify evaluation efforts based on previous test performance.

42. Use lecture technique when there is much factual material to be covered in a short period of time.
43. Monitor students' attitudes, interests, self-concepts and values related to the subject and school.
44. Identify alternative strategies to follow when a situation is not covered in the handbook.
45. Apply fair, consistent and clear procedures for assigning grades.
46. Give students the opportunity to practice newly learned information.
47. Construct valid, reliable tests.
48. Design an efficient system to record the attendance and behavior of students.
49. Utilize standardized tests when appropriate.

Scoring: (A) = if you have no knowledge or experience regarding this task; (B) = if you cannot perform the task at all; (C) = if you can do the task, but only with help and assistance; (D) = if you can do it, but have done it infrequently; and (E) = if you always perform the task easily.

Reprinted with permission of the author.

Self Efficacy

Teacher Efficacy Scale

Gibson, S. 1984. Teacher Efficacy Scale. *Journal of Educational Psychology* 76:569-582.

Comments: The 30-item rating scale is designed to allow teachers to evaluate their degree of personal efficacy or their conviction that they can successfully execute behavior necessary to produce desired outcomes. Self-efficacy beliefs would indicate that teachers' evaluations of their abilities can bring about positive student change.

Sample: The sample consisted of 208 teachers from 13 elementary schools within two neighboring school districts in California.

Validity: A multitrait-multimethod technique was employed to establish both convergent and discriminant validity on three traits—teacher efficacy, verbal ability, and flexibility.

Factor Analysis: A principal factoring solution was used with both orthogonal and oblique rotations. Two factors were produced suggesting that the two factors were relatively independent. One factor was named personal teaching efficacy; the second was teaching efficacy.

Data Analysis: Classroom observations related to academic focus and teacher feedback behaviors indicated differences between high- and low-efficacy teachers in time spent in whole class versus small group instruction, teacher use of criticism, and teacher lack of persistence in failure situations.

References:
Bandura, A. 1977. Self-efficacy: Toward a unifying theory of behavioral change. *Psychological Review* 84:191-215.

Bandura, A. 1978. Reflections on self-efficacy. *Advances in Behavioral Research and Therapy* 1:237-269.

Gibson, S., and R. Brown 1982. The development of a teacher's personal responsibility/self-efficacy scale. Paper presented at American Educational Research Association.

Teacher Efficacy Scale

1. When a student does better than usual, many times it is because I exerted a little extra effort.
2. The hours in my class have little influence on students compared to the influence of their home environment.
3. If parents comment to me that their child behaves much better at school than he/she does at home, it would probably be because I have some specific techniques of managing his/her behavior which they may lack.
4. The amount that a student can learn is primarily related to family background.
5. If a teacher has adequate skills and motivation, he/she can get through to the most difficult students.
6. If students aren't disciplined at home, they aren't likely to accept any discipline.
7. I have enough training to deal with almost any learning problem.
8. My teacher training program and/or experience has given me the necessary skills to be an effective teacher.
9. Many teachers are stymied in their attempts to help students by lack of support from the community.
10. Some students need to be placed in slower groups so they are not subjected to unrealistic expectations.
11. Individual differences among teachers account for the wide variations in student achievement.
12. When a student is having difficulty with an assignment, I am usually able to adjust it to his/her level.
13. If one of my new students cannot remain on task for a particular assignment, there is little that I could do to increase his/her attention until he/she is ready.
14. When a student gets a better grade than he usually gets, it is usually because I found better ways of teaching that student.
15. When I really try, I can get through to most difficult students.
16. A teacher is very limited in what he/she can achieve because a student's home environment is a large influence on his/her achievement.
17. Teachers are not a very powerful influence on student achievement when all factors are considered.
18. If students are particularly disruptive one day, I ask myself what I have been doing differently.
19. When the grades of my students improve, it is usually because I found more effective teaching approaches.
20. If my principal suggested that I change some of my class curriculum, I would feel confident that I have the necessary skills to implement the unfamiliar curriculum.
21. If a student masters a new math concept quickly, this might be because I knew the necessary steps in teaching that concept.
22. Parent conferences can help a teacher judge how much to expect from a student by giving the teacher an idea of the parents' values toward education, discipline, etc.
23. If parents would do more with their children, I could do more.
24. If a student did not remember information I gave in a previous lesson, I would know how to increase his/her retention in the next lesson.
25. If a student in my class becomes disruptive and noisy, I feel assured that I know some techniques to redirect him quickly.
26. School rules and policies hinder my doing the job I was hired to do.
27. The influences of a student's home experiences can be overcome by good teaching.
28. When a child progresses after being placed in a slower group, it is usually because the teacher has had a chance to give him/her extra attention.

29. If one of my students couldn't do a class assignment, I would be able to accurately assess whether the assignment was at the correct level of difficulty.

30. Even a teacher with good teaching abilities may not reach many students.

Scoring: 1 = Strongly Disagree to 6 = Strongly Agree.

Reprinted with permission of the author.

Principal Self-Efficacy Scale
Teacher Self-Efficacy Scale

Hillman, S.J. 1986. Measuring self-efficacy: Preliminary steps in the development of a multi-dimensional instrument. Paper presented at American Educational Research Association. ERIC ED 271 505.

Comments: Two parallel 16-item questionnaires were designed to measure either teachers or principals self efficacy, that is, the extent to which they feel positive or negative concerning their achievement and productivity in the classroom or in the school. Both instruments are the same except principal items relate to the achievement of the school, while teacher items have a focus on the classroom.

Scale Construction: Half of the items presented positive situations that might occur in the classroom or school. Each item has four possible responses: (1) the first attributed the situation to either the teacher's ability or inability to teach; (2) this attributed the situation to either their effort or lack of effort; (3) placed responsibility on materials—test or subject content not the teacher; (4) this assigned responsibility to either luck or lack of luck.

Sample: As part of a larger study, 758 fourth-grade students, 35 teachers, and 19 principals completed their respective version of the self-efficacy instruments. They were taken from 20 public schools–ten from high achieving schools and ten from low achieving schools with the state of Michigan.

Reliability: Each instrument has alpha coefficients that ranged from 0.81 to 0.93 on each of the four subscales.

Validity: Only content validity is discussed. Because of the relatively high alpha estimates for the total instrument and for each subscale, it was assumed that sufficient homogeneity existed among the items and scales to assume that a measure of construct validity was provided.

Factor Analysis: Apparently, correlations were used to form the four subscales. There is no evidence of any other (i.e., factor analysis) procedures being used to form the subscales. The four subscales were labeled positive and negative internal and positive and negative external.

References:
Bandura, A. 1981. Self-referent thought: A developmental analysis of self-efficacy. In J.H. Flavell and L. Ross (eds.), *Social cognitive development*. Cambridge: Cambridge University Press.

Fuller, B., et al. 1982. The organizational context of individual efficacy. *Review of Educational Research* 52:7-30.

Stipek, D.J., and J.R. Weisz. 1981. Perceived personal control and academic achievement. *Review of Educational Research* 51:101-137.

Principal Self-Efficacy Instrument

1. If the achievement level of your school is high, it would be because
   A. you possess a natural ability to be an effective instructional leader.
   B. as a principal, you put a great deal of effort into emphasizing academic achievement.
   C. the achievement test used to measure the achievement level of your students was too easy.
   D. you were lucky to get a good school.

2. If your school appeared to be strong in a particular skill such as "Language-Spelling Skills," it would be because
   A. you possess a natural ability to be an effective instructional leader.
   B. as a principal, you emphasize the importance of students acquiring this skill.
   C. the materials used in the classroom covering this skill area were too much like the items on the achievement test.
   D. you were lucky to get a good school.

3. If very few of the students in your school by the end of the year are able to master the basic statewide objectives established for their grade level it would be because
   A. you do not possess a natural ability to be an instructional leader.
   B. you lack of effort in emphasizing the importance of all students mastering the basic objectives.
   C. the statewide objectives are unrealistic and too difficult to attain.
   D. you were not lucky enough to get assigned to one of the better schools.

4. If your school, which has a history of being a low-achieving school, increases its achievement level this year to above the norm, this would be because of
   A. your natural ability to be an instructional leader.
   B. your effort in supporting and emphasizing the importance of students' achievement.
   C. a change in the achievement testing, making it easier for your students to succeed.
   D. your being lucky. Recent redistricting brought brighter students to your school.

5. If the achievement level of your school is below the norm, it would be because
   A. you do not possess a natural ability to be an instructional leader.
   B. you did not put in the effort needed to emphasize high achievement.
   C. the materials used in the classroom did not emphasize the areas tested by the achievement measure.
   D. you were not lucky enough to get a school of high achievers.

6. If you received a negative evaluation from your superintendent in the area of instructional leadership, this would be because
   A. you do not possess a natural ability to be an instructional leader.
   B. you do not feel this is an important part of your job; therefore, you do not emphasize it.
   C. the evaluation was not fair with the standards by which you were measured being too difficult for anyone to attain.
   D. your superintendent just happened to be in a critical mood the day he/she wrote the evaluation.

7. If a new science program is initiated in your school and the students' achievement in this area increases significantly, this would be due to
    A. your natural ability to be an effective instructional leader.
    B. the effort you put into promoting the program and assisting teachers in working with it.
    C. a good match between the objectives emphasized in the new science program and the achievement test.
    D. your being lucky. Recent redistricting brought brighter students to your school, particularly those having a high aptitude for science.

8. Twenty-five percent (25%) of the students in grades 1-3 were retained and not promoted to the next grade. This rate is higher than any other school in the area. This would be due to:
    A. your lacking natural ability in being an effective instructional leader.
    B. your lack of effort in emphasizing the need for all students to achieve.
    C. your school's standards for retention are more rigid than other schools.
    D. your not being lucky enough to get assigned to one of the better schools.

9. If students do well in your classes, it would be because
    A. you have the natural ability to be an instructional leader.
    B. you put a great deal of effort into emphasizing the importance of academic achievement.
    C. the basic material covered is designed so that even the slowest of students can get some right.
    D. you were lucky to get a bunch of kid this year who are smart and self-motivated.

10. Suppose your superintendent commended you on doing a fine job as evidenced by the high level of achievement demonstrated by your students. This would mean
    A. a great deal, because you feel you have a natural ability as an instructional leader in your school.
    B. a great deal, because you have put in a lot of effort and time into promoting and insuring a high level of achievement for all students.
    C. very little, because you suspect the test used to measure the academic achievement of your students was very easy and most should pass it anyway.
    D. very little, because you were simply lucky to be in a school where the majority of your students have a high enough IQ which enables them to achieve independently of anything you really do.

11. If your school scores very low in a particular subject area such as math on an achievement test, it would be because
    A. you do not possess a natural ability to be an instructional leader, particularly in the area.
    B. you did not emphasize the importance of achieving in this subject area as much as the other subjects.
    C. the math section of the achievement test did not test what was taught.
    D. you happened to get a school whose students don't have the ability to achieve in this area.

12. If 95% of the students in your school are mastering the basic objectives established for their grade level, this would be because
    A. you possess a natural ability to be an instructional leader.
    B. you have emphasized the importance of all students achieving at least the basic objectives before the end of the school year.

C. the basic objectives were established at such minimum level as to enable even the slowest of students to succeed in mastering them.

D. you were lucky to get a school whose student body tends to be very academically able.

Scoring: Strongly Agree = 5; Agree = 4; Unsure = 3; Disagree = 2; and Strongly Disagree = 1.

Teacher Self-Efficacy Instrument

1. If a student does well in your class, it is probably because
    A. of your natural ability to teach.
    B. of the effort you put into teaching.
    C. the assignments are easy.
    D. you were lucky to get at least a few good students.

2. When your class is having trouble understanding something you have taught, it is usually because
    A. you do not possess a natural ability to teach.
    B. you did not put in enough effort.
    C. the material you are teaching is difficult to comprehend.
    D. you were unlucky in getting a particularly slow class this year.

3. When most of your students do well on a test, it is more likely to be because
    A. of your natural ability to teach.
    B. of the effort you put into teaching.
    C. the test was easy.
    D. you were lucky to get a class composed of generally good students.

4. When students in your class forget something that you had already explained, it is usually because
    A. you do not possess a natural ability to teach.
    B. you did not put in enough effort in explaining the topic.
    C. the topic area is particularly difficult.
    D. you were unlucky in getting a particularly slow class this year.

5. Suppose your principal says you're doing a fine job. This is likely to happen because
    A. of your natural ability to teach.
    B. of the effort you put into teaching.
    C. the material you are teaching is quite basic and easy to learn.
    D. you were lucky to get a good academically able class this year.

6. If most of the students in your class are doing very well, it is probably because
    A. of your natural ability to teach.
    B. of the effort you put into teaching.
    C. the material you are teaching is quite basic and easy to learn.
    D. you were lucky to get a good class academically to begin with.

7. If you are working with a student who can't understand a concept and he suddenly "gets it," it is likely to happen because
   A. of your natural ability to teach.
   B. of the effort you put into teaching.
   C. the material takes a while to understand anyway.
   D. you were lucky at that moment.

8. If few of your students by the end of the year are able to master the basic objectives established for their grade level, it is most likely because
   A. you do not possess a natural ability to teach.
   B. you did not put in enough effort.
   C. the objectives were established unrealistically high.
   D. you were unlucky in being assigned a particularly slow class this year.

9. When a large percent of the students in your class are doing poorly, it usually happens because
   A. you do not possess a natural ability to teach.
   B. you did not put in enough effort.
   C. the topic area is particularly difficult.
   D. you were unlucky in being assigned a particularly slow class this year in understanding and learning.

10. Suppose you present some new material to your students and most of them remember it. This is likely to be because
    A. of your natural ability to teach.
    B. of the effort you put into teaching.
    C. the material is quite basic and easy to learn.
    D. you were lucky to have a good class academically to begin with.

11. When your students do poorly on a test, it is because
    A. you do not possess a natural ability to teach.
    B. you did not put in enough effort in teaching the material covered on the test.
    C. the test was too difficult.
    D. you were unlucky in being assigned a particularly slow class this year.

12. If a child does not do well in your class it is probably because
    A. you do not possess a natural ability to teach.
    B. you did not put in enough effort in helping this child.
    C. the material is particularly difficult.
    D. you happened to get some poor students this year who started off way below the others.

13. When you are having a hard time getting your students interested in a lesson, it is usually because
    A. you do not possess a natural ability to teach.
    B. you are not putting in enough effort.
    C. the lesson is particularly boring.
    D. you were unlucky in getting a group of students who generally are difficult to motivate.

14. If all of your students by the end of the school year are mastering the basic objectives established for their grade level, it is most likely because
    A. of your natural ability to teach.
    B. of the effort you put into teaching.
    C. the objectives are a minimum and easy for all to obtain.
    D. you were lucky to get students who, on the whole, are particularly bright.

15. When your students seem interested in your lesson right from the beginning, it is because
    A. of your natural ability to teach.
    B. of the effort you put into teaching the lesson.
    C. the topic is one which students generally find interesting.
    D. you were lucky to get students who are generally highly motivated to learn.

16. On those days when you are depressed and feel you are not doing as good a job as you would like, it is because
    A. you do not possess a natural ability to teach.
    B. you do not put in enough effort.
    C. the material you are covering is very difficult to teach.
    D. it is one of those unlucky days when everything goes wrong.

Scoring: See above.

Reprinted with permission of the author. (Copyright ©1983 by S.J. Hillman. No part may be reproduced or transmitted without permission from the author.)

Self-Esteem

Texas Social Behavior Inventory

Helmreich, R., and J. Stapp. 1974. Short forms of the Texas Social Behavior Inventory (TSBI), an objective measure of self-esteem. *Bulletin of the Psychonomic Society* 4:473-475.

Comments: The 32-item long form of the TSBI measures self esteem or social competence. Based on the results of factor and item analyses with over 1,000 people, two short forms each with 16 items were developed.

Sample: Over 8,000 students at the University of Texas at Austin have completed the TSBI.

Reliability: Based on a sample of 238 male and 262 female undergraduate students at the University of Texas at Austin, the following Alpha coefficients were reported. On Form A, they ranged from 0.85 (men) to 0.86 (women) and from 0.85 (men) to 0.88 (women) on Form B. The alpha coefficients on the original 32-item TSBI ranged from 0.92 (men) to 0.93 (women). Forms A and B are highly correlated with the original scale. The criteria for the two 16-item short forms were equivalence of part-whole correlations, equivalence of means between forms and between sexes, equivalence of score distributions, and parallel factor structures.

Validity: Factor analysis and part-whole correlations confirmed the similarity of the two forms. The TSBI has been correlated with the Personal Attributes Questionnaire. Correlations of 0.81 and 0.83 are reported with the masculinity subscale for men and women, and correlations of 0.42 and 0.44 are reported with the femininity subscale for men and women.

Factor Analysis: Principal axis rotation produced only one factor, whereas an oblique rotation yielded four factors: confidence, dominance, social competence, and social withdrawal (male) or relations to authority figures (female).

References:
Helmreich, R., et al. 1974. The Texas Social Behavior Inventory (TSBI): An objective measure of self-esteem or social competence. *Journal Supplement Abstract Service. Catalog of Selected Documents in Psychology* 4:79.

Spence, J.T., et al. 1974. The Personal Attributes Questionnaire: A measure of sex-role stereotypes and masculinity-femininity. *Journal Supplement Abstract Service. Catalog of Selected Documents in Psychology* 4:43.

Spence, J.T., et al. 1975. Ratings of self and peers on sex-role attributes and their relations to self-esteem and conceptions of masculinity and femininity. *Journal of Personality and Social Psychology* 32:29-39.

Texas Social Behavior Inventory (Form A)

1. I am not likely to speak to people until they speak to me.
2. I would describe myself as self-confident.
3. I feel confident of my appearance.
4. I am a good mixer.
5. When in a group of people, I have trouble thinking of the right things to say.
6. When in a group of people, I usually do what the others want rather than make suggestions.
7. When I am in disagreement with other people, my opinion usually prevails.
8. I would describe myself as one who attempts to master situations.
9. Other people look up to me.
10. I enjoy social gatherings just to be with people.
11. I make a point of looking other people in the eye.
12. I cannot seem to get others to notice me.
13. I would rather not have very much responsibility for other people.
14. I feel comfortable being approached by someone in a position of authority.
15. I would describe myself as indecisive.
16. I have no doubts about my social competence.

Scoring: (a) Not at all characteristic of me; (b) Not Very; (c) Slightly; (d) Fairly; (e) Very much characteristic of me. The lower self-esteem response receives a score of 0, while the higher self-esteem response receives a score of 4. The following items on Form A receive a 0: (1e, 2a, 3a, 4a, 5e, 6e, 7a, 8a, 9a, 10a, 11a, 12e, 13e, 14a, 15e, 16a). The following items on Form B receive a 0: (1e, 2e, 3a, 4a, 5a, 6a, 7a, 8a, 9a, 10a, 11a, 12e, 13e, 14a, 15a, 16a).

Reprinted with permission of the author.

Institutional Ethical Practices and
Faculty Professional Self-Esteem Survey

O'Hara, L.F. 1991. Institutional Ethical Practices and Faculty Professional Self-Esteem: Survey Report. ERIC ED 331 543.

Comments: The ten-item survey provides individual institutions with faculty perceptions about the following nine aspects that impact on faculty self esteem: administrative commitment, faculty input, information sharing, honesty, budget, classroom control, support services, professional development, and goal setting. The tenth item is open-ended.

Sample: The original sample consisted of 1,286 full-time faculty from 25 community college campuses representing 20 institutions of higher education in 13 states as well as the 25 chief executive officers for each institution.

Data Analysis: Based on site location, means are reported for each of the nine variables.

References:
O'Hara, L.F. 1991. Institutional Ethical Practices and Faculty Professional Self-Esteem Survey Report. *Community/Junior College Quarterly* 18:319-327.

Institutional Ethical Practices and
Faculty Professional Self-Esteem Survey

1. The administration of this college has stated, formally and/or informally, its commitment to promoting the professional self-esteem of the faculty.
2. Faculty are influential in ensuring that issues which will enhance their professional self-esteem are addressed.
3. All pertinent information dealing with college issues is openly and freely exchanged.
4. Faculty are dealt with in an honest and consistent manner.
5. Faculty have power in determining the institutional budget.
6. Faculty have control over all appropriate classroom-related matters.
7. The institution demonstrates sensitivity to the faculty need to devote the proper amount of time and attention to instructional matters.
8. The institution supports opportunities for faculty professional growth and renewal.
9. Faculty are meaningfully involved in institutional planning.
10. List any other institutional variable that is significant to the quality of the teaching-learning environment *at this institution*. Explain.

Scoring: A ten-point scale ranges from 0 = Does not describe to 10 = Describes.

Reprinted with permission of the author. (Instrument may not be used without the expressed, written permission of the author.)

Sex Roles (Gender Identification)

Women as Managers Scale

Peters, L.H., et al. 1974. Women as Managers Scale (WAMS): A measure of attitudes toward women in management positions. *JSAS Catalog of Selected Documents in Psychology*, Ms. No. 585.

Comments: The authors suggest using the WAMS in field settings. It might be interesting to adapt the WAMS to an educational setting.

Scale Construction: The original 55-item WAMS included general descriptive traits of managers and female-specific stereotypic traits that could impede their obtaining managerial positions. Based on the results of item analysis and a principal components analysis, the new scale contained 21 items (11 worded positively and ten worded negatively).

Sample: The original sample consisted of 541 advanced undergraduates from four universities in the Midwest and South. The validation sample consisted of 180 men and 100 women who worked for an international distributing company.

Reliability: The corrected split-half (odd-even) reliability was 0.91.

Validity: To establish the validity of the WAMS, six predictions were tested. Four out of six predictions were supported at the 0.05 level. One prediction was supported at the 0.10 level, while one prediction was not supported (work history of female participants' mothers). In addition, part of the sample was used in a cross-validation study.

Factor Analysis: Although a principal components factor analysis yielded three factors, additional analysis suggested a single factor.

Data Analysis: Descriptive statistics for the sample are provided. One-way ANOVAs were used to test the six predictions. A step-wise regression of attitudes on personal data and organizational data are reported.

References:
Crino, M.D., et al. 1981. A comment on the dimensionality and reliability of the Women as Managers Scale (WAMS). *Academy of Management Journal* 24:866-876.

Garland, H., and K.H. Price 1977. Attitudes toward women in management and attributions for their success and failure in a managerial position. *Journal of Applied Psychology* 62:29-33.

Terborg, J.R., et al. 1977. Organizational and personal correlates of attitudes toward women as managers. *Academy of Management Journal* 20:89-100.

Women as Managers Scale

1. It is less desirable for women than men to have a job that requires responsibility.
2. Women have the objectivity required to evaluate business situations properly.
3. Challenging work is more important to men than it is to women.
4. Men and women should be given equal opportunity for participation in management training programs.
5. Women have the capability to acquire the necessary skills to be successful managers.
6. On the average, women managers are less capable of contributing to an organization's overall goals than are men.
7. It is not acceptable for women to assume leadership roles as often as men.
8. The business community should someday accept women in key managerial positions.
9. Society should regard work by female managers as valuable as work by male managers.
10. It is acceptable for women to compete with men for top executive positions.
11. The possibility of pregnancy does not make women less desirable employees than men.
12. Women would no more allow their emotions to influence their managerial behavior than would men.
13. Problems associated with menstruation should not make women less desirable than men as employees.
14. To be a successful executive, a women does not have to sacrifice some of her femininity.
15. On the average, a women who stays at home all the time with her children is a better mother than a woman who works outside the home at least half time.
16. Women are less capable of learning mathematical and mechanical skills than are men.
17. Women are not ambitious enough to be successful in the business world.
18. Women cannot be assertive in business situations that demand it.
19. Women possess the self-confidence required of a good leader.
20. Women are not competitive enough to be successful in the business world.
21. Women cannot be aggressive in business situations that demand it.

Scoring: Strongly Disagree = 1; Disagree = 2; Slightly Disagree = 3; Neither Disagree nor Agree = 4; Slightly Agree = 5; Agree = 6; and Strongly Agree = 7. The scoring is reversed for the following items: 1, 3, 6, 7, 15, 16, 17, 18, 20, and 21.

Personal Attributes Questionnaire

Spence, J.T., et al. 1974. The Personal Attributes Questionnaire: A measure of sex-role stereotypes and masculinity-femininity. *JSAS Catalog of Selected Documents in Psychology* 4:42.

Comments: The 24-item PAQ measures attributes that differentiate between the sexes. In addition, Spence et al. developed the 55-item Attitudes toward Women Scale (the short form has 15 items), which has items that describe the privileges, rights, and roles that women should have or be allowed to have.

Scale Construction: The original 55-item PAQ contains three scales: a masculine scale (M) with 23 items, a feminine scale (F) with 18 items, and a masculine-feminine scale (M-F) with 13 items. One item could not be classified. The PAQ is based on over 130 items generated by students as characteristics that differentiate between males and females. The 55 items not only describe characteristics that differentiate between males and females, but also represent the actual ratings of university males and females. The current 24-item PAQ contains the same three scales with eight items in each scale.

Sample: One set of normative data is available based on the rounded mean of the medians of the men and women in the high school sample. Another set of normative data derived by using the same procedure (rounded mean of the medians of the men and women) is available based on 715 university students.

Reliability: Cronbach alpha reliabilities were 0.78 (M-F scale), 0.82 (F scale), and 0.85 (M scale). Correlations between the short form and the original scale were 0.91 (M-F scale) and 0.93 (M and F scales).

Validity: Factor analytic procedures confirmed the unidimensionality of the M and F scales. Information about concurrent and predictive validity is reported.

Definition of Scales: The *Masculinity Scale* consists of items that are socially desirable for both sexes, although men possess these characteristics more than women. The *Femininity Scale* consists of items that are socially desirable for both sexes, although women possess these characteristics more than men. The *Masculinity-Femininity Scale* consists of items whose social desirability varies between the sexes.

Data Analysis: Two samples of university students yielded significant differences between the means of men and women on every item of the PAQ. Males scored higher on the M and M-F items, and scored lower on the F items. In addition, part-whole correlations were computed between each of the item scores and each of the three scales.

References:
Jones, B.J.W. 1993. Career socialization, locus-of-control and perceptions of sex role stereotypes among female administrators in Georgia's technical institutes. Ph.D. dissertation, Georgia State University.

Waelde, L.C., et al. 1994. Stressful life events: Moderators of the relationships of gender and gender roles to self-reported depression and suicidality among college students. *Sex Roles: A Journal of Research* 30:1-22.

Personal Attributes Questionnaire

1. Not at all aggressive   Very aggressive
2. Very whiny   Not at all whiny
3. Not at all independent   Very independent
4. Not at all arrogant   Very arrogant
5. Not at all emotional   Very emotional
6. Very submissive   Very dominant
7. Very boastful   Not at all boastful
8. Not at all excitable in a major crisis   Very excitable in a major crisis
9. Very passive   Very active
10. Not at all egotistical   Very egotistical
11. Not at all able to devote self completely to others   Able to devote self completely to others
12. Not at all spineless   Very spineless
13. Very rough   Very gentle
14. Not at all complaining   Very complaining
15. Not at all helpful to others   Very helpful to others
16. Not at all competitive   Very competitive
17. Subordinates oneself to others   Never subordinates oneself to others
18. Very home oriented   Very worldly
19. Very greedy   Not at all greedy
20. Not at all kind   Very kind
21. Indifferent to others' approval   Highly needful of others' approval
22. Very dictatorial   Not at all dictatorial
23. Feelings not easily hurt   Feelings easily hurt
24. Doesn't nag   Nags a lot
25. Not at all aware of feelings of others   Very aware of feelings of others
26. Can make decisions easily   Has difficulty making decisions
27. Very fussy   Not at all fussy
28. Gives up very easily   Never gives up easily
29. Very cynical   Not at all cynical
30. Never cries   Cries very easily
31. Not at all self-confident   Very self-confident
32. Does not look out only for self; principled   Looks out only for self; unprincipled
33. Feels very inferior   Feels very superior
34. Not at all hostile   Very hostile
35. Not at all understanding of others   Very understanding of others
36. Very cold in relations with others   Very warm in relations with others
37. Very servile   Not at all servile
38. Very little need for security   Very strong need for security
39. Not at all gullible   Very gullible
40. Goes to pieces under pressure   Stands up well under pressure

Scoring: A bipolar scale is used. Each item receives a score of 0 to 4.

Reprinted with permission of the author.

Stress/Burnout

Work Stress Inventory

Barone, D.F., et al. 1988. The Work Stress Inventory: Organizational stress and job risk. *Educational and Psychological Measurement* 48:141-154.

Comments: The 40-item WSI assesses work stress. The inventory can be used to examine employee satisfaction, organizational development, organizational climate, and differences among occupations.

Scale Construction: Study 1 involved the development of the WSI. After a review of the literature, 99 items that represented work stressors (overload, role conflict, role ambiguity, nonparticipation, and interpersonal relationships) were generated. Based on the results of factor analysis, only 25 items were retained. Study 2 provided support for the validity of the WSI. Study 3 involved the development of a second scale for the WSI. After a review of the literature, 58 items that represented threats or risks (emergency responding, prolonged attention to detail, adverse conditions in the work environment, safety, and job security) were generated. Based on the results of factor analysis, only 20 items were retained. Study 4 provided additional support for the validity of the WSI.

Sample: The sample for Study 1 consisted of 300 workers (administrators/managers, nurses, police, teachers, social workers, counselors, and air traffic controllers). The sample for Study 2 consisted of 100 workers. The sample for Study 3 consisted of 231 workers. The sample for Study 4 consisted of 182 workers.

Reliability: The alpha coefficient for Study 1 was 0.94 and using a cross-validation sample (25 items), the alpha coefficient was 0.92. The alpha coefficient for Study 3 was 0.91. Test-retest reliabilities for the organizational stress scale in Study 4 were 0.88 (intensity), 0.83 (frequency), and 0.84 (composite). Test-retest reliabilities (over a one-month period) for the job risk scale in Study 4 were 0.90 (intensity), 0.91 (frequency), and 0.90 (composite).

Validity: Evidence for the construct and predictive validity of the WSI is provided in Study 2. The WSI was compared to questionnaires that assessed job satisfaction, anxiety, and daily stressors. Study 4 provides further evidence for validity by comparing the two scales of the WSI to questionnaires that assessed job satisfaction, anxiety, absenteeism/turnover and daily stressors.

Factor Analysis: A principal components factor analysis was conducted in Study 1 and one factor was identified (organizational stress). A principal components factor analysis was conducted in Study 3 and one factor was identified (job risk). A varimax rotation yielded two factors: organizational stress (OS) contains 20 items (1, 3, 4, 8, 9, 11, 12, 13, 16, 20, 22, 23, 25, 26, 29, 30, 31, 34, 38, and 40) and job risk (JR) contains 20 items (2, 5, 6, 7, 10, 14, 15, 17, 18, 19, 21, 24, 27, 28, 32, 33, 35, 36, 37, and 39).

Data Analysis: Correlation matrices (Study 2 and Study 4) are reported.

References:

Lee, R.T., and B.E. Ashforth. 1993. A longitudinal study of burnout among supervisors and managers: Comparisons between the Leiter and Maslach (1988) and Golembiewski, et al. (1986) models. *Organizational Behavior and Human Decision Processes* 54:369-398.

Page, R.A. 1988. Changing stressful work environments: Supervisory interventions with minority service workers. Ph.D. dissertation, Nova University.

Sarason, I.G., et al. 1983. Assessing social support: The Social Support Questionnaire. *Journal of Personality and Social Psychology* 44:127-139.

Simons, Y., and D.F. Barone. 1994. The relationship of work stressors and emotional support to strain in police officers. *International Journal of Stress Management* 1:223-234.

311

Work Stress Inventory

1. Not knowing what superiors expect of you.
2. Having to respond on an "emergency basis."
3. Disagreeing with superiors.
4. Not knowing how much authority you have.
5. Being injured as a result of the mistakes of others.
6. Having to deal with injury or death as part of your job.
7. Having to make decisions that will dramatically affect other peoples' lives.
8. Finding that rewards are not based on performance (e.g., promotions, raises).
9. Having to deal with several pressing problems at once.
10. Working in a "high crime area."
11. Not knowing what supervisors think of you.
12. Not having the opportunity to participate in decision-making.
13. Having conflicting job responsibilities.
14. Working without adequate safety standards.
15. Having inadequate personnel or equipment to respond in an emergency situation.
16. Feeling there is no clear chain of command.
17. Having periods of inactivity separated by periods of emergency response.
18. Having to physically restrain others.
19. Potential for being injured on the job.
20. Being held responsible for too many different activities.
21. Knowing that your error may harm another person.
22. Failing to receive recognition of achievement by superiors.
23. Having to do things on the job that are against your better judgement.
24. Never knowing when a potentially dangerous event might occur.
25. Feeling that your work ability is under rated.
26. Not being permitted to make decisions on your own.
27. Working for long periods of time without rest.
28. Performing duties that are potentially dangerous to others.
29. Receiving criticism from superiors.
30. Receiving conflicting requests.
31. Finding a lack of assistance or support from superiors.
32. Working in excess of eight hours per day.
33. Working with dangerous materials.
34. Having ideas considerably different from those of your superior.
35. Doing another person's job in addition to yours.
36. Having to maintain prolonged vigilance to protect the safety of others.
37. Potential for being the victim of a crime while on the job.
38. Being held responsible for mistakes made by co-workers.
39. Working while fatigued or tired.
40. Working under inconsistent policies and guidelines.

Scoring: Intensity (amount of stress) is scored as: 0 = None; 1 = A little; 2 = Moderate amount; 3 = Much; and 4 = Very much. Frequency is scored as: 0 = Never; 1 = Rarely (annually); 2 = Sometimes (at least monthly); 3 = Often (at least weekly); and 4 = Daily.

Reprinted with permission of the authors.

Dworkin Teacher Burnout Scale (Alienational Burnout)

Dworkin, G.A., et al. 1986. The effects of tokenism on work alienation among urban public school teachers. *Work and Occupations* 13:399-420.

Comments: The ten-item scale is based on the work by Seeman (1959). There are two items for each of the following five areas of alienation identified by Seeman: powerlessness, normlessness, meaninglessness, isolation, and estrangement.

Sample: The original sample consisted of 3,277 public school teachers from Texas in 1977. These teachers were surveyed prior to the implementation of any school reform initiatives. The second sample consisted of 1,060 public school teachers after the implementation of reform initiatives (1986-1987).

Reliability: The alpha coefficient was 0.83.

Validity: Factor analytic procedures confirmed the unidimensionality of the WSI. In addition, the WSI has been compared to the Maslach Burnout Inventory.

Factor Analysis: Although a principal factor analysis yielded two factors, the first factor accounted for 90% of the total variance. Another factor analysis was conducted and the results of this oblique factor analysis yielded one factor.

References:
Caram, D.F. 1982. An analysis of factors associated with job dissatisfaction and quitting behavior among urban public school teachers. Ed.D. dissertation, University of Houston.

Coughlin, R.J. 1970. Dimensions of teacher morale. *American Education Research Journal* 7:221-233.

Jackson, S.E., et al. 1986. Toward an understanding of the burnout phenomenon. *Journal of Applied Psychology* 71:630-640.

Maslach, C., and S.E. Jackson. 1981. The measurement of experienced burnout. *The Journal of Occupational Behavior* 2:99-113.

Seeman, M. 1959. On the meaning of alienation. *American Sociological Review* 32:273-285.

Dworkin Teacher Burnout Scale

1. Those who make the ultimate decisions in the school system really pay attention to my ideas and suggestions.
2. The longer I am in school, the more I realize how little control I have over things that happen here.
3. Teachers can get what they want without breaking the rules.
4. Many of the school rules are so rigid and/or absurd that a good teacher must defy regulations.
5. My experiences in school have proven that public school teaching is a rewarding career.
6. I see my job as contributing very little to the betterment of the world.
7. The people I work with and my students make me feel like I'm of vital importance to the school.
8. Sometimes I think a teacher could drop dead or quit and nobody would know or care.
9. I cannot imagine my choosing any other career than teaching.
10. I am seriously planning to leave the field of education.

Scoring: A five-point Likert scale ranging from 1 = Strongly agree to 5 = Strongly disagree is used for the first item in each of the five categories. The scoring is reversed for the second item in each of the five categories. A low score indicates low alienation or burnout.

Reprinted with permission of the author.

Teacher Stress Inventory

Fimian, M.J., and P.S. Fastenau. 1990. The validity and reliability of the Teacher Stress Inventory: A re-analysis of aggregate data. *Journal of Organizational Behavior* 11:151-157.

Comments: The 49-item TSI assesses occupational stress in teachers. It contains ten factors; the first five represent sources of stress, whereas the remaining five represent manifestations of teacher stress. The TSI presents evidence of validity and reliability. A Media Specialist Stress Inventory is also available.

Scale Construction: After reviewing the literature on teacher stress, a list of 135 items was written. Content analyses and editing reduced the number to 63 items. Additional content validation procedures, factor analyses, and tests of internal consistency were conducted, thereby reducing the number to 30 items. Twelve items were added, and then the TSI was administered to four samples. The TSI contained two dimensions: frequency and strength. The revised 41-item TSI was factor analyzed. An oblique six-factor solution was accepted. The number of items remaining was reduced to 38. Alpha coefficients ranged from 0.70 to 0.90.

Sample: The total sample consisted of 3,401 teachers from seven states in the eastern United States. These teachers represent 21 different samples. Overall, there were 962 regular education teachers and 2,352 special education teachers. Eighty-seven teachers did not identify themselves as either regular or special education teachers.

Reliability: Alpha coefficients (Cronbach) for the ten factors were: 0.75 (professional investment); 0.82 (behavioral manifestations); 0.83 (time management); 0.86 (discipline and motivation); 0.87 (emotional manifestations); 0.80 (work-related stressors); 0.88 (gastronomical manifestations); 0.78 (cardiovascular manifestations; 0.82 (fatigue manifestations); and 0.82 (professional distress). All alpha coefficients were greater than 0.75, and the alpha for the entire inventory was 0.93. Means and standard deviations are presented.

Validity: This study reexamined the factor structure and internal consistency of the TSI. Content validity was accomplished by having 92 experts in the field examine the TSI. Factor analyses were conducted to further refine the TSI.

Factor Analysis: Principal components factor analyses were conducted as well as oblique and varimax rotations. The results of these analyses yielded ten factors. The factors are: four items on professional investment (11, 13, 14, and 15); four items on behavioral manifestations (29, 28, 31, and 27); eight items on time management (47, 45, 44, 46, 48, 49, 43, and 42); six items on discipline and motivation (17, 16, 19, 18, 20, and 21); five items on emotional manifestations (22, 24, 23, 25, and 26); six items on work-related stressors (1, 3, 5, 4, 2, and 6); three items on gastronomical manifestations (35, 34, and 39); three items on cardiovascular manifestations (32, 33, and 30); five items on fatigue manifestations (40, 41, 38, 36, and 37); and five items on professional distress (7, 8, 9, 12, and 10). Factor loadings, communalities, alpha reliabilities, means and standard deviations are presented.

Definition of Factors: *Professional investment* refers to the feeling of distance that teachers feel on their jobs; it refers to a minimum investment in teaching careers for a variety of reasons. *Behavioral manifestations* refer to the variety of inappropriate ways that teachers deal with their stress. *Time management* refers to the "balancing act" features related to teaching. *Discipline and motivation* refer to two aspects of the teacher-student relationship. *Emotional manifestations* refer to the different ways that teachers respond emotionally to stress. *Work-related stressors* refer to a variety of environment-specific events that are sources of teacher stress. *Gastronomical manifestations* refer to a variety of stomach ailments related to teacher stress. *Cardiovascular manifestations* refer to different cardiovascular problems associated with stress. *Fatigue manifestations* refer to a variety of fatigue problems associated with stress. *Professional distress* refers to the ways that teachers see themselves as professionals; it is like a "professional self-concept" scale.

References:

Fimian, M.J. 1984. The development of an instrument to measure occupational stress in teachers: The Teacher Stress Inventory. *Journal of Occupational Psychology* 57:277-293.

Fimian, M.J. 1988. *The Teacher Stress Inventory and test manual.* Brandon, VT: Clinical Psychology Publishing Company.

Teacher Stress Inventory

1. There is little time to prepare for my lessons/responsibilities.
2. My personal priorities are being shortchanged due to time demands.
3. I have too much work to do.
4. My caseload/class is too big.
5. The pace of the school day is too fast.
6. There is too much administrative paperwork in my job.
7. I lack promotion and/or advancement opportunities.
8. I am not progressing in my job as rapidly as I would like.
9. I need more status and respect on my job.
10. I lack recognition for the extra work and/or good teaching I do.
11. My personal opinions are not sufficiently aired.
12. I receive an inadequate salary for the work I do.
13. I lack control over decisions made about classroom/school matters.
14. I am not emotionally/intellectually stimulated on the job.
15. I lack opportunities for professional improvement.
16. **I feel frustrated**...having to monitor pupil behavior.
17. ...because of discipline problems in my classroom.
18. ...attempting to teach students who are poorly motivated.
19. ...because some students would do better if they tried harder.
20. ...because of inadequate/poorly defined discipline policies.
21. ...when my authority is rejected by pupils/ administration.
22. **I respond to stress**...by feeling insecure.
23. ...by feeling unable to cope.
24. ...by feeling vulnerable.
25. ...by feeling depressed.
26. ...by feeling anxious.
27. ...by calling in sick.
28. ...by using prescription drugs.
29. ...by using over-the-counter drugs.
30. ...with rapid and/or shallow breath.
31. ...by using alcohol.
32. ...with feeling increased blood pressure.
33. ...with feelings of heart pounding or racing.
34. ...with stomach pain of extended duration.
35. ...with stomach cramps.
36. ...with physical exhaustion.

37. ...with physical weakness.
38. ...by becoming fatigued in a very short time.
39. ...with stomach acid.
40. ...by sleeping more than usual.
41. ...by procrastinating.
42. I rush in my speech.
43. There isn't enough time to get things done.
44. I have to try doing more than one thing at a time.
45. I become impatient if others do things too slowly.
46. I have little time to relax and enjoy the time of day.
47. I easily over commit myself.
48. I think about unrelated matters during conversations.
49. I feel uncomfortable wasting time.

Scoring: No Strength; not noticeable; not applicable = 1; Mild Strength; barely noticeable = 2; Medium Strength; moderately noticeable = 3; Great Strength; very noticeable = 4; and Major Strength; extremely noticeable = 5.

Reprinted with permission of the publisher. (Fimian, M.J., and P.S. Fastenau. 1990. The validity and reliability of the Teacher Stress Inventory: A re-analysis of aggregate data. *Journal of Organizational Behavior* 11:151-157. Reprinted by permission of John Wiley & Sons, Ltd.)

Student Stress Inventory

Fimian, M.J., et al. 1989. The measure of classroom stress and burnout among gifted and talented students. *Psychology in the Schools* 26:139-153.

Comments: Over 90% of the experts concluded that the items on the SSI were related to student stress. Interrater reliability was high. Factor analysis yielded five interpretable factors. The factors found in the SSI are similar to those found in the Teacher Stress Inventory. The authors suggest further work on content validation and adding items to two of the scales to increase their reliability.

Scale Construction: Based on a review of the literature, a pilot form of the SSI was created and completed by 311 gifted students. At the same time, a group of 14 experts assessed the content validity of the SSI by determining the relevancy between each item and student stress. Items with 60% agreement were retained. Relevancy mean scores were studied. Nineteen items were deleted because they had factor loadings of less than 0.35. Additional factor and reliability analyses were conducted to further refine the SSI. The final version contains 41 items.

Sample: The sample consisted of 311 gifted students from Florida, North and South Carolina, and Virginia who attended summer camp at Appalachian State University in North Carolina.

Reliability: Alpha coefficients (Cronbach) were 0.85 (student distress); 0.63 (social/academic problems); 0.83 (emotional manifestations; 0.76 (behavioral manifestations); and 0.80 (physiological manifestations). The total scale alpha was 0.80.

Validity: Items were written after a review of the observational and conceptual literature, thereby establishing face validity. Fourteen experts assessed the content validity of the SSI by comparing the items to the construct of student stress. A relevancy mean score for each subscale was computed. Expert ratings, means, percentages, and interrater reliabilities are reported. The concurrent validity of the SSI was determined by correlating student stress with student burnout (Maslach Burnout Inventory), student stress with tedium (the Tedium Measure), and student stress with Quality of School Life (Epstein and McPortland, 1978).

Factor Analysis: Principal components factor analyses were conducted with oblique and varimax rotations. The results of the oblique rotation yielded five factors. The five factors are: 14 items on student distress (27, 22, 28, 23, 3, 16, 13, 11, 4, 25, 15, 7, 1, and 10); six items on social/academic problems (20, 24, 26, 31, 18, and 21); ten items on emotional manifestations (37, 43, 36, 52, 55, 41, 47, 32, 49, and 35); six items on behavioral manifestations (56, 59, 53, 42, 48, and 60); and six items on physiological manifestations (45, 44, 57, 34, 50, and 54). Component loadings, means, and standard deviations are reported.

Definition of Factors: *Student distress* refers to negative feelings about school, including not having enough time to relax and enjoy the day and feeling unimportant in school. *Social/academic problems* refer to various social and academic problems in school that contribute to stress such as having to do the same things in school week after week. *Emotional manifestations* refer to the emotional ways students react to stress such as feeling cranky. *Behavioral manifestations* refer to the techniques that students use to respond to stress such as acting defensively with others. *Physiological manifestations* refer to reactions such as eating more or less than usual and breaking out in a cold sweat.

References:

D'Aurora, D.L., and M. J. Fimian. 1988. Dimensions of life and school stress experienced by young people. *Psychology in the Schools* 25:44-52.

Epstein, J.L., and J.M. McPortland. 1978. *Administration and technical manual: The Quality of School Life Scale.* Boston: Houghton-Mifflin.

Fimian, M.J., and A.H. Cross. 1986. Stress and burnout among preadolescent and early adolescent gifted students: A preliminary investigation. *Journal of Early Adolescence* 6:247-267.

Pines, A.M., et al. 1981. *Burnout: From tedium to personal growth.* New York: The Free Press.

Student Stress Inventory

1. I have enough time to relax and enjoy the school day.
2. I have to deal with too many people each day.
3. I am important in school.
4. I am excited about the things I learn in school.
5. There are too many interruptions in my daily classroom routine.
6. I am all alone when I am at school.
7. I know exactly what is expected of me in school.
8. The school day seems to go either too fast or too slow for me.
9. My teacher(s) doesn't have enough time for me.
10. How well I did before in school really matters to my teacher(s) today.
11. It is easy for me to talk to my teachers.
12. Every one else in my class gets the "lucky breaks."
13. I feel physically comfortable in my classroom or school.
14. My grades are good enough.
15. I feel comfortable with the different ways in which my teachers teach.
16. My teacher(s) likes me.
17. I am helpless or hopeless.
18. We seem to do the same things in my classes week after week.
19. I feel no pressure to get my school work done.
20. I don't remember everything that I learn in school.
21. Some of my classmates get better treatment than I do.
22. I easily make friends and follow up interests out of school.
23. The information my teacher(s) gives me helps me do better in school.
24. Some of my teachers have too much power over me.
25. I am learning a lot in school.
26. My parents expect too much of me in school.
27. I am accepted by the other students.
28. My classmates really care about what I think and feel.
29. Tests and quizzes make me nervous.
30. I am not progressing in my studies rapidly enough.
31. I have too much information to deal with on a daily basis.

I RESPOND TO STRESS AT SCHOOL BY/WITH...

32. feeling insecure.
33. not being able to sit still.
34. rapid breathing.
35. putting things off to another day.
36. feeling scared.
37. feeling worried.

38. crying.
39. feeling dizzy.
40. becoming tired in a very short time.
41. feeling anxious.
42. acting defensively with others.
43. feeling pressured.
44. stomach pain of extended duration.
45. stomach acid.
46. sleeping more than usual.
47. feeling unable to cope with school.
48. allowing my friendships to fall apart.
49. feeling vulnerable.
50. feeling of increased blood pressure.
51. feeling physically exhausted.
52. feeling depressed.
53. "bad mouthing" certain classmates, teachers, or school staff.
54. feeling my heart pounding or racing.
55. feeling angry.
56. picking on someone else.
57. getting stomach cramps.
58. not talking to anybody.
59. talking back to teachers.
60. calling in sick.

Scoring: No Strength; not noticeable = 1; Of Mild Strength; barely noticeable = 2; Of Medium Strength; moderately noticeable = 3; Of Great Strength; very noticeable = 4; and Of Major Strength; extremely noticeable = 5.

School Principal Burnout Scale (SPB-R)

Friedman, I.A. 1995. School principal burnout: The concept and its components. *Journal of Organizational Behavior* 16:191-198.

Comments: The 23-item SPB-R is a revised version of School Principal Burnout Scale, which assesses exhaustion, depersonalization, and accomplishment.

Scale Construction: Sixty elementary and secondary school principals described feelings and behaviors of burned-out principals. Their responses generated 228 items, which were field tested with a random sample of 571 principals. A second random sample of 410 principals completed a questionnaire with four major categories: exhaustion, aloofness, deprecation, and unaccomplishment. Response patterns, item-total correlations, and semantic content were examined before a 30-item scale was generated.

Sample: The final validation sample consisted of 502 elementary principals, 266 junior high and high school principals, and 53 principals who did not indicate school level.

Reliability: Alpha coefficients were 0.90 (exhaustion and depersonalization) and 0.84 (accomplishment). Test-retest reliability over a two-week interval was 0.83 with a sample of 37 principals.

Validity: Construct validity was established by conducting factor analytic procedures.

Factor Structure: A three-factor solution was accepted. The first factor, exhaustion (1-9) contains items related to "feelings of experienced cognitive, emotional, and physical fatigue." The second factor, depersonalization (10-16) contains items related to "negative, callous or excessively detached response to care service recipients." The third factor, accomplishment (17-23), contains items related to a "decline in ones feelings of competence and successful achievement in work, reduced productivity or capability, low morale, withdrawal, and inability to cope."

Reference:
Friedman, I.A. 1995. Measuring school principal experienced burnout. *Educational and Psychological Measurement* 55:641-651.

School Principal Burnout Scale

1. I feel tired of running the school to the extent that I wish to quit.
2. I feel burned out by my work as school principal.
3. I think I am no longer interested in running a school.
4. I feel emotionally worn out by running the school.
5. I feel that I would like a break from the problems brought to me.
6. I feel that my work as a principal gives me a lot of pleasure.
7. I feel it is difficult for me to always solve problems at school.
8. I feel full of energy and readiness to promote school matters.
9. I feel quite fresh at the end of a day's work at school.
10. I feel that in contrast with the past I care less about teachers' problems.
11. I feel that in contrast with the past I am less supportive or appreciative of my teachers.
12. I feel impatient with teachers and students at school.
13. I feel that my relationships with teachers and students are less personal than in the past.
14. I think that ideas and suggestions raised by teachers and staff members are not as interesting and good as they were in the past.
15. In contrast to the past, I tend to ignore things at school that I don't like.
16. I think that I am not as open to suggestions and ideas raised by teachers as I was in the past.
17. I feel I have to assist in solving problems at school and I do not find enough time for that.
18. During a day's work I find the time to encourage a teacher having problems and to assist him or her in solving them.
19. During a day's work I find the time to quietly think and plan future activities.
20. Teachers refer problematic students to me and I cannot find time to take care of them.
21. I find enough time to meet students during the day.
22. I find sufficient time to meet with the school counselor or psychologist to discuss issues of special interest to me personally.
23. I sit in on teachers' classes to an extent that seems to me most satisfactory and desirable.

Scoring: Never = 1; Very rarely = 2; Rarely = 3; Often = 4; Very often = 5; and Always = 6.

Reprinted with permission of the author.

Administrative Stress Index

Gmelch, W.H., and B. Swent. 1982. Management team stressors and their impact on administrators' health. Paper presented at American Educational Research Association. ERIC ED 218 761.

Comments: The 35-item ASI identifies major sources of administrators' stress by establishing clear categories of occupational stressors (stress-inducing situations). Comparisons were made among sources of stress and various administrative positions. In addition, the relationship between sources of stress and administrator physical health was examined.

Sample: All 1,211 participants in the study were members of the Confederation of Oregon School Administrators. Three hundred and fifty-four were elementary administrators, 397 were junior high and high school administrators, 151 were superintendents or superintendents/principals, 254 were assistant superintendents and central office staff, and 89 were curriculum directors, transportation supervisors, and athletic directors.

Validity: The ASI is comprised of the 15 items from the Job-Related Index (Indik, Seashore, and Slesinger, 1964) and 23 items developed from stress logs and a review of the literature that examined sources of administrator stress. The items were then placed in one of the five stress categories. The index was piloted using 25 school administrators. After the initial pilot study, the index was revised and piloted on another group of 20 administrators. The development of the ASI provides evidence for its content validity.

Factor Analysis: Each of the five factors contains seven items. The items have been rank ordered from 1 (highest) to 35 (lowest). For convenience, the rank order has been used as the item number. Administrative constraints consists of items 1, 2, 3, 8, 10, 17, and 23; administrative responsibilities 4, 6, 16, 18, 19, 22, and 29; interpersonal relations 5, 12, 14, 15, 20, 26, and 31; intrapersonal conflict 7, 9, 13, 24, 28, 31, and 34; and role expectations 11, 21, 24, 27, 30, 33, and 35.

Definition of Factors: *Administrative constraints* refer to inadequate time, meetings, and rules. *Administrative responsibilities* refer to the managerial tasks of evaluation, supervision and negotiation. *Interpersonal relations* refer to resolving differences among and between supervisors and colleagues. *Intrapersonal conflict* refers to conflicts between one's performance and one's internal beliefs and expectations. *Role expectations* refer to the difference in expectations of self and the various publics served.

Data Analysis: Mean scores for each of the 35 items and the five factors are provided. In addition, analysis of variance tests for significant differences between the factors and administrative position as well as mean scores and analysis of variance for the top seven stressors by administrative position are reported.

References:
Gmelch, W.H. 1982. *Beyond Stress to Effective Management.* New York: John Wiley and Sons.

Gmelch, W.H., and J.S. Burns. 1991. Sources of stress for academic department chairs: A national study. Paper presented at the Association for the Study of Higher Education.

Ogden, D.L. 1992. Administrative stress and burnout among public school administrators in Georgia. Ph.D. dissertation, Georgia State University.

Administrative Stress Index

1. Complying with state, federal, and organizational rules and policies
2. Feeling that meetings take up too much time
3. Trying to complete reports and other paperwork on time
4. Trying to gain public approval and/or financial support for school programs
5. Trying to resolve parent/school conflicts
6. Evaluating staff members' performance
7. Having to make decisions that affect the lives of individual people that I know (colleagues, staff members, students, etc.)
8. Feeling that I have too heavy a work load, one that I cannot possibly finish during the normal work day
9. Imposing excessively high expectations on myself
10. Being interrupted frequently by telephone calls
11. Feeling I have to participate in school activities outside of the normal working hours at the expense of my personal time
12. Handling student discipline problems
13. Feeling that the progress on my job is not what it should or could be
14. Feeling staff members don't understand my goals and expectations
15. Trying to resolve differences between/among staff members
16. Being involved in the collective bargaining process
17. Writing memos, letters and other communications
18. Administering the negotiated contract (grievances, interpretation, etc.)
19. Supervising and coordinating the tasks of many people
20. Trying to resolve differences between/among students
21. Thinking that I will not be able to satisfy the conflicting demands of those who have authority over me
22. Preparing and allocating budget resources
23. Having my work frequently interrupted by staff members who want to talk
24. Knowing I can't get information needed to carry out my job properly
25. Feeling pressure for better job performance over and above what I think is reasonable
26. Trying to influence my immediate supervisor's actions and decisions that affect me
27. Not knowing what my supervisor thinks of me, or how he/she evaluates my performance
28. Feeling that I have too little authority to carry out responsibilities assigned to me
29. Speaking in front of groups
30. Being unclear on just what the scope and responsibilities of my job are
31. Attempting to meet social expectations (housing, clubs, friends, etc.)
32. Trying to resolve differences with my superiors
33. Feeling that I have too much responsibility delegated to me by my superiors
34. Feeling that I am not fully qualified to handle my job
35. Feeling not enough is expected of me by my superiors

Scoring: A five-point Likert-type is used.

Reprinted with permission of the author.

Teacher Burnout Scale

Seidman, S.A., and J. Zager. 1986-87. The Teacher Burnout Scale. *Educational Research Quarterly* 11:26-33.

Comments: The 21-item TBS was designed specifically to measure teacher burnout.

Scale Construction: A 65-item scale was administered to 217 elementary and secondary school teachers from southern Indiana. The results were factor analyzed using a varimax rotation. Five factors emerged. The revised 23-item scale was administered to a sample of 365 teachers from northern Texas. The results were factor analyzed using a varimax rotation. Four factors emerged. The final version of the TBS contains 21 items.

Sample: The TBS was administered to 490 public school teachers from Fort Worth, Texas.

Reliability: Coefficients of internal consistency (Cronbach's alpha) were 0.89 for career satisfaction, 0.84 for perceived administrative support, 0.80 for coping with job-related stress, and 0.72 for attitudes toward students. Test-retest reliability coefficients over a six–to eight–week interval (89 public school teachers) were 0.82 for career satisfaction, 0.78 for perceived administrative support, 0.56 for coping with job-related stress, and 0.76 for attitudes toward students. All reliability coefficients were significant at the 0.001 level.

Validity: The factor analysis on the 490 teachers from Fort Worth established the existence of four orthogonal factors that are consistent with the literature. In addition, teachers who scored high on the four scales reported that they were more burned out than teachers who scored lower. The scores on the TBS were also correlated with the Maslach Burnout Inventory (frequency dimension). The correlations were low to moderately high (construct validity). The predictive validity of the TBS was determined by using an ANOVA to test whether or not the burnout scores of teachers in low-stress/burnout schools would be lower than the teachers in high-stress/burnout schools. Significant main effects were found on all four scales. A Tukey HSD was then performed indicating that all four comparisons were statistically significant at the 0.05 level.

Factor Analysis: A four-factor orthogonal varimax solution was accepted using criterion of eigenvalues greater than 1.0 and factor loading above 0.40. The four factors are: five items on career satisfaction (1, 5, 10, 12, and 19); six items on perceived administrative support (3, 8, 11, 15, 18, and 20); six items on coping with job-related stress (2, 4, 7, 9, 13, and 14); and four items on attitudes toward students (6, 16, 17, and 21).

Definition of Factors: *Career satisfaction* refers to the selection of teaching as a career. *Perceived administrative support* refers to whether or not teachers believe they receive adequate encouragement and assistance from their supervisors. *Coping with job-related stress* refers to feelings of lethargy, depression, and other negative manifestations of stress. *Attitudes toward students* refer to positive and negative teacher attitudes.

Reference:
Zager, J. 1982. The relationship of personality, situational stress and anxiety factors to teacher burnout. Ph.D. dissertation. Indiana University.

Teacher Burnout Scale

1. I look forward to teaching in the future.
2. I feel depressed because of my teaching experiences.
3. I get adequate praise from my supervisors for a job well done.
4. The teaching day seems to drag on and on.
5. I am glad that I selected teaching as a career.
6. The students act like a bunch of animals.
7. My physical illnesses may be related to my stress in this job.
8. I feel that the administrators are willing to help me with classroom problems, should they arise.
9. I find it difficult to calm down after a day of teaching.
10. Teaching is more fulfilling than I had expected.
11. I believe that my efforts in the classroom are unappreciated by the administrators.
12. If I had to do it all over again, I would not become a schoolteacher.
13. I feel that I could do a much better job of teaching if only the problems confronting me were not so great.
14. The stresses in this job are more than I can bear.
15. My supervisors give me more criticism than praise.
16. Most of my students are decent people.
17. Most students come to school ready to learn.
18. I feel that the administrators will not help me with classroom difficulties.
19. I look forward to each teaching day.
20. The administration blames me for classroom problems.
21. Students come to school with bad attitudes.

Scoring: Strongly Agree, Moderately Agree, Slightly Agree, Slightly Disagree, Moderately Disagree, and Strongly Disagree.

Reprinted with permission of Joanne Zager and Steven A. Seidman.

Supervisory/Managerial Behavior

School Principals' Perceptions of Evaluation/Compensation Factors

Cunningham, R.A. 1993. Principals' perceptions of evaluation/compensation factors. Ed.D. dissertation. Temple University.

Comments: The SPPECF examines administrator preparation (nine items), personal traits (14 items), conceptual skills (11 items), position characteristics (17 items), administrative processes (11 items), and performance/results achieved (ten items) in terms of whether or not they should be included in a district's evaluation/compensation program. Originally, administrators were also asked to rank the importance of the items on a five-point scale. However, this was not done and may be considered as a recommendation for future research.

Sample: The sample consisted of 265 elementary and secondary principals from four counties outside of Philadelphia.

Reliability: Test-retest reliability for the pilot study over a ten-day period is reported as number of response agreements at percentage ranges.

Validity: The original survey was critiqued by the author's advisor. Then a panel of seven experts in the field examined the modified survey. The revised survey was pilot tested on ten elementary and ten secondary principals.

Data Analysis: Frequency distributions, percentages, means, standard deviations, and standard or z scores are provided.

References:
Herman, J.J. 1988. Evaluating administrators—assessing the competencies. *NASSP Bulletin* 72:5-9.

Langlois, D.E., and R.P. McAdams. 1992. *Performance appraisal of school management*. Lancaster, PA: Technomic Publishing.

Murphy, J., et al. 1986. The administrative control of principals in effective school districts: The supervision and evaluation functions. *The Urban Review* 18:149-162.

Redfern, G.B. 1986. Techniques of evaluation of principals and assistant principals. *NASSP Bulletin* 70:66-74.

School Principals' Perceptions of Evaluation/Compensation Factors

PART II: ADMINISTRATIVE COMPETENCIES

PREPARATION:
1. Academic degrees held
2. In-service attended
3. In-service conducted
4. Professional growth
5. Certifications
6. Awards of distinction
7. Professional affiliations
8. Teaching experience
9. Administrative experience

PERSONAL TRAITS:
10. Creativity
11. Consistent attendance
12. Ability to use judgement
13. Sensitivity
14. Motivation
15. Personal interests
16. Health
17. Appearance
18. Enthusiasm
19. Intelligence
20. Energy level
21. Self control
22. Initiative
23. Technical skills-methods and procedures

CONCEPTUAL SKILLS:
24. Ability to work with people
25. Problem solving
26. Judgement
27. Personal stress management
28. Imagination
29. Cooperativeness
30. Integrity
31. Loyalty
32. Time management
33. Ability to adopt to change
34. Ability to resolve conflict

POSITION CHARACTERISTICS:
35. Level of authority
36. Degree of responsibility
37. Span of control
38. Amount of fiscal responsibility

39. Enrollment
40. Degree of interpersonal conflicts
41. Number of assigned tasks
42. Frequency of public contracts
43. Nature and composition of student body and community
44. Position expectations
45. Consequence of errors
46. Scope and complexity of skills required for the position
47. Number of special services provided by the school
48. Adequacy of staff performances
49. Staff turnover rate
50. Length of work year
51. Amount of additional time required beyond the regular work day

PART III: ADMINISTRATIVE PERFORMANCE INDICATORS

ADMINISTRATIVE PROCESSES:
52. Develop and execute plans
53. Organize work
54. Coordinate service
55. Implement policies
56. Attends to administrative routine
57. Ability to motivate
58. Decision making capabilities
59. Instructional leadership
60. Supervision of staff and students
61. Delegate responsibilities
62. Manage the administrative processes: finance, plant personnel, scheduling, etc.

PERFORMANCE/RESULTS ACHIEVED:
63. Attainment of goals
64. Contributions to the total effort
65. Performance objectives set by principals
66. Observations of evidence to measure productivity
67. Duties performed
68. Behaviors executed
69. Performance in a position as compared to a set of prior achievements accomplished by other principals
70. Performance of duties that exceed responsibilities (merit or incentive plans)
71. Accomplishments as compared to average performances

Scoring: For the first part of the item (Where should these factors be included in a district's evaluation/compensation process) A = Evaluation; B = Compensation; C = Evaluation and Compensation; and D = None of the Above. For the second part of the item (To what degree do you recommend the use of these factors in a district's evaluation/compensation process) A = (1) Of No Importance; B = (2) Of Little Importance; C = (3) Moderately Important; D = (4) Important; and E = (5) Critical.

Reprinted with the permission of the author, Dr. Richard A. Cunningham. (Temple University Dissertation 1993 Principals' Perceptions of Evaluation/Compensation Factors.)

Principal Instructional Management Rating Scale

Hallinger, P., and J. Murphy. Assessing the instructional management behavior of principals. *The Elementary School Journal* 86:217-247.

Comments: The 71-item PIMRS measures the instructional leader behavior of elementary and secondary school principals. Each item focuses on a specific job-related behavior of the principal, and according to the authors, is useful for school evaluation, staff development, research, and district policy analysis. Thus, the instrument may indirectly become a useful tool for the evaluation of a school's effectiveness. The design of the instrument attempted to remedy earlier measurement shortcomings by isolating the curriculum and instructional management functions from other managerial duties.

Sample: Teachers, principals, and central office supervisors from one school district with ten elementary schools in California responded to the initial development of the instrument.

Reliability: The lowest alpha coefficient for the 11 subscales was 0.75.

Validity: Content, discriminant, and construct validation of the instrument are provided and ample evidence of each procedure provided.

Factor Analysis: A factor analysis of the 71-item instrument yielded 11 interpretable factors, or subscales. The principal's behavior/performance can be evaluated separately on each of the following 11 subscales, which were named as follows: framing goals, communicating goals, monitoring student progress, supervising/evaluating instruction, coordinating the curriculum, protecting instructional time, maintaining high visibility, providing incentives for teachers, promoting professional development, enforcing academic standards, and providing incentives for learning.

Data Analysis: The data analysis indicated that individual principal profiles were obtained that discriminated substantially among principals as to their instructional management behavior. Principal and supervisory ratings generally supported those ratings provided by teachers.

References:
Hallinger, P. 1983. Assessing the instructional management behavior of principals. Ed.D. dissertation, Stanford University.

Hallinger, P., and C. Hausman. 1993. From Attila the Hun to Mary had a little lamb: Redefining roles in restructured schools. Paper presented at American Educational Research Association. ERIC ED 359 647.

Principal Instructional Management Rating Scale

To what extent does your principal...?

FRAMING THE SCHOOL GOALS

1. Develop goals that seek improvement over current levels of academic performance.
2. Frame academic goals with target dates.
3. Frame the school's academic goals in terms of staff responsibilities for meeting them.
4. Use needs assessment or other questionnaires to secure staff input on goal development.
5. Use data on student academic performance when developing the school's academic goals.
6. Develop goals that are easily translated into classroom objectives by teachers.

COMMUNICATING THE SCHOOL GOALS

7. Communicate the school's academic goals to people at school.
8. Refer to the school's academic goals in informal settings with teachers.
9. Discuss the school's academic goals with teachers at faculty meetings.
10. Refer to the school's academic goals when making curricular decisions with teachers.
11. Ensure that the school's goals are reflected in highly visible displays in the school (e.g., posters or bulletin boards indicating the importance of reading or math).
12. Refer to the school's goals in student assemblies.

SUPERVISING AND EVALUATING INSTRUCTION

13. Conduct informal observations in classrooms on a regular basis (informal observations are un-scheduled, last at least 5 minutes, and may or may not involve written feedback or a formal conference).
14. Ensure that the classroom objectives of teachers are consistent with the stated goals of the school.
15. Meet with teachers and aides to ensure that they are working toward the same objectives.
16. Review student work products when evaluating classroom instruction.
17. Evaluate teachers on academic objectives directly related to those of the school.
18. Point out specific strengths in teacher instructional practices in postobservation conferences.
19. Point out specific weaknesses in teacher instructional practices in post observation conferences.
20. Note specific strengths of the teacher's instructional practices in written evaluations.
21. Note specific weaknesses of the teacher's instructional practices in written evaluations.
22. Note student time on-task in feedback to teachers after classroom observations.
23. Note specific instructional practices related to the stated classroom objectives in written evaluations.

COORDINATING THE CURRICULUM

24. Make clear who is responsible for coordinating the curriculum across grade levels (e.g., the principal, vice principal, or a teacher).
25. Ensure that the school's academic goals are translated into common curricular objectives.
26. Draw on the results of schoolwide testing when making curricular decisions.
27. Ensure that the objectives of special programs are coordinated with those of the regular class-room.
28. Monitor the classroom curriculum to see that it covers the school's curricular objectives.
29. Assess the overlap between the school's curricular objectives and the achievement test(s) used for program evaluation.
30. Participate actively in the review and/or selection of curricular materials.

MONITORING STUDENT PROGRESS

31. Meet individually with teachers to discuss student academic progress.
32. Discuss the item analysis of tests with the faculty to identify strengths and weaknesses in the instructional program.
33. Use test results to assess progress toward school goals.
34. Distribute test results in a timely fashion.
35. Inform teachers of the school's performance results in written form (e.g., in a memo or newsletter).
36. Inform students of the school's performance results.
37. Identify students whose test results indicate a need for special instruction such as remediation or enrichment.
38. Develop or find the appropriate instructional program(s) for students whose test results indicate a need.

PROTECTING INSTRUCTIONAL TIME

39. Ensure that instructional time is not interrupted by public-address announcements.
40. Ensure that students are not called to the office during instructional time.
41. Ensure that truant students suffer specified consequences for missing instructional time.
42. Ensure that tardy or truant students make up lost instructional time.
43. Visit classrooms to see that instructional time is used for learning and practicing new skills and concepts.

MAINTAINING HIGH VISIBILITY

44. Take time to talk with students and teachers during recess and breaks.
45. Visit classrooms to discuss school issues with teachers and students.
46. Attend or participate in cocurricular or extracurricular activities.
47. Cover classes for teachers until a late or substitute teacher arrives.
48. Tutor or provide direct instruction to students.

PROVIDING INCENTIVES FOR TEACHERS

49. Reinforce superior performance by teachers in staff meetings, newsletters, or memos.
50. Compliment teachers privately for their efforts or performance.
51. Acknowledge special effort or performance by teachers in memos for their personal files.
52. Reward special efforts by teachers with opportunities for professional development (e.g., new roles or in-service training).

PROMOTING PROFESSIONAL DEVELOPMENT

53. Inform teachers of opportunities for professional development.
54. Select in-service activities that are consistent with the school's academic goals.
55. Support teacher requests for in-service that is directly related to the school's academic goals.
56. Distribute journal articles to teachers on a regular basis.
57. Actively support the use of skills acquired during in-service training in the classroom.
58. Ensure that instructional aides receive appropriate training to help students meet instructional objectives.
59. Arrange for outside speakers to make presentations on instruction at faculty meetings.
60. Provide time to meet individually with teachers to discuss instructional issues.
61. Sit in on teacher in-service activities concerned with instruction.
62. Set aside time at faculty meetings for teachers to share ideas on instruction or information from in-service activities.

DEVELOPING AND ENFORCING ACADEMIC STANDARDS

63. Set high standards for the percentage of students who are expected to master important instructional objectives.
64. Encourage teachers to start class on time and to teach to the end of the period.
65. Make known what is expected of students at different grade levels.
66. Enforce a promotion standard requiring mastery of grade-level expectations.
67. Support teachers when they enforce academic policies (e.g., on grading, homework, promotion, or discipline).

PROVIDING INCENTIVES FOR LEARNING

68. Recognize students who do superior academic work with formal rewards such as the honor roll or mention in the principal's newsletter.
69. Use assemblies to honor students for their academic work and/or behavior in class.
70. Recognize superior student achievement or improvement by seeing students in the office with their work products.
71. Contact parents to communicate improved student performance in school.

Scoring: 5 = Almost Always; 4 = Frequently; 3 = Sometimes; 2 = Seldom; and 1 = Almost Never.

Reprinted with permission of the author. (Developed and published by Philip Hallinger, 1983.)

Management Inventory on Modern Management

Kirkpatrick, D.L. 1989. Management Inventory on Modern Management. WI: Elm Grove.

Comments: The 80-item MIMM examines eight areas of modern management. Each area has ten items that deal with philosophy, principles, and approaches of effective managers. According to the author, the MIMM has the following uses: "to determine the need for training; as a tool for conference discussion, to evaluate the effectiveness of a training course; to provide information for on-the job coaching; and to assist in the selection of managers."

Categories: The eight management categories are: leadership styles (1-10); selecting and training (11-20); communicating (21-30); motivating (31-40); managing change (41-50); delegating (51-60); decision-making (61-70); and managing time (71-80).

Data Analysis: Mean scores are reported for 67 personnel/training managers and for 232 line managers.

References:
Gellerman, S. 1963. *Motivation and productivity.* New York, NY: Amacom.

Kirkpatrick, D.L. 1983. *A practical guide for supervisory training and development.* Reading, MA: Addison-Wesley Publishing Company.

Likert, R. 1961. *New patterns of management.* New York, NY: McGraw-Hill Book Company.

Management Inventory on Modern Management

Leadership Styles

1. In order to be effective, a manager must be able to perform all the jobs in the department.
2. "Management by Objectives," means that a manager sets objectives for subordinates and measures their results against those objectives.
3. Every manager should have the dual objectives of contributing to the effectiveness of the organization and maintaining high morale among subordinates.
4. Managers who are "employee-centered" are always more effective than those who are "job-centered."
5. According to Blake and Mouton in describing the "Managerial Grid," a manager who has high concern for both productivity and people is most apt to be successful in most situations on a long term basis.
6. According to McGregor, Theory "X" managers are more oriented to controls than are Theory "Y" managers.
7. According to Batten, an example of a "Tough-Minded Manager" is one who is "as hard as granite."
8. All employees prefer a manager who uses a democratic rather than an autocratic style.
9. "Quality Circles" and "Performance Circles" are practical examples of participative management.
10. In order to be effective a manager must have the same leadership style as his/her boss.

Selecting and Training

11. The person with the highest intelligence, best personality and most experience should always be selected for a job.
12. Performance, seniority, and cooperation are the three most important factors when considering a non-supervisory employee for promotion to first-level supervisor.
13. One of the most important qualifications for promoting a doer to a supervisor is the person's desire to be a supervisor.
14. Employees who have performed their job in an outstanding manner should be rewarded by being promoted.
15. There is some truth to the "Peter Principle" which states that employees tend to rise to their level of incompetence.
16. Managers are responsible for the growth and development of their subordinates.
17. If classroom supervisory training is to be effective, it must be supported by the managers to whom the supervisors report.
18. A performance appraisal system is primarily for the benefit of the personnel department.
19. An effective performance appraisal program must include a requirement that subordinates know what is expected of them by their manager.
20. Many of the practices used by successful athletic coaches can be used by managers.

Communicating

21. Good working relationships between manager and subordinate are an important foundation for effective communication.
22. The misunderstanding of an order or instruction can have serious results in terms of safety, production and cost.
23. A manager has failed to communicate unless the receiver understands the message the way the manager intended it.
24. In order to have an effective company communication program, top management must take an active part.

25. Significant organizational changes should be communicated to all employees.
26. When it is important that a new policy be understood by all employees, the best way to communicate is through channels of authority in the organization.
27. If employees do not understand, they will usually indicate lack of understanding by asking questions or by saying they don't understand.
28. The best way to get feedback is to ask, "Do you have any questions?"
29. It is worthwhile to conduct employee meetings in which employees are encouraged to ask questions, offer suggestions, and air their complaints.
30. If a manager is busy, it is best to tell a subordinate who wants to talk, "I'm busy right now, contact me later."

Motivating
31. Most employees are interested in doing work of which they can be proud.
32. It is possible for managers to motivate their subordinates.
33. Positive reinforcement is important not only for an outstanding job but also for any improvement in performance.
34. "Expect the best" from subordinates is good advice for managers.
35. When subordinates do not perform up to their potential, it is frequently because they encounter obstacles over which they have no control.
36. Very few employees will offer suggestions for improvement unless they are financially rewarded.
37. Money never motivates.
38. Freedom to make decisions is one of the highest forms of reward that can be given to outstanding performers.
39. According to Herzberg, the best way to increase the motivation of an employee is to enrich the job.
40. According to Maslow, the need to be accepted by peers is usually stronger than the needs for recognition and self satisfaction.

Managing Change
41. If you are promoted to a management job, you should make the job different than it was under your predecessor.
42. Empathy is one of the most important concepts in managing change.
43. Managers should welcome suggestions from all sources including subordinates and people from other departments.
44. If your boss tells you to implement an idea you think is a mistake, you should challenge it.
45. If your boss says "no" to an idea you've presented, you should not give up but should try to figure out a different approach to sell the idea.
46. Frequently, employees resist change because they think they will lose something.
47. Once you've decided on a change, you should implement it immediately.
48. It is better to communicate with a group concerning a change than to talk to each person individually.
49. A manager should encourage subordinates to try out any changes that they feel should be made.
50. "Ne Stupefaciamus" is good advice.

Delegating
51. Delegation means the same as job assignment.
52. Delegation should always include the results to be achieved as well as the activities to be performed.

336

53. Delegation should be accompanied by a clear explanation of the degree of authority that the subordinate is given by the manager.
54. When delegating to a subordinate, a manager should make it clear the reporting he/she wants from the subordinate.
55. Delegation should always provide frequent points of control so that progress can be monitored.
56. Delegation should always save time for a manager.
57. When delegating, a manager should always be sure that the person can do the job.
58. Before deciding to whom to delegate, the reason for delegation should first be determined.
59. Activities can be delegated upward in an organization as well as downward.
60. Final accountability for the work cannot be delegated to a subordinate.

Decision Making
61. Decisions should be based on opinions as well as facts.
62. In making decisions, a manager should carefully consider the quality of the decision as well as the level of acceptance on the part of those who will be affected.
63. When conflict arises between manager and subordinate, it is almost impossible for both of them to "win."
64. When there is conflict between manager and subordinate, the manager must make the final decision or else lose face.
65. Brainstorming is a practical tool for use in group problem solving.
66. Group problem solving meetings are usually an exercise in frustration and a waste of time.
67. In making a decision that involves a group, it is important to decide "what is right" rather than "who is right."
68. A group decision is always better than a decision made by one person.
69. Subordinates who are asked for their ideas and opinions regarding a decision are more likely to accept the final decision than those who aren't asked.
70. Reasons for a decision should always be communicated along with the decision itself.

Managing Time
71. Managers should be judged and rewarded on the basis of the amount of time and energy they devote to the organization.
72. A wise use of time for a manager is to tour the department and informally talk with employees.
73. All managers should know how to say "no" to bosses, subordinates, and all other members of management.
74. A manager should always do the most important things first.
75. It is all right for a manager to set his/her own working hours rather than adhere to the working hours of subordinates.
76. Proper planning can reduce the amount of time spent on crises and emergencies.
77. Finding more discretionary time should be a goal of a manager.
78. When a subordinate comes to a manager with a problem which he/she can't immediately solve, it's a good policy to say, "I'll look into it and let you know."
79. Non-productive meetings are one of the biggest time robbers.
80. It's a good idea to handle each piece of paper only once.

Scoring: Agree or Disagree. A separate answer booklet is provided. There is no incorrect answer for items 48, 49, and 75. The raw score is the total number of correct answers.

Reprinted with permission of Dr. Donald L. Kirkpatrick, 1929 Hawthorne Drive, Elm Grove, WI 53122.

Principal Perceived Autonomy Questionnaire

Lucas, S., G.C. Brown, and F.W. Markus. 1991. Principals' perceptions of site-based management and teacher empowerment. *NASSP Bulletin* 75:56-62.

Comments: The ten-item questionnaire examines who is responsible in schools and measures the perceptions of principals regarding their ability to make decisions.

Sample: Elementary and secondary school principals from 11 states in the southeast participated in this study. Responses were received from 542 principals. The participants were randomly selected.

Categories: The eight areas identified in this study were: perceived autonomy of self; perceived teacher autonomy; perceived teacher effectiveness qualities; perceived acceptance of student achievement levels; school climate; increased support for teacher autonomy; degree of external pressure to instructional personnel; and use of standardized tests as a measure of teacher performance.

Data Analysis: Mean scores for each of the eight categories listed above are presented for the total group, by ethnicity, and by size of school district. In addition, percentages of agreement are presented for the total group and by ethnicity for principal perceived autonomy, principal perceived teacher autonomy, principal view of effectiveness, and principal perceived need to increase teacher autonomy.

Principal Perceived Autonomy Questionnaire

1. I have sufficient autonomy over the following to create the best learning environment in my school:
   - district allocated funds
   - influencing educational reform activities
   - subject matter and methods of instruction
   - student personnel
   - support personnel
   - instructional personnel

2. Teachers in my school have sufficient autonomy in the following areas to create the best classroom environment for learning:
   - choice of subject matter to meet student need
   - choice of instructional procedures and strategies
   - use of financial and other resources

3. Teachers in my school show sufficient levels of:
   - professional competence to achieve desired goals
   - motivation to teach productively
   - caring for students

4. The level of student academic achievement is sufficiently high to meet community expectation.

5. The learning atmosphere in my school is sufficiently productive.

6. I would support teacher empowerment to:
   - make staffing decisions
   - manage resources allocated by the district
   - design and implement educational programs
   - "co-manage" the school
   - _____

7. I face greater external pressure than before to increase teacher and student productivity.

8. The use of standardized test results in my school is an appropriate measure of teacher performance.

9. How many layers of administration exist between you and your superintendent?

10. What "one prerogative" do you need to be more productive with students and teacher?

Scoring: Strongly Disagree; Disagree; Agree; Strongly Agree.

Reprinted with permission of the author.

Supervising Teacher Behavior Description Questionnaire

Sistrunk, W.E., et al. 1983. Investigations of supervisory behavior: A symposium. Paper presented at Mid-South Education Research Association. ERIC ED 238 203.

Comments: The 54-item STBDQ was modified from the Supervisory Behavior Description Questionnaire. Both instruments are useful in evaluating behaviors of supervisory educational personnel in terms of whether respondents prefer supervisors to behave in a directive, collaborative, or nondirective manner in relation to specific supervisory tasks. The STBDQ was designed specifically for supervising teachers in order to obtain feedback in the process of supervising student teachers.

Scale Construction: The instrument provides three broad dimension scores: Directive, Collaborative, and Nondirective; three subscale scores: Planning and organizing, Instructional management, and Instructional evaluation, as well as a total score.

Sample: The total sample of 227 was composed of 132 student teachers and 95 supervising teachers.

Reliability: Alpha coefficients for the dimensions were as follows: total score 0.97, directive 0.95, collaborative 0.95, and nondirective 0.96; and for the subscales 0.88, 0.94, and 0.93, respectively.

Validity: Attempts to obtain construct, content, and criterion related validity were provided.

Factor Analysis: Factor analysis in order to produce the dimensions and subscales was performed; however, details concerning this analysis were not provided.

Reference:
Sistrunk, W.E. 1982. The Supervisory Behavior Description Questionnaire (SBDQ) Forms 1 and 2 as research instruments. Paper presented at the Mid-South Educational Research Association.

Supervising Teacher Behavior Description Questionnaire
Form 2

1. The supervising teacher should write and plan units and lessons for the student teaching experience.
2. The supervising teacher should collaborate with the student teacher in writing and planning units and lessons.
3. The supervising teacher should permit the student teacher to plan and write his/her own units and lessons.
4. The supervising teacher should determine the educational objectives and how they are to be achieved.
5. The supervising teacher should collaborate with the student teacher in determining the educational objectives and how they are to be achieved.
6. The supervising teacher should permit the student teacher to determine the educational objectives and how they are to be achieved.
7. The supervising teacher should group students within the classroom for instructional purposes.
8. The supervising teacher should collaborate with the student teacher in grouping students within the classroom for instructional purposes.
9. The supervising teacher should permit the student teacher to group students within the classroom for instructional purposes.
10. The supervising teacher should tell and/or show the student teacher how to improve students' study and work habits.
11. The supervising teacher should collaborate with the student teacher in telling and/or showing the students how to improve their study and work habits.
12. The supervising teacher should permit the student teacher to tell and/or show the students how to improve their study and work habits.
13. The supervising teacher should require standard procedures and format of unit and lesson plans.
14. The supervising teacher should collaborate with the student teacher in developing standard unit and lesson plans.
15. The supervising teacher should permit student teachers to develop standard unit and lesson plans.
16. The supervising teacher should show the student teacher how to use machines and materials.
17. The supervising teacher should collaborate with the student teacher in learning how to use machines and materials.
18. The supervising teacher should permit the student teacher to learn how to use machines and materials.
19. The supervising teacher should assign specific instructional tasks to the student teacher.
20. The supervising teacher should collaborate with the student teacher in the choice of instructional tasks.
21. The supervising teacher should permit the student teacher to select his/her own instructional tasks.
22. The supervising teacher should preview and select curricular materials prior to their use by the student teacher.
23. The supervising teacher should collaborate with the student teacher in previewing and selecting curricular materials prior to their use by the student teacher.
24. The supervising teacher should permit the student teacher to preview and select his/her own curricular material.

25. The supervising teacher should decide if curricular materials are contributing to the desired educational objectives.
26. The supervising teacher and the student teacher should collaborate in deciding if curricular materials are contributing to the desired educational objectives.
27. The supervising teacher should permit the student teacher to decide if curricular materials are contributing to the desired educational objectives.
28. The supervising teacher should determine the areas of improvement needed by the student teacher and tell/show him/her how to improve.
29. The supervising teacher and the student teacher should collaborate in determining the areas of improvement needed by the student teacher and the means of improving.
30. The supervising teacher should permit the student teacher to determine the areas of improvement needed by the student teacher and how to improve.
31. The supervising teacher should provide a framework for implementation of educational innovations by the student teacher.
32. The supervising teacher and the student teacher should collaborate in providing frameworks for the implementation of educational innovations by the student teacher.
33. The supervising teacher should permit the student teacher to devise frameworks for implementing educational innovations in his/her classes.
34. The supervising teacher should identify instructional problems encountered by the student teacher.
35. The supervising teacher should collaborate with the student teacher in identifying instructional problems encountered by the student teachers.
36. The supervising teacher should permit the student teacher to identify his/her instructional problems.
37. The supervising teacher should require the student teacher to develop written long range instructional plans.
38. The supervising teacher and the student teacher should collaborate in the development of long range written instructional plans.
39. The supervising teacher should permit the student teacher to develop long range written instructional plans.
40. The supervising teacher should establish objectives and procedures for evaluating the student teacher's instruction.
41. The supervising teacher and the student teacher should collaborate in establishing objectives and procedures for evaluating the student teacher's instruction.
42. The supervising teacher should permit the student teacher to establish objectives and procedures for evaluating his/her instruction.
43. The supervising teacher should base the evaluation of the student teacher's progress on research.
44. The supervising teacher and the student teacher should collaborate in developing research-based criteria for evaluating the student teacher's progress.
45. The supervising teacher should permit the student teacher to develop research-based criteria for evaluating student teacher progress.
46. The supervising teacher should tell/show the student teacher how to teach more effectively.
47. The supervising teacher and the student teacher should collaborate in determining how the student teacher can teach more effectively.
48. The supervising teacher should permit the student teacher to determine how he/she can teach more effectively.
49. The supervising teacher should select instruments for evaluating student teacher progress.
50. The supervising teacher and the student teacher should collaborate in selecting instruments for evaluating student teacher progress.

51. The supervising teacher should permit the student teacher to select instruments for evaluating student teacher progress.

52. The supervising teacher should conduct action research about teaching on a regular basis.

53. The supervising teacher and the student teacher should collaborate in conducting action research about teaching on a regular basis.

54. The supervising teacher should permit the student teacher to conduct action research about teaching on a regular basis.

Scoring: It is a semantic differential scale that ranges from Satisfying/Dissatisfying; and/or Motivating/Nonmotivating.

Reprinted with permission of the author, Walter E. Sistrunk, Professor of Education Emeritus, Mississippi State University, P.O. Box JG, Mississippi State, MS 39762.

Principals' Analysis of Their Supervisory Styles
Teachers' Analysis of Their Principals' Supervisory Styles

Smalt, R.M. 1997. Measuring principals' styles of supervision. Ed.D. dissertation, Fordham University.

Comments: The 67-item PASS and the 69-item TAPSS assess principals' styles of supervision. The questionnaires, which were developed over a period of three years, were based on the work by McDonough (1991).

Sample: Thirty principals and 40 teachers completed the draft questionnaires. Demographic data are reported for the 51 principals who completed the principals' questionnaire as well as for the 56 teachers who completed the teachers' questionnaire.

Reliability: Alpha coefficients for the six subscales on the principals' questionnaire were: 0.78 (purposes of supervision); 0.91 (structure and procedures during supervision in my school); 0.80 (supervisory practices and behaviors); 0.81 (promoting trusting relationships); 0.93 (the transformational supervisor); and 0.86 (nurturing reflective thinking in my school). The total alpha was 0.95. Alpha coefficients for the six subscales on the teachers' questionnaire were: 0.94 (purposes of supervision); 0.92 (structure and procedures during supervision in my school); 0.74 (supervisory practices and behaviors); 0.89 (promoting trusting relationships); 0.96 (the transformational supervisor); and 0.60 (nurturing reflective thinking in my school). The total alpha was 0.98.

Validity: Content validity was established through a panel of experts who modified and refined the questionnaires. Statements with at least 80% agreement were retained. In addition, there was strong to moderate literature support for all six subscales. Construct validity was examined by studying the intercorrelations of the six subscales. Evidence is also provided for discriminant validity (principals' questionnaire).

Factor Analysis: Although factor analytic procedures yielded six interpretable factors for both questionnaires, the item numbers vary. The six subscales for the principals' questionnaire are: purposes of supervision (1-5); structure and procedures during supervision in my school (6-16); supervisory practices and behaviors (17-24); promoting trusting relationships (25-32); the transformational supervisor (33-54); and nurturing reflective thinking in my school (55-67). The six subscales for the teachers' questionnaire are: purposes of supervision (1-8); structure and procedures during supervision in my school (9-19); supervisory practices and behaviors (20-29); promoting trusting relationships (30-39); the transformational supervisor (40-59); and nurturing reflective thinking in my school (60-69).

References:
Barell, M.C. 1991. New York: The state of learning: Statewide profile of the educational system. A report to the governor and the legislature on the educational status of the state's schools for 1989-90. ERIC ED 334 252.

Costa, A.L., et al., ed. 1992. *If minds matter: A foreword to the future.* (Volumes I and II.) Palatine, IL: Skylight Publishing Inc.

McDonough, S. 1991. The supervision of principals: A comparison of existing and desired supervisory practices as perceived by principals trained in cognitive coaching and those without the training. Unpublished master's thesis. Sacramento State University.

Principals' Analysis of Their Supervisory Style

Part I: Purposes of Supervision

1. Teachers' formal classroom observations are used to promote instructional improvement.
2. Teachers' nonformal classroom observations are used to promote instructional improvement.
3. Teachers in my school generally speak positively about supervision.
4. I believe teachers benefit from my supervision.
5. Teachers believe the principal demonstrates supervisory leadership when he/she works with them during supervision rather than performing perfunctory duties.

Part II: Structure and Procedures During Supervision in my School

During the *preconference*, teachers in our building are encouraged to:

6. Clarify goals for their lessons.
7. Clarify objectives for their lessons.
8. Clarify teaching strategies for their lessons.
9. Clarify student achievement assessment techniques to be used during their lessons.
10. Clarify the data-gathering procedures to be used during their lessons.

During the *postconference*, teachers in our building are encouraged to:

11. Summarize formal and informal assessments from their lessons.
12. Recall data supporting formal and informal assessments from their lessons.
13. Compare what they had planned for their lessons with how the lessons actually went.
14. Infer relationships between their decisions and student achievement during their lessons.
15. Construct new ways to improve their lessons.
16. Reflect on the effects of the supervision process by suggesting improvements for the current supervisory process.

Part III: Supervisory Practices and Behaviors

As a principal, I:

17. Discuss the ground rules for the supervisory process in the preconference.
18. Attempt to respond favorably to teachers' responses in the preconference.
19. Correct my own communication patterns after expressing a negative value judgement.
20. Demonstrate an acceptance of teachers' ideas.
21. Rephrase, paraphrase, translate, and/or summarize teachers' ideas.
22. Help teachers clarify instructional strategies.
23. Invite teachers to become more specific by requesting that they elaborate or rephrase their ideas.
24. Invite teachers to analyze information recorded during the lesson.

Part IV: Promoting Trusting Relationships

As a principal, I:

25. Express my own feelings honestly.
26. Follow through on commitments to teachers.
27. Accept responsibility for my actions.
28. Exhibit an interest in teachers as individuals beyond my role as principal.
29. Focus on teacher concerns by listening actively, reflectively, and empathetically.
30. Express willingness to support teachers' ideas.
31. Support goals that are within teachers' abilities.
32. React to teachers in an appropriate manner when they need support.

Part V: The Transformational Supervisor

As a principal, I encourage teachers to:

33. Understand in greater depth their thinking regarding all aspects of their lessons.
34. Be cognizant of their educational goals, objectives, and/or instructional strategies.
35. Identify possible relationships between particular teaching strategies and desired outcomes.
36. Construct and sequence plans to meet desired student outcomes.
37. Construct and sequence plans to meet desired teacher outcomes.
38. Recall student and teacher behavior during their formal observations.
39. Compare their preplanned instructional strategies with those performed during lessons.
40. Analyze the achievement of goals, objectives, and outcomes during the lessons.
41. Hypothesize differences in their goals, objectives, and outcomes if alternative educational strategies had been used in lessons.
42. Plan future strategies based on their evaluations of the lesson's goals, objectives, and outcomes.

As a principal, I:

43. Identify educational resources needed to assist teachers in creating students' successes.
44. Demonstrate consistent supervisory behavior when I work with teachers who have personality types and/or learning styles.
45. Hold high expectations for myself.
46. Hold high expectations for teachers.
47. Invite teachers to identify appropriate modifications of their behaviors as a result of the supervisory process.
48. Am increasingly aware of how my behavior affects teachers.
49. Am thorough in my approach to professional activities.
50. Am continually examining ways to improve the supervisory process.
51. Am continually examining ways to improve my supervisory performance.
52. Encourage teachers to experiment with creative educational strategies, teacher and student behaviors.
53. Frequently hear from teachers about the spirit of cooperation that exists in our school.
54. Believe teachers and I are creating a learning environment that promotes success for all students.

Part VI: Nurturing Reflective Thinking in My School

55. When students pose unusual questions teachers ask, "What made you think of that?"
56. Teachers believe that textbooks do not have all the answers.
57. Teachers believe they should spend time on interesting student ideas rather than covering the content only.
58. Teachers encourage students to seek alternative solutions to problems.
59. Teachers encourage students to generate their own questions for and during class discussion.
60. Few questions posed during our teachers' classes can be answered with short or one-word answers.
61. Students in our teachers' classes spontaneously engage in critiquing each other's thinking.
62. Students in our teachers' classes relate subject matter to experiences in other subjects.
63. Teachers encourage students to be reflective.
64. Students often set goals and objectives for their own learning.
65. Students spend time working collaboratively to solve problems.
66. We talk about the nature of thinking.
67. We learn from colleagues by observing each other's teaching.

Teachers' Survey of Their Principals' Supervisory Practices

Part I: Purposes of Supervision

1. The principal clearly agrees with teachers about the purposes of supervision.
2. The principal's formal classroom observations are used to promote instructional improvement.
3. The principal's nonformal classroom observations are used to promote instructional improvement.
4. The principal's nonformal classroom observations are used for evaluation.
5. The principal decides which classes to visit during formal observations.
6. The principal generally speaks positively about supervision.
7. I believe I benefit from my principal's supervision.
8. The principal demonstrates supervisory leadership when he/she works with teachers during supervision rather than performing perfunctory duties.

Part II: Structure and Procedures During Supervision in My School

During the preconference, the principal encourages me to:

8. Clarify goals for my lesson.
9. Clarify objectives for my lesson.
10. Clarify teaching strategies for my lesson.
11. Clarify student achievement assessment techniques to be used during my lesson.
12. Clarify the data-gathering procedures to be used during my lesson.
13. Summarize formal and informal assessments from my lesson.
14. Recall data supporting formal and informal assessments from my lesson.
15. Compare what I had planned for my lesson with how the lesson actually went.
16. Infer relationships between my decisions and student achievement during my lesson.
17. Construct new ways to improve my lesson.
18. Reflect on the effects of the supervision process by suggesting improvements for the current supervisory process.

Part III: Supervisory Practices and Behaviors

My principal:

19. Discusses the ground rules for the supervisory process in the preconference.
20. Attempts to respond favorably to my responses in the preconference.
21. Responds frequently to me in the form of praise.
22. Corrects his/her own communication patterns after expressing a negative value judgement.
23. Uses silence effectively to elicit a response from me.
24. Demonstrates an acceptance of my ideas.
25. Rephrases, paraphrases, translates, and/or summarizes my ideas.
26. Helps me clarify my instructional strategies.
27. Invites me to become more specific by requesting that I elaborate or rephrase my ideas.
28. Invites me to analyze information recorded during my lesson.

Part IV: Promoting Trusting Relationships

My principal:

29. Expresses his/her own feelings honestly.
30. Volunteers personal information about himself/herself.
31. Maintains confidentiality.
32. Follows through on commitments to me.
33. Accepts responsibility for his/her actions.
34. Exhibits an interest in me as an individual beyond his/her role as principal.
35. Focuses on my concerns by listening actively, reflectively, and empathetically.
36. Expresses a willingness to support my ideas.
37. Supports goals that are within my abilities.
38. Reacts to me in an appropriate manner when I need support.

Part V: The Transformational Supervisor

My principal encourages me to:

39. Understand in greater depth my thinking regarding all aspects of my lessons.
40. Be cognizant of my educational goals, objectives, and/or instructional strategies.
41. Identify possible relationships between my particular teaching strategies and desired outcomes.
42. Construct and sequence plans to meet desired student outcomes.
43. Construct and sequence plans to meet desired teacher outcomes.
44. Devise multiple methods to assess student learning.
45. Recall student and teacher behavior during my formal observations.
46. Compare my preplanned instructional strategies with those performed during lessons.
48. Analyze the achievement of goals, objectives, and outcomes during my lessons.
49. Hypothesize differences in my goals, objectives, and outcomes if alternative educational strategies had been used in my lessons.
50. Plan future strategies based on my evaluations of my lesson's goals, objectives, and outcomes.

My principal:

51. Identifies educational resources needed to assist me in creating students' successes.

52. Demonstrates consistent supervisory behavior when he/she works with me irrespective of my personality type and/or learning style.
53. Holds high expectations for himself/herself.
54. Holds high expectations for me.
55. Invites me to identify appropriate modifications of my behaviors as a result of the supervisory process.
56. Is increasingly aware of how his/her behavior affects me.
57. Is thorough of his/her approach to professional activities.
58. Is continually examining ways to improve the supervisory process.
59. Is continually examining ways to improve his/her supervisory performance.

Part VI: Nurturing Reflective Thinking in My School

60. Encourages me to experiment with creative educational strategies, teacher and student behaviors.
61. Frequently hears from teachers about the spirit of cooperation that exists in our school.
62. Believes he/she is creating with teachers a learning environment that promotes success for all students.
63. When students pose unusual questions I ask, "What made you think of that?"
64. I encourage students to seek alternative solutions to problems.
65. I encourage students to generate their own questions for and during class discussion.
66. When teaching, I usually move around the classroom.
67. I encourage students to be reflective.
68. Students spend time working collaboratively to solve problems.
69. We learn from colleagues by observing each other's teaching.

Scoring: Never = 1; Infrequently = 2; Frequently = 3; and Always = 4.

Reprinted with permission of the author.

Audit of Principal Effectiveness

Valentine, J.W., and M.L. Bowman. 1988. The Audit of Principal Effectiveness: Instrumentation for principalship research. ERIC ED 311 554.

Comments: The instrument was designed to provide useful feedback to principals about their administrative skills. The development of the various scales was based on the effective school literature, which indicates that principals of more effective schools possess the following characteristics: (1) are assertive instructional leaders, (2) are goal and task oriented, (3) are well organized, (4) convey high expectations for students and staff, (5) define and communicate policies effectively, (6) visit classrooms frequently, (7) are visible and available to students and staff, (8) provide strong support to teachers, and (9) are adept at parent and community relations. Thus, the literature and research of principal effectiveness is used as a foundation for the instrument.

Scale Construction: Operating with the guidelines above, 162 items describing effective principal behavior were identified. These were categorized under 12 theoretical constructs. Because of the length of the instrument, it was divided into two forms—Form A and B with 81 items each.

Sample: The two forms of the instrument were mailed to 3,660 teachers across the United States. The teachers were randomly selected based on seven geographic regions and by elementary, middle, and high school.

Validity: Studies dealing with congruent and discriminant validity were provided.

Factor Analysis: The sample of 3,660 teacher responses was submitted to factor analysis with a varimax rotation. A factor loading of 0.40 or higher was used to retain an item on the factor. A 110-item instruments survived this procedure—55 items on each of Forms A and B. Form A extracted five factors and Form B four factors. The five factors on Form A are instructional management, teacher relations, directional leadership, affective involvement, and affective congruence. Form B produced student orientation, organizational development, organizational linkage, and adaptive leadership.

References:
Edmonds, R.R. 1982. Programs of school improvement: An overview. *Educational Leadership* 40:4-11.

Sweeney, J. 1982. Research synthesis on effective school leadership. *Educational Leadership* 39:346-352.

Audit of Principal Effectiveness

Sample Items:

1. The principal has high professional expectations and standards for self, faculty, and school.
2. The principal encourages changes in the school program that lead to a better school for the students.
3. The principal utilizes resources from outside the school to assist in the study, development, implementation, and/or evaluation of the school.
4. The principal informs staff of new developments and ideas in education.
5. The principal is able to anticipate the effects of decisions.
6. The principal utilizes a systematic process for change which is known and understood by the faculty.
7. When deserving, teachers are complimented by the principal in a sincere and honest manner.
8. The principal takes the time to listen to teachers.
9. The principal finds the time to interact with students.
10. The principal positively reinforces students.
11. The principal keeps teachers informed about those aspects of the school program of which they should be aware.
12. The principal communicates to teachers the reasons for administrative practices used in the school.
13. The principal works with other leaders of the school in the implementation of a team approach to managing the school.
14. The principal encourages faculty to be sensitive to the needs and values of other faculty in the school.
15. The principal is knowledgeable of the varied teaching strategies teachers might appropriately utilize during instruction.
16. The principal maintains an awareness and knowledge of recent research about the learning process.
17. The principal promotes the diagnosis of individual and group learning needs of students and application of appropriate instruction to meet those needs.
18. The principal uses objective data such as test scores to make changes in curriculum and staffing.

Scoring: Respondents are asked to indicate the degree to which each item is descriptive of the skill of an effective principal.

Reprinted with permission of the author. (© Jerry W. Valentine and Michael L. Bowman.)

Teacher Attitudes/Beliefs

Faculty Beliefs about Grades Inventory

Barnes, L.B. 1997. Development of the Faculty Beliefs About Grades Inventory. *Educational and Psychological Measurement* 57:459-468.

Comments: The 24-item FBGI assesses faculty beliefs about norm-referenced and criterion-referenced grading systems as well as their beliefs about the gatekeeping purpose of grades.

Scale Construction: Items were written based on a thorough review of the literature, interviews with faculty, and personal observations. The pilot inventory had 62 items and was tested on 75 faculty members using alternate forms. As a result of the pilot study, 40 items were retained.

Sample: The original random sample consisted of 243 tenure-track undergraduate faculty from two universities in the Midwest.

Reliability: Coefficients of internal consistency were 0.86 for frame of reference and 0.83 for gatekeeping.

Validity: Content validity was established through the development of the FBGI. Construct validity was obtained through factor analysis.

Factor Analysis: Although an oblique rotation yielded four factors that accounted for 39% of the variance, only the first two factors were interpretable. Therefore, a two-factor solution was accepted. The first factor, frame of reference, contains 13 items (1, 2, 4, 7, 8, 10, 13, 14, 18, 20, 22, 23, and 24). The second factor, gatekeeping, contains 11 items (3, 5, 6, 9, 11, 12, 15, 16, 17, 19, and 21).

References:
Geisinger, K.F., and W. Rabinowitz. 1982. Individual differences among college faculty in grading. *Journal of Instructional Psychology* 7:20-27.

Goldman, L. 1985. The betrayal of gatekeepers: Grade inflation. *Journal of General Education* 37:97-121.

Milton, O., et al. 1986. *Making sense of college grades: Why the grading system does not work and what can be done about it.* San Francisco, CA: Jossey-Bass.

Faculty Beliefs about Grades Inventory

1. The highest scoring student should receive an "A" no matter what the highest score is.
2. Differentiating among students on the basis of achievement is a primary purpose of grading.
3. The distribution of scores on a well-written major exam following effective instruction should be "piled up" at the upper end of the scale range.
4. Instructors should determine cutoffs for grades from the distribution of their students' scores.
5. Courses in which students learn the most are typically those with many high grades.
6. Students have little respect for instructors who assign many high grades.
7. Comparative grading methods such as grading "on the curve" are the fairest ways of evaluating student performance.
8. Preset performance standards developed by instructors for assigning grades are, for the most part, arbitrary and meaningless.
9. A final exam in which all students score quite high is probably too easy, no matter how well students know the material.
10. Grades should indicate to students where they stand relative to their peers.
11. Leniency in grading constitutes inaccurate feedback and is detrimental to student progress.
12. Generally, a high percentage of "As" in class indicates low standards or a lack of rigor in assessing achievement.
13. A grade should reflect the degree to which a student has mastered course objectives, without regard for his/her ranking in the class.
14. The highest scoring student on an exam should receive an "A" only if that student's score is above a pre-established cutoff.
15. Departments with high grade point averages generally have lower academic standards.
16. Leniency in grading reduces the value of a college degree.
17. Even with effective instruction the idea that half the class deserves "As" is unreasonable.
18. To be fair, an instructor should try to avoid making comparisons among students in evaluating achievement.
19. The distribution of scores on a well-written major exam following effective instruction should be approximately bell-shaped.
20. A student's grade should be determined by his/her own performance and not be influenced by how well classmates do.
21. It is theoretically possible for every student in my class to earn an "A."
22. When I assign course grades, the number or percentage of students in each grade category is an important factor in grading decisions.
23. If the class average on an exam is quite a bit lower than expected, I would adjust the grades upward.
24. I do not believe in "curving" the grades.

Scoring: Strongly Agree = 7; Agree = 6; Unsure but tend to Agree = 5; Neither Agree nor Disagree = 4; Unsure but tend to Disagree = 3; Disagree = 2; and Strongly Disagree = 1. For scoring purposes, the following items are reversed: 3, 5, 13, 14, 18, 20, 21, and 24.

Reprinted with permission of the author.

Affective Work Competencies Inventory

Brauchle, P.E., et al. 1983. The factorial validity of the Affective Work Competencies Inventory. *Educational and Psychological Measurement* 43:603-609.

Comments: The 45-item AWCI measures five work attitudes and habits that represent intrinsic value components. According to the authors, it is possible that the most effective method of teaching affective work competencies for job success is through student emulation of teacher behavior.

Sample: The AWCI was administered to 798 industrial workers, 567 industrial supervisors, and 120 vocational educators. The responses of 1,485 people were examined to study their perceptions of affective work competencies.

Reliability: Kuder-Richardson formula 20 estimates for the five factors were: 0.64 (ambition), 0.80 (self-control), 0.76 (organization), 0.89 (enthusiasm), and 0.79 (conscientiousness). They ranged from a high of 0.89 (enthusiasm) to a low of 0.64 (ambition).

Validity: Content validity was established through the development of the AWCI. The original instrument contained 95 items in 15 competency clusters. Factor analysis was undertaken as a way of establishing the construct validity of the instrument.

Factor Analysis: A principal components factor analysis with a varimax orthogonal rotation yielded five factors with loadings above 0.35. The five factors accounted for 76.3% of the variance. The five factors are: four items on ambition (31, 46, 1, and 32); eight items on self-control (65, 82, 55, 10, 69, 40, 36, and 94); four items on organization (57, 80, 92, and 83); 16 items on enthusiasm (86, 75, 89, 77, 70, 95, 93, 64, 78, 66, 48, 79, 88, 71, 67, and 76); and 13 items on conscientiousness (30, 39, 19, 16, 58, 68, 60, 81, 24, 72, 90, 45, and 74).

References:
Brauchle, P.E. 1979. Self and supervisor perceptions of affective work competencies in CETA trainees: A comparative study. Ph.D. dissertation, University of Missouri, Columbia.

Morgan, K.R. 1980. The relative effect of two different methods of instruction upon the affective work competencies of trade and industrial students. Ph.D. dissertation, University of Missouri, Columbia.

Petty, G.C. 1978. Affective work competencies of workers, supervisors, and vocational educators. Ph.D. dissertation, University of Missouri, Columbia.

Affective Work Competencies Inventory

1. Setting personal work/job goals
2. Setting goals for self-improvement
3. Acquiring new skills to advance in job
4. Participating in group activities
5. Becoming angry at others
6. Blowing my stack
7. Getting angry
8. Controlling temper
9. Staying angry or upset all day
10. Maintaining even temperament
11. Complaining
12. Complaining about job tasks
13. Keeping work area clear
14. Keeping work area clean and organized
15. Keeping supplies neatly arranged
16. Keeping records and files in order
17. Working hard to accomplish new goals
18. Accepting challenging assignments
19. Putting forth extra effort
20. Adjusting to change
21. Completing difficult tasks
22. Performing work eagerly
23. Speaking favorably of future work assignments
24. Completing work without constant supervision
25. Responding to greetings from co-workers
26. Listening to instructions
27. Adjusting to various work situations
28. Reading directions
29. Organizing work activities
30. Returning material and equipment to places
31. Practicing safe work habits
32. Volunteering suggestions
33. Avoiding work
34. Disturbing others who try to work
35. Reminded by others to begin work
36. Pushing work onto other workers
37. Saying one will do something and not doing it
38. Talking out of turn at group meetings
39. Gazing out the window or at the clock
40. Annoying other people
41. Interrupting others
42. Being late for work or meetings
43. Working hard only when someone is watching
44. Losing interest in work
45. Arguing about job assignments

Scoring: A Likert scale is used to measure work attitudes, values, and habits.

Reprinted with permission of Gregory Petty.

Minnesota Teacher Attitude Inventory

Cook, W.W., et al. 1951. Minnesota Teacher Attitude Inventory. Psychological Corporation, 555 Academic Court, San Antonio, TX 78204-2498.

Comments: The 150-item MTAI is used to assess attitudes that determine how well a teacher will get along with students. MTAI scores have been reported as unstable during the time between preservice and regular classroom teaching. The scores can be used to identify attitudes along a continuum that ranges from traditional to progressive.

Scale Construction: Leeds wrote 378 items in both positive and negative statements based on a review of the literature on teacher-pupil interaction. Two groups of 100 teachers (identified as superior or inferior) responded to the statements. One hundred sixty-four items differentiated between these two teacher groups. Another sample of 100 teachers participated. The final form of the MTAI contains 129 items that were developed by Leeds and 21 items developed by Callis.

Sample: The original sample consisted of 100 teachers who were identified as superior teachers and 100 teachers who were identified as inferior teachers. Another sample of 100 teachers in grades 4 through 6 responded to the inventory.

Factor Analysis: Yee and Fruchter factor analyzed the MTAI. Orthogonal varimax rotations yielded five factors. Only items with factor loading above 0.42 are reported. Sixty items met this criterion. Children's irresponsible tendencies and lack of self-control contains 20 items (19, 21, 23, 24, 35, 36, 52, 54, 63, 65, 75, 76, 80, 92, 109, 110, 114, 116, 126, and 128); conflict between teachers' and pupils' interests contains 15 items (20, 34, 99, 119, 121, 124, 131, 132, 133, 134, 136, 137, 141, 144, and 149); rigidity and severity in handling pupils contains 12 items (13, 27, 47, 72, 81, 85, 86, 88, 103, 115, 118, and 129); pupils independence in learning contains seven items (15, 16, 53, 64, 71, 77, and 93); and pupils' acquiescence to the teacher contains six items (1, 90, 101, 107, 113, and 146). The first three factors are related to traditionalism, while the last two factors are related to progressivism.

Validity: Based upon Leed's study, correlations with principals' ratings were 0.46, 0.59 with observers' ratings, and 0.31 with students' ratings. Based upon Callis' study, correlations were 0.19 with principals' ratings, 0.40 with observers' ratings, and 0.49 with students' ratings.

Reliability: Corrected split-half reliability was 0.93.

References:
Johnson, W.A. 1983. Personality correlates of preferences for preprofessional training by special education and regular class trainees. *Education* 103:360-368.

Yee, A.H. 1970. Do principals' interpersonal attitudes agree with those of teachers and pupils? *Educational Administration Quarterly* 6:1-13.

Yee, A.H., and B. Fruchter. 1971. Factor content of the Minnesota Teacher Attitude Inventory. *American Educational Research Journal* 8:119-133.

Scoring: Strongly Agree; Agree; Undecided or Uncertain; Disagree; and Strongly Disagree. Responses are scored +1, 0, or -1. Therefore, scores range from -150 to +150. Yee and Kriewall scored items +2, +1, 0, -1, and -2.

Sample Items:

5.   Teaching never gets monotonous.

106. A teacher should not be expected to do more work than he is paid for.

144. Teachers can be in the wrong as well as pupils.

Behavior Intervention Rating Scale

Elliott, S.N., and M.V.B. Treuting. 1991. The Behavior Intervention Rating Scale: Development and validation of a pretreatment acceptability and effectiveness measure. *Journal of School Psychology* 29:43-51.

Comments: The 24-item BIRS assesses teachers' perceptions of treatment acceptability and effectiveness. Nine new statements that measure treatment effectiveness were added to the 15-item Intervention Rating Scale (Martens, et al., 1985) to create this scale. The IRS measures treatment acceptability and has a reliability coefficient of 0.98.

Sample: The original sample consisted of 216 teachers who were enrolled in graduate courses at two universities in Louisiana. Over 80% were regular education teachers, while the others were special education teachers. All the teachers were volunteers.

Reliability: The alpha coefficients were 0.97 (acceptability), 0.92 (effectiveness), and 0.87 (time). The total scale alpha was 0.97.

Validity: Content validity was established through operationalizing the constructs of treatment acceptability and treatment effectiveness. Construct validity was established through factor analytic procedures. Concurrent validity was established through correlational comparisons between the Semantic Differential (Osgood, Suci, and Tannenbaum, 1957) and the BIRS.

Factor Analysis: Three factors were extracted with an oblique rotation. The three factors accounted for 73.6% of the total variance. Only items with loadings greater than 0.50 were retained on the factor. In addition, factor loadings had to be 0.30 or less on the other two factors to be retained. The three factors are: acceptability (all 15 statements from the IRP), effectiveness (seven of the new statements), and time (the remaining two new statements). Factor matrices are presented.

References:
Clark, L., and S.N. Elliott. 1988. The influence of treatment strength information on knowledgeable teachers' evaluation of two social skills training methods. *Professional School Psychology* 3:241-251.

Martens, B.K., J.C. Witt, S.N. Elliott, and D.X. Darveaux. 1985. Teacher judgments concerning the acceptability of school-based interventions. *Professional Psychology: Research and Practice* 16:191-198.

Sheridan, S.M., T.R. Kratochwill, and S.N. Elliott. 1990. Behavioral consultation with parents and teachers: Delivering treatment for socially withdrawn children at home and school. *School Psychology Review* 19:33-52.

Witt, J.C., S.N. Elliott, and B.K. Martens. 1984. Acceptability of behavioral interventions used in classrooms: The influences of amount of time, severity of behavior problems, and types of intervention. *Behavioral Disorders* 9:95-104.

Behavior Intervention Rating Scale

1. This would be an acceptable intervention for the child's problem behavior.
2. Most teachers would find this intervention appropriate for behavior problems in addition to the one described.
3. The intervention should prove effective in changing the child's problem behavior.
4. I would suggest the use of this intervention to other teachers.
5. The child's behavior problem is severe enough to warrant use of this intervention.
6. Most teachers would find this intervention suitable for the behavior problem described.
7. I would be willing to use this in the classroom setting.
8. The intervention would not result in negative side-effects for the child.
9. The intervention would be appropriate intervention for a variety of children.
10. The intervention is consistent with those I have used in classroom settings.
11. The intervention was a fair way to handle the child's problem behavior.
12. The intervention is reasonable for the behavior problem described.
13. I like the procedures used in the intervention.
14. This intervention was a good way to handle this child's behavior problem.
15. Overall, the intervention would be beneficial for the child.
16. The intervention would quickly improve the child's behavior.
17. The intervention would produce a lasting improvement in the child's behavior.
18. The intervention would improve the child's behavior to the point that it would not noticeably deviate from other classmates' behavior.
19. Soon after using the intervention, the teacher would notice a positive change in the problem behavior.
20. The child's behavior will remain at an improved level even after the intervention is discontinued.
21. Using the intervention should not only improve the child's behavior in the classroom, but also in other settings (e.g., other classrooms, home).
22. When comparing this child with a well-behaved peer before and after use of the intervention, the child's and the peer's behavior would be more alike after using the intervention.
23. The intervention should produce enough improvement in the child's behavior so the behavior no longer is a problem in the classroom.
24. Other behaviors related to the problem behavior also are likely to be improved by the intervention.

Scoring: Strongly Disagree = 1; Disagree = 2; Slightly Disagree = 3; Slightly Agree = 4; Agree = 5; Strongly Agree = 6.

Reprinted with permission of Stephen N. Elliot, Professor, University of Wisconsin-Madison.

Teachers' Beliefs about Administrators Scale

Feldman, D., and L.H. Gerstein. 1988. A factor analytic study of three teacher belief scales. *Measurement and Evaluation in Counseling and Development* 21:72-80.

Comments: The 12-item TBA scale can be used to determine how teachers feel about their administrative support systems. In addition to the TBA scale, the authors also developed the Teachers' Beliefs about Parents Scale and the Perceptions of Parental Beliefs Concerning Teachers. Psychometric information for all three scales is included in the article. All three scales could be used to determine the content and quality of the relationships among teachers, parents, and administrators.

Scale Construction: A review of the literature on administrative responsibilities and previous studies on teacher attitudes toward administrators were studied in order to identify concepts. Five education professors and six doctoral students sorted concepts (100% interrater agreement).

Sample: The sample consisted of 462 teachers who were taking graduate courses at three state universities in Arizona, Indiana, and Texas.

Reliability: The scale had an alpha (Cronbach) coefficient of 0.92.

Validity: Content validity was established by scale construction. Construct validity was established by factor analytic procedures.

Factor Analysis: Principal components factor analysis with a varimax rotation yielded one factor with 12 items. The final factor solution was cross-validated. These beliefs centered on administrative leadership, administrative partnership, and administrative support.

Data Analysis: Factor analysis was undertaken to establish a meaningful factor structure and to eliminate items. Tests for reliability were run to determine the internal consistency of the scale. Factor loadings, means, and standard deviations were reported.

References:
Hoy, W.K., and J.E. Henderson. 1983. Principal authenticity, school climate, and pupil-control orientation. *Alberta Journal of Educational Research* 29:123-130.

Robson, D.L. 1981. Administering educational services for the handicapped: Role expectations and perceptions. *Exceptional Children* 47:377-378.

Teachers' Beliefs about Administrators

I believe that ADMINISTRATORS

1. Know that beginning teachers need time to become master teachers.
2. Realize that teacher training in classroom discipline does not imply that teacher's sovereign territory of total management of problem behavior.
3. Support both parents and teachers, seeking to develop common ground with mutual regard and respect.
4. Seek to discover on a firsthand basis, in the environment of noted conflict, possible solutions.
5. Resolve problems between parents and teachers that maintain the "face" or "egos" of both parties.
6. Serve as an equivalent partner in behavior management responsibility.
7. Display academic leadership.
8. Display school discipline leadership.
9. Develop positive school climate.
10. Want to improve their interactions with parents.
11. Want to improve their interactions with teachers.
12. Are partners in the educational process.

Scoring: A percentage likelihood scaling format (0%-100%) with ten-point intervals is used.

(Reprinted with permission of Feldman, D., and L.H. Gerstein. 1988. Teachers' beliefs about administrators scale. Yorktown, IN: Educational Technology Resources.)

Middle School Attitude Inventory

Gillan, R.E. 1978. The Middle School Questionnaire. ERIC ED 160 617.

Comments: The Middle School Questionnaire is made up of five measures. They are: a Professional Description Survey, Middle School Employment Survey, Professional Recommendations Survey, Middle School Concept List, and the Middle School Attitude Inventory. The focus in this description is on the Middle School Attitude Inventory. The 30-item Middle School Attitude Inventory assesses teachers' attitudes toward the middle school.

Scale Construction: The surveys were constructed as a result of meetings with school administrators, middle school teachers, university faculty, and a thorough review of the literature on middle schools. A pilot study was conducted to refine the surveys. In addition, college faculty were involved in content validation.

Sample: The sample for the pilot study consisted of 30 middle school teachers. They were instructed to select 15 items that they strongly agreed with and 15 items that they strongly disagreed with out of a total of 60 items. Based on the results of group consensus (Delphi technique), 30 bipolar statements were developed. A field study was conducted with 45 certified middle school teachers and 45 teachers who were certified at a different school level.

Data Analysis: One-way analysis of variance was conducted on the Middle School Attitude Inventory to decide whether or not significant differences existed between the two groups. Chi-square analysis was performed on the School Concept List to decide whether or not significant differences existed between the two groups. Significant differences were found in four domains.

Middle School Attitude Inventory

1. The development of the middle school has given improved status to intermediate grade education.
2. A competitive atmosphere in the academic program as well as co-curricular activities will best prepare the student for real life.
3. The middle school teacher is responsible for the establishment of an effective learning environment and the student for learning.
4. The middle school provides an environment which specializes in helping the student make a smooth transition from childhood to adolescence.
5. Flexible scheduling provides for efficient use of teacher time and permits more effective instructional planning.
6. The middle school facilitates the reorganization of teacher education to provide 3 areas of specialized training (elementary, middle, and secondary).
7. Present undergraduate education programs adequately prepare both elementary and secondary teachers for the middle school.
8. In the middle school organization it is probably best that the lower grades (5 and 6) remain as self-contained classes.
9. The effective teacher must be able to anticipate change and adjust to changing situation, and to help the student do the same.
10. Since children in grades 6-9 are undergoing common experiences, little developmental difference is noted.
11. The middle school program stresses academic exploration as opposed to subject centered concentration.
12. The diagnosing and prescription for individual learning problems can best be accomplished through formal evaluation by the counselor or a testing team.
13. The middle school allows the student to begin studying academically challenging subjects under a subject specialist at a younger age.
14. The academic program of the middle school should emphasize how to learn through student exploration.
15. The six period day should be introduced by grade 7 in order to prepare the students for the Carnegie Unit in high school.
16. Individual reading skills can be best developed by a separate middle school course in reading and spelling.
17. The nature of the middle school program requires that each teacher also function as a guidance counselor.
18. The middle school should place emphasis on student self direction and learner independence through joint student teacher planning.
19. The academic purpose of the middle school is to provide the student with a strong background for high school studies in the four basic academic disciplines.
20. The teacher should help the student develop a learning sequence appropriate to his level based on formal and informal diagnosis of ability and achievement.
21. The only difference between a middle school and a junior high school is the grade organization.
22. Future education (education for change) should be confined to high school grades as most preadolescence have not developed the conceptual processes such education requires.
23. Developmentally, children in grades 6-8 are probably more alike than children in grades 7-9.
24. Since most elementary and secondary teacher training programs overlap at the middle school grades, there is little need for a special program at this level.

25. The middle school facilitates the introduction in grades 5 and 6 of some specialization and team teaching in staff patterns.
26. Content area reading instruction should be a primary responsibility of each middle school teacher.
27. One of the most serious problems of the middle school program is the lack of teachers trained specifically for the middle school.
28. The mastery of concepts and skills in the 4 basic academic disciplines should be the primary goal of the middle school program.
29. Guidance and counseling in the middle school program should be practiced by and limited to those professionally prepared and certified in the field.
30. The middle school program should strive to lessen competition in all phases of the student's life.

Scoring: A five-point Likert scale ranging from Strongly Agree to Strongly Disagree is used on the Middle School Attitude Inventory. A "right" response has a value of plus one, while a "wrong" response has a value of minus one. On the Middle School Concept List, respondents are instructed to select ten concepts that are the most important to a middle school program.

Reprinted with permission of Dr. Robert E. Gillan, Northwestern State University.

Teacher Attitude Inventory

Glascock, C.H. 1996. Teachers' perceptions of the principal/superintendent relationship and school climate: Do they correlate? Ph.D. dissertation, Louisiana State University.

Comments: The 14-item TAI examines the perceptions of teachers regarding the relationship between their principal and their superintendent. The TAI is currently being further refined.

Sample: A multistaged sampling procedure was used to select elementary and high schools. Study one involved 252 teachers from five elementary and three high schools. Study two involved 270 teachers from 19 elementary and seven high schools.

Reliability: For study one, the Alpha coefficient was 0.77 with items 1-5 and 7 deleted. For study two, the alpha coefficient was 0.78 with items 1-5 and 7 deleted.

Validity: A panel of six experts analyzed the TAI on at least three occasions. According to the author, the purpose of study one was to establish the construct validity and reliability of the TAI, while the purpose of the second study was to validate the factor analytic results of the first study.

Factor Analysis: A desired two-factor solution (independence and influence) was not confirmed. The TAI is a general measure of the relationship between the principal and the superintendent. The one-factor solution with eight items accounts for almost 31% of the variance in both studies.

Data Analysis: Means and standard deviations by item (6 and 8-14) are included.

References:
Hallinger, P., et al. 1990. What makes a difference in school context, principal leadership, and student achievement. NCEL Occasional Paper No.3. Nashville, TN: National Center for Educational Leadership.

Molm, L.D. 1990. Structure, action, and outcomes: The dynamics of power in social exchange. *American Sociological Review* 55:427-447.

Okeafor, K.R., and R.M. Frere. 1992. Administrators' confidence in teachers, leader consideration, and coupling in schools. *Journal of Research and Development in Education* 25:204-212.

Smith, J.B., M.L. Maehr, and C. Midgley. 1992. Relationship between personal and contextual characteristics and principals' administrative behaviors. *The Journal of Educational Research* 86:111-118.

Whaley, K.W., and T.G. Hegstrom. 1992. Perceptions of school principal communication effectiveness and teacher satisfaction on the job. *Journal of Research and Development in Education* 24:224-231.

Teacher Attitude Inventory

1. When teachers in our school push for curriculum changes, principal must get the approval of the superintendent before agreeing to these changes.
2. If the principal thinks it's better for our school, he/she will modify some district policies without consulting the superintendent.
3. The superintendent transfers teachers into and out of our school without consulting the principal.
4. When it comes to hiring teachers at our school, the principal usually gets whom he/she wants.
5. The principal determines how some funds are spent at our school without consulting the superintendent; for example, funds raised by the school for staff development or supplies.
6. When parents, who have difficulty with a teacher in our school, go over the principal's head to the superintendent, the superintendent usually intervenes and tells the principal what to do.
7. The principal must have the superintendent's permission before raising money from businesses in the community.
8. Teachers can get needed resources, such as overhead projector and materials, because the principal has a good working relationship with the superintendent.
9. The principal's explanations about parental concerns are disregarded by the superintendent when making decisions.
10. When teachers in our school want permission to try new instructional techniques, the principal is able to convince the superintendent to allow it.
11. When teachers ask the principal to request extra resources for our school, like new computers, the principal is able to get those resources from the superintendent.
12. The principal is able to persuade the superintendent to support new programs for our school.
13. The principal does not seem able to influence the superintendent in hiring teachers for our school.
14. The superintendent seldom supports the principal's requests or additional funding for our school.

Scoring: A five-point Likert scale ranges from Strongly Disagree to Strongly Agree. There is a No Opinion response that receives a score of zero. A low score shows that teachers don't observe a high level of independence and influence occurring in relationship between the principal and superintendent.

Reprinted with permission of Catherine H. Glascock © 1996.

Teaching Behaviors Questionnaire

Marchant, G.J., and N.D. Bowers. 1990. An attitude inventory for research-based effective teaching behaviors. *Educational and Psychological Measurement* 50:167-174.

Comments: The 36-item TBQ could be used for preservice and postservice teacher training. In addition, it could also be used to select and screen teachers and principals. Teacher education programs might use the results to identify areas for training.

Scale Construction: The research on effective teaching was reviewed and the following six categories related to teaching generated the items for the TBQ: instructional design and structure; active teaching; giving information; questioning the student; reacting to student responses; and handling seatwork and homework assignments. A pilot test was conducted on four graduate classes of 60 teachers.

Sample: Three hundred teachers, 100 principals, 50 college education faculty, and 50 undergraduate education students from Illinois, Indiana, and Wisconsin participated in the study.

Reliability: The alpha coefficient for the TBQ was 0.76. Reliabilities for each group are provided. They ranged from a high of 0.78 (college education faculty) to a low of 0.62 (undergraduate education students).

Data Analysis: Means and standard deviations are presented for each group in the sample. Item-total correlations were computed. The distribution of the data was studied to prove normality. Significant differences among the various groups have been identified.

References:
Marchant, G.J. 1988a. Attitudes toward research-based effective teaching behaviors. Ph.D. dissertation. Northwestern University.

Marchant, G.J. 1988b. Attitudes toward research-based effective teaching behaviors from teachers, principals, and college faculties and students. Paper presented at Mid-Western Educational Research Association. ERIC ED 303 449.

Marchant, G.J., and N.D. Bowers. 1988. Teacher agreement with research-based effective teaching behaviors. Paper presented at American Educational Research Association. ERIC ED 302 503.

Teaching Behaviors Questionnaire

1. The teacher should allow the students to figure out the main idea of a lesson on their own.
2. The teacher should provide drill and practice after each skill or section taught.
3. The teacher should explain assignments and go over practice examples with the students before they are allowed to work independently.
4. The teacher should monitor the progress of each student daily.
5. The teacher should spend most of the class time teaching the student as one whole group.
6. The teacher should sit at the teacher's desk while the students are doing seat work, and have students come up to the desk when they need help.
7. The teacher should call on both volunteering and non-volunteering students after asking a question in class.
8. The teacher should redirect relevant student questions to the class and incorporate comments into the lesson.
9. The teacher should expect all of the students to master the course content.
10. The teacher should quickly ask the class another question when a student gives an incorrect answer to a question asked in class.
11. The teacher should not let the students know which assignments are for a grade and which are for practice.
12. The teacher should introduce classroom rules and procedures one-at-a-time as they become necessary throughout the year.
13. The teacher should make class presentations of less than 20 minutes.
14. The teacher should wait at least 3 seconds after asking a question in class before calling on a student.
15. The teacher should convey a strong sense of enthusiasm to the students.
16. The teacher should receive 60 to 80 percent correct by most of the students on assignments that the students are expected to work on independently.
17. The teacher should rephrase the question to the student when an incorrect answer is given in class.
18. The teacher should continue to work on problem material when performance on assignments is poor.
19. The teacher should only call on volunteering students after asking a question in class.
20. The teacher should move around the classroom during the time that the students are working independently at their seats.
21. The teacher should stick to the lesson regardless of student comments.
22. The teacher should primarily emphasize academic instruction in the classroom.
23. The teacher should expect about half of the students to master the curriculum.
24. The teacher should not use praise excessively in the classroom.
25. The teacher should save drill and practice until the students have a number of skills to practice.
26. The teacher should often use unfamiliar and abstract words in classroom lessons and presentations.
27. The teacher should inform the students exactly what determines the grade on an assignment.
28. The teacher should overtly acknowledge correct answers that a student gives to a question asked in class.
29. The teacher should expect the students to figure out instructions as part of an assignment.
30. The teacher should identify the main ideas of a lesson during the lesson and at the end of the lesson.
31. The teacher should continue to the next scheduled unit when performance is poor, and in the future the teacher should avoid material similar to that which the students had problems.
32. The teacher should receive 90 to 100 percent correct by most of the students on assignments that students are expected to work on independently.
33. The teacher should spend time at the beginning of the school year teaching classroom rules and procedures.
34. The teacher should monitor the progress of each individual student every two to four weeks.

35. The teacher should begin lessons and presentations to the class with a review or an overview of the material.
36. The teacher should immediately call on a student after asking a question in class.

Scoring: Strongly Disagree = 4; Disagree = 3; Agree = 2; and Strongly Agree = 1. The scoring is reversed for the following items: 2, 3, 4, 5, 7, 8, 9, 13, 14, 15, 17, 18, 20, 22, 24, 27, 28, 30, 32, 33, and 35.

Reprinted with permission of Gregory J. Marchant, Educational Psychology, Ball State University, Muncie, IN 47306-0595.

Attitudes and Beliefs on Classroom Control Inventory (ABCC)

Martin, N.K., Z. Yin, and B. Baldwin. 1997. Attitudes and beliefs regarding classroom management style: Differences between male and female, urban and rural secondary level teachers. Paper presented at the American Educational Research Association. ERIC ED 404 738.

Comments: The 26-item inventory assesses teachers' perceptions of their classroom management attitudes and behaviors. The ABCC was previously known as the Inventory of Classroom Management Style. Items were written based upon actual classroom experiences and observations as well as suggestions from experts in the field.

Sample: The sample consisted of 282 teachers from three school districts located in the southwestern part of the United States.

Reliability: The alpha coefficients were 0.82 (instructional management), 0.69 (people management), and 0.69 (behavior management).

Validity: Structural validity was confirmed by means of factor analytic procedures. The concurrent validity of the ABCC was examined by comparing the scores on the ABCC with the scores of the 16 Personality Factor Questionnaire (16PF) Form A.

Factor Analysis: The results of an orthogonal varimax factor analysis yielded three subscales: 14 items on instructional management (1, 2, 5, 6, 7, 8, 10, 11, 14, 18, 21, 22, 24, and 26); eight items on people management (3, 4, 9, 12, 15, 17, 23, and 25); and four items on behavior management (13, 16, 19, and 20).

Data Analysis: Scale means and standard deviations are presented as well as the results of an item analysis.

References:
Martin, N.K., and B. Baldwin. 1996. Helping beginning teachers foster healthy classroom management: Implications for elementary school counselors. *Elementary School Guidance and Counseling* 31:106-113.

Martin, N.K., Z. Yin, and B. Baldwin. 1998 (in press). Construct validation of the Attitudes & Beliefs on Classroom Control Inventory. *Journal of Classroom Intervention*.

Wolfgang, C.H., and C.D. Glickman. 1986. *Solving discipline problems: Strategies for classroom teachers*. Boston, MA: Allyn and Bacon.

Attitudes and Beliefs on Classroom Control (ABCC) Inventory

1. I believe the teacher should direct the students' transition from one learning activity to another.
2. I believe it's important to continuously monitor students' learning behavior during seatwork.
3. I believe students should create their own daily routines as this fosters development of responsibility.
4. I believe students will be successful in school if allowed the freedom to pursue their own interests.
5. I believe the teacher should decide what topics the students study and the tasks used to study them.
6. During the first week of class, I will announce the classroom rules and inform students of the penalties for disregarding the rules.
7. The teacher knows best how to allocate classroom materials and supplies to optimize learning.
8. When a student bothers other students, I will immediately tell the student to be quiet and stop it.
9. I believe class rules stifle the students' ability to develop a personal moral code.
10. While teaching a lesson on library skills, a student begins to talk about the research she is doing for her book report. I would remind the student that the class has to finish the lesson before the end of the class period.
11. I believe teachers should require student compliance and respect for law and order.
12. When moving from one learning activity to another, I will allow students to progress at their own rate.
13. If students agree that a classroom rule is unfair, then I would replace it with one that students think is fair.
14. I believe students need the structure of a daily routine that is organized and implemented by the teacher.
15. I allow students to select their own seats.
16. When students behave appropriately, I will provide a reward of some kind such as points toward a party or free time.
17. I believe students should judge the quality of their own work rather than rely on what the teacher tells them.
18. I believe students will be successful in school if they listen to the adults who know what's best for them.
19. I believe students should choose the learning topics and tasks.
20. During the first week of class, I will allow the students to come up with a set of classroom rules.
21. I believe the primary purpose of homework is to provide drill and practice of skills learned in the classroom.
22. I believe that students need direction in how to work together.
23. Students in my classroom are free to use any materials they wish during the learning process.
24. I specify a set time for each learning activity and try to stay within my plans.
25. I believe friendliness, courtesy, and respect for fellow students is something that students have to learn first-hand through free interaction.
26. I believe class rules are important because they shape the student's behavior and development.

Scoring: There are four responses for each item: Describes me very well = 4; Describes me usually = 3; Describes me somewhat = 2; and Describes me not at all = 1. The scoring is reversed for statements 3, 4, 9, 12, 13, 15, 17, 19, 10, 13, and 25. The higher the score, the more controlling (interventionist). Three separate scale scores are produced. Reprinted with permission of the author.

Occupational Work Ethic Inventory

Hill, R.B., and G.C. Petty. 1995. A new look at selected employability skills: A factor analysis of the occupational work ethic. *Journal of Vocational Education Research* 20:59-73.

Comments: The 50-item OEWI (Petty, 1991) assesses the intrinsic aspect of the workplace. The work ethic factors provide a research base for educators who are preparing students for the transition from school to work. It has been validated with over 2,279 workers.

Sample: The sample for the most recent study consisted of 1,151 employees in private and public organizations in the Southeast. In a previous study (1994), over 2,220 employees from six occupational groups were surveyed.

Reliability: In a pilot study, the alpha correlation was 0.95. In additional studies, the alpha coefficients ranged from 0.90 (Hatcher) to 0.95 (Hill).

Validity: Content validity was established by choosing items from a review of the literature on work attitudes, work values, and work habits. The items were reviewed by a panel of experts. Another panel of experts sorted the original items into categories. This process was repeated until consensus was reached. The four categories were: dependable, ambitious, considerate, and cooperative. Several factor analytic studies were conducted to establish the construct validity of the OWEI.

Factor Analysis: A principal components factor analysis with a varimax orthogonal rotation yielded four factors. The four factors are: 15 items on interpersonal skills (17, 22, 28, 29, 31, 32, 33, 37, 41, 42, 43, 46, 47, 48, and 50); 16 items on initiative (5, 6, 7, 10, 11, 14, 15, 18, 20, 27, 35, 36, 38, 40, 45, and 49); seven items on being dependable (1, 3, 4, 8, 12, 16, and 23); ten items on reversed items (9, 13, 21, 24, 25, 26, 30, 34, 39, and 44.).

Data Analysis: Factor loadings, item means, and standard deviations are reported.

References:

Hatcher, T. 1993. The work ethic of apprentices and instructors in a trade union apprenticeship training program. Ph.D. dissertation. University of Tennessee, Knoxville.

Hill, R.B. 1992/1993. The work ethic as determined by occupation, education, age, gender, work experience, and empowerment. Ph.D. dissertation. University of Tennessee, Knoxville.

Petty, G.C., and R.B. Hill. 1994. Are men and women different? A study of the occupational work ethic. *Journal of Vocational Education Research* 19:71-89.

Petty, G.C. 1995. Adults in the work force and the occupational work ethic. *Journal of Studies in Technical Careers* 15:133-140.

Petty, G.C. 1995. Vocational-technical education and the occupational work ethic. *Journal of Industrial and Teacher Education* 32:45-58.

Occupational Work Ethic Inventory

At work I can describe myself as:

1.	dependable	26.	negligent
2.	stubborn	27.	persevering
3.	following regulations	28.	likable
4.	following directions	29.	helpful
5.	independent	30.	apathetic
6.	ambitious	31.	pleasant
7.	effective	32.	cooperative
8.	reliable	33.	hardworking
9	tardy	34.	rude
10.	initiating	35.	orderly
11.	perceptive	36.	enthusiastic
12.	honest	37.	cheerful
13.	irresponsible	38.	persistent
14.	efficient	39.	hostile
15.	adaptable	40.	dedicated
16.	careful	41.	devoted
17.	appreciative	42.	courteous
18.	accurate	43.	considerate
19.	emotionally stable	44.	careless
20.	conscientious	45.	productive
21.	depressed	46.	well groomed
22.	patient	47.	friendly
23.	punctual	48.	loyal
24.	devious	49.	resourceful
25.	selfish	50.	modest

Scoring: 1 = Never; 2 = Almost Never; 3 = Seldom; 4 = Sometimes; 5 = Usually; 6 = Almost Always; and 7 = Always.

Reprinted with permission of the author. (For additional information contact George C. Petty, Department of Human Resource Development, University of Tennessee at Knoxville, Knoxville, TN 37996-2755.)

Teacher Multicultural Attitude Survey (TMAS)

Ponterotto, J.G., et al. 1998. Development and initial score validation of the Teacher Multicultural Attitude Survey. *Educational and Psychological Measurement* 58:1002-1016.

Comments: The 20-item TMAS assesses the multicultural awareness of teachers (K-12).

Scale Construction: Based upon a thorough review of the literature, the initial item pool consisted of 50 items dealing with multicultural sensitivity and competence. After the research team (professor and three graduate students) evaluated the items, 31 items were left. Ten additional graduate students then evaluated these items (80% agreement). The original version of the TMAS contained 30 items. In addition, two focus groups were held. The TMAS was revised as a result of factor analytic procedures.

Sample: There were a total of 429 (teachers and teacher education students) people from New York, New Jersey, and New Hampshire who participated in Study 1. Study 2 consisted of 227 teacher education graduate students.

Reliability: The alpha coefficient for the 30-item TMAS was 0.82. The alpha coefficient for the 20-item TMAS was 0.86. The theta coefficient was 0.89. Test-retest reliability over a three-week period (16 students) was 0.80.

Validity: Evidence for construct and criterion validity are provided.

Factor Analysis: Although the results of a principal components factor analysis yielded four factors, the first factor accounted for 32.5% of the common variance. Therefore, a forced, one-factor procedure was employed (18 items had factor loadings above 0.35). These results were consistent with the findings in Study 1 that multicultural awareness is a single factor.

Data Analysis: Means, standard deviations, factor structure coefficients, and item-total correlations are reported.

References:
Phinney, J.S. 1992. The Multigroup Ethnic Identity Measure: A new scale for use with diverse groups. *Journal of Adolescent Research* 7:156-176.

Ponterotto, J.G., et al. 1995. Development and initial validation of the Quick Discrimination Index (QDI). *Educational and Psychological Measurement* 55:1016-1031.

Ponterotto, J.G., and P.B. Pedersen. 1993. *Preventing prejudice: A guide for counselors and educators*. Newbury Park, CA: Sage.

Teacher Multicultural Attitude Inventory

1. I find teaching a culturally diverse student group rewarding.
2. Teaching methods need to be adapted to meet the needs of a culturally diverse student group.
3. Sometimes I think there is too much emphasis placed on multicultural awareness and training for teachers.
4. Teachers have the responsibility to be aware of their students' cultural backgrounds.
5. I frequently invite extended family members (e.g., cousins, grandparents, godparents, etc.) to attend parent-teacher conferences.
6. It is not the teacher's responsibility to encourage pride in one's culture.
7. As classrooms become more culturally diverse, the teacher's job becomes increasingly challenging.
8. I believe the teacher's role needs to be redefined to address the needs of students from culturally diverse backgrounds.
9. When dealing with bilingual students, some teachers may misinterpret different communication styles as behavioral problems.
10. As classrooms become more culturally diverse, the teacher's job becomes increasingly rewarding.
11. I can learn a great deal from students with culturally different backgrounds.
12. Multicultural training for teachers is not necessary.
13. In order to be an effective teacher, one needs to be aware of cultural differences present in the classroom.
14. Multicultural awareness training can help me work more effectively with a diverse student population.
15. Students should learn to communicate in English only.
16. Today's curriculum gives undue importance to multiculturalism and diversity.
17. I am aware of the diversity of cultural backgrounds in my classroom.
18. Regardless of the racial and ethnic makeup of my class, it is important for all students to be aware of multicultural diversity.
19. Being multiculturally aware is not relevant for the subject I teach.
20. Teaching students about cultural diversity will only create conflict in the classroom.

Scoring: Strongly Disagree = 1; Disagree = 2; Uncertain = 3; Agree = 4; and Strongly Agree = 5. The scoring is reversed for items 3, 6, 12, 15, 16, 19, and 20. High scores represent greater appreciation and awareness of issues regarding multicultural teaching.

Educational Beliefs Questionnaire

Silvernail, D.L. 1992. The development and factor structure of the Educational Beliefs Questionnaire. *Educational and Psychological Measurement* 52:663-667.

Comments: The 20-item EBQ measures beliefs about five educational concepts by using five educational philosophies. Additional research will determine whether the three-factor solution is viable. The author suggests using a structured interview in addition to the EBQ to see if the verbal beliefs and written beliefs of participants are congruent. This would provide an alternate way of determining the validity of the EBQ.

Scale Construction: This 67-item pilot instrument was built upon the work of Kerlinger and Kaya. A 5x5 item grid was developed using five educational philosophies (essentialism, traditionalism, progressivism, reconstructivism, and existentialism) and five educational concepts (the purpose of schools, curriculum content, methods of instruction, the role of the teacher, and the role of the student). After a panel of three educational theorists reviewed the items, the 25-item EBQ was administered to a group of volunteers.

Sample: The sample consisted of 610 volunteer teachers K-12 from 11 schools in a state in northern New England.

Reliability: Alpha coefficients were 0.71 (perennialism orientation), 0.72 (romanticism orientation), and 0.64 (progressivism) with a total scale coefficient of 0.73.

Validity: Face validity was established by the panel of judges who reviewed the items for clarity and accuracy. Construct validity was determined through various factor analytic procedures.

Factor Analysis: Factor analysis with a varimax rotation yielded a final three-factor solution. The three factors are: seven items on perennialism orientation (1-7); nine items on romanticism orientation (8-16); and four items on progressivism (17-20). Factor loadings are reported.

Definition of Factors: *Perennialism orientation* refers to the philosophies of essentialism and traditionalism; it contains items that relate to the importance of schools in transmitting cultural heritage and strong authority roles for teachers. *Romanticism orientation* refers to the philosophies of reconstructivism and existentialism; it contains items that relate to the importance of schools as sources of new social ideas and individual self-awareness and the role of teachers as facilitators in the natural development of youngsters. *Progressivism* refers to the progressive philosophy found in the instruments developed by Kerlinger and Kaya; it contains items that relate to the role of schools in developing socially conscious adults and the importance of acquiring problem-solving skills and knowledge.

References:
Kerlinger, F., and E. Kaya. 1959. The construction and factor analytic validation of scales to measure attitudes toward education. *Educational and Psychological Measurement* 19:13-29.

Silvernail, D.L., and L. Goldsberry. 1992. The development and validation of an Educational Philosophy Beliefs Questionnaire: Work in Progress. Paper presented at American Educational Research Association.

Educational Beliefs Questionnaire

The following are not complete statements. In the total instrument, an appropriate cue is provided for each of the item stems listed below.

1. Students need more supervision
2. Drill/factual knowledge important
3. Demonstration/recitation essential
4. Teacher strong authority
5. Student receiver of knowledge
6. Need highly structured environment
7. Subjects should represent heritage
8. Curriculum focus on social problems
9. Schools should promote self-awareness
10. Students should have more freedom
11. Students should design program
12. Students should learn from peers
13. Schools sources of new ideas
14. Personality of students important
15. Learning should be experimental
16. Schools should preserve values
17. Students should learn essential skills
18. Students should learn essential knowledge
19. Teachers should be facilitators
20. Schools should foster intellectual

Scoring: A six-point Likert scale is used.

Reprinted with permission of the author.

Attitudes about Merit Pay

Weber. L. 1988. An instrument for assessing attitudes about merit pay. *Educational Research Quarterly* 12:2-7.

Comments: This 16-item instrument addresses two problems associated with merit pay: definitions and criteria. In addition, it provides information about reliability and validity.

Sample: The original instrument was administered to 237 teachers and 86 administrators in northern Virginia. Two months later, 193 teachers, 107 administrators, and 135 parents participated in a replication study in Virginia.

Reliability: In the replication study, the total group alpha for the 16 items was 0.92; 0.93 for the teachers, 0.87 for the administrators, and 0.91 for the parents.

Validity: Five aspects of merit pay were identified through a review of the literature. These aspects were examined by 12 public school educators and a 34-item instrument was developed to assess merit pay; its effect on morale and instruction; methods for deciding on merit; and monetary issues (content validity).

Factor Analysis: Linkage and factor analyses were performed and yielded similar results: one factor emerged that assessed a general attitude toward merit pay.

Reference:
Carter, E.L. 1983. Merit pay programs for teachers: Perceptions of school board members in Virginia. Ed.D. dissertation, Virginia Polytechnic Institute and State University.

Attitudes about Merit Pay

1. A merit pay program will attract better qualified people to the teaching profession.
2. Merit pay would not enhance the positive relationship among teachers and administrators.
3. A merit pay system will have a negative impact on the morale of teachers in the system.
4. Nominees for a merit pay increase can be objectively identified.
5. Merit pay will positively affect teacher morale.
6. Competition for merit pay will inhibit spontaneity and innovation by teachers within classrooms.
7. A merit pay plan has no place in the public school setting.
8. Teachers working under merit pay will be less cooperative with their peers.
9. A merit pay system should be included in the salary schedule.
10. Students standardized test scores results should be a factor used when evaluating teachers for merit purposes.
11. Standardized test scores in the school system would improve if a merit system of pay were adopted.
12. Accord between administrative and instructional staff will be negatively affected if a merit system is adopted.
13. Merit pay should not be implemented in the public schools.
14. A merit pay program will improve the quality of instruction for gifted students.
15. A merit pay program will result in a higher retention rate of better teachers.
16. Tenured teachers receiving unsatisfactory evaluations should be denied automatic salary increases so that funds will be available for merit pay.

Scoring: Agree = 1; Tend to Agree = 2; Tend to Disagree = 3; Disagree = 4. Scoring is reversed for negative items (2, 3, 6, 7, 8, 12, and 13). Low mean values (equal to or less than 2.5) represent a favorable attitude.

Reprinted with permission of Educational Research Quarterly.

Attitudes Toward Inclusive Education Scale (ATIES)

Wilczenski, F.L. 1995. Development of a scale to measure attitudes toward inclusive education. *Educational and Psychological Measurement* 55:291-299.

Comments: The 16-item ATIES assesses attitudes toward including students with disabilities in regular education classrooms. The scale contains four statements in each of the following categories: academic, behavioral, physical, and social integration. The basis for this scale is the Attitudes Toward Mainstreaming Scale that was developed by Berryman (1988).

Sample: The participants consisted of 445 regular education teachers from urban, suburban, and rural school districts in New Hampshire.

Data Analysis: Rasch analysis was conducted through BIGSTEPS (a computer program used to analyze the data on a rating scale). Therefore, the nonlinear scores were changed into linear scores. Infit and outfit statistics as well as calibrations and standard errors are reported. According to the author, the item-fit statistics were acceptable, indicating a unidimensional construct.

References:
Berryman, J.D. 1988. Attitudes Toward Mainstreaming Scale: Factorial validity for a lay population. *Educational and Psychological Measurement* 48:231-236.

Wilczenski, F.L. 1992. Measuring attitudes toward inclusive education. *Psychology in the Schools* 29:306-312.

Wright, B.D., and J.M. Linacre. 1993. BIGSTEPS: Rasch-model computer program. Chicago, IL: MESA Press.

Attitudes Toward Inclusive Education Scale

1. Students whose academic achievement is 2 or more years below the other students in the grade should be in regular classes.
2. Students who are physically aggressive toward their peers should be in regular classes.
3. Students who cannot move without help from others should be in regular classes.
4. Students who are shy and withdrawn should be in regular classes.
5. Students whose academic achievement is 1 year below the other students in the grade should be in regular classes.
6. Students whose speech is difficult to understand should be in regular classes.
7. Students who cannot read standard print and need to use Braille should be in regular classes.
8. Students who are verbally aggressive toward their peers should be in regular classes.
9. Students who have difficulty expressing their thoughts verbally should be in regular classes.
10. Students who need training in self-help skills and activities of daily living should be in regular classes.
11. Students who use sign language or communication boards should be in regular classes.
12. Students who cannot control their behavior and disrupt activities should be in regular classes.
13. Students who need an individualized functional academic program in everyday reading and math skills should be in regular classes.
14. Students who cannot hear conversational speech should be in regular classes.
15. Students who do not follow school rules for conduct should be in regular classes.
16. Students who are frequently absent from school should be in regular classes.

Scoring: Strongly Agree = 6; Agree = 5; Agree Somewhat = 4; Disagree Somewhat = 3; Disagree = 2; Strongly Disagree = 1.

Reprinted with permission of the author.

Pupil Control Ideology Form

Willower, D.J., et al. 1967. *The school and pupil control ideology.* University Park, PA: Penn State Studies Monograph No. 24.

Comments: The 20-item PCI provides an operational measure for pupil control orientation. Control ideology ranges on a continuum from custodial to humanistic. The authors state that as a result of the item analysis, only two items out of 20 were representative of the humanistic orientation. Another instrument, the Pupil Control Behavior Form was developed by Helsel and Willower. The PCB measures educators pupil control behavior on the same continuum as the PCI. The PCB is usually completed by students.

Scale Construction: Based upon a review of the literature, the author's experience in the public schools, the operational definition of pupil control ideology, and field notes from a prior study, 57 items were written. This original form of the PCI was administered to a sample of 58 people. Through item analysis, a 38-item form was developed. As a result of the pilot studies, the number of items that were positive to the humanistic orientation was eliminated. Based on the item analysis, 20 out of 38 items were retained because they had biserial correlation coefficients greater than 0.325.

Sample: The original sample consisted of a combination of 58 graduate students in education and in-service teachers. The revised form was administered in seven schools in New York and Pennsylvania. Five elementary and two secondary schools participated from urban, suburban, and rural areas. One elementary and one secondary school were selected because of their reputation as "humanistic" schools. Overall, 170 teachers responded.

Reliability: A split-half reliability coefficient of 0.91 was obtained by correlating even-item subscores with odd-item subscores. The corrected reliability coefficient was 0.95. An additional reliability test was done using only one elementary school and one secondary school (55). This yielded a coefficient of 0.83 and a corrected coefficient of 0.91.

Validity: Principals identified approximately 15% of their faculties as having either a custodial ideology or a humanistic ideology. Then, the mean scores of these teachers on the PCI was compared. T-tests were performed to see if teachers considered to have a custodial ideology differed from those teachers considered to have a humanistic ideology. The results were significant at the 0.01 level. In addition, a cross-validation study using the seven schools was conducted. The results were significant at the 0.001 level.

Definition of Dimensions: *The custodial orientation* is similar to the traditional school, which is characterized by a highly controlled setting; the maintenance of order; students are considered to be irresponsible and undisciplined; relationships with students are impersonal; pessimism and mistrust prevail; the school is viewed as an autocratic organization; and power and communication flow downward. The *humanistic orientation* views the school as an educational community in which interaction and experience guide its members; learning is viewed as a worthwhile activity in and of itself; relationships with students are personal; teachers are optimistic; teachers want to make the classroom climate democratic; and there are open channels of communication.

Data Analysis: Means, standard errors squared, and the results of t-tests for each major hypothesis tested are presented.

References:

Appleberry, J.B., and W.K. Hoy. 1969. The pupil control ideology of professional personnel in "open" and "closed" elementary schools. *Educational Administration Quarterly* 5:74-85.

Helsel, R.R., and D.J. Willower. 1974. Toward definition and measurement of pupil control behavior. *Journal of Educational Administration* 12:114-123.

Schilling, K.J. 1988. The relationship among the conflict management styles utilized by the elementary school administrators, the organizational climate of an elementary school, and the pupil control orientation of the elementary teachers. Ed.D. dissertation, Loyola University, Chicago.

Vitagliano, J.A. 1985. Pupil control ideology and pluralistic ignorance in a residential facility for the hearing impaired: Hearing and non-hearing teacher perspectives. Ph.D. dissertation, Louisiana State University and Agricultural and Mechanical College.

Woolfolk, A.E., et al. 1990. Teachers' sense of efficacy and their beliefs about managing students. *Teaching and Teacher Education* 6:137-148.

Pupil Control Ideology Form

1. It is desirable to require pupils to sit in assigned seats during assemblies.
2. Pupils are usually not capable of solving their problems through logical reasoning.
3. Directing sarcastic remarks toward a defiant pupil is a good disciplinary technique.
4. Beginning teachers are not likely to maintain strict enough control over their pupils.
5. Teachers should consider revision of their teaching methods if these are criticized by their pupils.
6. The best principals give unquestioning support to teachers in disciplining pupils.
7. Pupils should not be permitted to contradict the statements of a teacher in class.
8. It is justifiable to have pupils learn many facts about a subject even if they have no immediate application.
9. Too much pupil time is spent on guidance and activities and too little on academic preparation.
10. Being friendly with pupils often leads them to become too familiar.
11. It is more important for pupils to learn to obey rules than that they make their own decisions.
12. Student governments are a good safety valve, but should not have much influence on school policy.
13. Pupils can be trusted to work together without supervision.
14. If a pupil uses obscene or profane language in school, it must be considered a moral offense.
15. If pupils are allowed to use the lavatory without getting permission, this privilege will be abused.
16. A few pupils are just young hoodlums and should be treated accordingly.
17. It is often necessary to remind pupils that their status in school differs from that of teachers.
18. A pupil who destroys school material or property should be severely punished.
19. Pupils cannot perceive the difference between democracy and anarchy in the classroom.
20. Pupils often misbehave in order to make the teacher look bad.

Scoring: A five-point Likert-type scale is used. Strongly Agree = 5; Agree = 4; Undecided = 3; Disagree = 2; and Strongly Disagree = 1. The scoring is reversed for the two positive items representing the humanistic ideology (5 and 13). The higher the score, the more custodial the orientation. The lower the score, the more humanistic the orientation.

(Reprinted with permission of Willower, D.J., et al. 1967. *The school and pupil control ideology.* University Park, PA: Penn State Studies Monograph No. 24.)

Total Quality Management

TQM: Stakeholders Perceptions

Currie, T.A. 1997. Total quality management in Georgia postsecondary technical institutes. Ed.D. dissertation. University of Georgia.

Comments: The 37-item survey measures the magnitude of four key aspects of total quality management (leadership, empowerment, strategic quality planning, and human resource development) in postsecondary technical schools based upon the perceptions of administrators, faculty, and support staff.

Sample: A sample of 157 administrators, 280 faculty, and 131 support staff from postsecondary technical schools was surveyed.

Reliability: A reliability coefficient of 0.92 was obtained with the pilot study of 45 administrators and faculty.

Validity: Content validity was established based upon a thorough review of the literature. Face validity was accomplished through a panel of experts.

Core TQM Tenets: The following four key aspects were examined: nine items on leadership (1, 2, 4, 5, 7, 24, 26, 30, and 31); ten items on empowerment (3, 6, 11, 13, 20, 23, 28, 33, 35, and 36); nine items on strategic quality planning (8, 10, 12, 14, 15, 22, 29, 34, and 37); and nine items on human resource development (9, 16, 17, 18, 19, 21, 25, 27, and 32).

Data Analysis: Scale means and standard deviations are presented as well as average composite scores for each item, for each group, and for each of the four components. Results of multivariate analysis of variance are reported.

References:
Cornesky, A. 1992. Using Deming to improve quality in colleges and universities. ERIC ED 354 838.

Hixson, J., and K. Lovelace. 1992. Total quality management's challenge to urban schools. *Educational Leadership* 50:24-27.

Kaufman, R., and A. Hirumi. 1992. Ten steps to "TQM Plus." *Educational Leadership* 50:33-34.

Marchese, T. 1991. TQM reaches the academy. *AAHE Bulletin* 44:3-9.

Tribus, M. 1993. TQM in education: The theory and how to put it to work. ERIC ED 370 168.

TQM: Stakeholder Perceptions

1. The President is personally and visibly involved in quality improvement projects.
2. My supervisor is personally and visibly involved in quality improvement projects.
3. I am allowed to make those decisions and instigate action in areas that effect my job.
4. The practices of my supervisor regularly demonstrate and communicate a commitment to exceptional customer service.
5. The practices of the President regularly demonstrate and communicate a commitment to continuous quality improvement of programs and services.
6. All staff in the institute are provided an opportunity to participate on quality teams.
7. The President communicates his commitment to customer focus and quality values to all employees.
8. Periodic reviews of quality plans and performance are conducted with all employees.
9. The institute provides time and other resources to develop continuous quality improvement initiatives.
10. The institute collects and utilizes data on service quality and customer satisfaction to develop improvement plans.
11. My input is always welcomed concerning quality initiatives and process improvement.
12. The institute has operational (one to two year) and strategic (three to five year) plans that describe overall quality and performance goals and strategies for achieving those goals.
13. Collaboration among employees to improve the quality of programs and services is encouraged.
14. There is a plan to communicate quality expectations to all personnel at my institute.
15. The institute has developed a plan for committing resources for quality initiatives.
16. My job has changed significantly as a result of "redirection" of institute funds.
17. The job of someone with whom I work has changed significantly as a result of "redirection" of institute funds.
18. Employees are recognized for achievement of quality goals and strategies.
19. Employees are provided incentives to encourage them to contribute to quality improvements.
20. The President promotes employee authority to act.
21. Training in quality improvement techniques is part of each employee's staff development plan.
22. Training is based upon a thorough analysis of employee staff development needs.
23. I am able to access the education and training I need to improve my contribution to my work unit.
24. Employees who pursue training in quality methods beyond the scope of that offered by the institute are rewarded through leadership opportunities.
25. Employees are rewarded for the achievement of quality goals and objectives.
26. The President measures institute success by the quality of programs and services provided rather than by a cost per credit hour ratio.
27. There is evidence that continuous improvements have been made in the reward systems to promote quality in my institute.
28. Employees in the institute are given the freedom to act without fear of retribution.
29. Plans and strategies are being developed to build and maintain positive relationships with institute customers.
30. The President utilizes total quality management principles in leading the institute.
31. The day-to-day practices of the institute's administrators demonstrate commitment to total quality management principles.
32. My job provides me with a great deal of satisfaction.
33. Changes have been made in our organizational structure to facilitate employee empowerment.

34. My input is valued and incorporated in the long range planning for my unit.
35. Team initiative and innovation by employees are encouraged in my organization.
36. I feel free to take risks in an effort to improve the quality of my unit's performance.
37. The institute employs systematic methods of evaluating the quality of products and services.

Scoring: There are four responses for each item: 1 = strong disbelief; 2 = disbelief; 3 = moderate belief; and 4 = strong belief.

Reprinted with permission of the author.

Instruments Available through Commercial Organizations

Sex Role Egalitarianism Scale
King, L.A. and D.W. King. 1993.

The 95-item SRES assesses attitudes toward the equality of men and women. There are five scales with 19 items in each scale. One scale measures educational roles. Reliability and validity are provided as well as descriptive statistics for many sample groups.

Available: Sigma Assessment Systems, Inc.
511 Fort Street, Suite 435
P.O. Box 610984
Port Huron, MI 48061-0984

Occupational Stress Inventory
Osipow, S.J. and A.R. Spokane. 1981, 1983, 1987, and 1992.

The 140-item OSI contains three questionnaires that assess occupational stress, psychological strain, and coping resources. There are 14 different scales. Reliability estimates range from 0.71 to 0.94 for the 14 scales. Norms are provided for 130 jobs.

Available: Sigma Assessment Systems, Inc.
511 Fort Street, Suite 435
P.O. Box 610984
Port Huron, MI 48061-0984

Culture-Free Self-Esteem Inventory
Battle, J. 1981, 1992.

The 40-item CFSEI-2 assesses the following four aspects of self-esteem: general, social, personal, and lie (defensiveness). Norms are provided.

Available: Sigma Assessment Systems, Inc.
511 Fort Street, Suite 435
P.O. Box 610984
Port Huron, MI 48061-0984

The Empowerment Profile
Jones, J.E. and W.L. Bearley

The EP assesses a manager's/supervisor's perceptions along eight categories including autonomy, climate, and control.

Available: HRDQ
2002 Renaissance Boulevard #100
King of Prussia, PA 19406-2756

Participative Management Profile
Jones, J.E. and W.E. Bearley

The PMP contains 20 workplace situations. Managers/Supervisors select the best decision-making method for each situation.

Available: HRDQ
2002 Renaissance Boulevard #100
King of Prussia, PA 19406-2756

Supervisory Skills Questionnaire
Russo, E.M.

The SSQ contains 30 situations that supervisors typically encounter. Each situation has three alternatives that correspond to the following five skill categories: guiding the work, organizing the work, developing your staff, managing performance, and managing relations.

Available: HRDQ
2002 Renaissance Boulevard #100
King of Prussia, PA 19406-2756

Problem Solving Style Inventory
Phillips, K.R.

The 30-item PSSI identifies the following five styles: ego-oriented, deferred, other-oriented, I/W-oriented, and We-oriented.

Available: HRDQ
2002 Renaissance Boulevard #100
King of Prussia, PA 19406-2756

Conflict Strategies Inventory
Russo, E.M. and M. Eckler

The CSI contains ten brief cases of work-related conflict. It assesses the following five conflict strategies: avoiding, smoothing, competing, compromising, and integrating.

Available: HRDQ
2002 Renaissance Boulevard #100
King of Prussia, PA 19406-2756

Thomas-Kilmann Conflict Mode Instrument
Thomas, K.W. and R.H. Killman. 1974.

The TKI contains 20 pairs of statements that measure a person's behavior in conflict situations. Five methods for understanding conflict are identified. They are: competing, collaborating, avoiding, compromising, and accommodating. Detailed information is provided on scoring and interpreting scores.

Available: Consulting Psychologists Press, Inc.
3803 E. Bayshore Road
P.O. Box 10096
Palo Alto, CA 94303

Power Base Inventory
Thomas, K.W. and G.F. Thomas. 1985, 1991.

The PBI contains 30 pairs of statements that identify the sources of power (power bases) that may be used to influence other people. Six power bases are identified. They are: information, expertise, goodwill, authority, reward, and discipline. Detailed information is provided on scoring and interpreting scores.

Available: Consulting Psychologists Press, Inc.
3803 E. Bayshore Road
P.O. Box 10096
Palo Alto, CA 94303

TQManager Inventory
Schmidt, W.H. and J.P. Finnigan. 1994.

The 25-item TQM measures an individual's level of skill in the following five areas: developing relationships of openness and trust, building collaboration and teamwork, managing by fact, supporting results through recognition and rewards, and developing a learning and continually improving organization. Detailed information is provided on scoring and interpreting scores.

Available: Consulting Psychologists Press, Inc.
3803 E. Bayshore Road
P.O. Box 10096
Palo Alto, CA 94303

Empowerment Inventory
Thomas, K.W. and W.G. Tymon, Jr. 1993.

The 24-item EI assesses four types of empowering feelings as an individual performs various tasks at work. The four empowering feelings are choice, competence, meaningfulness, and progress. Detailed information is provided on scoring and interpreting scores.

Available: Consulting Psychologists Press, Inc.
3803 E. Bayshore Road
P.O. Box 10096
Palo Alto, CA 94303

Kilmann-Saxton Culture Gap Survey
Kilmann, R.H. and M.J. Saxton

The CGS contains 28 pairs of norms that assesses the cultural norms of groups within various organizational settings. It identifies the difference between desired norms and actual norms. The CGS is based on more than 400 norms from over 25 different organizations. Four categories of culture-gaps are identified: task support, task innovation, social relationships, and personal freedom. Detailed information is provided on scoring and interpreting scores.

Available: Consulting Psychologists Press, Inc.
3803 E. Bayshore Road
P.O. Box 10096
Palo Alto, CA 94303

Maslach Burnout Inventory
Maslach,C. and S.E. Jackson

The MBI measures the intensity and frequency of perceived burnout in three areas: emotional exhaustion, personal accomplishment, and depersonalization.

Available: Consulting Psychologists Press, Inc.
3803 E. Bayshore Road
P.O. Box 10096
Palo Alto, CA 94303

School Assessment Survey
Wilson, B.L., et al. 1985.

The 48-item norm-referenced SAS assesses the following nine areas of school climate: goal consensus, facilitative leadership, classroom instruction, curriculum and resources, vertical communication, horizontal communication, staff conflict, student discipline, and teaching behavior. Profiles and item analysis are available. Information about validity is also available as well as a technical manual. Scoring and interpretation is available from RBS.

Available: Research for Better Schools
444 North Third Street
Philadelphia, PA 19123

Dimensions of Excellence Scales: Survey Instruments for School Improvement
Dusewicz, R.A. and F.S. Beyer. 1991.

The three survey forms of the DOE (staff, parents, and students) assess the following eight areas related to effective school performance: school climate, leadership, teacher behavior, curriculum, monitoring and assessment, student discipline, staff development, and parent involvement. A technical manual is available as well as scoring and interpretation from RBS.

Available: Research for Better Schools
444 North Third Street
Philadelphia, PA 19123

Sizing Up Your School System: The District Effectiveness Audit
Buttram, J.L., T.B. Corcoran, and B.J. Hansen. Reprinted 1989.

Interviews and surveys are used to measure the effect of the actions of boards of education and district administrators in the following seven areas: goal setting, curriculum, quality assurance, resource allocation, work environment, school improvement, and community relations. Instructions for analysis are provided.

Available: Research for Better Schools
444 North Third Street
Philadelphia, PA 19123

Environment Assessment Questionnaire
Kinlaw, D.C. 1986.

Assesses clarity, fairness, appreciation, responsiveness, and involvement of a work group's environment.

Available: Talico Inc.
2320 South Third Street, Suite #5
Jacksonville, FL 32250

Employee Opinion Survey
Talico Inc.

Assesses attitudes toward management effectiveness, supervisory practices, communication effectiveness, nondiscrimination, pay and benefits, interpersonal relations, policies and work rules, job interest, work performance, and general level of job satisfaction.

Available: Talico Inc.
2320 South Third Street, Suite #5
Jacksonville, FL 32250

Author Index

Instrument Index

About the Authors

Dr. Paula E. Lester brings to this handbook almost 30 years of experience as a classroom teacher, educational administrator, department chairperson, and college professor. She received a Ph.D. in organizational and administrative studies from New York University. Her more than 25 publications include four books and articles in *Educational and Psychological Measurement, Principal, Clearing House*, and other periodicals. She has been on the faculty of Long Island University since 1985 and a full professor since 1994. She teaches the course Fundamentals of Administration and supervises administrative interns.

Dr. Lloyd K. Bishop has been a professor of education for more than 30 years. He received his Ph.D. in education and organizational behavior from Claremont Graduate School. His many publications include seven books and articles published in the *Review of Education, Educational Administration Quarterly, Administrative Science Quarterly*, and other periodicals. He has been a professor, department chair, and program director at various universities including New York University, the University of Nevada, and Dowling College, New York. He teaches doctoral courses in research methodology, measurement, and statistics. His expertise in applied research has resulted in numerous guest lectures and long-range planning studies in more than 150 school districts throughout the United States.

PHYSICIAN ASSISTANT

A Guide to Clinical Practice